THE LEGAL RIGHTS MANUAL

The Legal Rights Manual

A Guide for Social Workers and Advice Centres

Jeremy Cooper

Gower

Published by
Gower Publishing Company Limited
Gower House
Croft Road
Aldershot
Hants GU11 3HR
England

Gower Publishing Company
Old Post Road
Brookfield
Vermont 05036
USA

British Library Cataloguing in Publication Data
Cooper, Jeremy, *1950–*
   The legal rights manual: a guide for social workers and
   advice centres.
   1. England.   Law
   I. Title
   344.2

ISBN 0 566 05507 4

Filmset by Speedset Ltd, Ellesmere Port
Printed in Great Britain by
Billing & Sons Ltd, Worcester

Contents

Abbreviations

ABWOR	Advice by Way of Representation
ACAS	Advisory Conciliation and Arbitration Service
ACE	Advice Centre for Education
AIMS	Association for Improvements in Maternity Services
ASW	Approved Social Worker
BASW	British Association of Social Workers
BGS	British Geriatrics Society
BT	British Telecom
CAB	Citizens' Advice Bureau
CCE	Counsel and Care for the Elderly
CCETSW	Central Council for Education and Training in Social Work
CCG	Community Care Grant
CHAR	Housing Campaign for Single People (formerly Campaign for the Homeless and Rootless)
CLH	Common Lodging House
CPAG	Child Poverty Action Group
CRE	Commission for Racial Equality
CSA	Central Services Agency
CSDPA	Chronically Sick and Disabled Persons Act 1970
CSE	Centre for Studies on Integration in Education
DHSS	Department of Health and Social Security
DOE	Department of the Environment
	Department of Employment
DOH	Department of Health

DPSCRA	The Disabled Persons Services, Consultation and Representation Act 1986
DRO	Disablement Resettlement Officer
DSS	Department of Social Security
EAT	Employment Appeal Tribunal
ECC	Electricity Consumers' Council
ECT	Electro-Convulsive Therapy
EEC	European Economic Community
EHO	Environment Health Officer
EOC	Equal Opportunities Commission
EPA	Equal Pay Act
ESW	Exceptionally Severe Weather (payment)
FC	Family Credit
FIAC	Federation of Independent Advice Centres
FPC	Family Practitioner Committee
FRU	Free Representation Unit
GDC	General Dental Council
GIA	General Improvement Area
GLAD	Greater London Association for Disabled People
GOQ	Genuine Occupational Qualification
GP	General Practitioner
HA	Housing Association
HAA	Housing Action Area
HASAW	Health and Safety at Work 1974
HAT	Housing Action Trust
HB	Housing Benefit
HMO	House in Multiple Occupation
HMSO	Her Majesty's Stationery Office
HRP	Home Responsibilities Protection
HSE	Health and Safety Executive
IB	Invalidity benefit
ICA	Institute of Consumer Advisers
	Invalid Care Allowance
IS	Income Support
IYSH	International Year of Shelter for the Homeless
LEA	Local Education Authority
MAT	Medical Appeal Tribunal
MENCAP	Royal Society for Mentally Handicapped Children and Adults
MHAC	Mental Health Act Commission

MHRT	Mental Health Review Tribunal
MIND	The National Association for Mental Health
MSC	Medical Services Committee
NACAB	National Association of Citizens' Advice Bureaux
NAFD	National Association of Funeral Directors
NAHA	National Association of Health Authorities
NCC	National Consumer Council
NCIP/HNCIP	Non-Contributory Invalidity Pension
NCVO	National Council for Voluntary Organizations
NHS	National Health Service
NI	National Insurance
NISP } NSP	Notice Seeking Possession
NSPCC	National Society for the Prevention of Cruelty to Children
OFTEL	Office of Telecommunications
OPAS	Occupational Pensions Advisory Service
OUP	Oxford University Press
PACE	Police and Criminal Evidence Act 1984
PAYE	Pay As You Earn
PCA	Police Complaints' Authority
PCC	Professional Conduct Committee of the Bar
RAC	Rent Association Committee
RMO	Responsible Medical Officer
RRA	Race Relations Act
SB	Sickness Benefit
SDA {	Sex Discrimination Act Severe Disablement Allowance
SEPACS	Sheltered Employment Procurement and Consultancy Services
SERPS	State Earnings Related Pension Scheme
SFC	Social Fund Commissioner
SFI	Social Fund Inspector
SFO	Social Fund Officer
SHAC	The London Housing Centre
SOSR	Some Other Substantial Reason (for dismissal)
SSAT	Social Security Appeal Tribunal
SSP	Statutory Sick Pay
TPAS	Tenant Participation Advisory Service

Abbreviations

TUC	Trades Union Congress
UB	Unemployment Benefit
UHH	Unfit for Human Habitation
UPIAS	Union of the Physically Impaired Against Segregation

Acknowledgements

This book has grown from my work as a teacher of law and legal rights to social work students, first at Middlesex Polytechnic and now at the Polytechnic of East London. It was my students who consistently reported the need for a book such as this, as an initial reference point on the legal rights of their clients over a range of common problems. It was the same students who persuaded me to write the book. It is therefore only natural that it is to them that I now dedicate it, with thanks.

Many people gave generously of their time and expertise in reading and commenting upon various sections of the book. In particular I would like to express my thanks to Norman Cooper, Tim Hellings, Raymond Jack, David James, Liliane Kott, Malcolm Leder, Howard Levenson, Pat Reddin, Tony Riley, Ruth Robins and Stuart Vernon. Clare Picking read the entire manuscript and her comments were especially valuable, as they are on everything. Juliet and Douglas did not read the manuscript and no doubt will not read the book. But they have helped me in more important ways, and to them I send a very special thank you.

Chapter 7 on Legal Rights in the Workplace was written entirely by David Lewis, Principal Lecturer in Law at Middlesex Polytechnic.

Grammatical purists will notice that throughout the book I have used the pronoun 'they' rather than 's/he' in a way that some might argue is grammatically incorrect. This is deliberate and I make no apologies. Unlike the Latin based languages of Southern Europe, the English language does not have a non-gender specific third person singular pronoun, such as the French 'on'. Faced with a choice between unacceptable sexism, tedious and ugly repetition, or grammatical impurity, I opted for impurity.

I gratefully acknowledge permission from the Police Complaints Authority to reproduce Table 2.1 on page 37; to MIND to reproduce Table 5.1 on page 58 and to the Benefits Research Unit (Service) Ltd to reproduce tables 8.1 and 11.1 on pages 285 and 411.

1

Introduction

'Law!' said Bunce, with all the scorn he knew how to command –
'Law! Did ye ever know a poor man yet was the better for law, or a
lawyer?'
From *The Warden* by Anthony Trollope.

The splendid Mr Bunce, in the first of Anthony Trollope's six
Barsetshire novels, expressed in these few words sentiments that are
echoed today in many of the offices and workplaces of those carrying
out social work and related professions throughout the length and
breadth of the United Kingdom. It is unfortunately true that the great
majority of those who receive social work assistance in some form are
at the lower end of the socio-economic scale. Few in these circumstances ever envisage the law as a positive instrument to improve
their position. All too frequently the law has been identified with the
source of their greatest discomfort: a brush with the police, care
proceedings against their children, a 'section' under the Mental
Health Act, or an intransigent, rule-bound DSS officer refusing
financial assistance. Confronted with the law, they feel at best
powerless, at worst afraid. It is the purpose of this book to present the
law in a different perspective and to encourage those engaged in such
work to use it positively and creatively for the benefit of their clients.
The task is not simple as the prejudice against law runs deep. But
after many years engaged first in the practice of welfare law and
latterly in the teaching and training of social work students in the
ways that law can be used for the benefit of their clients, I remain
convinced that ignorance of the law is not bliss, but folly, and that a
greater understanding of its uses can only be for the good of the
client.
   Another of the common prejudices concerning the law and its uses

1

is articulated in the course of the Barsetshire novels in the words of the zealous young reformer John Bold who 'wanted law from a lawyer as he did a coat from a tailor: because he could not make it so well himself'. For many engaged in social work, law is something that is done by lawyers. If they also become knowledgeable in its scope and uses they fear they may somehow become surrogate lawyers, which will in turn restrict their freedom to exercise a wider range of social work and advice skills. This view I believe to be seriously misguided and I offer this book as an opportunity for social workers and others in the caring and advice professions, to embark upon a reappraisal of this common perception.

Although I write the book as a lawyer, I write it for use by those who are not, in the firm belief that some of the best and most imaginative use of the law is made by those who are not themselves lawyers. Lawyers all too frequently take the narrow view, the cautious interpretation, too influenced at times by their sense of the mathematical risk of failure which is bred in them by their training. The possibility of success must always be balanced against the risk of failure: the scales of justice on the roof of the Old Bailey are more than mere metaphor. Above all lawyers seem to be little concerned with justice, confirming Samuel Johnson's observation that 'a lawyer has no business with the justice or injustice of the cause he undertakes. The justice or injustice is to be decided by the judge'. In contrast, those who work at the social work coalface have no need to exercise the same restraint in their endeavours to assist their clients and need specifically to help their clients in the active enforcement of their legal rights. If their client has legal rights it is surely the duty of the social worker to help the client obtain them. But to embark upon this task of encouraging client self-assertion the adviser must have an appropriate level of knowledge of the possibilities that the law presents either to consolidate or to improve their client's situation. The *CCETSW Law Report* published in 1988, which exposed the serious inadequacies in the teaching of law to trainee social workers throughout the country, serves as a clear indication that too many social workers are entering practice poorly prepared to assist in the assertion of clients' legal rights. The independent advice sector is equally concerned with such training issues. I hope this book may help to address this inadequacy.

In designing the structure and content of the book I inevitably had

2

to make a number of choices: essentially choices of what to leave out. A deliberate decision was taken at an early stage to leave out all the areas of strict 'statutory' work for which some specialized social workers have responsibility, e.g. child care work, child abuse, and participation in the process of the committal of people to detention in a mental institution. There are two reasons for this decision. The first is because to include such material would be to focus on professional specialisms within social work, which is not my intention and in any event a number of specialized manuals on these areas already exist. The second is more complex but essential in order to expose the central philosophy of the book. It is premised upon the belief that there is a basic core of legal knowledge that should be available to all who are engaged in caring for people in trouble, whatever their particular specialism. The style and layout of the book reflects the level I believe that knowledge should reach. I do not believe that all those doing social work should have *specialist* legal knowledge. What I do believe is that it is essential for all those doing social work or advice work to be able to recognize the general circumstances in which the law can be of assistance to their client; to be able to provide their client with a basic outline of their legal rights and to be in a position to help them explore in more detail their legal position with the aid of appropriate specialized assistance. It is for this latter reason that the book provides at every stage, details of where to go for further assistance either in the form of specialized agency advice or in further written advice.

My selection has deliberately omitted one important area, that of family law, i.e. the laws on divorce, cohabitation, custody, access, maintenance, wardship, adoption and so forth. The principal reason for this omission is that by and large the solicitor's profession is very well placed to provide detailed legal advice and assistance under the *legal aid scheme* (see page 5) in this field, for largely historical reasons connected with the way in which legal aid was developed in this country. As this very extensive, skilled and heavily subsidized legal advice service exists for those with problems in this area, it seems unnecessary to include it in this book. I hope that the experiences of those who use the book do not prove me wrong.

In fulfilment of the goals set out above I have thus selected what appear to me to be the areas in which the great majority of social work client problems fall, and in which clear legal advice concerning legal rights can be given by social workers and other lay advisers, without any recourse to lawyers. Inevitably a great deal of the focus of the book is upon the problems of those experiencing poverty. There is more than a grain of truth in Oliver Goldsmith's comment in *The Traveller* that 'laws grind the poor, and rich men rule the law'. Social workers and advice workers know that most of their clients are poor. And poverty is not just about a shortage of money. It is also about relative deprivation compared to the other members of the society in which we live. As the Church of England Report on inner city deprivation 'Faith in the City' observed in 1985 'poverty exists . . . if people are denied access to what is generally regarded as a reasonable standard and quality of life in that society'. Elsewhere in the same Report is another statement whose message provides the motivation for this book and the approach that it adopts: 'Poverty is not only about shortage of money. It is about rights and relationships; about how people are treated and how they regard themselves; about powerlessness, exclusion and loss of dignity. Yet the lack of an adequate income is at its heart.'

One of the key themes that runs through the book is the need to be aware of the precise pressure point at which to press a claim. Knowing where an adverse decision was made, knowing in which department, in which office, and by which individual, can all be key factors in the pursuit of a challenge on behalf of a client. A very large number of the decisions that affect the lives of social work clients are made in the offices of departments of central and local government. Two invaluable reference works that are annually updated and provide a mass of detailed addresses and other information about all such departments are *The Municipal Yearbook* (Municipal Publications Ltd) and *The Social Services Yearbook* (Longman).

Wherever appropriate throughout the book, details have been provided of where to go for further assistance. But how does the adviser know when they have gone as far as their knowledge will safely allow them in giving assistance and it is therefore time to refer the client to a specialist? This is a difficult question to answer and will always be a matter of individual judgement. As the aim of the book is to encourage self help, both on the part of the lay adviser and the client, the general answer is that you can normally go a lot further than you realized! Nevertheless, it should be stressed that there are in particular two large scale networks of professional legal advice provision that are always available for referral at the appropriate moment: The Citizens' Advice Bureau Network (CABs) and Legal Aid Solicitors.

CABs. There are close on 1000 CABs in operation in England, Wales and Northern Ireland (Scotland has its own separate though similar system). CABs provide a wide range of general advice, much of it legal advice, free of charge to anybody who requests it. The quality and accuracy of the advice is maintained by the fact that every CAB has to register as a member of the National Association of CABs (NACAB) in order to operate and NACAB has an extensive programme of training, research, information retrieval and back up that it makes available to all its local offices. NACAB itself operates from a central office in London and 22 area offices throughout the regions. It is essential that any person engaged in social work makes contact with their local CAB in order to familiarize themselves with the range of matters upon which the CAB is able to advise and also on any secondary specialist services they may operate such as the use of the services of local solicitors, accountants, surveyors and so forth on a volunteer basis. In some rural areas peripatetic CABs also operate. For further information on the operation of the service contact NACAB, 115 Pentonville Road, London N1 9LZ (Tel: 01 833 2181).

In addition to CABs a number of *independent advice centres* exist throughout the country which, though not affiliated to NACAB, often provide a similar sort of service to a CAB. To discover if there is an independent advice centre in your area contact The Federation of Independent Advice Centres (FIAC), 4th Floor, Concourse House, Lime Street, Liverpool L1 1NY (Tel: 051 709 7444) or 13 Stockwell Road, London SW9 9AU (Tel: 01 274 1839/1878), or consult the *FIAC Directory of Independent Advice Centres 1988.* For Scottish FIAC contact Rights Office, 12 Viewfield Terrace, Dunfermline, Fife (Tel: 0383 732320).

Legal aid solicitors. Since 1949 solicitors (and if necessary barristers), have been able to represent clients in the civil courts on a subsidized basis as a result of the legal aid scheme. They have been able to represent clients on this basis in the criminal courts for a much longer period. Although no solicitor is obliged to participate in the scheme, the majority do, particularly those working in small to medium sized firms. Thus if a client has a problem that may involve an

5

action in the civil court (county or High Court) either as the plaintiff or the defendant, it is always advisable to refer them to a local legal aid solicitor.

Legal aid is not automatically granted to a person involved in a civil court action. The client (or their solicitor) will have to apply for it to the local legal aid committee. They will also have to submit to a means test. The legal aid committee, which is composed of solicitors and barristers, will grant legal aid if they think there is a reasonable chance of success and that the case can be financially justified (i.e. a person would still engage in the litigation if they had to pay for it themselves!). It can, however, take a few weeks for the decision to be made and legal aid is not backdated. The means test is at present conducted by correspondence with a special division of the DSS, though this is likely to change in the future. If the client satisfies the means test they will be granted legal aid, which means that all or some of their legal fees will be met by the state. The amount, if any, that they will be asked to contribute to the cost will depend upon their income. On current figures, approximately 60 per cent of the population of the country would be entitled to at least partial assistance. Legal aid is not, however, available to cover the cost of legal representation in most tribunals, although limited financial support known as ABWOR (Advice By Way Of Representation) is available in Mental Health Review Tribunals (see Chapter 5, p. 155); for the representation of parents or guardians in certain child care proceedings and in proceedings before boards of visitors of custodial institutions.

Legal aid in criminal cases (Magistrates and Crown Courts) is granted by the clerks or the magistrates at the first appearance of the defendant in those courts. It is also subject to a means test, albeit a more generous one. In addition a magistrate need only grant legal aid if s/he considers that the defendant is at risk of losing their liberty, or would be unable to follow the proceedings without a lawyer representing them, or if there is a point of law to argue. The great majority of magistrates' courts (and a few county courts) also operate a Duty Solicitor Scheme (see Chapter 6, p. 212) whereby a duty solicitor will represent any unrepresented defendant who turns up at the court and who requires their services.

Parallel to the legal aid scheme there has been in existence since 1973 the legal advice and assistance scheme, commonly referred to as the *green form scheme*. Under this scheme a solicitor can give advice and assistance (e.g. write a letter, make a telephone call and so forth) to a client on any matter of English law, subject to a simple means test that the solicitor will carry out in the office. If the client satisfies the means test the solicitor can give a limited amount of advice and assistance to the client free of charge and recoup the cost from the state. It is possible that in the near future the green form scheme may be extended to include other advice agencies, in particular the CABs.

The Law Society has produced each year a detailed booklet for each region of England and Wales providing details of all the solicitors in that region who provide services under the legal aid scheme. The booklet is called the *Legal Aid Referral List*. A copy should be obtained by all those engaged in social work. The area legal aid committee can provide a copy (address in local telephone book). Alternatively, local CABs and libraries normally have their own copies. For further information on the legal aid scheme contact Legal Aid Board, Newspaper House, 8–16 Great New Street, London, EC4 3BN (Tel: 01 353 7411). For a detailed practical guide on legal aid consult Hansen, O. and Levenson, H. (1985) *Legal Aid: How to Use It* (Legal Action Group) and Hanson, O. (1989) *Using Civil Legal Aid* (LAG).

The two networks described above are by no means the only sources of specialist front line legal advice and assistance. A number of specialist agencies cover specific subject areas and offer a limited back-up service to advisers who cannot solve the problem themselves. Where appropriate these have been referenced in the text of the book. In some parts of the country (particularly large cities) there may also be an independent law centre, which can offer some form of free legal service to clients in their catchment area. Law centres normally prioritize the matters on which they are able to help, to reflect the major concerns of their local area, but most law centres offer assistance in the areas of housing, social security, family, employment and immigration law. To find out whether there is a law centre in your area contact The Law Centres Federation, Duchess House, 18–19 Warren Street, London W1P 5EB (Tel: 01 387 8570).

Finally, mention should be made of four organizations who provide specialist advice in specific areas which are not covered in the chapters of this book. First, Community Relations Councils (CRCs) which exist in most regions of the country to help foster good race relations and which can therefore advise on ways of trying to resolve disputes in this field. If the address of the local CRC cannot be found in the local telephone directory contact the Commission for Racial Equality (CRE), Elliot House, 10–12 Allington Street, London SW1E 5EH (Tel: 01 828 7022). Second, The Children's Legal Centre exists as a pressure group to provide legal advice, back-up and research on any issue that involves the legal rights of children. They can be contacted at 20 Compton Terrace, London N1 2UN (Tel: 01 359 6251). Third, the Family Rights Group provides a limited telephone advice service (mornings only, Monday, Wednesday and Friday) to families with children in care or the subject of other related proceedings. They can be contacted at 6–9 Manor Gardens, London N7 6LA (Tel: 01 272 7308). Fourth, the Women's Legal Defence Fund, 3rd Floor, 29 Great James Street, London, WC1 3ES, provides advice, assistance and free representation to women in equal pay, discrimination and harassment cases.

This book is devoted largely to the legal rights of social work clients in England and Wales and to a lesser degree in Scotland. For historical and political reasons the law-making process in Northern Ireland is a little different from that in the mainland, which accounts for the fact that whilst the law in that country is in general terms broadly similar to that in England and Wales there remain sufficient differences of detail for a different book to need to be written, were it to accommodate the law of that country. Scotland, with its own very different legal system, presents another set of problems to anyone writing a book of this nature. However, as many of the laws of England apply in more or less the same way to Scotland the book is more accessible to the Scottish reader, and the text will indicate where appropriate if the law in Scotland differs in any way.

One final point should be made regarding this book and national boundaries. The only courts that will have any direct interest for the great majority of social work clients and their advisers are the domestic courts of the United Kingdom, and of course the large number of administrative tribunals. There are, however, two other courts outside the United Kingdom whose deliberations can have a considerable impact on the lives of those living in this country. These are the European Court in Luxembourg and The European Court of Human Rights in Strasbourg.

The *European Court* is the final Court of Appeal, whose decisions will bind the courts of the United Kingdom, on matters relating to the

Treaty of the European Community (EC). This may not at first sight appear to have much to do with the daily life of those doing social work. But occasionally the European Court has been used by pressure groups working within the United Kingdom to challenge the legality of a government action, on the grounds that it is in breach of EEC law. The most spectacular example of this in recent years has been the challenge by the Child Poverty Action Group (CPAG) to the provision in the Social Security Act 1975 preventing a married or cohabiting woman from receiving invalid care allowance (see Chapter 4, p. 122), a weekly benefit paid to the carers of disabled people. The CPAG successfully argued that this provision was in breach of an EEC Directive concerning the Equal Treatment of Women and in consequence the government was obliged to extend the benefit to married and cohabiting women at a cost in excess of £70m.

The *European Court of Human Rights* is a very different institution which is based in the Council of Europe and is concerned with the upholding of human rights in European countries, in accordance with the Convention for the Protection of Human Rights and Fundamental Freedoms of 1950. Unlike EEC law, this Convention does not form part of the law of the United Kingdom although the Court of Appeal has stated that United Kingdom courts should 'have regard' to it when applying national law. The Convention, which is essentially a human rights charter, covers a wide range of rights including the right to life, the right not to be subjected to torture or to inhuman or degrading treatment or punishment, the right to a fair hearing, the right to respect for private life and freedom of correspondence and the right to freedom of thought and expression.

A person who believes that one of these rights has in their case been violated can apply to the *European Commission on Human Rights*, setting out the basis of their claim. They can only do this, however, if they have first exhausted all legal remedies in this country. If the Commission believes that the applicant has a strong case they may then refer the matter to the European Court of Human Rights which will decide whether the alleged conduct has violated the Convention. If the Court finds in favour of the applicant, it will become the duty of the member state concerned to enforce their decision, although the only sanction for failure to enforce is suspension of membership of the Council of Europe. More cases have been brought against the United Kingdom than any other

9

member state and in many case violations of the Convention have been found to have occurred. In three areas of particular concern to those engaged in social work the Court rulings have had a significant impact in the United Kingdom: the recognition and development of prisoners' rights; the rights of mentally disordered patients (see Chapter 5) and in areas of legislation relating to immigration. Those who are interested in learning more about the operation and the potential use of this court should write to Interights, Kingsway Chambers, 46 Kingsway, London WC2B 6EN. (Tel: 01 242 5581)

Finally, those with the confidence to 'go it alone' who simply need to know what to do, should obtain the following invaluable guide: *Taking Your Own Case to Court or Tribunal* (1985) The Consumer Association.

An excellent ongoing update to much of the material in this book (and more) is *The Adviser* magazine published jointly by NACAB and Shelter at regular intervals.

2

How to Help Your Client Complain

The right to complain, if a service is inadequate, should be considered a fundamental human right. All too frequently, that right to complain remains unexercised, because people are unaware of the procedures that are available for making a complaint. There are in fact a surprisingly large number of complaints procedures in this country, that are little used. Not only do the major providers of professional services such as doctors, nurses, lawyers, psychiatrists, paramedicals, teachers, surveyors, architects, banks, local authorities, estate agents, travel agents and the police have their own internal complaints procedures, but increasing numbers of trades are also developing Codes of Practice within their own associations, that include procedures for handling complaints from customers. This chapter will provide the social worker with an outline of the complaints procedures that exist for dealing with some of the more common types of complaint their clients might wish to make. As in other chapters, the chapter will demonstrate how the law provides a much wider framework through which common frustrations can be expressed than is often supposed. Although it may often be the case that the most effective way of addressing a problem is by collective action, this chapter will concentrate upon the procedures available for individual complaints. Complaints about local authority employees, including social workers, are dealt with in Chapter 3.

The particular complaints procedures to be outlined in this chapter are as follows:

1. complaints about public utilities: gas (p.12), electricity (p.15), water (p.19), telephone (p.19), postal service (p.22);
2. complaints about faulty goods and services;
3. complaints about police misconduct;

4. complaints about lawyers: solicitors (p.38) and barristers (p.44).
5. complaints about medical services and paramedical services: general practitioners (p.48), dentists (p.51), hospital staff and paramedical professions (p.52).

Whatever the subject, whether it be an unhelpful doctor, an aggressive police officer, a badly mended washing machine, a ruined holiday, or poor legal advice, dissatisfaction with a service invariably gives rise to a sense of injustice in the person on the receiving end. This sense of injustice normally manifests itself in the desire to complain. This chapter sets out to clarify the relevant procedures.

COMPLAINTS ABOUT PUBLIC UTILITIES

Although an increasing number of the utilities in this section have passed into private ownership as part of the policies of the Thatcher government, they can still be described as *public utilities* in the sense that the great majority of households in this country receive these services as a matter of course. This is of increasing importance, as more and more utilities are passed from a state monopoly to a 'private' monopoly. The economic theorist Hayek, whose writings inform much of Thatcher government policy, has argued that even if in given circumstances only Government is able to supply particular services, there is no reason to prohibit private agencies from trying to find methods of providing these services. Every one of the public utilities in this section has its own complaints procedures, details of which can be obtained free of charge by writing to the addresses provided.

Gas

Responsibility for gas provision rests with British Gas, which is divided into geographical regions. A number of the legal duties, both of the consumer, and British Gas are set out in the Gas Act 1986. They can be summarized as follows:

General duties of British Gas. To supply gas to any occupier of premises within 25 yards of a live gas main who so requests; and not to disconnect that supply unless a bill is unpaid for at least 28 days, and 7 days' notice of disconnection has been given (see also p.17 on effects of Code of Practice on Disconnection), or in an emergency. Although normally British Gas employees need a warrant to enter private premises, they may enter without a warrant in an emergency to take steps to avert danger to life or property.

General duties of consumer. To ensure that air is freely available to a gas appliance; to have gas appliances fitted by a competent installer; not to use a gas appliance that might be unsafe; if there is a gas leak, to shut off the supply and contact the local gas emergency service (number in telephone book under British Gas). Failure to do any of these things is an offence carrying a heavy fine.

Can a consumer be made to pay for gas, after they have vacated the premises?

If a consumer is vacating premises to which gas is supplied they must give British Gas 24 hours' notice of their departure, otherwise they may be obliged to pay for gas used up to whichever of the following first occurs:
- the 28th day after notice is eventually given;
- the date of the next meter reading;
- the date on which a subsequent occupier requires a supply of gas.

What can you complain about?

Clearly, a customer is entitled to complain if British Gas fail to comply with any of their legal duties set out above. They may in addition wish to complain about faulty maintenance by British Gas contractors, faulty goods purchased from a British Gas showroom (on this see also 'complaints about faulty goods', p.25), or mistakes in a gas bill. Any failure on the part of British Gas to follow their Code of Practice regarding disconnection (see below) will automatically give rise to grounds for complaint.

If the customer is a tenant, paying for gas through a meter, the law regulates exactly how much a landlord can charge for the gas. The up-to-date figures are contained in a leaflet which can be obtained from any gas showroom or *Gas Consumers' Council*. If the landlord is overcharging, the tenant is entitled by law to a refund when the meter

13

is emptied. For further information see the Gas Consumers' Council leaflet *Gas: How Much Can Your Landlord Charge?*, and the National Consumer Council paper (1987) *The Maximum Resale Price of Gas*.

Finally, the Gas Act 1986 requires British Gas to send to any consumer on request a copy of a statement issued by the Secretary of State for Energy relating to the tests of the gas supplied to the consumer during the preceding quarter.

Who do you complain to?

Initially, all complaints should be made either to the local British Gas showroom, or if this is inconvenient, to the relevant British Gas Regional Office whose address will be on the customer's last gas bill. If the matter cannot be resolved over the telephone the complaint should be put in writing. If the matter is not resolved by this method, the next stage is to write to the regional Gas Consumers' Council, whose address should also be on the customer's last gas bill. This Council is an independent body, which represents customers' interests in disputes with British Gas.

For serious complaints contact: National Gas Consumers' Council, Abford House, 15 Wilton Rd, London SW1V 1LT (Tel: 01 931 0977). The equivalent body for Scotland is at 86 George St, Edinburgh EH2 3BU (Tel: 031 226 6523), and for Wales is at Caradog House, St Andrew's Place, Cardiff CF1 3BE (Tel: 0222 226547). There are a further 9 regional offices.

These gas consumer councils are independent consumer watchdog organizations that represent the interests of gas consumers in a whole range of ways, lobbying the government for change, ensuring that any price increases are scrutinized, and representing individuals with grievances against British Gas that have not been resolved at a local level.

Is there a time limit?

There is no time limit for complaints about British Gas services. If, however, the complaint is serious enough to lead to possible legal action, as for example when the customer has been injured by the negligence of British Gas employees, any legal action must normally be commenced within 3 years of the incident.

14

How do you make the complaint?

If a complaint is not immediately satisfied, it should always be put in
the form of a letter, copies being kept by the complainant.

Will you need help to make the complaint, and will it cost anything?

Gas Consumer Councils (regional and national) should normally
handle the complaint once it has been made. There is no charge.
Further help will be needed if the complaint might lead to legal
action. A Citizens' Advice Bureau, or Consumer Advice Centre, will
advise on the likelihood of this.

What remedies are available?

For further information see the leaflet *Help and Advice from the Gas
Consumers' Councils* which can be obtained from any British Gas
showroom.

Electricity

The procedures governing complaints about electricity services are
very similar to those governing complaints about gas services.
Responsibility for the provision of electricity rests with the Electricity
Board, which like British Gas, is divided into regions. The legal
duties of both the Electricity Board and the consumer are laid down
by several statutes which can be summarized as follows:

General duties of Electricity Board. To provide a supply of
electricity to any occupier of premises who so requests providing they
live within 50 yards of a distributing main; to continue to supply the
electricity unless the customer fails to pay for it. There is no statutory
procedure for disconnection as for gas (but see p.17 on the Code of
Practice on Disconnection). Electricity Board employees may only
enter private premises without a warrant in an emergency to take
steps to avert danger to life or property, e.g. to prevent an imminent
fire.

General duties of consumer. There is no special requirement by
law that electricity consumers ensure that their appliances are safe,
although it is obviously in their own interests that they do so!

15

Can a consumer be made to pay for electricity after they have left the premises?

By law the consumer must inform the Electricity Board in writing at least 24 hours before they move so that the meter can be read. If they do not do this they will be liable to pay for any electricity up to the next meter reading or the time the next person moves in, whichever is the first to occur.

If a customer has a complaint about any aspect of their electricity service, they should follow exactly the same procedures as set out above for complaints about gas. The equivalent of the regional Gas Consumers' Council is the *Area Electricity Consultative Council,* whose address can be found in the local telephone directory or on the last electricity bill. If the complaint is serious and has not been resolved by the Area Electricity Consultative Council, the national policy making body for the supply of electricity, the Electricity Council, should be contacted. (There is no such Council for Scotland or Northern Ireland but see below).

Every consumer of electricity has *by law* the right to make representations to the Electricity Council on a matter affecting the distribution of electricity by an Area Electricity Board (see s.7[8A] Electricity Act 1947). This right only becomes exercisable once the Area Electricity Consultative Council has not been able to resolve the matter. Further information on this procedure can be found in the Electricity Council leaflet *Statutory Representations to the Electricity Council: a Guide for Consumers who Want to Make a Representation about their Local Electricity Board.*

The Electricity Council also has the power to investigate group complaints about the Bulk Supply Tariff, the structure of electricity tariffs for domestic and commercial use, the efficiency of the industry, methods of helping consumers to meet their electricity bills, policy on disconnection, consumer education on energy conservation. The address of the Electricity Council is: Electricity Council, 30 Millbank, London SW1P 4RD (Tel: 01 834 2333). For assistance with complaints of this nature in Scotland ring 031 225 1361 (North) or 041 637 7171 (South) and in Northern Ireland ring 0232 661100.

Completely independent of all the above bodies, is the *Electricity Consumers' Council (ECC)*, set up as a watchdog to 'represent the

16

interests of electricity consumers in England and Wales at national level'. The ECC does not normally take up individual cases, but it is a very useful body to approach concerning any general or persistent difficulties or problems experienced by clients in connection with their electricity supply. The ECC has direct access to the policy making level of the electricity industry and is willing and able to lobby hard and effectively on behalf of dissatisfied electricity consumers. Its particular areas of concern are the cost of domestic electricity, methods of helping consumers to meet their electricity bills, the circumstances in which Area Boards can disconnect customers, consumer education on the wise use of electricity and energy conservation. The address of the ECC is: The Electricity Consumers' Council, Brook House, 2–16 Torrington Place, London WC1E 7LL (Tel: 01 636 5703). (For equivalent complaints in Scotland and Northern Ireland ring numbers set out above.)

Special rules on disconnection of services (gas and electricity) for non-payment of bills

One of the most distressing problems facing clients of those engaged in social work is the threat of disconnection of gas or electricity services for non-payment of bills. In 1985–86 101 379 people were disconnected from their electricity supplies and 42 468 people were disconnected from their gas supplies. In 1987 disconnections increased by a further 30 per cent. For an excellent handbook, covering the whole range of problems associated with the fuel industries consult *The Fuel Rights Handbook* latest edition (SHAC), or Phillips, B. (1987) *Pay Less, Keep Warm* (Optima) or Colesby, J. and Townsend, P. (1981) *Keeping Warm for Half the Cost* (2nd edition) (Prism Press).

Since 1982 the electricity and gas industries have operated a joint Code of Practice for domestic users of their services regarding disconnection for non-payment of bills. The Code of Practice is essential reading for anybody engaged in social work. It can be obtained from any gas or electricity showroom. Reference to the Code of Practice will be invaluable if a social worker is negotiating on behalf of a client threatened with disconnection. Failure to comply with the Code will give rise to an automatic grounds for lodging a complaint.

The most important points contained in the Code of Practice are, in summary, as follows:

17

- Once either service has been informed that the DSS or Social Services are involved in trying to help the customer, no supply will be disconnected for at least 14 days. If necessary a longer period than 14 days can be negotiated, in which case written confirmation should be requested. Longer periods should always be sought where possible to enable the agency to try and find ways to alleviate the problem. It is particularly important that this right is observed where children are in the home. The statistics on the effects of cold weather on children make grim reading. For example, in the winter quarter of 1980, there were 51 per cent more deaths of male children and 21 per cent more deaths of female children than in the summer quarter of that year. Social services departments are empowered to make financial payments to families in emergencies if this is likely to reduce the risk of their children being taken into care.
- If the house is lived in by a person who is blind, severely sick or disabled, the Code states 'we will try to agree with you a payment arrangement to avoid disconnection'. The clear implication of this section is that only in quite exceptional circumstances (e.g. blatant refusal to pay) can disconnection occur to people in these categories.
- If all the people living in the house, who have incomes are old age pensioners (see Chapter 9) the supply will not be disconnected between 1 October and 31 March. This rule does not, however, apply if the people can pay but refuse to do so. In the latter case not only can disconnection take place but the supply may not be reconnected for the following winter. (For general advice to elderly people on ways of paying for fuel and insulation consult Age Concern *Your Rights* which provides many useful ideas.)
- The actual disconnection should not take place if there is no adult at home at the time, unless warning has already been given that disconnection will take place after a certain date, that date has passed, and the employee who has come to disconnect the service has an entry warrant.
- Disconnection will not take place because of a debt in the name of a previous customer, nor if it is safe and practical to install a slot meter which can be set to incorporate payment of the debt in the future, nor if the debt is only for a hire purchase item nor if the customer has made and kept to a proposal in writing to pay off the debt by instalments over a reasonable period.

18

- If the debt is in the name of a landlord to whom the tenant has paid money for the use of gas and electricity, disconnection will not take place for at least 14 days. This is to enable the customer to apply to their local council (if in England or Wales) to pay the landlord's debt, and reclaim the sums from him. It is very important, if these are the circumstances, that the council are informed promptly in writing by the consumer (or their adviser) of the request. For general advice on ways of tackling fuel related poverty contact Neighbourhood Energy Action, 2–4 Bigg Market, Newcastle-upon-Tyne, NE1 1UB (Tel: 091 261 5677) or The Rights to Fuel Campaign, 318 Summer Lane, Birmingham, B19 3RL (Tel: 021 359 3562) which is a national voluntary organization committed to the abolition of disconnection powers for reasons of debt.

Water

The administration of the provision of water supplies in the United Kingdom, at the time of going to press, is divided up as follows:

England and Wales: the local water authority.
Scotland: the regional council (see Chapter 3).
Northern Ireland: DOE for NI.

As each area has its own regulations and bye-laws, any customer wishing to complain about their water service should obtain details about the local situation before taking any action. This information can be obtained from the local water office, whose address can be found on the last water rates bill. Once the water industry has passed into private ownership it is to be hoped an appropriate complaints mechanism is created.

Telephone

A convenient starting place to consider whether to make a complaint about the telephone service is to read the *British Telecom Code of Practice for Consumers*, which is printed in full in the back of the local Telephone Directory (A–D if in the London area). This explains in some detail the rights of the consumer of telephone services, and the practice that should be followed by British Telecom, the public company licensed by the Government to run the telecommunications services throughout the United Kingdom.

What can you complain about?

The Code of Practice deals with the standards of service that can be expected in a number of areas as follows:

- installation (including connection charges and deposits);
- provision of telephone books, and entries of name and address of subscribers;
- explanation of content of bills, and procedures for payment;
- procedures for querying of bills;
- procedures when subscriber has difficulty paying bills;
- disconnection and reconnection of telephone;
- the fault repair service (repairs normally to be effected within 2 days of complaint, if not, financial compensation is paid to the customer (under the Customer Service Guarantee);
- procedures for reimbursement of calls where difficulties are experienced after connection.

The Code of Practice should be consulted for further details of the above, together with the BT leaflet *What We're Doing to Improve our Service for You.*

Selling by telephone

Another telephone usage that often provokes a wish to complain is the use of the telephone for selling unsolicited services or goods. The Office of Fair Trading in a report published in October 1984 (*Selling By Telephone*) has set out Guidelines for companies engaging in this type of selling, laying down what it considers to be fair and unfair practice. These Guidelines are published in full at the back of the Telephone Directory. In summary, they state there should be no telephone selling at the customer's place of work; no selling after 9 p.m. at night; no calls to ex-directory numbers; a 'cooling-off' of 7 days between the date of the call and the receipt of any papers relating to any agreement to purchase; and a rule that all calls should begin with the caller explaining who they are, and the purpose of the call. If a customer feels that this particular practice code is not being followed by an unsolicited caller, they should obtain the name and address of the caller and complain to: The Office of Fair Trading, Field House, 15–25 Bream's Building, London EC4A 1PR (Tel: 01 242 2858).

Who do you complain to?

The Code of Practice answers this question as follows:

> All problems should be taken up with the local British Telecom Office . . . who will try to solve your difficulties. You may also obtain independent advice from a Citizens' Advice Bureau, Consumer Advice Centre or Trading Standards Department. British Telecom is very happy to work together with any of the independent advisory bodies if you decide you need their help to resolve your problem.

The telephone numbers of all local British Telecom Offices are listed in the Telephone Directory after the Code of Practice.

For more serious complaints, or complaints that are not satisfied by the above method, contact the Regional Advisory Committees on Telecommunications, which are the independent bodies set up to monitor and regulate Telecommunications in the United Kingdom. There are offices in Glasgow (041 248 2855), Cardiff (0222 374028), Belfast (0232 244113) and London (01 822 1650). The addresses are listed in the Telephone Directory after the Code of Practice. The central office for the United Kingdom is in London: OFTEL, Atlantic House, Holborn Viaduct, London EC1N 2HQ (Tel: 01 822 1650).

If the complaint is serious enough to be likely to lead to legal action, and the customer does not wish to engage in court proceedings, British Telecom offers an alternative to court action in the form of legally binding arbitration through the Chartered Institute of Arbitrators, who can be contacted at: International Arbitration Centre, 75 Cannon St, London EC4N 5BH (Tel: 01 236 8761) (covering the whole of the United Kingdom).

Is there a time limit?

It is naturally best to complain as early as possible after the problem has occurred. Complaints to the Chartered Institute of Arbitrators should normally be made within 12 months of the cause of the complaint, and the Institute will only accept complaints after that period in exceptional circumstances.

How do you make the complaint?

The method of pursuing initial complaints has already been described above. If the arbitration service is to be used, application in writing for the relevant application forms, and explanatory leaflet, should be made directly to the Chartered Institute of Arbitrators.

Will you need help to make the complaint and will it cost you anything?

The arbitration procedure is very simple, and based entirely on what is written by the complainant and British Telecom on the relevant forms. It is thus important to fill out the application form with great care, putting in all relevant details, dates, charges, costs and so forth, after consultation with any relevant documents, such as diaries. There will be a registration fee of £15. The arbitrator may refund the fee in the light of the outcome of the arbitration.

What remedies are available?

The arbitrator has the power to come to a decision that is legally binding on both parties, which includes the power to award compensation of up to £1000. Any claim in excess of this will probably have to go to the county court, which will involve the employment of a solicitor.

For a detailed appraisal and criticism of the standard contract conditions for the provision of services by British Telecom see the National Consumer Council Response to the OFTEL Consultation Document PD 41/87, which can be obtained from the NCC, 20 Grosvenor Gardens, London SW1W 0DH (Tel: 01 730 3469).

Postal services

Unlike the other services outlined above, there is no contractual relationship between the Post Office and its customers. This means that the areas of legal complaint are rather limited. There is however a Code of Practice governing most areas of Post Office contact with the public and a failure to follow the Code of Practice will give grounds for a complaint. A copy of this Code of Practice can be obtained from most large post offices.

What can you complain about?

The most common type of complaint relates to late delivery. Unfortunately there is no legal redress for such a complaint. If the delay is flagrant or persistent, it is nevertheless worth registering dissatisfaction by writing to the local Head Postmaster who will at the very least acknowledge the complaint. If it can be shown that the Post Office was in some way negligent in its handling of the relevant delivery, and damage was suffered by the complainant, compensation may be paid.

The other common type of complaint relates to lost or damaged mail. Post Office leaflet P58 *Enquiry about a missing or damaged letter or parcel* explains the procedure for such a complaint, and can be obtained from any post office. The level of compensation payable will depend on whether the item was sent by ordinary mail, recorded delivery, registered mail, or special delivery. Evidence that the item was actually sent must be produced. This should be in the form of a certificate of posting, which can be obtained from the post office at the time the item is posted (it obviously will not be given retrospectively). N.B. Complaints about standards of direct mail operations (including misleading information) should be addressed to the Direct Mail Services Standards Board (see p. 24).

Who do you complain to?

In the first instance all complaints should be addressed to the local Head Postmaster, whose address can be obtained from the local post office. If still dissatisfied, the complainant can complain to the Regional Director, of which there are seven in England, and one each in Scotland, Wales and Northern Ireland. The national, independent advisory bodies dealing with complaints about the Post Office are as follows:

Post Office Users' National Council (England), Waterloo Bridge House, Waterloo Rd, London SE1 8UA (Tel: 01 928 9548).
(Wales) Caradog House, St Andrew's Place, Cardiff CF1 3BE (Tel: 0222 374028).
(Scotland) Alhambra House, 45 Waterloo St, Glasgow G2 6AT (Tel: 041 248 2855).

(Northern Ireland) Chamber of Commerce, 22 Great Victoria St, Belfast BT2 7BJ (Tel: 0232 244113).

The Chartered Institute of Arbitrators is also available as an alternative method for resolving any dispute. For details of this procedure see p. 21 under British Telecom.

The Direct Mail Services Standards Board is at 26 Eccleston Street, London, SW1N 9PY (Tel: 01 824 8651).

Is there a time limit?

The usual advice applies about the desirability of making a complaint as soon as possible after the event. The Head Postmaster normally takes at least 6 weeks to reply to a complaint. If the complaint relates to a lost or damaged item, and court proceedings become necessary, they must be initiated within 12 months of the date the item was posted. If an application is to be made to the Chartered Institute of Arbitrators it must be filed within 18 months of the date the item was posted.

How do you make the complaint?

Complaints should be addressed to the Head Postmaster in a letter, or if still dissatisfied to the regional Director, also in a letter. If arbitration is being used, follow the procedure set out on p. 22 under British Telecom.

Will you need help to make the complaint and will it cost you anything?

See p. 22 under British Telecom (same answer).

What remedies are available?

Both the Post Office and the arbitrators can make offers of money compensation, if they feel the complaint is justified. In the latter case the offer is legally enforceable.

COMPLAINTS ABOUT FAULTY GOODS AND SERVICES

The law relating to faulty goods and services is quite complicated, and cannot be dealt with in any detail in this book. In addition, it should be made clear that for Scotland and Northern Ireland whilst the general principles set out below apply, there are differences of detail that ought only to be referred to local experts. As a starting point advisers should obtain from the Office of Fair Trading (address below) the relevant general pamphlet:

How to Put Things Right (England and Wales).
Dear Shopper in Scotland (Scotland).
Dear Shopper in Northern Ireland (Northern Ireland).

An excellent and readable summary of the various ways to complain about faulty goods and services can be found in a book by Brigid Avison (1986) *How to Complain* (Longman Self Help Guide). A more detailed and comprehensive account of the main legal rights of consumers, together with procedures for redress and useful addresses is the *Handbook of Consumer Law* (1989) produced by the National Federation of Consumer Groups and published jointly by Which/Hodder and Stoughton. A Citizens' Advice Bureau (and, if one exists in the area, a Consumer Advice Centre) is normally a good place to go to seek more detailed advice on how to complain about faulty goods or services. There is, however, set out below, a summary of the main factors of importance, when considering complaints of this nature.

Trade Associations

Some traders belong to Trade Associations. Most of these Trade Associations have Codes of Practice, which members are supposed to follow in their dealings with customers. A typical Code of Practice would be likely to cover most of the common areas of customer complaint, such as shoddy work, overcharging, slowness, and incompetence. Most of these Codes of Practice contain internal arbitration procedures that the dissatisfied customer may decide to use to resolve their dispute rather than engage in lengthy correspondence or legal proceedings. At the time of writing, official Codes of Practice (i.e. those drawn up in consultation with the Office of Fair Trading) exist for the purchase of all the following goods: mail-order catalogue goods, party plan selling, cars and motor cycles (including parts and accessories), electrical goods, furniture, shoes, glass and glazing, and photographic equipment.

In addition official Codes of Practice exist in connection with all the following services: repair and servicing of cars and motor cycles and body repairs to cars and caravans; repair and servicing of electrical goods, furniture, shoes and other footwear; laundry, dry cleaning, double glazing and photographic services.

All these Codes of Practice can be obtained from the Office of Fair Trading (see below) who will also provide an updated list. (N.B. If the complaint is about selling by telephone, see p. 20).

The addresses of all the Trade Associations concerned with all the above goods and services can be found in Avison (see above) and can also be obtained from the Office of Fair Trading. It must be stressed, however, that a trade or retailer is under no obligation to belong to the relevant Trade Association, and will only be bound by the Code of Practice if they are a member of that Trade Association or if they pretend that they are.

If a client is about to employ somebody to do work in their house such as home improvements or repairs (e.g. builders, plumbers, electricians) they are well advised *before employing any such person* to obtain the pamphlet *Home Improvements* from the Office of Fair Trading, which sets out in simple language how to avoid legal pitfalls so often associated with such work.

Goods bought from a trader (including shop, but excluding private sales)

All purchases of goods from a trader (i.e. person selling goods in the course of a business) have the following terms *automatically* implied into the sale, whatever the trader may or may not say to the contrary. If it subsequently transpires that one of these terms was not complied with by the seller, the purchaser has a legal remedy against the seller and should complain direct to them, either rejecting the goods in exchange for a refund or seeking financial compensation. The purchaser may need to seek legal advice on which of these various remedies is the most appropriate in the circumstances of their case as the law here can be complicated. If they do not obtain satisfaction, they should consult a Citizens' Advice Bureau or a Consumer Advice Centre. In addition, if the complainant's income is below a certain level, they can ask a solicitor to write a letter of complaint for them, under the Green Form Scheme (see Chapter 1). Ultimately, if they obtain no satisfaction they may have to take legal proceedings in the local county court. They will be most unlikely to receive legal aid for such a claim, whatever their income.

The terms that are *automatically* implied into a contract are as follows:

- that the trader has the legal right to sell the goods (i.e. they are not stolen). There are special rules extending the protection of the purchaser of goods in a 'market overt', i.e. a market held on days and at times prescribed as market days by charter, custom or statute.
- that the goods match their description (e.g. in size, colour, quality, shape, smell and so forth). Description may be by label, advertisement, or by the word of the trader themselves. (e.g. if the trader describes an item to the purchaser as a waterproof coat, it must be waterproof).
- as they are sold in the course of a business (i.e. not a private sale), that they are of *merchantable quality* and they are *fit for the purpose for which they were bought*. These terms need further explanation:
  - *of merchantable quality*. This means that they are in a suitable condition to be sold, given the circumstances in which they are offered. The question of the suitability of the goods will be decided by reference to a number of factors including their age, their price and their alleged quality, so that a second hand item need not be as 'merchantable' as one that is brand new. The case law here is extensive and the Law Commission has recently recommended that a far more detailed and clearer definition of the phrase should be developed by parliament (see *Sale and Supply of Goods*, Law Commission No. 160, May 1987). One case alone illustrates the subtleties of judicial interpretation. A pork chop containing a parasite worm that caused illness when eaten was not considered 'un-

27

merchantable' because the court found that the worm would have been killed had the chop been properly cooked!

Purchasers should further note that the trader is not liable for any defects specifically drawn to the attention of the purchaser prior to the purchase nor is the trader liable for any defects that the purchaser, having examined the goods prior to purchase, ought to have discovered.

- *fit for the purpose for which they are bought*. In order to rely upon this condition the purchaser must have communicated to the trader the purpose for which they were purchasing the goods unless the trader can show that the purchaser did not rely upon the trader's skill or knowledge, or that it would have been unreasonable to have done so.

For more detailed information on all the above implied terms consult Harvey, B. and Parry, D. (1987) *The Law of Consumer Protection and Fair Trading* (Butterworths) or Leder, M. (1986) (2nd edn.) *Consumer Law* (Pitman).

Note that if any goods are bought *on credit* the whole transaction is subject to a set of special rules under the Consumer Credit Act 1974. Details on these rules, which are designed amongst other things to protect the consumer from being rushed into credit sales, are set out in the leaflet *Shop Around for Credit* (Office of Fair Trading). A short summary of the rights of consumers to know what credit reference agencies say about them is contained in *No Credit?* (Office of Fair Trading). Details of the risks involved in paying in advance for goods and services are contained in *Don't Wave Your Money Goodbye* (Office of Fair Trading). For details on the protection of consumers who make 'doorstep purchases' and then wish to withdraw consult Consumer Protection SI 1987 No. 2117 (HMSO), or a simple leaflet *How to Cope With Doorstep Salesmen* (Office of Fair Trading).

There are also a number of criminal offences that may be committed under the Trade Descriptions Act 1968 in connection with false or misleading descriptions of goods that are offered for sale. Convictions can lead to heavy fines and compensation orders. Misleading price indications are covered by the Consumer Protection Act 1987 (see Harvey and Parry, above).

The responsibility for enforcing these criminal laws on trade

28

description and misleading prices rests with the Trading Standards/ Consumer Protection Department of the local authority (see Chapter 3) which should be consulted on any problem that may arise.

Services

There are further laws which protect the consumer of services. Any goods supplied as part of a service will be subject to what has been written above. But in addition the service has to reach certain basic standards. The law is set out in the Supply of Goods and Services Act 1982. The Act states that any supplier of a service to a consumer must provide that service:

- with reasonable care and skill, i.e. the standard expected of a reasonably competent practitioner of that trade;
- within a reasonable time, if it is implied in the contract that time is an essential part of the deal;
- for a reasonable charge, unless there is something to the contrary in the contract.

If a customer feels that they have been given a service that falls short on one or more of the above criteria, they will probably be entitled to claim some compensation from the person who provided the service. A Citizens' Advice Bureau, Consumer Advice Centre or solicitor can advise on such a claim. If not settled informally the claim will have to be settled in the small claims division of the local county court. Most county courts provide initial advice to claimants on how to make an application. Legal costs cannot be claimed if the amount of compensation is less than £500 (rising soon to £1000).

Note on exclusion clauses

None of the implied terms set out above can be excluded by a trader from a contract for the sale of consumer goods so long as the purchaser is dealing 'as a consumer' which means quite simply that the purchaser is a private purchaser and the seller is a trader. The main exception to this rule is a sale by auction, in which case the exclusion clause is effective if shown to be reasonable in the circumstances.

For further information on all the above aspects of consumer rights contact the Office of Fair Trading, Field House, 15–25 Bream's Building, London EC4A 1PR (Tel: 01 242 2858). A further valuable source of up to date information is the quarterly journal of the National Consumer Council, *Consumer Voice*.

All the leaflets and booklets of the OFT described above can be obtained from this address or in Northern Ireland from the Department of Economic Development, Trading Standards Branch, 176 Newtownbreda Road, Belfast BT8 4QS (Tel: 0232 647151). Stocks of these publications should also be available in CABs, Consumer Advice Centres and Trading Standards (or Consumer Protection) Departments.

General assistance with consumer complaints

Since 1974 there has been in existence the Institute of Consumer Advisers, (ICA) 14 Delawyk Crescent London SE24 9JB (Tel: 01 403 5867). The membership comprises people who are professionally employed as consumer advisers within consumer advice centres. The ICA aims to encourage, maintain and seek to improve standards of consumer services. Whilst it does not deal with individual complaints it can refer enquiries to advisers in the relevant area.

The Institute of Trading Standards Administration (ITSA), County Offices, Kendal, Cumbria L79 4RQ (Tel: 0539 21000 extension 4327) is the professional body for trading standards officers, and is able to advise members of the public with regards to the problems encountered in the commercial transactions of everyday life. Finally, the *Consumer Congress Directory* produced by the National Consumer Council, 20 Grosvenor Gardens, London, SW1W 0DH (Tel: 01 730 3469) provides details, including addresses and telephone numbers, of 295 organizations involved in the consumer movement in the United Kingdom. It is an invaluable reference source on a very wide range of consumer issues as a means to finding the best back-up assistance available for a particular problem.

Over the coming 5 years, the gradual implementation of the Civil Justice Review should have a significant impact upon the processing through the courts of small consumer claims.

COMPLAINTS ABOUT POLICE MISCONDUCT

This section deals only with the position in England and Wales and does not extend to Scotland or Northern Ireland which operate under a different system. For details of the complaints systems in these countries consult:

Scotland: the Police (Discipline) (Scotland) Regulations 1967 available from any Scottish Police Station or from the Scottish Police Federation (041 332 5234/6268). There is no independent complaints authority in Scotland equivalent to the Police Complaints' Authority in England (see p. 35).

Northern Ireland: the Independent Commission for Police Complaints (0232 244821) should be contacted for further information on the complaints system currently in operation in Northern Ireland.

England and Wales: Any person who is a victim or a witness of misconduct by a police officer has a right to lodge a complaint against that officer. If a person suffers actual physical harm, damage to their property or is wrongfully arrested or imprisoned by a police officer, they may also be able to sue that officer or the relevant police authority in the county or High Court. Whilst the decision whether or not to sue the officer is best taken following legal advice, the lay adviser should be able to advise a client as to whether or not to make an official complaint about police misconduct.

An adviser whose work brings them into regular contact with clients who are frequently in brushes with the police should obtain a copy of the best existing guide on the subject Harrison, J. (1987) *Police Misconduct: Legal Remedies* (Legal Action Group). The book also includes PACE Codes of Practice (see Chapter 6) and the Police Discipline Code 1985. This book contains detailed information on the procedures available, draft complaints letters, explanations of how to present evidence and find witnesses, examples of successful outcomes, and a range of interesting statistics concerning the effectiveness of police complaints. For the adviser whose work only occasionally brings them into contact with alleged police misconduct the following outline should suffice.

Also of interest is English, J. *The Police Training Manual.*

The police complaints procedure

Any person whether victim or witness of alleged police misconduct has the right to lodge a formal complaint about the misconduct. The complaint must relate to the action of an identifiable officer, or officers, and not just to 'police action in general'. 'Misconduct' means any breach by a police officer of the *Police Discipline Code* (Police Discipline Regulations 1985 SI No. 518 Sch 1). The Code should be consulted in detail if possible before deciding whether to lodge a complaint. Offences under the Code are in summary as follows:

- discreditable conduct (e.g. acting in a disorderly manner);
- misconduct towards another member of the police force (e.g. abusing or assaulting a colleague);
- disobedience to orders (e.g. any breach of the Code of Practice, see Chapter 6 on Civil Rights and the Police);
- neglect of duty (e.g. failing to react promptly to a request for assistance from a member of the public);
- falsehood or prevarication (e.g. making up or destroying evidence);
- improper disclosure of information (e.g. handing over confidential police records to a third party);
- corruption (e.g. accepting bribes);
- abuse of authority (e.g. being violent, oppressive or abusive to any member of the public);
- racially discriminatory behaviour;
- neglect of health (e.g. not carrying out doctor's instructions when off sick);
- improper dress or untidiness while on duty;
- damage to police property, wilfully or through lack of due care;
- drunkenness while on duty or preventing officer coming on duty;
- drinking on duty or soliciting drink;
- entering licensed premises without good cause, on duty, or off duty if still in uniform;
- criminal conduct;

- being an accessory to a disciplinary offence.

The Police Discipline Code is clearly extensive, even draconian, demanding from officers very high standards of behaviour. Some 16 000 complaints are filed each year against police officers for alleged breaches of the Code. It should be noted however that, of these complaints, an average of less than 10 per cent are upheld. Less than 1 per cent lead to any disciplinary action against the officer involved. It is indeed immensely difficult to succeed in attributing blame to any police officer under the existing complaints procedures. In the words of Sir Cecil Clothier, Chairman of the Police Complaints Authority, writing in the *Guardian* in response to criticism of this low 'success' rate (17 April 1987): 'It remains the fact that in the great majority of cases no disciplinary proceedings follow investigation, either because there is no cause for them or, more commonly, because there is insufficient evidence.'

Information on police computers

In 1988 the Association of Chief Police Officers published a detailed *Code of Practice for Police Computer Systems* which states that 'any failure to comply with the Code could amount to disciplinary offence'. The Code can be obtained from the Communications Department, Merseyside Police, PO Box 59, Liverpool L69 1JD (see also Chapter 6, p. 178).

Procedure for making a complaint

The procedure for making a complaint about a police officer who is alleged to have breached the Police Discipline Code is very straight-forward. It costs nothing. The complainant, or somebody acting on their behalf, simply writes a letter addressed to the Chief Constable (or to the Commissioner of Police if in London) setting out the circumstances of the complaint. The letter should give the date, time and place of the incident. It should identify the officer or officers involved, either by name, by number, or if that is not possible, by description. It should describe the incident fairly and concisely, including details of any damage or injuries sustained. It should also give details of any other witnesses to the incident. A copy should always be kept of this letter.

Once the complaint has been received by the relevant police chief, there are two possible paths they may take, either an *informal resolution or a formal resolution*.

Informal resolution

This is only permissible if the conduct complained of, if proved, would not justify a criminal or disciplinary charge *and* the complainant agrees that the matter can be resolved informally. The Home Office has suggested the following as examples of misconduct that should be investigated informally: 'the use of obscene language or the disciplinary offence of incivility, or an assault in the nature of a mere push without aggravating features such as an endeavour to obtain an admission'.

If the officer appointed by the police chief to investigate the complaint feels that informal resolution is the best way of dealing with the complaint, an interview will be arranged between that investigating officer and the complainant to discuss this possibility. An adviser can be present at this interview to ensure that undue pressure is not placed upon the complainant. It is important to ask the investigating officer *before the interview begins* for an agreement that the complainant will be sent a photocopy of any statement they may make in the course of the interview. Any statement made by either party in the course of an interview for informal resolution will be inadmissible in any future criminal trial, so all parties can express themselves freely.

If, following the interview, the complainant is willing to drop the complaint, or is satisfied with the investigating officer's explanation or apology, the matter will have been informally resolved. If the complainant is not satisfied with the informal resolution, they must make this clear. In these circumstances the complaint will follow the formal complaints procedure.

Formal investigation

If a complaint cannot be resolved informally, or is not appropriate for informal resolution because of its serious nature, it will be investigated formally in one of two ways, either by an *Internal Formal Investigation* or by an *Investigation Supervised by the Police Complaints' Authority (PCA)*.

Internal formal investigation

This procedure runs along similar lines to the informal resolution procedure, but if there has already been an informal resolution attempt which has failed, a different investigating officer will be appointed. Investigating officers are always appointed by the police chief who received the initial complaint. They may be from another force, but this is not essential. The officer will always be a senior officer of at least the rank of chief inspector. The investigating officer will arrange an interview in the same way as for the informal resolution. The complainant can be accompanied at this interview by a person of their choice.

Investigation supervised by the Police Complaints' Authority (PCA)

The most serious types of complaints are referred to the PCA, a special independent body set up in 1985 with wide powers to investigate serious complaints against the police. Broadly speaking, these will be where it is alleged that the conduct complained of:

- resulted in death;
- resulted in serious injury (a fracture, damage to an internal organ, a deep cut or laceration, or an impairment of bodily function);
- amounted to an assault occasioning actual bodily harm;
- amounted to corruption;
- constituted a *serious arrestable offence* (see Chapter 6, p. 195).

A police chief may refer any other complaint to the PCA but is under no obligation to do so. Controversial cases are often referred to the PCA in an attempt to allay public anxiety about the independence of the enquiry. In addition, the PCA may itself require a police chief to submit a particular complaint to its supervision. A complainant may themselves request the PCA to investigate their complaint. This is only likely to be allowed if there are special 'disadvantages' in the complainant's position, e.g. they are very elderly, mentally ill, or a juvenile.

The role of the PCA is supervisory, i.e. it does not carry out the investigation itself. It does, however, have wide powers to dictate the way in which the investigation is carried out, for example by requesting that certain witnesses be interviewed, by requiring specific forensic tests to be carried out, or by insisting on vetting the choice of investigating officer.

When the investigating officer has completed the investigation they will send a report to the PCA. The PCA will then send a statement to the relevant police chief in which they will indicate whether they feel the investigation is satisfactory. A copy of this statement should normally be sent to the complainant (unless, for example, criminal charges are being advised). For a critical appraisal of the work of the PCA read Christian, L. (1989) 'PCA Worse than useless' *Socialist Lawyer,* No. 7, Winter/Spring, 15–17.

What are the possible outcomes of any of the above investigations?

The purpose of the investigation is to decide whether the officer(s) in question breached the Police Discipline Code. There may be three possible findings:

- there has been no breach of the Police Discipline Code;
- there has been a breach but no action will be taken (because it was too minor, or the officer has left the force or cannot be identified);
- there has been a breach and disciplinary and/or criminal proceedings will be initiated against the officer(s).

The PCA can be contacted at 10 Great George St, London SW1P 3AE (Tel: 01 273 6450).

Will the complainant receive any compensation?

It should be noted that the complainant will not receive any compensation under any of the above procedures even if their claim is substantiated and action is taken against the officer. If the complainant wishes compensation (because, for example, they have suffered some injury, damage to their property, or have suffered the indignity of false imprisonment) they will have to initiate court proceedings against the police (see Chapter 6, p. 187). This should

Table 2.1 Analysis of disciplinary outcome of complaints[1]. Period 1 January–31 December 1988. From the Annual Report of the Police Complaints Authority 1988

Type of complaint	No disciplinary charges preferred	Disciplinary charges preferred by chief officer and admitted by accused S.91(2)	Disciplinary charges preferred by chief officer (not admitted by officer)		Disciplinary charges recommended by PCA		Dispensation		Total
			Complaints	Charges[2]	Complaints	Charges[2]	Refused	Granted	
1. Incivility	1 420	—	16	16	2	2	—	209	1 647
2. Assault	2 721	—	45	40	10	13	4	541	3 321
3. Irregularity in Procedure	1 175	—	6	8	1	1	1	118	1 301
4. Traffic Irregularity	273	3	—	—	1	1	—	11	285
5. Neglect of Duty	1 261	—	21	24	13	8	—	94	1 392
6. Corruption	58	—	15	10	—	—	—	14	87
7. Mishandling of Property	286	—	2	3	—	—	—	67	355
8. Irregularity of Evidence	727	—	1	2	2	3	—	47	777
9. Oppressive Conduct	988	—	9	8	1	3	2	316	1 316
10. Irregular Arrest	715	—	5	5	—	—	—	40	760
11. Irregular Stop/Search	67	—	2	2	—	—	—	7	76
12. Irregular Search	234	—	—	—	—	—	—	7	242
13. Other	919	—	15	15	2	1	1	27	964
Total	10 844	3	137	133	32	32	9	1 498	12 523

[1] For distinction between complaints and cases see Chapter 5 paragraph 5.2
[2] These figures are not included in TOTAL.

only be done after careful consultation with a solicitor. In really serious cases of police misconduct involving wider questions of civil liberties the National Council for Civil Liberties, 21 Tabard St, London SE1 4LA (Tel: 01 403 3888) may be able to help.

COMPLAINTS ABOUT LAWYERS

Legal services are provided by lawyers who are either solicitors or barristers. They may be in private practice, or they may be working for a law centre, a Citizens' Advice Bureau or an independent advice agency, in which case they are paid a salary from public funds. Although in private practice, the solicitor or barrister may receive payment for the case from the government, through the legal aid scheme (see Chapter 1). Regardless of the nature or the place of the lawyer's practice, or form of remuneration, every solicitor or barrister is expected to provide a service of high professional skill. Any client who feels that in their particular case they have not received such a service, has the right to make a formal complaint. The complaint will always be against the individual lawyer, and not against the practice, the chambers or the organization for which they work. For every lawyer is personally responsible for their own standards of work.

This section deals first with lawyers practising in England and Wales and second with lawyers practising in Northern Ireland and Scotland.

England and Wales

Solicitors

As a starting point advisers should obtain 2 leaflets from the N W Legal Services Committee, 2nd Floor, Elizabeth House, 16 St Peter's Square, Manchester M2 3DA entitled as follows: *Good Practice by Solicitors* (for advisers) and *How to Get the Best out of your Solicitor* (for clients).

What can you complain about?

A complaint about a solicitor is likely to be one of three types:

- a complaint about the solicitor's bill;
- a complaint that the solicitor has proved incompetent, as a result of which the client has suffered some loss;
- a complaint about the way a solicitor has handled a case but no financial loss has been suffered by the client.

A COMPLAINT ABOUT THE SOLICITOR'S BILL

Solicitors run a business and therefore have to make a profit in order to pay their salaries and meet their overheads. It is perfectly proper, therefore, that anybody visiting a solicitor for the first time should enquire as to how much the solicitor's service is going to cost. If the client is eligible for legal aid, a special procedure will be followed (see Chapter 1). If, however, the client is not eligible for legal aid, or the matter is not one for which legal aid is available (e.g. conveyancing, and making of wills) the client will have to pay. It is essential that a client is aware from the outset that solicitors charge for all the time they spend on the case, including time spent perusing letters and making telephone calls at an hourly rate. This means that even the friendly, reassuring chat on the telephone may end up as an item on the bill! Solicitors' bills are thus often higher than the client expected at the outset. Nevertheless, if a client feels that they have been overcharged there are two procedures they may follow to challenge their bill:

1. *Apply for a remuneration certificate.* This procedure is only available for work that has not involved court proceedings. The client who, having received a bill, feels they have been overcharged, should ask their solicitor within 1 month of receiving the bill for a Remuneration Certificate from the Law Society. They can make this request in writing to their solicitor to avoid embarrassment, and in the meantime, should not pay the bill. The solicitor must then write to the Law Society enclosing their file and justifying the bill. The client will be given the opportunity to comment on the solicitor's justification. Eventually the Law Society will reply to the client enclosing a certificate stating the amount they feel should be paid. The client

The legal rights manual

cannot challenge this certificate and will have to pay whatever amount is shown.

It should be noted that where the bill concerns any conveyancing charges the solicitor should have followed the procedure laid down by the Law Society in their *Fact Sheet on Solicitors' Conveyancing Charges* which is available free of charge from the Law Society, 113 Chancery Lane, London WC2A 1PL (Tel: 01 242 1222).

2. *Apply for taxation of the bill.* This procedure is available whether or not the work has involved court proceedings. It could involve the client in expense, however, and is a procedure that is not advisable for relatively minor matters. It is probably best to seek advice from a Citizens' Advice Bureau before embarking upon the procedure. Under the procedure, which involves an application to the court by the client (which court will depend on the size of the bill), the court may reduce the bill, having listened to representations from both sides. The procedure is complicated because the court cannot reduce every aspect of the bill, and in addition if they only reduce the bill by 20 per cent or less, they can order the complainant to pay the solicitors' costs of defending the application. There is thus a very real danger that the client will end up paying more than the original bill, even if the bill is reduced! In addition, the procedure is slow and cumbersome.

A COMPLAINT THAT THE SOLICITOR HAS PROVED INCOMPETENT AS A RESULT OF WHICH THE CLIENT HAS SUFFERED LOSS.

Under this procedure, the client is in fact suing their solicitor for negligence. One can therefore imagine the reluctance of a client who has already suffered loss as a result of their solicitor's alleged incompetence, to embark upon yet more legal proceedings. In recent years, however, the Law Society has tried to make the system more accessible to such complaints, in an attempt to improve the image of the profession, and allay public criticism.

What can you complain about?

A client can complain about any action (or inaction) by their solicitor, that has caused them loss for which compensation should reasonably be paid. The missing of deadlines for the issue of court proceedings;

failure to seek expert advice that might have increased the client's claim; the giving of negligent advice leading to the client losing money are all common grounds for negligence claims against solicitors. But the issues here are complex and certainly need legal advice. If in any doubt, seek the advice of the Negligence Panel (and see below).

What is the procedure?

As the complaint is one whereby the client is seeking compensation directly from the solicitor, the complaint has to be directed to the solicitor in question. The solicitor is unlikely to accept the complaint without a fight and it is thus advisable to seek legal assistance in the drafting of such a complaint before it is formally made. But where can you seek that advice? Since 1986 a scheme has been in operation whereby a client who is considering making such a complaint can receive a one hour diagnostic interview with an experienced solicitor free of charge, to decide whether grounds for such a claim exist. The diagnostic interview will be with a member of the *Negligence Panel*. For access to this panel the complainant must write directly either to their local law society (address in telephone book, or obtainable from the Law Society, see above), or to: Solicitors' Complaints Bureau, Portland House, Stag Place, London SW1E 5BL (Tel: 01 834 2288).

The solicitor on the Negligence Panel may recommend a number of alternative options:

- no action, if having heard the story, they believe there is no case in law;
- the use of the independent Arbitration Scheme which might be proposed as a simple way of resolving small disputes where the alleged loss is minimal;
- legal action against the solicitor in question. If this is the conclusion of the Negligence Panel member, they will advise the client to obtain legal representation, for which legal aid will be available (see Chapter 1). Otherwise the client will have to pay. The Negligence Panel solicitor is allowed to offer to take the case for the client;
- no legal action should be taken but the matter should be referred to the Solicitors' Complaints Bureau as 'shoddy work' (see below).

41

A COMPLAINT ABOUT THE WAY A SOLICITOR HAS HANDLED A CASE BUT
WHERE NO LOSS HAS BEEN SUFFERED

What can you complain about?

It sometimes happens that the client does not actually suffer direct
financial loss as a result of the way their solicitor has handled their
case, but they feel that their solicitor has generally given them a
service that is below the standard they are entitled to expect. The Law
Society gives the following as examples of the type of situation where
the circumstances may give rise to a right to lodge a complaint under
this head. The list is not exhaustive:

- failure or delay in answering letters;
- delay in dealing with the case;
- failure to deal properly with the client's money;
- acting for both sides in a case, where there is a conflict of
  interest;
- overcharging (see also p. 39);
- dishonesty or deception;
- failure to hand back papers when client has asked for them
  having paid the bill;
- 'shoddy work'. This is generally defined as work which is
  substandard, causing distress and inconvenience though no
  entitlement to compensation.

Who do you complain to?

The procedure for making one of the above complaints was
introduced in 1986 and is relatively straightforward. The complaint
must be made by the complainant in writing, direct to the *Solicitors'
Complaints Bureau* (see p. 43 for address). The Bureau is a body of
lawyers and lay representatives. Its complaints work is itself
monitored by an internal Investigation Committee, and by the
external Lay Observer (see p. 43). Once the Bureau has received the
complaint, they will send a copy of it to the solicitor involved, inviting
comment. They may also ask the complainant for more information.
Having considered all sides of the argument they may then choose to
take no further action, or they may report the matter to the Solicitors'
Disciplinary Tribunal. This latter body has wide powers, including

the power to fine a solicitor, to suspend the solicitor from further practice and the ultimate sanction of preventing the solicitor from continuing in practice at all. In 1986 160 solicitors were referred to the Disciplinary Tribunal and in 1987 102 solicitors were referred.

Can anybody help you to lodge your complaint?

The Interview Panel. Another innovation in the complaints system is the Interview Panel. This service is available to clients of solicitors who wish to make a complaint, but who have difficulty explaining their case. In these circumstances an appointment can be made with a solicitor who will help write out the complaint. It is potentially an innovation of great assistance to those engaged in social work, many of whose clients might not be conversant in legal jargon and procedures. Most parts of the country have now established their Interview Panels. All appointments with a member of the Interview Panel are made by the Solicitors' Complaints Bureau, and are free. Bureau staff will not themselves give interviews for this purpose.

The Lay Observer. The Lay Observer, appointed by the Lord Chancellor, exists as a further tier in the complaints system. The Lay Observer cannot be either a solicitor or a barrister. The first two Lay Observers were in fact retired senior officers of the armed forces. The Lay Observer exists to investigate complaints about the complaints procedure itself. If, once a client's complaint has been investigated, they are still dissatisfied either with the way in which it has been investigated, or with the outcome of the investigation, they may complain to the Lay Observer. They should write a letter to the Lay Observer setting out the reason for their dissatisfaction at the following address: The Lay Observer for England and Wales, Royal Courts of Justice, Strand, London WC2A 2LL (Tel: 01 936 6000).

The complaint must be lodged within 3 months of receiving the decision of the Solicitors' Complaints Bureau. It will be necessary to inform the Lay Observer of the file number of the complaint. S/he will then investigate the complaint and decide whether it has been investigated fully and fairly. If s/he concludes that this is not the case, s/he can order a further investigation. The 1986 Report of the Lay Observer revealed that 225 legitimate allegations concerning the Law Society's treatment of complaints have been investigated and had

43

been resolved in a wide variety of ways. The 1987 Report reveals a further 15 per cent rise in complaints from the previous year.

Finally, it is worth noting that in 1989 the Investigation Committee of the Solicitors' Complaints Bureau argued in a report that complaints should ideally be handled by a new consumer orientated board, independent of the Law Society, with powers to award compensation. This approach was echoed by the Lord Chancellor in the Green Paper on the future of the legal profession.

Barristers

A consumer of legal services will rarely have direct contact with a barrister. This is because under an ancient tradition of the legal profession it is to a solicitor that a client goes for the first line of legal advice and assistance. A barrister will only be engaged if the case requires certain specialist services, such as representation in the higher courts or a legal opinion on a complicated area of law. Even then it is the solicitor and not the client who engages the barrister, and the client may still have no direct contact with the barrister involved in their case. Nevertheless, if the client is in some way dissatisfied with the service provided by their barrister, there are procedures available for them to register a formal complaint which will be investigated. Social workers engaged in court work frequently tell of the frustration felt by themselves or their client when the barrister who has been working with the client on the case is replaced at the last minute by another barrister. This is the type of matter for which complaints procedures exist. These procedures are available regardless of whether the client is paying for the service or receiving legal aid.

What can you complain about?

As with the service of solicitors, a client who has suffered some financial loss as a result of a barrister's negligent work may wish to sue the barrister for damages. This right is, however, limited to the work that a barrister does *outside* the courtroom, e.g. giving written opinions that are inaccurate on points of law, or preparing faulty documents. A barrister cannot be sued for losses suffered by their court performance, however inadequate it may have been. If a client

44

is considering suing their barrister they should consult a solicitor following the procedures for suing solicitors set out on p. 40.

The more likely circumstances in which a client may wish to register dissatisfaction are where the client feels that their barrister has acted unprofessionally, been guilty of inadequate preparation, sloppy conduct and so forth. All barristers are subject to a Code of Professional Conduct which they are obliged to follow. Failure to attend court in good time, refusal to take a brief for inadequate reason, unseemly behaviour in court, inadequate preparation, demanding of fees direct from the client, are all examples of behaviour that might give rise to a complaint. The *Code of Conduct for the Bar of England and Wales* (4th edn.) can be obtained from the General Council of the Bar (p. 47).

Who do you complain to?

Complaints against barristers are investigated by the Professional Conduct Committee of the Bar (PCC). The PCC consists of members of the Bar and lay representatives who are drawn from a panel appointed by the Lord Chancellor. *The Bar Council Notes for Guidance* to complainants advise as follows:

- The complaint should be made in writing.

As there is no equivalent of the solicitors' Interview Panel for barristers, it is likely that the complainant will need assistance for another source such as a CAB or a social worker, in order to draft this letter.

- The complaint should identify the barrister and set out in detail the respects in which it is alleged s/he was guilty of professional misconduct or a breach of professional standards.

Since 1989 the General Council of the Bar has made readily available an account of what standards are expected of the profession. If in doubt, the complainant should insist on being sent a copy of the Code of Conduct.

- Any witness who can support the complaint should either provide a statement or be identified.

Once this information has been received by the PCC they will then obtain any further information that they feel might be appropriate, e.g. they might seek more evidence from the complainant or witness, and they will write to the barrister against whom the complaint is made.

Having obtained all the necessary information, the PCC will review the evidence. They have a number of options available to them:

- They may dismiss the complaint (but only if the lay represent-atives on the PCC agree).
- They may accept the complaint but determine that no action should be taken on it (because, for example, of its trivial nature).
- They may decide to deal with the complaint informally, and direct the barrister to arrange a meeting with the Chairman of the PCC.
- They may refer the matter to be dealt with by the Leader of the Court circuit to which the barrister belongs, or the Treasurer of the Inn of Court to which they belong.
- In serious cases, they may order a formal hearing of the complaint either before a Summary Tribunal (minor matters), or before a Disciplinary Tribunal. The Tribunal will consist of a judge, a lay representative and three practising barristers. The complainant will normally be called as a witness to the hearing which will normally be in private. The Tribunal has wide powers to discipline the barrister if they find the allegation to be proved including disbarrment.

The creation of a summary tribunal chaired by a QC which could respond more swiftly to complaints by judges about the conduct of a barrister, and also to complaints by members of the public of professional misconduct was a response to widespread public criticism of the Bar before 1989. This tribunal has powers both to fine and to order that the barrister foregoes a fee, in appropriate circumstances.

The address to write to for further information and a complaint form is: The General Council of the Bar, 11 South Square, Gray's Inn, London WC1R 5EL (Tel: 01 242 0082).

Complaints should normally be made within 12 months of the incident.

Scotland and Northern Ireland

Both the Scottish and the Northern Irish legal professions operate their own complaints procedures which are similar to those operating in England and Wales but differ in certain aspects of detail. For further information on these procedures contact:

Scotland: For complaints against solicitors, contact: Law Society of Scotland, Law Society Hall, PO Box 75, 26 Drumsheugh Gardens, Edinburgh EH3 7YR (Tel: 031 226 7411). For complaints against barristers (advocates) contact: Faculty of Advocates, Office of Clerks, Parliament House, Edinburgh EH1 1RF (Tel: 031 226 2881).

Northern Ireland: For complaints against solicitors contact: Law Society of Northern Ireland, Law Society House, 90/106 Victoria Street, Belfast BT1 3JZ (Tel: 0232 231614). For complaints against barristers contact: The Secretary to the General Council of the Bar of Northern Ireland, Bar Library, Royal Courts of Justice, Chichester Street, Belfast BT1 3JX (Tel: 0232 241523).

It should further be noted that both countries operate a Lay Observer system for dealing with complaints about the Law Societies' handling of complaints as follows:

The Lay Observer for Scotland, 30 Castle St, Edinburgh EH2 3HT (Tel: 031 226 2503).

The Lay Observer for Northern Ireland, Clarendon House, Room 407, Adelaide St, Belfast BT2 8ND (Tel: 0232 244300).

COMPLAINTS ABOUT MEDICAL SERVICES AND PARA-MEDICAL SERVICES

For more general information, consult Consumer Association (1983) *Patients' Guide to the NHS*.

N.B. All complaints procedures relating to mental health services are dealt with in Chapter 5.

General practitioners (GPs)

GPs generally provide an excellent service to their patients. It sometimes happens, however, that a patient is not satisfied with the way their GP is treating them, or they may even claim to have suffered injury as a result of their GP's incompetence. In these circumstances it is important that the patient is aware that there are procedures that allow them to make formal complaints. The procedures should be explained to a patient when they first register with a GP. In practice this is rarely the case. The various procedures are therefore set out below.

Before dealing with complaints, it would be helpful to set out the basic procedure by which a patient comes to be registered with a particular GP in the first place. Every resident of the United Kingdom is entitled to be registered with a GP. Family Practitioner Committees (FPCs) (England and Wales), Health Boards (Scotland) and the Central Services Agency (CSA) (Northern Ireland) are the bodies with statutory responsibility to ensure that every person resident in the United Kingdom, who so requests, is registered with a GP. Every practising GP in the United Kingdom has a contract with one of these bodies to look after a given number of patients, normally between 2000 and 3000. Their names and addresses are published by the above bodies. Every patient has a right to change their GP without giving any reason. In these circumstances the local body has a duty to find them an alternative GP. A GP also has a right to remove a particular patient from their list without giving any reason. The addresses of the local FPC (or equivalent) can be found in the local telephone directory or on the back of a client's NHS medical card.

Despite the existence of this legal right to change GPs, there is evidence that in practice the procedure is not as straightforward as it seems. In May 1987 the Consumers' Association published the results of a survey of 2600 patients and 1300 GPs in which they claimed that:

> nearly 4 out of 10 doctors in our survey told us they had refused to accept new patients in the last 12 months. The most common reason for such refusal was that the GP already had a full list of patients. A minority of refusals were however on the grounds that the GP thought the patient was likely to be difficult' . . . 'difficult' was all too often defined as a patient who was transferring from a neighbouring practice, or was known to have fallen out with their last GP. (*Which*, May 1987)

What can you complain about?

A dissatisfied client is entitled to complain about any aspect of their treatment, about the way in which a practice is run, and about any professional or ethical misconduct by their GP.

Who do you complain to?

The nature of the complaint will determine the way in which the complaint should be made.

- *Allegation that the GP has not shown proper skill or care, as a result of which the patient has suffered injury*. This complaint should be made directly to the GP, or their solicitor, and should normally only be made after seeking careful legal advice, as the allegation is one of professional negligence, and is thus extremely serious for the GP in question.
- *Allegation that the GP has breached their contract with the FPC (or the Health Board or the CSA) in their dealings with their patient*. This complaint should be made in writing, to the relevant body (see above), within 8 weeks of the alleged incident (6 weeks in Scotland or Northern Ireland). If a patient wishes to check whether their GP has breached the contract, they will obviously wish to know what the contract actually says. If the FPC (Health Board or CSA) cannot provide a copy, the full text of the contract can be found in *Statutory Instrument 1974 No. 160* available from HMSO. The matters in the contract that most directly affect the patient are the duty to provide 'proper and sufficient accommodation' at the practice;

the duty to render to patients 'all necessary and appropriate medical services of the type usually provided by general medical practitioners'; the duty to provide this care at a surgery or at the patient's residence 'if their condition so requires'; and the restrictions on the types of service for which a GP may charge.

- *Minor complaint falling short of allegation of breach of contract.* This complaint should be made in writing, to the same body as for complaints of breach of contract.
- *Allegations of serious professional or ethical misconduct.* Any allegation of this nature must be made in writing directly to the General Medical Council, the statutory body set up to ensure standards of medical training and practice. The Council's address is 44 Hallam St, London W1N 6AE (Tel: 01 580 7642). If the complaint amounts to an allegation of 'serious professional misconduct', the complainant will be asked to make a sworn statement (called a 'statutory declaration') before a Commissioner for Oaths or Notary Public, that their allegation is true. The following examples illustrate conduct that could give rise to complaints under this procedure. The list is not exhaustive.

  - improperly disclosing information about a patient;
  - abuse of drugs or alcohol;
  - indecent behaviour with a patient;
  - prescribing addictive drugs when not necessary;
  - failing to visit or treat a patient when necessary;
  - asking fees for services that should be provided free of charge;
  - entering into an emotional or sexual relationship with a patient that disrupts the patient's family life, or that damages or distresses the patient.

Procedures

ALLEGATION OF BREACH OF CONTRACT

Once the relevant body has received the letter of complaint (see p. 49), a formal investigation procedure has to be carried out by their Medical Services Committee (MSC). The Committee is composed of doctors and laypersons, the latter group having the majority. The GP will be sent a copy of the complaint and given the chance to respond.

If there appears to be any grounds for the complaint, a date will be fixed for a formal hearing of the complaint before the MSC, with at least 21 days notice (14 days in Scotland or Northern Ireland). Both patient and doctor may attend the hearing, which will be in private. Either side may be assisted by another person, such as a social worker or a lawyer. Having heard the complaint, the MSC will compile a report to the relevant body, which has a number of courses of action available to it, ranging from dismissing the complaint to recommending that part of the GP's pay be withheld, or even that the GP appear before the National Health Service Tribunal with a view to being stopped from practising.

MINOR COMPLAINTS FALLING SHORT OF BREACH OF CONTRACT

Once the statutory body has received the letter of complaint, they should appoint from their panel a 'layperson with tact and sympathy' who will try to resolve the matter informally, with the assistance of a doctor who will explain any medical aspects.

ALLEGATIONS OF SERIOUS PROFESSIONAL OR ETHICAL MISCONDUCT

Allegations of this nature can be dealt with in a variety of ways depending on the nature of the allegation. If the GMC decide to hold a formal enquiry, evidence will have to be given on oath, and will be subjected to cross examination as in a court of law. The most serious allegations may lead to the GP being struck off the register of practitioners.

ACCESS TO MEDICAL REPORTS

Since 1989 all patients have a right of access to reports written about themselves by medical practitioners for employment or insurance purposes, on payment of a small fee. Doctors can refuse patients access only if they believe access would cause them, or others, physical or mental harm, reveal the identity of a third party, or indicate the doctor's intentions.

Dentists

The procedures for complaining about dentists are rather more straightforward than those for complaints about doctors. There is no formal procedure for registration with a particular dentist, and subsequently changing to another for whatever reason, so long as the particular course of treatment has been completed, is perfectly simple.

How do you complain?

Complaints about the standard of service should be addressed to the local Family Practitioner Committee (Area Health Board or Central Services Agency) within 8 weeks of the incident. The subsequent procedures will be exactly the same as those for complaints alleging that a GP has breached their contract of employment (see above).

Complaints of serious professional misconduct (broadly similar to those relating to GPs) should be addressed to the Registrar of the General Dental Council (GDC), 37 Wimpole St, London W1M 8DQ (Tel: 01 486 2171). A recent court ruling has decided that in such cases the GDC must establish 'conduct connected with the dentist's profession in which they have seriously fallen short of the standards of conduct expected among dentists'.

Complaints of professional negligence that have caused injury or loss should only be made having sought the advice of a solicitor.

For further information consult National Consumer Council (1987) *You and Your Dentist* (HMSO), a paperback guide to patients' rights.

Hospital staff and paramedical professions

These complaints will normally be in one of two categories, each category having its own procedures for complaint:

1. Complaints about the quality of the service.
2. Complaints about the clinical judgement of hospital staff.

Complaints about the quality of service (including conduct or behaviour of a member of hospital staff)

Complaints should always be made in the first instance to the person involved. If this proves impossible or too embarrassing, or the

52

complaint is sufficiently serious, the patient should complain to a senior member of staff, preferably the member of staff responsible for the work of that particular individual. If the matter still remains unresolved, the patient, or somebody on their behalf, should write a formal letter of complaint to the Hospital Administrator, who will then be bound to investigate the complaint. Such complaints should normally be lodged within a year of the incident complained about.

Complaints about the clinical judgement of hospital staff

A three-stage procedure exists for the patient who wishes to complain about the clinical judgement of any member of the medical staff responsible for their treatment.

Stage 1. The patient should formally complain, verbally or in writing, to the consultant responsible for their treatment, or alternatively to their district health authority. The consultant in charge must then look into the complaint, and seek the opinion of the members of staff involved in the complaint. The consultant should try to resolve the matter by informal discussion with the patient.

Stage 2. If the patient is still dissatisfied, they must renew their complaint, at which stage the Regional Medical Officer will be informed (in Wales the Medical Officer for Complaints, in Scotland the Chief Administrative Medical Officer, and in Northern Ireland the Chief Administrative Officer). The consultant will be asked to try once more to resolve the matter informally, having received the views of this officer.

Stage 3. If the matter remains unresolved, and the patient is not considering any other proceedings (e.g. an action for negligence) the Regional Medical Officer (or equivalent: see Stage 2) can set up an independent professional review of the case. This will only happen if the complaint is of a serious nature. The review will be carried out by the independent consultants at a time fixed in advance. The patient can invite their GP, or a relative or friend (including, if appropriate, a social worker) to this review. The consultants will try to resolve the problem at the review, and will also submit a written report of the review and their findings to their district administrator, who will then write formally to the patient setting out their opinions.

Serious professional misconduct or unethical behaviour by a hospital doctor of whatever rank should be reported to the General Medical Council following the procedures set out on p. 50.

The Health Service Commissioner (Ombudsman)

This is an independent body set up by the Government to investigate complaints of maladministration concerning the health services. A separate office exists for England, Wales, Scotland and Northern Ireland (known as the Commissioner for Complaints). The Ombudsman is a place of last resort for the complainant as the office will not investigate matters until all other complaints procedures have been exhausted, and they have an undertaking that no legal proceedings are pending. Normally complaints should reach the Ombudsman within a year of the incident, though this can be extended. The Ombudsman has wide powers of investigation, but will not investigate any matter directly involving the clinical judgement of a doctor (see p. 53). In broad terms the sort of complaints the Ombudsman will investigate concern alleged failures of health authorities to provide services they have a duty to provide, and any maladministration. Each national office produces leaflets setting out their procedures and the scope of their activities in more detail. The addresses are as follows:

(England) Church House, Great Smith St, London SW1P 3BW(Tel: 01 212 7676).
(Wales) 4th Floor, Pearl Assurance House, Greyfriars Rd, Cardiff CF1 3AG (Tel: 0222 394621).
(Scotland) 11 Melville Crescent, Edinburgh EH3 7LU (Tel: 031 225 7465).
(Northern Ireland) 33 Wellington Place, Belfast BT1 6HN (Tel: 0232 233821).

Further assistance (including complaints about paramedical professions)

A detailed handbook to be consulted on most of the above is *Patients' Guide to the NHS*. Consumer Association (1983).

The best short booklet setting out the main procedures and addresses for making complaints on this nature is *Patients' Rights* produced in 1983 by the National Consumer Council. It covers the position in the whole of the United Kingdom. As well as dealing with complaints it also sets out patients' rights concerning such matters as home visits, urgent treatment, refusal to consent to treatment, maternity and contraceptive services, abortions, hospital treatment, sterilization, second opinions and alternative medicine.

The Patients Association, 18 Victoria Park Square, London E2 9PE (Tel: 01 981 5676) is a registered charity providing an advice service and collective voice for patients. It also publishes a quarterly newssheet – *Patient's Voice*.

On the procedures for handling complaints by staff about patient care see *Protecting Patients: Guidelines for Handling Staff Complaints about Patient Care* (1985) which is available from the National Association of Health Authorities in England and Wales, Garth House, 47 Edgbaston Park Rd, Birmingham B15 2RS (Tel: 021 471 4444). Available from the same address is an excellent book providing a detailed stage by stage account of the procedures for complaints about medical services in general, viz. Capstick, B. (1985), *Patient Complaints and Litigation*.

Complaints involving the nursing, midwifery or health visiting professions, where there is an allegation of professional misconduct should be addressed to:

(England) The English National Board for Nursing, Midwifery and Health Visiting, Victory House, 170 Tottenham Court Rd, London W1P 0HA (Tel: 01 388 3131).
(Wales) The Welsh National Board for Nursing, Midwifery and Health Visiting, 13th Floor, Pearl Assurance House, Greyfriars Road, Cardiff CF1 3AG (Tel: 0222 395535).
(Scotland) The National Board for Nursing, Midwifery and Health

Visiting for Scotland, 22 Queen St, Edinburgh EH2 1JX (Tel: 031 226 7371).
(Northern Ireland) The National Board for Nursing, Midwifery and Health Visiting for Northern Ireland, RAC House, 79 Chichester St, Belfast BT1 4JE (Tel: 0232 238152).

Instances where it appears that a nurse is practising unsafely due to physical or mental illness should be reported directly to: United Kingdom Central Council for Nursing, Midwifery and Health Visiting, 23 Portland Place, London W1N 3AF (Tel: 01 637 7181).

Complaints involving speech therapists should be addressed to: The College of Speech Therapists, Harold Poster House, 6 Lechmere Rd, London NW2 5BU (Tel: 01 459 8521). A voluntary organization offering advice to parents of speech impaired children is AFASIC, 347 Central Markets, Smithfield, London, EC1A 9NH (Tel: 01 236 3632).

Complaints involving other registered health professionals (e.g. physiotherapists, radiotherapists, chiropodists, occupational therapists) should be addressed to: The Council for the Professions Supplementary to Medicine, Park House, 184 Kensington Park Rd, London SE11 4BU (Tel: 01 582 0866).

For a general specialist work covering many aspects of the use of the law to cover disputes in medicine and nursing, advisers should consult Cole, A., Tingle, J. *et al.* (1988) *Medicine, Nursing and the Law* (Blackstone Press Ltd).

Community Health Councils

These Councils have been set up since 1981 (one per health district) to represent the interests of the public in the running of the health services of their district. In Scotland, their equivalent is the Local Health Council, and in Northern Ireland their (limited) equivalent is the District Committee. The Councils normally have between 18 and 24 members, drawn from local authority nominees, regional and district health authority nominees and voluntary organizations. Councils should be consulted by district health authorities on any proposals for 'substantial development' or 'substantial variation' of existing health services. Councils can also pass on to their district health authorities all general complaints about services, and will often provide representation to individual complainants involved in any of the above procedures. For the address of the local Community Health Council see the local telephone directory.

National Association for Patient Participation

This voluntary organization encourages patients to form or develop patient participation groups. There are currently over 100 such groups in the United Kingdom. Groups are normally formed by the patients of one particular practice or health centre, with the co-operation of the doctors involved. Their work might include health education, preventive care, and representation of patients' views to the doctors in the practice. For further information on how to set up such a group contact: Mrs Joan Mant, 6 Landsdowne, 1 Sydney Road, Guildford, Surrey, GU1 3LJ (Tel: 0483 65882) or Anne Smith, 50A Wallasey Village, Wallasey, Wirral L45 3NL (Tel: 051 639 0083).

The Association produces a useful booklet, which explains the work of patient participation groups and gives practical advice on how to start one, called *Patient Participation in General Practice*, which can be obtained from the above addresses.

Association for Improvements in Maternity Services (AIMS)

This is a pressure group working from London, with twelve UK branches, which offers publications, information, support and advice to parents about all aspects of maternity care including parents' rights, technological interventions, natural childbirth and complaints procedures. For further information contact AIMS, 40 Kingswood Avenue, London NW6 6LS.

The Maternity Alliance

This is a voluntary, campaigning organization concerned to improve health care and legal rights of parents-to-be, mothers, fathers and babies. It provides an information resource to organizations, groups and individuals with an interest in maternity rights and services. Contact Maternity Alliance, 15 Britannia Street London WC1X 9JP (Tel: 01 837 1265).

3

Dealing with Council Services: Rights and Responsibilities

This chapter will examine the structure of local authorities, more commonly known as councils, with a view to explaining the various ways in which the users of council services can:

- exercise their legal right to find out more about the decision making processes in their local council;
- express their dissatisfaction with any service, and if appropriate seek some form of redress.

By its very nature, the chapter differs from most of the other chapters in this book, in that it deals with an area of rights in which the adviser may themselves be the subject of the complaint. Whether advising on the making of a complaint or responding to a complaint, it remains, however, a matter of great importance that anybody engaged in social work has a clear understanding of how councils work and of the relevant procedures for investigating and challenging their decisions. A social worker may be, at the same time, both the subject of a complaint about an aspect of their own work, and actively engaged in assisting a client in making a complaint about another council department. They may even be a councillor themselves in another council, in which case their experience will be that of employer in one council and employee in another. As will be seen later in this chapter, councillors have a particularly important role in dealing with complaints about services in their own council.

Although social workers are given special attention in this chapter, the procedures, rights and responsibilities referred to will relate equally to any council employee, and will thus be of equal relevance to housing officers, environmental health officers, solicitors, occupational therapists, social work assistants and any other council employee engaged in providing some sort of service to the public.

Where appropriate, the chapter will deal with collective action as well as individual action.

WHAT IS A COUNCIL?

A council is an organization created by Parliament to supply a number of services to the public in its area. In England and Wales councils are divided into a three-tier system, with a division of responsibilities across the tiers. In Scotland there are just two tiers. The current system of local government in Northern Ireland is based largely upon district and borough councils. Most of the material in this chapter relates to the prevailing situation in England and Wales. Where the material also has specific application to Scotland or Northern Ireland the text indicates accordingly.

England and Wales. The county or city councils (47 in total) are normally responsible for such matters as education, personal social services, highways, consumer protection, arts and leisure facilities, libraries and the police and fire services. The district or borough councils (36 metropolitan, 31 London and 333 non-metropolitan in total) are normally responsible for such matters as housing, planning, public health, some social services, refuse collection, cemeteries, markets, local licensing and a whole range of local matters such as the allocation of allotments, coastal protection and so forth. In Greater London most of the functions of county and district councils are combined together in the London boroughs. Parish or town councils (known in Wales as community councils) have minor local responsibilities in such matters as footpath protection, public lavatories, recreation and parking.

Scotland. In Scotland the equivalents of the county councils are called regional councils, and district councils are the same. There are no parish councils.

For those who wish to acquire a deeper knowledge of the precise distribution of power between various types of council, the following books are recommended reading: Davies, K. (1983) *Local Government Law* (Butterworths) and Jefferies, R. (1982) *Tackling the Town Hall: a Local Authority Handbook* (RKP). Neither book, however, includes reference to the effects of the abolition in the recent past of the Greater London Council and the six 'metropolitan' counties. A more recent, shorter book is Hutt, J. (1988) *Opening the Town Hall Door: an Introduction to Local Government* (Bedford Square Press). A concise and practical guide to the law governing access to local authority held information and meetings is Harrison, T. (1988) *Access to Information in Local Government* (Sweet and Maxwell). For those requiring a very detailed and specialist knowledge the best book is *Cross on Local Government* (1986) (Sweet and Maxwell).

A council is made up of councillors, who are elected by the local populace for a period of 4 years, and officers, who are the employed staff who administer the council services and carry out the decisions of the councillors.

There are a number of features common to all councils, based in constitutional law:

- Most of the legal powers and duties of councils (e.g. under the Mental Health Act, Child Care Law, and Disability laws) are vested in the elected councillors, not the officers.
- A number of these powers and duties are delegated by the full council to its committees and sub-committees, made up of councillors and officers. Some powers are further delegated to officers. Some duties, such as the fixing of the annual rate, cannot be delegated, and remain the responsibility of the full council.
- All council committees and sub-committees will operate according to standing orders which are drawn up by the council and which must be available to the public for inspection.
- All council committee and sub-committee meetings are open to the public, subject to the limited exceptions set out below.
- Questions coming before any council meeting must be decided by a majority of those present and voting.
- Names of those present at all council meetings must be recorded and minutes taken which must be available for public inspection (see below).
- Every council has the power to appoint staff, of which some appointments are mandatory (e.g. Director of Social Services and Chief Education Officer).

- Every council has agreed to be bound by the National Code of Local Government Conduct which expands and clarifies a number of the rules by which they operate. The full text of the Code can be found in Report of the Redcliffe Maud Committee, *Conduct in Local Government* (HMSO Cmnd. 5636 1974). The Code begins with the following statement:

This Code is a guide for all councillors elected or co-opted to local authorities in England, Wales and Scotland. It supplements both the law enacted by Parliament and the standing orders made by individual councils. It has been agreed by the Associations representing local authorities in all three countries and by the Government.

The Code covers the following areas: Standing Orders, Public Duty and Private Interest, Disclosure of Pecuniary and Other Interests, Membership and Chairmanship of Council Committees and Sub-Committees, Councillors and Officers, Use of Confidential and Private Information, Gifts and Hospitality, Expenses and Allowances, and the Use of Council Facilities.

What services does a council have responsibility to provide?

The range of services that a council provides is vast and there is insufficient space to list them all here. As indicated above, these services are also often distributed between different types of council. Housing, social services, education, environmental health, public health, public libraries and recreation facilities are examples of some of the most important council services. It is always important to distinguish between the service that a council provides through political preference and the service that a council provides through *legal obligation*. Failure to provide the latter type of service always leaves open the possibility of legal action against the council for a breach of statutory duty (see p. 81), whereas failure to provide the former does not.

It is seldom a simple matter to determine whether a service is a council's legal obligation or political preference. Only a thorough knowledge of the subject area will ultimately answer this question.

There are, however, some clear areas of councils' legal obligation that are examined in this book:

- obligations to mentally disabled people (see Chapter 5);
- obligations to physically disabled people (see Chapter 4);
- obligations to homeless people (see Chapter 10);
- obligations relating to disrepair and public health (see Chapter 11);
- obligations to elderly people (see Chapter 9).

How are decisions regarding council services made?

Because it would be impossible for a full council meeting to make all the decisions regarding the provision of services, the formal way in which councils operate is through a committee system. Committees will be set up to cover all the main areas of council activity, e.g. housing, planning, social services, education, staff employment, recreation, public health and finance. Each committee will have its own rules of conduct (standing orders). A number of the council's decision-making powers will be delegated to committees, e.g. decisions about council house allocation, planning permission, care proceedings, and the acquisition of property. Each committee will be made up of a selection of councillors, who are advised by the relevant council officers. The chairperson of the committee will be the vital link between the officers and the committee in the periods between meetings.

WHAT IS A COUNCILLOR?

A councillor is somebody who has been elected by the local populace to serve as a member of the council for a period of 4 years (less if elected in a by-election). Councillors have collective responsibility for making all the policy decisions of their council, and for ensuring that the council officers carry out these decisions. Nowadays councils invariably operate on party political lines that follow national party politics fairly closely. This means that once all the votes have been counted, the majority group within the council will automatically have an in-built political majority in the council, and on all its committees. Like a member of parliament, however, a councillor is elected to serve all the constituents whatever their politics. There is no doubt that, within any council, a councillor is a powerful figure.

Anybody fitting the following description may stand for election as a councillor: a British subject or Irish citizen who is 21 or over on the day of the election and who has a local connection with the authority in which they are standing for election. If a candidate is not registered as a voter in the area of the council they must demonstrate substantial living or working connections with the area for at least the previous 12 months.

Even if a person fits the above description, they may be disqualified from standing for election for a number of other reasons, e.g. bankruptcy, or a recent prison sentence. The full details on disqualification from standing for office are set out in the Local Government Act 1972. For more information on the powers and responsibilities of councillors see Turner, B. (1986) *Law For Councillors* (Sweet and Maxwell), which contains a wealth of information on such questions as privilege and protection, corrupt practices, and the legal limits to councillors' powers.

What happens if a councillor does not attend any council meetings?

Failure of a councillor to attend any meetings of the council and its committees for a period of at least 6 months without good cause (such as illness) renders that councillor liable to be disqualified from office.

What powers do councillors have to investigate the work of their officers?

Because one of the primary collective functions of councillors is to employ staff to carry out their policies it follows that councillors must have powers to check that their policies are actually being carried out. This employer's right is, however, subject to all the general laws of the workplace (see Chapter 7). The existence of these powers does not mean that councillors have the right of random access to officers' files. Any request for access to an officer's files must be justified by the councillor as reasonably necessary in order for that councillor to carry out their duties. If a member of the public complains to a councillor about the actions of a particular officer, however, the position becomes clearer. Because councillors have a legal responsibility to keep themselves informed of all matters necessary for them to perform their duties, they have a basic right to inspect any files relevant to the matter they have been asked to investigate. This gives councillors who are investigating complaints very wide powers to inspect files. But are there any limits to these powers? The question has come up in a number of High Court cases in recent years. According to the House of Lords (*R. v. Birmingham District Council ex parte O.* 1983 1 AC 578), the answer to this question is now as follows:

> a councillor is entitled by virtue of his office to have access to all written material in the possession of the local authority of which he is a member provided that he has good reason for the access.

Since this case was decided, the Local Government (Access to Information) Act 1985 has come into force in England, Wales and Scotland (but not in Northern Ireland). This Act lists 15 categories of 'exempt information' to which the public can be denied access (see below). It seems that a councillor not concerned with the issue that is the subject of the exemption can also be denied access to such information. It seems likely, however, that the 'good reason' argument set out by the House of Lords and quoted above could be successfully used by a councillor, to enable them to obtain access even to 'exempt information' in appropriate cases, probably if the councillor can show that it is in the public interest that they should have access to the particular piece of information. This does not mean that the councillor has the automatic right to show the information to the person whom it concerns (see below).

If an officer refuses to show a councillor a file, the line or senior manager should be consulted. If this manager upholds the refusal, the councillor has the right to take the matter to the full council for a decision, and ultimately to challenge any refusal in court.

To whom may the councillor divulge any confidential information that they have obtained?

Having obtained information, a councillor has then to decide

65

whether to divulge its contents. The Data Protection Act 1984 and the Access to Personal Files Act 1987 may in any event entitle the *client* to automatic access (see p. 70). Otherwise, it will be a matter for the councillor to decide whether or not to divulge the contents of the file. If the document is contentious or is marked 'confidential' it is advisable for the councillor to seek legal advice before divulging its contents, as the document may be the subject of legal privilege, its contents may be defamatory, or it may contain confidential inform- ation about other people. In any of these cases, revealing the contents of the document may render the councillor liable to legal action.

For further discussion on this subject see an interesting booklet by Ron Bailey, *Guide to Councillors' Rights to Information* (Community Rights Project).

FINDING OUT ABOUT COUNCIL SERVICES AND ACTIVITIES

The Redcliffe Maud Committee on councils stated in 1974 that to secure public confidence, the workings of a local authority should in general 'be both visible and intelligible'. This committee was set up to investigate local authority openness, or lack of it, in the wake of a series of spectacular prosecutions involving corruption charges against councillors and local businessmen. The central philosophical drive of the report towards more open access to council activity has underpinned much of the subsequent legislation in this area. The following section examines the extent to which these goals have been achieved.

Obtaining general information

Most councils have information departments usually based in their town hall, which employ officers skilled in guiding enquirers in the right direction. These departments will usually be able to indicate which particular section of the council is responsible for any service. In addition to providing general information councils have a statutory duty to provide certain specific information if requested, as follows:

- details of the council's housing allocation policy;

66

- details of forthcoming meetings of council committees and sub-committees (including the agenda, copies of any reports that will be publicly discussed, together with copies of any relevant background papers. A reasonable fee may be charged for copies provided);
- similar details of similar meetings that have taken place together with the minutes of any such meeting;
- a register of councillors, including each councillor's address, and the ward or division they represent;
- the name and address of every member of each committee and sub-committee of the council;
- details of any powers that have been delegated for more than 6 months to a council officer, together with a description of the rank of that officer.

Rights of a member of the public to attend council meetings

A member of the public has the right to attend any council meeting, committee or sub-committee meeting, unless the council has exercised its power to exclude the public from all or part of that meeting. This power to exclude can only be exercised in the following circumstances:

- *either* the presence of the public would result in a breach of confidence by the disclosure of confidential information supplied to the council on confidential terms by a government department or whose disclosure is prohibited by court order or statute;
- *or* the item(s) of business to be discussed may involve the disclosure of 'exempt information'.

The power to exclude is exercised by a simple resolution proposed at the time that the need to exclude arises.

Exempt information

There are 15 categories of 'exempt information', including inform-ation about any of the following: council employees and councillors past, present and future; council tenants or licensees; recipients of council services or financial assistance from the council; the adoption, care, fostering or education of any child. The full list can be found in the Local Government (Access to Information) Act 1985.

Exclusion occurs after a resolution by the council, which is taken in the light of one of the above matters.

Disorderly behaviour

The chairperson of any council meeting has the power to ask any member of the public to refrain from 'disorderly behaviour' and if necessary, arrange for them to be removed from the meeting with such reasonable force as is necessary to eject them. The police have no power to enter council premises in these circumstances, unless invited by the council to do so. They may, however, enter without permission if they have reasonable grounds to suspect that a breach of the peace is imminent. If the 'disorderly behaviour' is by a councillor, the councillor should be asked to withdraw voluntarily, and if they refuse to do so, the meeting can be adjourned or suspended.

For further information on the running of council meetings, and the procedures that can be adopted within meetings see Ward, S. (1985) *A–Z of Meetings* (Pluto Handbooks). For a more formal account see Moore, M. (1979) *The Law and Procedure of Meetings* (Sweet and Maxwell). See also Harrison p. 61.

Obtaining information about council expenditure: public rights of access to council accounts

Every council's financial year ends on 31 March each year. A council is obliged by law to have their accounts audited by an external auditor appointed by the Audit Commission and to publish thereafter a summary of the accounts. Jefferies (see p. 60) provides much useful guidance on what can be found in this summary – information that may be essential to the pursuance of a complaint. Every council elector has the right to purchase from their council a copy of this summary, together with any explanatory tables, diagrams and statistical information that may accompany it.

If an elector wishes to make a more detailed examination of the council's accounts (including related books, deeds, contracts, bills and vouchers) they have the right to do so, and to make copies, provided they do so in a period of 7 clear days before a date fixed and published annually by the district auditor. A period then follows during which an elector may question the auditor on the accounts and express any objections. In the event of objections being made, the auditor may call an informal meeting at which the objector(s) can pursue their objections further. Under the Local Government Finance Act 1982 a number of powers are given to auditors to declare as unlawful any item of council expenditure, and new formal procedures are also available to the public to challenge an auditor's action, or failure to act. These procedures are complex and time consuming and advice should be sought before invoking them. For further information see Turner, B. (1986), *Law for Councillors* (Sweet and Maxwell).

It should be noted that, in all the above circumstances, the rights of councillors of access are even more extensive than those of members of the public (see Turner, p. 64).

Obtaining information on personal council files: client rights of access

For many years the arguments have raged as to the desirability of open access of clients to the files held on them by council officers. On the one hand it has been argued that the willingness of officers to record their true impressions will be restrained by open access; on the other hand it has been argued that open access will encourage greater openness between officer and client and help reduce the possibility of inaccuracy or misunderstanding, particularly in the personal social services. After the introduction of open files in the United States in 1974, a study 3 years later of those files to which access had been sought revealed that inaccuracies had been discovered by clients in 90 per cent of files.

More recently, the general trend in British social services has been towards an acceptance of the principle of open access. In 1983 both the British Association of Social Workers (BASW) in *Effective and Ethical Recording*, and the DHSS in *Circular LMAC(83) 14* came out in favour of open access, subject to limited exceptions. Despite this support, research demonstrated that by January 1987 only 39 local authorities had actually implemented an open access policy. Furthermore, in almost all those social services departments that operated an open files policy, their internal regulations excluded certain documents from this policy (e.g. information provided by third parties). It can be a matter of some difficulty for the individual officer to decide whether or not a particular document is excluded.

For further discussion on the above, see also Birkinshaw, P. (1985) *Open Government: Freedom of Information and Local Government* (Local Government Legal Society) and Harrison (p. 61).

A move away from voluntary to compulsory access has recently been initiated by two important pieces of legislation, the Data Protection Act 1984 and the Access to Personal Files Act 1987. The position is now as follows.

Files and records held on a computer (England, Scotland, Wales and Northern Ireland)

Any person who is the subject of files or records held by a council authority on a computer has the right of access to those files or records. There are a number of exemptions to this right. Some of these are of relevance to those engaged in social work (for full details see SI 1903/4 1987 HMSO). Every local authority holding information on clients on a computer has to be registered with the Data Protection Registrar and will appoint a Data Protection Officer whose duty it is to ensure that the authority complies with the Data Protection Act.

If a client wishes to have access to information held on them on a computer by any council department they should apply in writing for access to the council's Data Protection Officer. A small fee will be charged for the service. Having requested the information, the client must be given access to it unless it is claimed that the information falls within one of the following exemptions:

- It is held by a local authority social services department, health authority, education welfare service, probation committee or the NSPCC and revealing it would *either* prejudice the carrying out of social work by seriously harming the health or emotional condition of that client or some other person *or* would lead to the identification of other individuals not employed in social work (e.g. informants) (SI 1904).

- It is held by a health professional (see below) and supply of the information would be likely to cause serious harm to the physical or mental health of the client or to lead to the identification of another person (SI 1903).

Health professionals include doctors, dentists, nurses, health visitors, midwives, various forms of therapists, and paramedical professionals such as speech and occupational therapists and physiotherapists.

For further advice and information on this subject contact: Data Protection Registrar, Springfield House, Water Lane, Wilmslow, Cheshire SK9 5AX (Tel: 0625 535777).

For useful guides to the Data Protection Act consult Elbra, R. (1984), *Guide to the DPA* (National Computing Centre); Savage, N. and Edwards, C. (1984), *Guide to the DPA* (Financial Training) or Charlton, S. and Gaskill, G. (1988) *Data Protection Law* (Sweet and Maxwell).

Personal files which are not held on a computer (England, Wales and Scotland)*

Partly in response to a lengthy campaign by the Freedom of Information Campaign (see p. 85 for address) there is now on the statute book an Access to Personal Files Act 1987. This act now allows individuals the right to see their housing or social services files, on payment of a small fee in order to:

- secure access to any *personal information* contained on their files, *and*
- have erased or rectified any inaccuracies contained in that information.

Personal information is defined as 'information which relates to a living individual who can be identified from that information (or from that and other information in the possession of the authority keeping

*For future implementation in Northern Ireland see Standing Committee C Col 59 1.4.87: 'to be implemented by order in Council'.

the record) including any expression of opinion about the individual but not any indication of the intentions of the authority towards that individual'.

The local authority can still withhold access on similar grounds to the Data Protection Act (p. 70). Thus the course of action proposed for a particular client need not be disclosed, although there may be some difficulties where the course of action is based upon an expression of opinion. Also the identities of third parties will be protected. For fuller details see *Access to Personal Files* (Social Services Regulations) (1989) HMSO and DOH Circular LAC (89)2.

COMPLAINING ABOUT A COUNCIL SERVICE

How do you complain about a council service?

It is always helpful as an adviser to draw up your own formula concerning priorities of complaint on a sliding scale of seriousness. In the same way that an individual does not take a case to the European Court of Human Rights until they have proceeded through the hierarchy of the United Kingdom appeal system, an individual with a complaint about a council action, or inaction, should be encouraged to pitch the initial level of their complaint at an appropriate level. The general rule should always be to make the initial complaint at the lowest appropriate level, and only if that does not achieve the desired result, should higher level complaints be considered.

As a preliminary rule a potential complainant should first enquire from the council information officer whether the council has a formal *complaints procedure*, what matters it covers and whether it is appropriate for the particular matter in question. Some councils produce a booklet setting out their procedures, others adopt a much more informal approach.

How to use a council complaints procedure

The general rule should be that if there is a complaints procedure that is appropriate for the particular complaint, then it should be used. At the present time however, only about half the social services departments in the country have formal procedures for the investigation of complaints by clients (see *National Consumer Council Survey*, December 1986). It is fair to say that the Social Services Inspectorate is concerned at the comparatively small number of such procedures and is taking steps to remedy this problem. In 1988 the National Consumer Council and the National Institute for Social Work jointly produced a detailed argument in favour of complaint procedures within social services, together with guidelines on how to operate such procedures: NCC/NISW (1988) *Open to Complaints* (National Consumer Council).

Alternative methods of complaint

Complain to relevant officer

Although it is the elected councillors who have overall responsibility for the services that their council provides (which is why they are named as the defendants in any legal action against the council) it is the council officers who carry out all the day-to-day work of the council, and it is normally to them that any complaint should first be addressed. Because of their geographical proximity to the 'coal face' of their work, council officers tend to have a much higher public profile than do government civil servants, although their constitutional position of neutrality is basically the same.

A complaint can either be addressed to a particular officer (for example a social worker, housing official, or estate manager) or to that officer's line manager. As a general rule, complaints should always begin at this level, to give the person most closely involved in the complaint the opportunity to resolve the problem or at least provide some explanation to the complainant. A complaint will always be more sympathetically received at a higher level if it has first been made at the level it has originated. Complaints should always be made in writing, with a copy retained by the complainant. Complaints about policy are best directed to the relevant *council committee* (see below).

If the officer or their line manager fails to resolve the complaint satisfactorily the complainant then has two choices: a) go to a higher level of officer management, or b) complain to a councillor.

Complain to higher level of officer management

The first problem will be to establish the particular hierarchy in the council in question. Most council information departments provide a booklet explaining the hierarchy of each department. Every department will have a head, who has ultimate responsibility for the work of every member of their department (e.g. the Director of Social Services, Chief Education Officer, Director of Housing, or the Chief Environmental Health Officer). The chief officer of the entire council is called the Chief Executive, who should be reserved only for the most serious complaints. If the complainant is not sure to which department to address their complaint, however, they should address it to the Chief Executive who will ensure that it ends up in the right department.

Complain to a councillor

As it is councillors who have ultimate responsibility for the work of council officers it is to them that a complaint should be addressed, if it has not been resolved by one of the above two methods. As a general rule, it is better to complain to a councillor only when a complaint has been made to the officers and the complaint has not been resolved. As has been shown above, councillors have wide powers to investigate a complaint, including the right of access to relevant files. An important consideration will be which councillor to complain to? There are two main possibilities. The first is to approach a councillor representing the ward where the complainant lives. The second is to approach the chairperson of the appropriate council committee. This latter course would normally only be taken if the matter involved a major complaint about the department, which would include a complaint about departmental policy.

Presentation of petitions and deputations

If the subject matter of the complaint affects a number of people, e.g. the closing of a school or day centre, or a refusal to install a pedestrian crossing, the raising and presentation of a *petition* may sometimes be an effective way of airing the complaint. Most councils have strict rules regarding the presentation of a petition which can be found in the standing orders of the council (see p. 61). Normally the following procedure should be adopted:

- The petition should have a clear and precise preamble which sets out the issue of concern and provides the names and addresses of the petition organizers.
- All those who sign the petition should give their name and address.
- The petition must be presented by a councillor, on behalf of the petitioners, to a full council meeting. The councillor will indicate the nature of the petition, and hand it in. There may then be a debate on the petition, or if appropriate it may be remitted to the next meeting of the committee dealing with the subject matter of the petition. The petitioners will *not* be allowed to speak in the debate.

If the complainants are anxious to be given the opportunity to address the full council or one of its committees on the issue in question, an alternative course of action would be to organize a *deputation*. A deputation is when a group of complainants are given the opportunity to confront the council directly with their problem. It is particularly useful when a group of people are anxious that the full council should be aware of the particular issue, as for example when a very local campaign has failed to influence the council decision and insufficient publicity has been given to the issues involved. Again the standing orders of the council should be consulted for details of the procedure. A typical procedure would be as follows:

- A written request must be addressed to the Chief Executive setting out the reasons for seeking a deputation, the names and addresses of those concerned in the deputation and nominating one of their number to speak on their behalf. The subject matter of the deputation must come within the general powers and duties of the council.
- The Chief Executive will convey the request to the mayor or chairperson of the council who has absolute discretion whether or not to allow the deputation. If the mayor or chairperson decides to allow the deputation, they can also decide whether it should be heard before the full council or before an appropriate council committee.

- If the deputation is allowed, limits can be placed upon the length of time the presenter will be allowed to speak, and the numbers that will be allowed onto the council floor. At the designated meeting (either the full council or committee) the presenter will be invited to address the members, and can then be cross-examined by any of them.

Complain to the Commissioner for Local Administration (the Local Ombudsman)

In 1974 the Ombudsman system that had been in operation since 1967 in relation to central government departments was extended to complaints about local authorities under the control of Commissioners for Local Administration, usually known as Local Ombudsmen. The Local Ombudsman operates as an independent investigator of any allegation by a member of the public, that they have suffered injustice as a result of council maladministration. Maladministration is a very broad term that includes undue delay, bias, discrimination, failure to apply rules of procedure, and general misconduct or incompetence. There are currently three Local Ombudsmen in England, and one each in Wales, Scotland and Northern Ireland. Each operates from a regional office with a full-time staff. Their addresses are as follows:

(England) 21 Queen Anne's Gate, London SW1H 9BU (Tel: 01 222 5622) (*two* covering Midlands and South); 29 Castlegate, York YO1 1RN (Tel: 0904 30151) (*one* covering East Anglia and North).
(Wales) Denven House, Court Road, Bridgend, Mid Glamorgan, Wales (Tel: 0656 61325).
(Scotland) Princes House, 5 Shandwick Place, Edinburgh EH2 4RG (Tel: 031 229 4472).
(Northern Ireland) 33 Wellington Place, Belfast BT1 6HN (Tel: 0232 233821).

The procedure for laying a complaint as set out below is the procedure for complaints in England and Wales, although the procedures in Scotland and Northern Ireland are broadly similar.

How do you complain?

A complainant, or somebody on their behalf, can initiate a complaint by writing directly to the Ombudsman, setting out the nature of the alleged maladministration – a letter will suffice. Normally the complaint should be lodged within 12 months of the alleged maladministration, although exceptionally, if for good reason, this requirement can be waived. The following are matters that the Ombudsman is *not* empowered to investigate:

- matters where there is an existing right of appeal to a tribunal, minister or court which has not yet been used, e.g. a decision to evict a council tenant where the tenant has grounds to defend the eviction;
- commercial transactions, other than those involving the purchase or sale of land, e.g. a council's decision to sell its office equipment;
- education matters affecting teaching in, or the internal organization of, schools;
- personnel matters;
- matters affecting most or all of the inhabitants (e.g. the level of the rates or community charge);
- matters relating to the investigation or prevention of crime;
- the commencement or conduct by the council of civil or criminal proceedings.

How does the Ombudsman deal with the complaint?

The first stage of the procedure, assuming that the complaint is one that the Ombudsman has power to investigate, will be for the Ombudsman to invite the relevant council officer(s) or councillor(s) to give their side of the story. If the Ombudsman feels there is a case to answer, s/he will despatch an investigator from the regional office to the council to interview the officers or councillors involved, and to look at all relevant files. The council must allow the Ombudsman access to all relevant files unless they claim that the 'public interest' demands that the files remain confidential to them. This may raise complicated legal questions on which the advice of the council legal department will be sought. If the Ombudsman wishes to resist such a claim s/he may apply to the court for the right of access to the files.

The court will have to decide whether the 'public interest' that certain council documents remain confidential outweighs the 'public interest' that the Ombudsman can carry out a full and thorough investigation. This may well be relevant in cases involving the personal social services where sensitive questions have been raised prior to making a decision on, for example, the suitability of a foster parent. The investigator will also visit the complainant and any other relevant parties. All these visits and interviews are intended to be fairly informal. The Ombudsman has the power to reimburse any expenses incurred by those taking part in the investigation. All interviews are conducted in private.

Having completed all these interviews and investigations the investigator will compile a 'statement of facts' which will be sent in draft form to both parties for their agreement.

The final stage of the investigation will be the preparation by the Ombudsman of a report which will decide whether maladminist- ration has taken place. If the answer is affirmative, the Ombudsman may also suggest an appropriate remedy, e.g. some form of com- pensation. The Ombudsman has no power to enforce this remedy other than the pressure that comes from the status of the office, and public opinion. The final report on the case will be made available to the public. It will not, however, identify the parties unless the Ombudsman rules it to be in the public interest to do so.

The largest category of complaints to the Local Ombudsman relate to housing and planning, followed by highways, education and environ- mental health matters. Complaints range from allegations of excessive delay in the processing of council house applications to failures to take correct action or consult the right people, to racial and personal bias or simply gross incompetence. Perhaps the biggest problem facing those who complain to the Local Ombudsman is the problem of the time that it takes to process the complaint: the average time is around 47 weeks from lodging the complaint to resolution. In England and Wales complaints to the Local Ombudsmen about social services are compara- tively rare: in the first 2 years of the Local Ombudsmens' work only 20 of the 466 reports issued related to social services departments. In general Local Ombudsmen receive between 2000 and 3000 complaints a year upon which on average around 12 per cent do they find initial grounds to investigate. Once a formal investigation has occurred about 60 per cent lead to a finding of injustice.

For further information consult the *Annual Reports of the Commissions for Local Administration* and Justice (1980) *The Local Ombudsman: Review of the First Five Years*. Both Hutt (see p. 60) and Jefferies (see p. 61) provide useful guidance on how to complain to a Local Ombudsman. The Ombudsmen offices in all four countries provide useful introductory leaflets on how they operate.

Sue the council

Suing the council means issuing proceedings in the county court or the High Court against a council officer, or against the council itself, for compensation to cover injury or damage that has been suffered as a result of their negligence or incompetence. This tactic should only be used as a last resort when all else has failed, and should never be adopted without first taking professional legal advice. In appropriate cases legal aid will be available (see Chapter 1). This form of action against social workers or social services departments is on the increase in the United States, even though at the present time it is relatively uncommon in the United Kingdom. However, according to one Social Services Director in England:

> One of the characteristics of the last five years has been the very significant increase in the extent to which solicitors are engaging in correspondence with [social service] departments about clients' rights and criticising the service and the way in which it is provided. (*Insight*, 20 February 1987)

In what sort of circumstances might somebody sue? The possibilities are endless, but will cluster around situations where councils have a statutory duty to provide a service which they have failed adequately to provide: for example, assistance to the disabled, adequate protection for children in care, or adequate after-care for those discharged from mental institutions. This book has demonstrated that the areas of statutory responsibility in which councils are involved are very broad.

IS THE OFFICER PERSONALLY LIABLE?

An officer is personally liable for his or her own negligence. However, as a general rule an employer is also vicariously liable (legally responsible) for the negligent acts of their employees, and thus the council rather than the officer will normally be the defendant in any court action, for the simple reason that they have more money to pay any compensation award. But even if this is the case, the officer does remain personally liable and can be jointly sued, which is the reason why most paramedical professionals (though not social workers) have compulsory insurance policies to cover this eventuality. Vicarious liability does not extend to the work of independent social workers or independent paramedics (i.e. those who are 'brought in' by the council for a specific task, but are not normally employed by that council). Such people remain personally liable for their negligent acts, and are strongly advised to take out private insurance against such an eventuality.

Vicarious liability for the negligence of employees also has its limits, which are essentially that the employee must have been 'acting in the course of their employment' even though their work was not up to professional standard. This point is well illustrated by one social services director as follows:

> The line I would draw is that the . . . council would defend anyone against whom we would not have wanted to take disciplinary action for gross misconduct. If a social worker in good faith is providing a service we would defend them. If, however, the social worker were to physically assault someone or steal their money the . . . council would not defend them against the client. We can't indemnify everyone against everything . . . they must have acted in good faith. (*Insight*, 20 February 1987)

Specialized complaints: discrimination on grounds of race or sex

It is unlawful for any council to discriminate against a person or group in the provision of any council services or facilities, including housing. Discrimination means treating a person less favourably than others on grounds of their colour, race, nationality, sex or ethnic or national origins. It also extends to 'indirect' discrimination which is the policy of applying a similar requirement for obtaining a service or facility to all members of the population, knowing that certain groups are less able to meet that requirement because of their colour, race, nationality, sex or ethnic origins. (For further details on the the concept of both direct and indirect discrimination as it relates to employment, see Chapter 7.)

Discrimination is notoriously hard to prove, as the evidence is rarely overt or written. The widening access to information described above will, however, make it easier to obtain evidence of discrimination and the powers vested in the Local Ombudsman (see p. 77) to obtain information and read files are another potential source of proof. Complaints about discrimination have to be brought in the local county court, within 6 months of the alleged act of discrimination. Anybody who believes they are the subject of discrimination in any of the above forms should seek further advice and assistance from one of the following organizations:

Equal Opportunities Commission (EOC) (sex), Overseas House, Quay Street, Manchester M3 3HM (Tel: 061 833 9244); Women's Legal Defence Fund (p. 8); Commission for Racial Equality (CRE) (race, colour, nationality, etc.), Elliot House, Allington St, London SW1 5EH (Tel: 01 828 7022).

For a clear, comprehensive and accurate book on the key provision of the 'equality legislation' see Gregory, J. (1987) *Sex, Race and the Law* (Sage).

High Court challenge on legality of council action

Over the past 20 years there has been a considerable increase in the number of people using the High Court in an attempt to force a local authority to do something they are legally obliged to do, or to prevent them from a particular course of action. The procedure involved in such action is called *judicial review*, a procedure whereby the High Court literally reviews the legality of a council's particular course of action. A series of complicated rules have been developed over the years to govern the circumstances in which judicial review can be requested. Nobody should contemplate an action for judicial review without first seeking expert legal advice. Legal aid is available for judicial review so long as the local legal aid committee consider that there is a reasonable chance of success, and that the action is justifiable in cost terms (see generally Chapter 1). The lay adviser should, however, be aware of the following general principles governing judicial review before advising a client to seek further legal assistance.

1. An applicant for judicial review must have 'sufficient interest in the matter to which the application relates' before the courts will entertain the application, i.e. a *direct* interest in the subject matter of the application. Thus a homeless person, or a disabled person would be entitled to initiate an action for judicial review of a council's decision, or failure to act if it concerned them personally. If the action to be reviewed involves significant expenditure, then a local ratepayer (or community charge payer) will also probably be able to argue that they have 'sufficient interest' to justify an application. But an applicant with no interest, other than a moral or political interest, is unlikely to be able to persuade the court to allow them to initiate judicial review proceedings.

2. A judicial review case can only be initiated if the applicant is first given *leave to apply* for judicial review by the High Court. The application for leave must be made 'promptly and in any event within three months from the date when grounds for the application arose'.

3. There are only certain types of council action (or inaction) that the court is willing to review as follows:
   * *either* when the council has exceeded or abused its legal powers;
   * *or* when it has failed to carry out its mandatory legal duty.
   There is a further restriction, which is that judicial review will not normally be considered until all existing internal appeal procedures have been followed. Thus, a disabled applicant seeking judicial review of their council's alleged failure to carry out their legal responsibilities under the Chronically Sick and Disabled Persons Act 1970 was refused permission as they had not gone through the existing appeal procedure to the Secretary of State, prior to making the application (for more detail on this case see Chapter 4, p. 90).

4. The description *exceeding or abusing power* is itself quite a complicated legal issue. The applicant must show one or more of the following:

a) The council had no power to make the decision that it made; for example because the committee making the decision was inquorate.

b) The council decision was based on an error in law; for example, the council misinterpreted the meaning of a statute.

c) The council decision was in breach of *natural justice*; for example, a councillor who was involved in the decision had a personal financial interest in the outcome, or the council only listened to one side of the argument before reaching a major decision.

d) The council has exercised its discretion in a way that no rational body could have done, which Lord Scarman has interpreted as meaning the council 'has taken leave of its senses'. This is a highly complex provision, as it involves a number of subtle interpretations of the words 'reasonable' and 'rational'. For example, it is quite reasonable for a council to follow its political philosophy, according to the case law, so long as the decision based upon that philosophy is 'rational'! Many people engaged in social work, with experience of the courts, will be slow to suggest this particular course of action, given their experiences of the views of some judges on what constitutes reasonable action!

5. Even if leave is granted to apply to the High Court for judicial review of a council decision, it may take between 6 months and a year before the application is finally heard, and a further lengthy period if the case goes to appeal.

6. If the applicant wins the case against the council, and the court finds that the council acted in some way unlawfully, it is by no means certain that the council will then make the decision that the applicant wishes them to make. This is because of the form taken by the *remedies* that are available to the High Court, in a *judicial review* case. The most common outcome of such cases, if the applicant is successful, is for the court to make either an order of *certiorari* or an order of *mandamus*. The former will declare the council decision to be null and void, the latter will order the council to take a particular course of action, e.g. reconsider the matter afresh. But in both cases, it may well be open to the council, having considered the matter, either again or for the first time, to reach the same decision! In which cases the unhappy

litigant will have won a battle but lost the war, and will be likely to feel extremely disillusioned by the whole process.

It probably goes without saying that some of the most controversial cases in recent years have been those using the judicial review procedure, giving rise to many allegations of the political bias of some members of the judiciary. This is a very volatile, creative and potentially useful use of the law for those engaged in social work. But a number of warnings need to be given to the client before they decide to embark upon this journey, for a lost case is more painful than one that has never been fought.

For those who are interested in looking in more detail at the issues surrounding this particular use of the law, the following books are of particular interest: Aldous, G. and Alder, J. (1985) *Applications for Judicial Review* (Butterworths); Prosser, T. (1983) *Test Cases for the Poor* (CPAG); Harlow, C. and Rawlings, R. (1984) *Law and Administration* (Weidenfeld and Nicholson); and Cooper, J. and Dhaven, R. (1986) (eds) *Public Interest Law* (Basil Blackwell).

FURTHER SOURCES OF INFORMATION

The three books mentioned most frequently in this chapter, Jefferies, Davies and Hutt, provide good accounts of how local government works. On the legal liabilities of those who work in the paramedical professions towards their clients see Finch, J. (1985) *Aspects of Law Affecting the Paramedical Professions* (Faber and Faber) and Cole, A. and Tingle, J. (1988) *Medicine, Nursing and the Law* (Blackstone Press Ltd). Finally, although directed primarily at occupational therapists, there is an excellent series of articles by Bridgit Diamond in the *Occupational Therapy Official Journal* (August, September and November 1986) which deal with a number of the legal aspects of working in the caring/paramedical professions, including civil actions by clients, professional registration, health and safety regulations (see also Chapter 7), the legal aspects of community care, liability for instructing or supervising others, and confidentiality. These articles are useful points of reference for anybody working in the caring professions, seeking information on their legal position in relation to their clients' rights.

For further information on the developments in the law on access to information, contact the Campaign for Freedom of Information, 3 Endsleigh St, London WC1H 0DD (Tel: 01 278 9686). A comparative overview of this issue across many parts of the world has been produced by Marsh, N. (1987) *Public Access to Government Held Information* (Stevens).

For information on the development of formal complaints procedures in social services departments contact the Social Services Inspectorate of the DSS, 19th Floor, Euston Tower, 286 Euston Road, London NW1 3DN (Tel: 01 388 1188), or the National Institute for Social Work, *either* at Mary Ward House, 5–7 Tavistock Place, London, WC1H 9SS (Tel: 01 387 9681), *or* Lawns House, Lawns Lane, Leeds LS12 5ET (Tel: 0532 798250).

Finally, for those with their sights on influencing parliament to bring about change for their particular cause, a useful guide has been produced: Dubs, A. (1988) *Lobbying: an Insider Guide to the Parliamentary Process* (Pluto).

4

The Legal Rights of Physically Disabled People

GENERAL INTRODUCTION

Government statistics suggest that over 6 million citizens of the United Kingdom suffer from severe physical and mental disability. In these circumstances a great responsibility lies with social workers, doctors, occupational and speech therapists, physiotherapists and other professionals to ensure that those with physical disabilities are aware of the special legal rights the law has created for their benefit. The dedication and perseverance of a number of individuals and groups working with disabled people has borne them considerable fruit in the legislative field. Since the end of the Second World War, over 45 Acts of Parliament have contained specific reference to the particular rights of physically disabled people. As a result of this legislation the legal rights of physically disabled people are now substantial. Enforcing these rights is a different matter.

This chapter will outline the special rights given by law to physically disabled people. It will begin by setting out the general statutory duties of local authorities towards disabled people. It will go on to describe in detail the specific legal rights of disabled people in the fields of employment, housing, financial benefits and education. As with the other chapters, addresses of useful organizations and details of helpful publications will be provided where appropriate.

STATUTORY DUTIES OWED BY LOCAL AUTHORITIES TOWARDS DISABLED PEOPLE

There are two statutes which lay down a series of legal duties owed by local authorities towards disabled people. The first is the Chronically Sick and Disabled Persons Act 1970 (CSDPA). The second (which is currently only partially in force) is the Disabled Persons (Services, Consultation and Representation) Act 1986 (DPSCRA).

Chronically Sick and Disabled Persons Act 1970 (CSDPA).

Under this Act a local authority has the following statutory duties.

The local authority must inform itself of the number of disabled persons in their area. For the purposes of this Act 'disabled' means 'suffering with a permanent and substantial handicap'. The definition clearly extends beyond physical disability to include those with mental handicap or disability so long as it is 'permanent or substantial'. A local authority will satisfy this duty by keeping a register of disabled people in their area. Any person who thinks they qualify as 'disabled' under the Act should contact their local social services department and ask to be registered. Councils employ occupational therapists, occupational therapy assistants and some social work assistants specially trained for this task. Although registration is not a precondition to receive special services it is clearly administratively useful in organizing and prioritizing limited resources.

The local authority must assess the needs of each disabled person within their area for any one of a list of services below.

If the local authority is satisfied that any disabled person in its area has a need for any of the services listed below, and that need is not being met, the local authority must inform that person of any welfare services it provides that could satisfy that need, and if necessary must make arrangements for the service to be provided to that person. Although the statute does not state who is responsible for paying for any services that are provided, the general consensus amongst lawyers is that lack of resources does not provide legitimate legal grounds for a local authority either to refuse to provide the service or to insist that it will only be provided if the client pays for it. Advisers should be astute to detect the local authority that is using the barrier of policy to avoid its legal responsibilities.

The services referred to above are as follows:

- practical help in the home, which might include the support of a home help to do cleaning and shopping;

- the provision of a television or radio, and help in using the local library;
- assistance towards attending educational facilities, games or outings, and, if available, council day centres, where a variety of activities might take place;
- adaptations to the home such as ramps for wheelchair access, extensions, and the provision of other specialist equipment;
- help towards a holiday;
- meals at home, or in a day centre;
- provision of a telephone, and any special equipment needed to operate it.

The Disabled Persons (Services, Consultation and Representation) Act 1986 (DPSCRA).

This Act, like the CSDPA 1970, began its life as a Private Members' Bill, so by the time it reached the statute book in 1987, it had undergone considerable embellishment. The parliamentary draughtsmen did not, however, change the essential philosophy of the Bill, which was to recognize more overtly than previously the role of the friend, carer and close relatives of disabled people in determining the nature of the services they might receive and to enshrine good administrative practices into statutory rights.

Although the Act entered the statute book in April 1987, only parts of it are currently in force, with no clear statement from the DSS at what date the remaining sections of the Act will become law. For further information on the progress of the implementation of more sections of the Act contact the Act Now Campaign, c/o RADAR (address on p. 131 and see Parrat, D. (1989) 'The DPA 1986: Myth or Reality' in *Contact*, Summer 1989, pp. 13–17.

At present, the Act has introduced the following statutory changes:

- If a local authority fails to assess the needs of a disabled person for any of the services listed above, it can be ordered to do so by a court.
- Where a disabled person is living at home and receiving a substantial degree of care from a carer (who is not a person employed to care for them by a statutory body), the views of this carer, and the extent of the carer's willingness and ability to

88

continue giving such care, *must* be taken into account when assessing the disabled person's future needs. The principal aim of this change appears to be to promote the concept of genuine shared care between informal carers and social services, where feasible.

- The local authority *must* inform a disabled person, whose needs it has assessed, of *all* relevant welfare services of which it has knowledge, from which that person might benefit. This duty extends beyond those services provided by the local authority to include all the relevant services from the voluntary sector, of which the local authority has knowledge. Many councils produce comprehensive booklets, setting out details of such services. The onus is clearly on those who provide a specialist service for the disabled to ensure that their local authority is aware of it.

- From 1990 onwards all disabled school leavers will receive statutory assessment by their local authorities prior to leaving school.

There are two other provisions in the 1986 Act, which have not yet come into force, but which will have a considerable impact when they do.

1. The first provision will enable a disabled person, who is not able to make representations on their own behalf, to appoint their own 'authorized representative' concerning any claim they may have under the CSDPA 1970. This representative, once appointed, will have to be consulted at every stage of an assessment and will be allowed to make representations to the local authority on the disabled person's behalf. Regulations are to be drawn up by the Secretary of State concerning the method for appointing an 'authorized representative'.

2. The second provision relates to those who are due to be discharged from a mental institution, following in-patient treatment for 'mental disorder'.

For a useful summary and commentary on the 1986 Act see the *Handbook for Voluntary Organisations on the Disabled Persons (Services, Consultation and Representation) Act 1986* produced jointly by MIND and RADAR (see Further Advice and Assistance,

p. 131). See also *Act Now: Handbook For Local Authority Social Services* (RADAR).

Miscellaneous duties

In addition to the above specific duties, a local authority must generally consider the needs of the disabled people in its area when designing new housing schemes (DOE Guidelines suggest that Wheelchair Housing and Mobility Housing are particular priorities that should be considered, see DOE Circular 59/78).

Finally, under a series of statutes, local authorities have a number of responsibilities to try to improve the general facilities for disabled people in buildings to which the public have access. The powers and duties generally apply only to new buildings, and they are by no means comprehensive, nor in general are they significantly grant aided. DOE Circular 10/82 does encourage each local authority to designate one of its staff as an 'access officer' to provide a clearly identified point of contact on questions of access for the disabled, from members of the public and it is important that local authorities should be pressed to make such an appointment.

For further information on what legal regulations exist and how they might be enforced see: *Access: Regulations and Guidelines* obtainable from GLAD, 336 Brixton Road, London SW9 7AA.

How can a local authority be forced to carry out its statutory duties?

Since the 1986 Act it seems likely that any failure by a local authority to assess the needs of a disabled person could be enforced through the courts. Ensuring that those needs, once discovered, are provided for is, however, a different matter. The only procedure available to disabled people who believe that they are not receiving the services to which they are legally entitled under the above legislation is to appeal in writing to the Secretary of State. The Court of Appeal decided, in the case of *Wyatt v. Hillingdon LBC* in 1978 (see *78 Local Government Reports 727*), that it is not open to a complainant to take the local authority to court for failure to carry out their statutory duties under the Act, unless the complainant has first gone through this written appeal procedure. This is unfortunate, as research by RADAR (see Further Advice and Assistance, p. 131), suggests that not only is the procedure extremely slow, taking up to 1 year from complaint to resolution, it is also extremely rare for a complainant to persuade the Secretary of State that a local authority is in default.

Another factor to take into consideration before mounting a complaint to the Secretary of State is that only individual complaints can be considered, even if a large number of people in one area have an identical complaint. This leaves the way open for large scale non-compliance by hard pressed, or negligent, local authorities who can refuse to carry out some of their duties, in the knowledge that it is most unlikely that they will be brought to task.

What can the Secretary of State do, if a complaint is justified?

The actual powers given to the Secretary of State, in the event of a finding that the local authority is in breach of their statutory duty to provide a particular service are vague. They appear to be limited to making a declaration that the local authority is 'in default', which is clearly a serious defect in the whole system, as it effectively means that a local authority can be found in default, but the complainant may receive no relief unless they are prepared to take subsequent legal action through the courts.

Throughout the early 1980s RADAR (see p. 131) conducted an extensive research project into the level of dissatisfaction with local authority provision under the 1970 Act. Its conclusions, published in an interim report entitled *Putting Teeth Into the Act*, make depressing reading. Commenting on the complaints procedure to the Secretary of State the report states:

> Referral to the Secretary of State has not led to the resolution of any problem if a general issue has been involved. Even when there is a cut-and-dried individual case the procedure may mean that provision is made several months, or even years, after the need originally arose, when the time taken by the Secretary of State is added to the delay on the part of the local authority.

Perhaps more serious is the potential conflict of interest high-lighted by the report for a Secretary of State who may be:

91

a member of a Government which is forcing local authorities to cut back generally on their expenditure. When in practical terms the provisions a local authority can make are largely dependent upon central Government decisions, the Secretary of State may be required to pass judgement on a local authority for actions for which he, as a member of the Cabinet, is largely responsible.

Is there any alternative complaints procedure?

If the complainant considers that their failure to receive a proper service from their local authority is a result of maladministration by the relevant officers it is always open to them to complain to the Local Government Ombudsman, although the Ombudsman does not have any powers of enforcement (for further details see Chapter 3, p. 76).

RIGHTS OF PHYSICALLY DISABLED PEOPLE IN THE FIELD OF EMPLOYMENT

The rights of disabled people to special employment consideration are poor and remain largely unenforced. The Department of the Environment continues to investigate ways of improving the situation. Both the National Audit Office and the Public Accounts Committee of the House of Commons have recently voiced criticism of the system and called for strong action to reform the system. A partial response has been the revision of the Government's *Code of Good Practice on the Employment of Disabled People* (1988) (Employment Service).

Legal rights to employment

According to the Disabled Persons (Employment) Acts of 1944 and 1958, certain categories of employer are obliged to operate a quota system whereby a minimum of 3 per cent of their workforce must be drawn from the Register of Disabled Persons. This Register is the general responsibility of the Department of Employment, working through the Employment Service (see p. 97). It is a different Register from the register kept by the social services department under the CSDPA 1970 (see p. 87). At the local level the Register is the responsibility of the *Disablement Resettlement Officer (DRO)*, who will normally be based in the local Job Centre.

The definition of a disabled person for the purposes of this Register is extremely long-winded. It reads as follows:

a person who on account of injury, disease (including a physical or mental condition arising from imperfect development of any organ) or congenital deformity, is substantially handicapped in obtaining or keeping employment, or in undertaking work on his own account, of a kind which apart from that injury, disease or deformity would be suited to his age, experience and qualifications.

In addition to falling within this definition the disabled person must be likely to remain disabled for at least 12 months and be actively looking for work, with some prospect of finding work. It is presumed that the prospect of finding work refers to the degree of impairment suffered by the disabled person and not to the general employment conditions in the area.

How does a disabled person get on the Register?

The applicant has to fill out a form provided by the DRO at their local Job Centre, describing the nature of their disability. If the conditions described above are clearly satisfied, the DRO will immediately register the applicant and grant them a Green Card (certificate of registration). The certificate may be granted for a period of from 1 to 10 years, or until retirement. It can be renewed on further application. The registered person can apply to remove their name from the Register at any time they wish by writing to the Job Centre or Employment Service.

What happens if the DRO refuses to place them on the Register?

If there is any doubt as to the applicant's eligibility, the application will go before a panel of the Committee for the Employment of Disabled People. This Committee includes representatives of employers and workers, doctors and people interested in the

93

problems of disablement. The panel will include a representative of each of the categories listed above. The applicant will be invited to attend before the panel, and can be accompanied by a representative of their choice, e.g. a social worker, trade union representative or advice worker. The panel will require medical evidence – normally a letter from the applicant's GP. Alternatively the Job Centre can arrange a special medical examination. Any loss of earnings or travelling expenses incurred by this medical examination can be met by the Job Centre. The hearing is in private. After the hearing, the panel will make a recommendation to the DRO. If accepted, registration will take place as above (p. 93).

For further information on this procedure see MSC Pamphlet DPL 1 (Employment Division) or *Employing People with Disabilities* (DRO) (Employment Service).

Which employers are covered by the Act?

Any employer with a workforce of 20 or more is subject to the Act, with the exception of the Crown and government departments. In the latter case *informal* agreements often exist with the Training Commission, concerning the employment of disabled people. It is possible for an employer to apply to the local DRO for a temporary permit exempting them from compliance with the quota, normally for a period of 6 months. Such a permit should only be granted if the employer has produced convincing evidence why no job suitable for a disabled employee is likely to become available within the following 6 months. Official government figures published in 1988 stated that in 1986 only 27 per cent of employers met the 3 per cent quota while 56 per cent had obtained exemption permits.

What happens if an employer does not comply with the Act?

Being below the quota is not an offence in itself. Being below quota when a suitable disabled person is available to do a job is, however, an offence, punishable on conviction in a magistrate's court by a fine, not exceeding £400. If the employer is a corporate body, the maximum fine is £2000. But since 1944 there have only been 10 prosecutions under the Act. Not surprisingly, the Public Accounts

Committee (see p. 92) concluded that the quota system was 'ineffective, unenforceable and out of date'.

For further information on this procedure see *MSC Employers' Obligations: Notes for Guidance* DPL(2), and *Code of Practice* (p. 97).

Are any categories of work reserved specifically for disabled people?

Vacancies for electric lift operators and car park attendants must be offered by law in the first instance to registered disabled people. Only if no such person is available for the job should it be offered to non-disabled people. The failure to add any more substantial jobs to this list is a serious inadequacy of the system.

How can employers be encouraged to comply with the spirit of the Act?

The low prosecution rate for offenders is a clear indication that disabled people are not generally getting a fair deal under the terms and spirit of the Act. There are a number of factors that discourage employers from seeking out disabled employees, many based on ignorance or prejudice. Unfortunately, attempts to extend the anti-discrimination laws to include disabled people have so far failed. It is ultimately a job for government nationally, and DROs locally, to encourage greater compliance with the Act. There are, however, practical sources of help to employers that may act as an incentive to employ more disabled people.

- Under the Job Introduction Scheme the Employment Service will make a contribution of £45 per week for 6 weeks to an employer who agrees to engage a selected disabled employee.
- Employers can gain assistance in improving their premises in such a way that compliance with the Act need not cost them much money. For example, they can apply for grant aid from the Employment Service to adapt their premises to accommodate the particular needs of disabled employees; generous capital grants are available to enable employers to install access ramps, special toilets, rails or other adaptations.

95

- The Employment Service can loan employers special tools, or other 'high-tech' equipment such as braille typewriters, talking calculators, hoists and hearing aids in appropriate cases.

What can advisers do to help?

Advisers to the physically disabled should encourage more disabled people to register under the Act, and seek out, monitor and lobby employers who are below the quota. They should be willing to report defaulting employers to the Employment Service Commission. They can encourage the local DRO to offer to pay the fares to work of disabled employees, a power which they have in appropriate cases up to 75 per cent cost of taxis to and from work 5 days per week (maximum ceiling approximately £65).

What are sheltered placements and Employment Rehabilitation Centres?

Finally, there is an alternative scheme offered by many local authorities in conjunction with their local DRO known as the *Sheltered Placement Scheme*. Under this scheme, certain disabled people (normally those who are able to do a particular job but at a very slow pace) are employed by a sponsor (normally the local authority or a charity) then 'leased out' to an employer offering suitable work. The employer will simply pay the employee for the work done, and their salary will then be 'topped up' by the sponsor, who should have this sum refunded. For further information on these schemes contact SEPACS, Matilda Street, Sheffield, S1 4PQ or Remploy Ltd, 415 Edgware Road, London, NW2 6LR.

As an alternative preliminary to returning to work after suffering from a new disability, the Training Commission offers short retraining courses at government financed Employment Rehabilitation Centres. These have been criticized, however, by the Public Accounts Committee which has reported that only 40 per cent of people who attended the Centres in 1986–87 were employed, or on the community programme, 3 months later. It was also pointed out that there were still large areas of the country without access to a Centre. For a series of leaflets on the above contact Training Policy and Programmes Division, Moorfoot, Sheffield, S1 4PQ (Tel: 0742 753275).

For further information on all the above schemes consult the Employment Service or the local Disablement Advisory Service (see p. 98).

Duty of companies to state their policy concerning disabled employees

Any company employing more than 250 people is obliged under the 1985 Companies Act to include in the Director's Report a statement of the company's policy for that year concerning disabled employees. If the company has no policy, it should say so. Only the civil service, nationalized industries, health authorities and local authorities are exempted from this legal duty. Directors' reports are available for public inspection at: Companies Registration Office, 55–71 City Road, London EC1Y 1BB (Tel: 01 253 9393).

For further general information on all the above contact: Training Commission, Moorfoot, Sheffield, S1 4PQ (Tel: 0742 753275), asking in particular for their leaflet *Code of Practice on the Employment of Disabled People*.

Further information and help

The principal government agency responsible for coordinating and improving efforts to assist disabled people in finding employment is the Employment Service, Rockingham House, 123 West Street, Sheffield S1 4ER (Tel: 0742 739190). From this service can be obtained a host of leaflets and booklets providing further information on all of the above as follows:

- *The Code of Practice on the Employment of the Disabled*
- *Employing People with Disabilities (Sources of Help)*
- *Employing People with Disabilities (DROs)*
- *The Job Introduction Scheme*
- *The Disabled Persons Register*
- *Adaptations to Premises and Equipment for People with Disabilities*
- *Travel to Work Grants for People with Disabilities*
- *Working at Home with Technology: Employing People with Disabilities*

- *Special Aids to Employment: Employing People with Disabilities*
- *Personal Reader Service: for People with Disabilities*

There are also a number of leaflets dealing with the specialist difficulties associated with the employment of those with mental illness or handicap, with epilepsy, with multiple sclerosis and those who are visually or hearing impaired.

Another major source of government sponsored assistance is the Disablement Advisory Service. There are 71 teams covering the country, and the address of the nearest DAS can be obtained from the local Job Centre. The aim of the service is to help employers of all sizes and in all types of industry, commerce and so forth, to adopt and implement good policies and practices in the employment of people with disabilities. There is a special advisory service for large employing organizations whose central office is the DAS Major Organizations Development Unit, Room 628, DOE, Caxton House, Tothill St, London SW1H 9NF.

For further information and assistance on all the above matters consult the local DRO.

Finally, Thomson, M. *Employment for Disabled People* (Kegan Paul) gives details of many different schemes and alternatives to work and recounts the experiences of disabled people.

HOUSING FOR DISABLED PEOPLE

For a disabled person a home can be a prison. Whilst some disabilities do not affect the mobility of a person, the majority do, and consequently the internal arrangements for comfort and mobility within a home take on a special significance.

If the home of a disabled person is unsuitable in some way for their particular needs, there are two possible ways of coping with the problem. The first is to carry out adaptations to their home to render it more suitable and comfortable for them. The second is to enable them to move to more suitable accommodation. What part do legal rights play in both these two alternative courses of action?

Adapting the existing accommodation

If a local authority is satisfied that the home of a disabled person is in

98

some way failing to meet the special needs arising from their disability (e.g. no access for a wheelchair, inaccessibility of toilet and bathing facilities) it is under a statutory duty by virtue of the CSDPA 1970 (see p. 87) to ensure that those needs are met, by arranging for any necessary adaptations to be made. Any person on the local authority Register of Disabled People can apply for assistance of this nature. Although it is not strictly necessary to be on the Register to receive help with housing adaptations it is advisable, as it is possible to obtain other benefits as a result of registration, e.g. travel passes. Applications to go on the Register are usually processed by social services departments and occasionally by the area health authority.

What sort of adaptations are available?

DOE Circular 59/78 sets out in detail the sorts of housing adaptations that are possible under the above legislation. In particular, Appendix I to the circular lists a large number of structural changes to property that might be made for the benefit of a disabled occupant, which would also be eligible for inclusion in an application for an *improvement grant* when proposed for a disabled person in private sector housing (see p. 101 on 'Improvement Grants'). The list includes building extensions, widening access areas and doors, constructing handrails, installing stairlifts, refixing water and electricity sources, acoustic insulation, kitchen conversion, and the installation of special baths and toilets.

Detailed technical advice on the availability of appropriate equipment for such adaptations may be obtained from the occupational therapist who is working through the social services department and is also usually appointed to assess need and make recommendations as to the work to be carried out. Further ideas, particularly on up to date equipment can be sought from: the Disabled Living Foundation, 380–384 Harrow Rd, London W9 2HU (Tel: 01 289 6111).

Who will pay for these adaptations?

The local authority has a legal power to recover the cost of the adaptation if it so chooses. If it chooses to exercise this power, it cannot do so by making the installation of the adaptation conditional upon prepayment for the service by the applicant. Its duty is to provide the adaptation, if it is necessary, without regard to the question of who will pay for it. In practice, of course, the question of who will pay for the adaptation looms large in every decision, both from the point of view of the applicant and the local authority.

Can anybody apply for grant aid for adaptations?

At the time of writing, one very useful way of obtaining financial assistance to pay for adaptations to a home is to apply for either an *intermediate* or an *improvement grant*. Any disabled person whose home is being adapted can apply, whether they are a council tenant, a private tenant or an owner occupier. An owner occupier, with a disabled person living in their home may also apply. A council tenant can only apply for a grant if the council supports the application. Similarly, although a private tenant may apply individually for a grant to carry out the work themselves, it must be with their landlord's consent and it will normally be better to persuade the landlord to apply instead. In particular, the details of the subsequent rent should be agreed in advance of the work being carried out. It should be noted, however, that the Local Government and Housing Act 1989 is likely to introduce significant new methods of financing adaptations, which will also be means tested. Consult the local occupational therapy unit for up to date information.

What adaptations do these grants cover?

- Improvement grants are available to help with 'major alterations and enlargements' in a home.
- Intermediate grants are available to help with the provision of *standard amenities* in a home, or to make existing standard amenities more accessible to a disabled occupant. Standard amenities are:
    - fixed bath or shower (normally in a bathroom),
    - wash-hand basin,
    - sink,
    - hot and cold water supply at a fixed bath or shower, wash-hand basin, or sink,
    - WC (normally inside the dwelling).

Insulation grants are available for the insulation of lofts, hot water tank jackets, and cold water tank and pipe lagging (Home Insulation Act 1978). The grants are paid at a higher level for pensioners, and people claiming mobility or attendance allowance (see below pp. 110–18). They are, however, discretionary and an annual ceiling is fixed on the amount of such grants by central government.

For more details consult *Your Rights* (Age Concern) or obtain the leaflet *Save Money on Loft Insulation* from the local town hall.

For further information on types of adaptation for which improvement grants are available see DOE Circular 59/78. Consult also the Local Government and Housing Act 1989.

Are the grants mandatory?

Improvement grants are discretionary. If one or more 'standard amenity' is lacking, an intermediate grant is mandatory if the property is in a Housing Action Area or a General Improvement Area (consult local authority on this) but is otherwise discretionary. If the amenity is present but inaccessible, the intermediate grant is discretionary. Although improvement grants are not normally available for owner occupiers whose property has a rateable value in excess of £225 (£400 in Greater London), local authorities must ignore these limits where the adaptations are for the benefit of disabled occupants. Where a grant is discretionary, the decision whether to approve the grant will normally be made by a special committee within the local authority, on the basis of the recommendations of their occupational therapists. See also the effects of the Local Government and Housing Act 1989.

How much are the grants and are they means tested?

The money for both types of grant comes from the Department of the Environment (2 Marsham St, London SW1P 3EB. Tel: 01 212 3134). Each year the Government sets maximum capital ceilings for each type of grant. Details of current maximums can be obtained direct from the Department of the Environment. Neither grant is means tested, though the fact that an improvement grant is discretionary means that some local authorities do effectively carry out a means test, in the discretion that they exercise in the choice of successful applicants.

For both types of grant the total amount paid to the applicant will normally be 75 per cent of the total cost of the adaptation, up to the maximum capital ceiling set by the Government. In cases of hardship this percentage can be increased to 90 per cent.

Various government circulars suggest that the degree of disability of an applicant should be an important factor in determining the percentage level of either grant. One particular circular urges local authorities to give 'maximum help for works for the disabled' unless 'a significant proportion of the eligible work is not directly related to the needs of the disabled occupant' (DOE Circular 38/81). 'Maximum help' means a 90 per cent grant. Government circulars have no legal force, but can be used persuasively by anybody arguing the case for a higher percentage. Another circular urges local authorities to give 'very sympathetic consideration to any person whose main source of income is a retirement pension or a disability pension' (DOE Circular 21/80).

Where can an applicant go to top up their grant?

It should be noted that in cases of hardship in exceptional circumstances, local authority social services departments, and a range of charities, may be willing to cover all or part of the difference between the grant and the total cost of the work, so that the applicant pays nothing at all. For a list of relevant charities consult the *Charities Digest* available from the Family Welfare Association, 501–5 Kingsland Road, Dalston, London E8 4AU (Tel: 01 254 6251). Any tenant applying for either grant should note that they will be required to meet 10 per cent of the cost of the adaptation themselves, and that it will be open to the landlord subsequently to raise the rent to reflect the improvement (see Chapter 11 on 'Rent Registration', p. 401).

Does the applicant ever have to pay the grant back?

If the applicant is an owner occupier (whether or not they are the disabled occupant for whom the adaptation is to be made) they must certify that either they intend to remain in occupation of the house for at least 5 years or (if a landlord) that they will continue to make the house available for renting for the next 5 years. If a landlord fails to honour this commitment at any time during the 5-year period, penalties may be exacted, including the repayment of the grant with interest. If, however, the owner occupier moves within that period, no penalty will be exacted so long as the original declaration was made in good faith, and the house has been sold to another owner occupier, who need not necessarily be disabled.

Is a disabled person entitled to special rate relief on their home?

If a home has been adapted for the benefit of a disabled person it is possible for the occupier of the premises to apply to the council for a rate rebate on that part of the premises of which the disabled person makes special use, and also that part of the premises not used because of the occupier's disability (Rating [Disabled Persons] Act 1978). For the purposes of this relief any person who qualifies as a disabled person under the CSDPA 1970 will be eligible to apply. There is no means testing involved in the rebate. The amount of the rebate will be a standard deduction from the rates bill. The property in question must, however, be the 'usual residence' of the disabled person. The kind of adaptations that have given rise to successful applications in the past have been additional lavatories, bathrooms and ground floor bedrooms made necessary by the particular disability of the occupant; stair lifts, garages, car ports; in short, anything that is provided specifically for the disabled occupant. It is not necessary to show that the adaptation was made for the particular occupant, just that it is now used for that person's particular benefit. (This right will cease once the community charge is fully implemented.)

What is the procedure for applying for rate relief?

The applicant fills out a simple form obtainable from the local rates department. This is a different form from the normal rate rebate form. If the applicant is unhappy with the outcome, an appeal lies to the county court within 21 days. The time may be extended at the court's discretion. Alternatively, it is always open to challenge the rateable value set on a property by application to the local valuation officer, with a further appeal to the Lands Tribunal.

Once the community charge is fully implemented the above relief will no longer be available.

Moving to other accommodation

There are few legal obligations on local authorities to provide accommodation to disabled people. If a disabled person is actually homeless, their homelessness is not 'intentional', and they are considered to be 'vulnerable', the local authority will have a duty to house them (for details on these rights and duties see Chapter 10, p. 322). Once such accommodation has been provided, the disabled person will be able to apply to the council for any necessary adaptations to the new home, following the procedures set out above.

The only other circumstances in which a local authority will be *legally obliged* to provide accommodation to a disabled person will be if that person's existing accommodation is unfit for human habitation, and the council have placed a demolition order, or a closing order on it (see Chapter 11, p. 389). Otherwise, the provision of alternative accommodation to a disabled person who already has accommodation, however unsatisfactory, is entirely a matter for the council's discretion.

Every local authority must by law publish the details of the allocations procedure that it follows concerning its vacant housing stock (for details see Chapter 10, p. 333). The most common procedure is the points system. A disabled person will almost certainly acquire extra points by virtue of their disability. The exact number of points awarded for a particular disability will normally be set out in a leaflet published by the local authority housing department. If no such leaflet is available, the local authority is under a duty to provide any enquirer with details of their allocations policy.

In addition to the points system or other allocations procedures, a council must by law consider the needs of disabled people in any new housing scheme it designs, and also in any new public building. DOE Guidelines set out examples of ways in which the former duty may be satisfied (DOE Circular 59/78). The commonest way in which this duty is satisfied is in the form of Wheelchair Housing Projects or Mobility Housing Projects.

Wheelchair Housing Projects are designed principally for those confined to a wheelchair, to enable them the maximum mobility within their home. Mobility Housing Projects are principally for those who use wheelchairs but are not confined to them. Whilst it lies entirely within the local authority's discretion how much housing of this nature they provide, it is clear that if they provide nothing at all, they are failing to fulfil their statutory obligations. In these circumstances legal advice should be sought from a solicitor to investigate whether the local authority could be taken to court for failure to carry out its statutory obligations.

Finally, some housing associations specialize in providing accommodation adapted for disabled people, and direct application to these associations should always be encouraged. Local authorities frequently work closely with such associations in the allocation of this specialist accommodation.

Further sources of information

For further information on grant aid see *DOE Housing Booklet No. 14*; more detailed information on home grants can be found in the booklet *Housing Grants and Allowances* published by RADAR; on rate relief see DOE leaflet: *Rate Relief for Disabled Persons*; on specialized charitable help in adaptation see the *Charities Digest* (p. 104).

All the DOE Circulars mentioned above can be obtained direct from the Department of the Environment.

SPECIAL FINANCIAL BENEFITS

A number of the financial benefits referred to in Chapter 8 will also be available to a disabled person who satisfies the eligibility criteria. In particular, a disabled person who has to leave work because of their disability should check their eligibility for *statutory sick* pay, *sickness benefit*, or *invalidity benefit*. All claimants should pay careful attention to the additional benefits available to disabled people in receipt of *income support* (Chapter 8).

It is unfortunately the case that very many disabled people are ineligible for the benefits referred to in the above paragraph for the simple reason that they have not paid any, or sufficient, national insurance contributions. This is normally through no fault of their own: they may have been unable to work, or unable to work long enough to acquire the appropriate number of contributions to become eligible. But even those disabled people who have not paid national insurance contributions are, however, entitled to claim a number of special financial benefits connected with their disability, subject only to satisfying the criteria laid down by law for the particular benefit. The benefits that fall into this category are as follows:

- benefits to compensate disability brought about by industrial injury or disease;
- war disablement pensions;
- attendance allowance;
- mobility allowance;
- severe disablement allowance (SDA);
- invalid care allowance (ICA);
- vaccine damage payments.

For detailed information on the effect of hospitalization on claims consult the *Hospital Patients' Handbook* (Disability Alliance).

What are the payment rates of each of these benefits?

The actual amount of each benefit is not included in this chapter as it will change from year to year. For the current levels advisers should consult the latest edition of the CPAG *Handbook* (see below at Further Assistance, p. 130) or *Disability Rights Handbook*. Alternatively, consult DHSS Leaflet: NI 196 which contains the full list of current social security benefit rates. See also the summary chart on p. 285.

Benefits to compensate disability brought about by industrial injury or disease

This section sets out the position in outline only. An excellent book to consult for a more detailed appraisal is *Compensation for Industrial Injury*, published in 1987 by Professional Books. Since 1948 there has been in existence in this country a scheme to compensate any employee who suffers disability as a result of an accident at work or an industrial disease. This scheme does not depend upon national insurance contributions. All that needs to be proved is that the claimant was gainfully employed under a contract of service (for clarification of this term see Chapter 7, p. 218 and see also the *Rights Guide to Non-Means Tested Social Security Benefits*). In addition, a person who suffers injury or disability as a result of the negligence of another (including employers, car drivers and so forth) can sue that person in the civil courts. Legal aid is available. For an excellent, detailed guide to the details of making such claims see Noble, P., Fanshawe, F. and Hellyer, B. (1988), *Special Damages for Disability* (Sweet and Maxwell).

Industrial injury

MUST THE ACCIDENT THAT LEADS TO THE DISABILITY OCCUR AT THE WORKPLACE?

To qualify for compensation the accident must have arisen out of and in the course of employment. This will therefore include accidents which occur travelling to and from work, so long as it can be shown that this was 'employer's time', i.e. time when the employee was still being paid. If the employee was doing something outside the terms of their employment, or in contradiction of express instructions from their employer at the time of the accident they may be denied the benefit.

HOW IS THE BENEFIT CLAIMED?

As soon as practicable after the accident the employee should report the details of the accident to their employer. By law, every employer of 10 or more employees should have an accident book for this purpose. If not, a letter setting out the details will be a sufficient record. If the employer disputes the accident the employee should apply to the DSS for a declaration that they have had an industrial accident. This can be done on DSS Form BI 95.

Once it becomes clear that the accident may have caused some disability to the employee (see below for definition of *disability*) the employee should apply for *disablement benefit* on DSS Form B100A. The benefit is not payable until 16 weeks after the date of the accident. The benefit should be claimed within 3 months of the day on which entitlement begins, though later claims will be considered. If the claim is late, arrears of only 3 months can be paid and only if there is 'continuous good cause' for the lateness.

107

WHAT DEGREE OF DISABILITY IS NECESSARY TO CLAIM DISABLEMENT BENEFIT?

This benefit is paid to those who have suffered disablement from a loss of physical or mental faculty. The amount of the benefit will vary according to the degree of disability. The degree of disability is determined according to a complicated scale of injuries drawn up by the DSS (for full details consult the *Disability Rights Handbook or the Rights Guide to Non-Means Tested Social Security Benefits*). The scale ranks severity of injuries from 0 to 100 per cent. In order to be eligible for the benefit, the claimant must be assessed as being at least 14 per cent disabled as a result of the accident.

HOW IS THE ASSESSMENT CARRIED OUT?

The assessment is carried out by a special medical board consisting of two or more doctors. The doctors will assess the extent and likely duration of the disablement by comparing the condition of the claimant with a normal healthy person of the same age and sex. They will make either a *provisional* or a *permanent* assessment, the former being subject to reassessment at a later date, the latter being for life. An appeal lies within 3 months to a Medical Appeal Tribunal. For further details see *DHSS Handbook for Industrial Injuries Medical Boards* (2nd edn.) (HMSO). For details on social security appeal tribunals generally see Chapter 8, p. 259.

HOW IS THE BENEFIT PAID?

The benefit is paid weekly as a percentage of the disablement benefit in force for that year (e.g. a person assessed as 50 per cent disabled will receive 50 per cent of the current rate of disablement benefit). It is not taxable, but it is treated as income for the purposes of claiming income support (see Chapter 8, p. 262). It will continue regardless of whether the claimant is in work.

N.B. A person claiming disablement benefit may be entitled to additional benefits in certain situations. For example, if their disablement is assessed at 100 per cent, and they require constant attendance, they may be entitled to claim *constant attendance* allowance (paid at a higher rate than the normal attendance allowance), and *exceptionally severe disablement allowance*. In addition, if the disability is likely to lead to reduced earnings in the future for the claimant they may be entitled to claim a reduced earnings allowance. For details on these benefits see the *Disability Rights Handbook* or the *Rights Guide to Non-Means Tested Social Security Benefits*.

Industrial diseases

The alternative grounds for claiming disablement benefit are that the claimant has suffered disablement from a loss of physical or mental faculty caused by an industrial disease. The industrial disease must be one of the 50 or more diseases prescribed as industrial diseases by the DHSS in DHSS Leaflets NI 2, NI 3 (pneumoconiosis and byssinosis) NI 237 (occupational asthma) and NI 207 (occupational deafness). The actual claim for disablement benefit should be made on DHSS forms B1 100 (pn) (pneumoconiosis or byssinosis); B1 100 (OD) (occupational deafness); B1 100 (OA) (occupational asthma); and B1 100B for all the other prescribed diseases.

IS THE PROCEDURE FOR APPLYING THE SAME AS FOR INDUSTRIAL INJURY?

The procedure is similar though not identical. The case is initially appraised by a combination of the DSS adjudication officer and a consultant. If they both believe there is grounds for a claim, they will refer the matter to a medical board who will operate in the same way as for an application based on industrial accident. Although the general time limits are similar as for industrial accident claims, there are complex details that vary according to the particular disease.

FURTHER DETAILS

For further details on disablement benefit consult DSS Leaflet NI6 or the *Disability Rights Handbook* or *Rights Guide to Non-Means Tested Social Security Benefits*.

War disablement pensions

There is a special scheme of benefits for people whose disability has been caused or aggravated by military service. Merchant seamen injured in either World War, and civilians whose disability was caused (though not aggravated) by the Second World War are also covered. The scheme is administered by the DSS and further details plus claim forms can be obtained from the Controller, Central Office (War Pensions) DSS, Norcross, Blackpool FY5 3TA. The basic payment takes the form of a tax-free weekly disablement pension. There are also a number of special related benefits. For further information see DSS leaflet NI 50 *National Insurance Guidance for War Pensioners*. There are also a number of leaflets available free of charge from War Pensioners' Welfare Offices as follows: *Rates of War Pensions and Allowances* (MPL 154); *Help for the War Disabled* (MPL 153); *War Widows* (MPL 152); *War Pensioners' Mobility Supplement* (MPL 155); *War Pensioners: Help with Transport* (NI 211A); *War Pensioners and Widows Going Abroad* (MPL 120).

Attendance allowance

This allowance is paid to severely disabled people, aged 2 or over, who need very frequent attention either in connection with their bodily functions, or to prevent them from injuring themselves. It is an important benefit that is claimed by over 500 000 people.

Who can claim it?

The allowance is paid to the disabled person themselves, or if they are under 16, to their mother, or if relevant, to any foster parents, or to the claimant's carer or other nominee, If the claimant is unable to make the claim themselves. The claimant must be ordinarily resident in Great Britain, and have been in the country for at least 26 weeks in the period immediately prior to the date of the application.

To be eligible, the claimant must be so severely disabled that they require from another person:

either (Daytime)
>   frequent attention in connection with their bodily functions or continual supervision to avoid substantial danger to themselves or others
or   (Night-time)
>   prolonged or repeated attention in connection with their

bodily functions *or* in order to avoid substantial danger to themselves or others, they require another person to be awake for a prolonged period or at frequent intervals for the purpose of watching over them.

The start of 'night-time' is not defined by law but is generally assumed to be approximately between the hours of 11 p.m. and 7 a.m. The criterion is what a claimant reasonably needs, thus they are entitled to receive attendance allowance even if they are not actually receiving the care that they need. To be eligible a claimant must have been in this condition for at least 6 months, although they can submit their claim before the 6 months have expired. It does not matter that during the 6 months the claimant was not eligible for other reasons, e.g. they were in hospital (see below) or were under 2 years of age.

What does *frequent attention in connection with bodily functions* mean?

This means that the claimant needs regular assistance throughout the day to carry out any of a number of personal activities such as going to the toilet, washing all over, eating, drinking, washing hair, shaving, or dressing. It does not extend to assistance with cooking or shopping. The severely deaf qualify if they need frequent attention in connection with their deafness. The payment can be paid to people living alone.

How much is attendance allowance?

There are two rates of payment, the higher rate and the lower rate. The higher rate is only payable if the claimant satisfies both night-time and daytime conditions.

Is the payment taxable?

Attendance allowance is not taxable, nor does it count as an income resource for the purposes of a claim for income support (see Chapter 8).

Can attendance allowance be backdated?

A claim for attendance allowance cannot be backdated. However, the Secretary of State has a discretion to treat a claim for income support as a claim for attendance allowance (or invalid care allowance). This will normally only be allowed if it is clear from the file that the DSS had sufficient information from the claimant at the time of their income support assessment to have led them to advise a claim for attendance allowance, but they failed to give such advice. A claim under this head should be made in a special letter to the Attendance Allowance Unit (see below).

How is attendance allowance claimed?

A claim should be made on DSS Form NI 205. If the form is not readily available an initial claim may be made by letter. If the claim is accepted, payment will be from the date of the form or the letter, whichever is the earlier. The claim will be decided by the Attendance Allowance Board, a central administrative body which normally delegates the decision making to one of a panel of doctors. The panel doctor who makes the decision will request another doctor to visit the applicant at their home, and carry out an examination, to determine whether in the view of that doctor the claimant is entitled to the allowance.

Does an appeal lie against an adverse decision?

Any dissatisfied claimant may ask for a review of the Board's decision within 3 months of receiving it. Approximately two out of every three reviews are successful. In a review there is a fresh determination with a different doctor, and the Board will give detailed reasons for its subsequent decision. If these reveal an error of law, a further appeal lies to a Social Security Commissioner (see Chapter 8, p. 261).

Are there any particular legal problems to look out for?

The majority of the problems surrounding refusal to grant attendance allowance centre on the interpretation of particular words in the definition of entitlement: for example such items as 'bodily function', 'danger' or 'frequent attention'. Anybody seeking further advice or clarification should consult one of the specialist agencies listed below (see 'Further Assistance').

How long will attendance allowance continue?

The allowance will be paid for as long as the claimant remains in need of it. It will cease, however, if the claimant is in hospital for more than 4 weeks, until they return home. It will also cease if the claimant is in accommodation provided for wholly, or partly, out of public funds for more than 4 weeks. If, therefore, the disabled claimant receives occasional respite care in an institution, they must be careful to ensure that they occasionally break the pattern of visits to avoid accumulating the 4-week period. For details on how to work this out contact the Disability Alliance (see p. 131). For special problems associated with claiming attendance allowance whilst in residential care see Ashton, G. (1989) 'Attendance Allowance and Residential Care' *Legal Action* 21–23 May.

Special rights of renal dialysis patients

Any person regularly receiving renal dialysis (more than twice a week) on a machine requiring supervision from another will automatically receive attendance allowance, unless the treatment is received as an out-patient in a hospital.

For further information write to: Attendance Allowance Unit, DHSS, North Fylde Central Office, Norcross, Blackpool FY5 3TA.

The Independent Living Fund

In 1988 the Government, together with the Disablement Income Group (DIG), set up a special trust fund open to severely disabled people in receipt of attendance allowance and on low incomes (i.e. income support level) who have to pay for domestic care. The details of the fund are complex and payments will be discretionary. The aim of the fund would appear to be to keep people living in the community who would otherwise have to go into residential care. It has been criticized as seeking to replace with a discretionary fund services that local authorities ought to be providing as a matter of right under the CSDPA 1970 (see p. 87). ILF is at PO Box 183, Nottingham NG8 3RD.

Mobility allowance

Mobility allowance is an allowance designed to help severely disabled people become more mobile. It is non-contributory and is not means tested.

Who can claim mobility allowance?

Any person can claim this allowance if they have a physical disability such that they are unable or virtually unable to walk. A first-time claimant must be between 5 and 65, and be likely to remain in the same condition for the next 12 months. It must also be clear that they will be in a position to benefit from the allowance, were it to be paid, i.e. they will be able to get outside of their home, albeit transported by another person. The residence conditions are similar to those for attendance allowance, except the claimant must have been resident in the country for 52 weeks in the 18 months immediately prior to the date of the application.

What is the meaning of *virtually unable to walk*?

This definition includes a number of possible claimants:

- a person for whom the exertion required to walk would in itself constitute a danger to their health or would be likely to lead to a serious deterioration in their health;
- a person who experiences such severe discomfort after walking about 50 yards that they have to give up;
- a person whose walking speed is so slow that they are virtually not walking at all.

In each of the above examples 'walk' means 'walk unaided'. The definition does not extend to those who are unable to walk outside because of agoraphobia.

There are many legal difficulties surrounding the question of the

114

mentally handicapped applicant, as for example in the case of the claimant with severe behavioural mobility problems, or with severe Down's syndrome. Although the House of Lords has considered the point, the answer still remains unclear. The best that can be said at present is that the answer will depend upon how often and to what extent the claimant suffers from 'temporary paralysis as far as walking is concerned'. The extent to which they can be coaxed or encouraged to continue walking, having stopped, will be a relevant factor.

For further discussion of this point see Smith, R. (1985) 'Mobility Allowance After Lees' *Legal Action,* July 1985 and *Disability Rights Handbook 1986*. For the most up to date information on this question contact the Child Poverty Action Group or the Disability Alliance (for addresses see pp. 130–31).

Is mobility allowance taxable?

Mobility allowance is not taxable nor does it count as an income resource for the purposes of a claim for income support (see Chapter 8).

Can mobility allowance be backdated?

Mobility allowance is payable only from the date of the claim.

How is mobility allowance claimed?

A claim should be made on DSS Form NI 211. The claimant fills out the form and sends it to the DSS Mobility Allowance Unit (see below for address). In almost all cases a medical examination will be arranged at a place near the claimant's home, or if they are unable to get out at all, in their own home. Travelling expenses to the examination can be claimed. The decision whether to grant mobility allowance will be made by the DSS adjudication officer on the basis of the written application and the medical report.

115

Does an appeal lie against an adverse decision?

An appeal against the decision of an adjudication officer is possible, if the decision was taken on non-medical grounds (e.g. failure to satisfy residential requirements). If, however, the application is refused on medical grounds (e.g. the doctor doubted the degree of disablement), the procedure is more complicated. As the adjudication officer will presumably have refused the application on the basis of a medical report, the appeal will be against this report, and will be decided by a medical board.

The appeal must be lodged with this medical board within 28 days of the notification of the decision (exceptionally, the Secretary of State may extend this period, if there are good reasons for the delay). This medical board will consist of two or more doctors, and will be accustomed to hearing such applications. The board is willing to receive any written evidence or opinions, including the views of any relevant social workers, occupational therapists, physiotherapists or other interested parties.

If a medical board does not allow the appeal a further appeal is permissible within 3 months of receiving notification of the board's refusal, to a Medical Appeal Tribunal. This Tribunal will consist of a lawyer chairperson and two doctors. Whereas the medical board makes its decision on the basis of written representations alone, the Medical Appeal Tribunal will have a full hearing of the matter which may be attended by both the claimant and their chosen representative. (The procedure at tribunals is outlined at Chapter 8.)

Are there any particular legal problems to look out for?

As with the other benefits outlined in this section, most of the legal problems will centre on the interpretation of particular words. If there is any doubt about the eligibility the claimant should consult a specialist agency which will offer free, expert advice (see 'Further Assistance').

How long will mobility allowance continue?

Mobility allowance will be paid so long as the claimant remains eligible (i.e. their disability continues).

Are there other benefits specifically available to a person in receipt of mobility allowance?

EXEMPTION FROM ROAD TAX

A person in receipt of mobility allowance can claim exemption from road tax (Vehicle Excise Duty) and rate relief on their garage, if they are unable to leave their home without assistance from another person. (This latter right will discontinue once the community charge is fully implemented.)

When receiving mobility allowance a claimant should automatically receive a road tax exemption form from the DSS which they must produce at the post office, in order to claim a tax exemption disc. Technically, the vehicle is only exempt whilst it is being used solely by or for the use of the disabled person. But if the vehicle is being used by another to do something for them, e.g. shopping, that would seem to be quite legal.

A person in receipt of mobility allowance may alternatively nominate another person's vehicle (e.g. their spouse) for exemption so long as that vehicle is used 'by or for the purposes of the claimant'.

If exemption appears to have been wrongfully refused for any purpose the claimant should write a letter of complaint to Room D9, Driver Vehicle and Licensing Centre, Longview Rd, Swansea SA6 7JL, setting out the details of the complaint.

ACCESS TO THE ORANGE BADGE SCHEME

A mobility allowance claimant may also apply to their local authority for an 'Orange Badge' which gives them certain parking privileges. Details on this scheme can be obtained from local social services departments. It is in the discretion of the local social services department whether or not to grant an Orange Badge. Even if the applicant is not in receipt of mobility allowance they are entitled to consideration for an Orange Badge if they are registered blind or have a permanent and substantial disability which causes inability to walk or very considerable difficulty in walking.

Orange Badges cannot be used in the Cities of London and Westminster (Central London) nor in parts of the London Borough of Camden.

ACCESS TO SCHEMES TO ASSIST IN ACQUIRING SPECIAL VEHICLES

Finally, there are also a number of schemes designed to assist people with mobility problems in obtaining specially adapted cars. The most prominent of these schemes is the *Motability Scheme*, whereby the claimant can rent a car from a private trust at favourable rates by trading in their mobility allowance. The address of Motability is: Motability, Boundary House, 91–3 Charterhouse Street, London EC1M 6BT (Tel: 01 253 1211).

For further details on this and several other schemes see the *Disability Rights Handbook*.

Severe disablement allowance (SDA)

This benefit was introduced in 1984 to replace non-contributory invalidity pensions (NCIP and HNCIP). Anybody receiving these pensions prior to the introduction of SDA is automatically entitled to receive SDA. The benefit is broadly designed as a weekly benefit for people with severe disabilities, who have not paid the necessary national insurance contributions, to claim the contributory benefits outlined at Chapter 8 ('statutory sick pay, sickness benefit, and invalidity benefit'). Inevitably, the level of SDA is lower than that of these three benefits. SDA is neither contributory, nor is it means tested. Although this benefit is often described as highly complex, the label arises more because of the number of different ways in which it can be claimed than because of any inherent complexity in the benefit itself. Nevertheless, it is normally advisable to consult a good manual before applying for the benefit, and in particular the *Disability Rights Handbook* is recommended in this respect (see 'Further Assistance', p. 130).

Who can claim SDA?

In addition to those already receiving NCIP/HNCIP when the benefit was introduced (November 1984), there are two other categories of claimant. To succeed, a claimant must fall into one of these categories:

- *Category 1*: The claimant must have been *incapable of work* for

118

at least 28 consecutive weeks prior to the date of the application, the relevant period commencing before the claimant's 20th birthday. The claimant must be aged 16 or over (and if in full-time education, aged 19 or over). (There are special – very complex – rules governing claimants in Category 1 who manage to find work for a brief period, then find, on reaching 20, they are being asked to reapply for SDA and establish 80 per cent disability. For a clear exposition of these rules see the *Disability Rights Handbook*.

- *Category 2*: The claimant must have been *incapable of work* for at least 28 weeks and disabled to the extent of 80 per cent. The claimant must be below pensionable age, unless they were entitled to SDA (or NCIP/ HNCIP) immediately prior to reaching pensionable age but for some reason failed to claim the benefit. If a claimant over pensionable age does receive SDA they will be entitled to receive it for the rest of their life. It should not be forgotten, however, that if a claimant is incapable of work (as above) but has *previously worked* and paid the appropriate number of national insurance contributions, they will be better off claiming statutory sick pay, sickness benefit and invalidity benefit.

Further general points are listed below.

INCAPABLE OF WORK

For an explanation of this term see Chapter 8, p. 254.

RESIDENCE REQUIREMENTS

At the time of claiming a claimant must be present in Great Britain, and have been present for 24 of the previous 28 weeks. In addition, they must have been resident in Great Britain for at least 10 of the previous 20 years (or if under 20, for at least 10 years since birth). No continuing residence requirement applies once the claimant is in receipt of SDA. Certain categories of claimant are exempted from these resident requirements, e.g. members of the armed forces (for full list see either of the reference handbooks mentioned below at 'Further Assistance').

80 PER CENT DISABLEMENT

The DSS has published a list of industrial injuries setting out prescribed percentages of disablement (Schedule 2[GB]Regs 82). It is essentially the same list that is used for assessing the degree of disability for a claim for disablement benefit (see p. 108). This list is reproduced in both the handbooks mentioned below at 'Further Assistance'. The list sets out standard percentage degrees of disablement for particular disabilities ranging from 2 per cent to 100 per cent. If a claimant's disability does not fall into any clear existing category it will be up to the adjudicating medical officer (see below) and ultimately the Medical Appeal Tribunal to determine whether the disability amounts to 80 per cent. It seems that a 75 per cent assessment is always rounded up to 80 per cent.

Certain claimants will automatically be assumed to have 80 per cent disability. These include claimants in receipt of attendance allowance (p. 110), mobility allowance (p. 114), a vaccine damage payment (p. 124), a DSS invalid car or private care allowance, a 75–80 per cent (or more) disability benefit under the industrial injuries scheme (p. 108), and those who are registered as blind or partially sighted.

Is SDA taxable?

SDA is not taxable, but it counts as an income resource in full for the purposes of a claim for income support (see Chapter 8).

Can SDA be backdated?

A claim for SDA can be backdated if the claimant has 'good cause' for the lateness. Given the inevitable disability of the claimant (which may also include a mental disability) the 'good cause' clause is normally treated fairly liberally. SDA cannot, however, be backdated for more than 1 month.

How is SDA claimed?

A claim should be made on DSS Form NI 252. An application may be made by a person acting on the claimant's behalf, if the claimant is unable to make the claim themselves. The application will be processed by an adjudication officer. If the question of a percentage disability arises the matter will be looked at by specialist adjudicating medical officers, who will always be doctors. These are the same people who decide a number of medically based claims relating to industrial injuries and diseases. The procedure for an SDA claim is the same as for the other claims dealt with by the adjudicating medical officers (see Chapter 8).

Does an appeal lie against an adverse decision?

If the adjudication officer refuses the application on a technical ground, e.g. residential qualifications, an appeal lies in the normal way against that officer's decision. An appeal on any other grounds lies to a Medical Appeal Tribunal, within 3 months of the claimant receiving notification of that decision. The procedure is the same as that for appeals concerning mobility allowance (see p. 116).

Are there any particular legal problems to look out for?

The main legal problems will concern the meaning of the term *incapable of work* and if relevant the *percentage disability*. On the former question, the case law on invalidity benefit, which uses the same term, will be applied (see Chapter 8). On the latter question, assistance may be gained from the case law concerning claims for disablement benefit (see p. 108). The CPAG Citizens Rights Office or the Disability Alliance should be consulted when in doubt.

How long will SDA continue?

SDA will continue so long as the claimant's disability renders them incapable of work. The additions for dependants will cease if the claimant's partner earns above a certain level. The claimant will normally be entitled to SDA if of 'pensionable age' (see Chapter 9, p. 302) if they were entitled to receive SDA immediately before reaching that age. If they are still entitled to SDA when they reach 'retirement age' (see Chapter 9, p. 302) they will continue to receive

SDA for the rest of their life even if they cease to be incapable of work.

Further information

In addition to the two handbooks detailed at the end of this chapter, there are two publications by the DSS that are particularly helpful in explaining how the 80 per cent test is carried out: *DHSS Handbook on Non Contributory Benefits for Disabled People* (DHSS), and *DHSS Handbook for Adjudicating Medical Authorities* (DHSS).

Invalid care allowance (ICA)

This allowance is an allowance paid to certain carers, engaged full-time in caring for a severely disabled person.

Who can claim ICA?

Any person can claim this allowance if they are caring for a person who is receiving either attendance allowance or constant attendance allowance in respect of industrial or wartime disablement. The claimant must not be gainfully employed, nor in full-time education. They must be 16 or over, and under 65, unless in the latter case they were receiving or eligible to receive ICA at the time they reached 65. Originally, married women were excluded from claiming ICA. This exclusion of married women from eligibility has recently been ruled unlawful in an historic case brought before the European Court of Justice in Luxembourg. Thus it is now open to married and cohabiting women to apply for the allowance.

To be eligible a claimant must be both present and ordinarily resident in Great Britain, and have been in Great Britain for 26 weeks of the year immediately prior to the application.

What do the phrases *caring for* and *gainfully employed* mean?

As with all benefits the legal problems invariably centre on the interpretation of particular words. The words 'caring for' have been held to mean 'regular and substantial caring' which may be satisfied by being around and available for most of the day to help when necessary with the disabled person's personal needs. Once a pattern of caring has been established, temporary breaks will not cause the carer to lose their benefit. In practice, a carer can have 4 weeks' holiday in any 6 months without losing their benefit. The words 'gainfully employed' have been held to mean 'earning £12 a week or more gross' (see Chapter 8 for explanation on how 'earnings' are calculated). For further advice on the precise meaning of each word, consult as for attendance allowance and SDA.

Is ICA taxable?

ICA is taxable, with the exclusion of any amount paid to the carer in respect of any dependent children. When receiving ICA the claimant is credited with Class I national insurance contributions (see Chapter 8, p. 256 and Chapter 9, p. 301 on relevance to pension rights). ICA counts as an income resource for the purposes of a claim for income support.

Can ICA be backdated?

ICA can be backdated for 3 months from the date of the application, or longer if the application can show 'good cause' for the delay. A claim for income support can be treated as a claim for invalid care allowance if the officer dealing with the income support claim ought to have advised the applicant to apply for ICA, on the basis of the available evidence but did not do so (see Attendance Allowance, p. 112).

How is ICA claimed?

A claim for ICA should be made on DSS Form NI 212. The claim will be decided by the Invalid Care Allowance Unit, (same address as Attendance Allowance Unit: see p. 113). A written decision regarding the claim will be sent directly to the claimant.

Does an appeal lie against an adverse decision?

An appeal lies to the social security appeal tribunal in the normal way (see Chapter 8).

How long will ICA continue?

ICA will continue for as long as the person for whom the carer is caring receives attendance allowance. Thus ICA will stop once the disabled person has been an in-patient in hospital for more than 4 weeks.

For further information and assistance regarding the problems of carers contact:

The Association of Carers, 243 Mortlake Road, Richmond, Surrey TW9 2LS (Tel: 01 948 3946). This is an organization that helps to set up local carer groups and support networks. It also provides information on services and benefits.

The National Council for Carers and their Elderly Dependants, 29 Chilworth Mews, London W2 3RG (Tel: 01 724 7776). This organization provides information, advice and a newsletter for carers. It gives information about carers' needs to government, local authorities and voluntary organizations and acts as a campaigning pressure group for carers.

Vaccine damage payments

This scheme is designed to compensate victims of vaccine damage. It is non-contributory and non-means tested. It does not affect the claimant's rights to pursue independent legal action for negligence. Any damages award in a successful claim will, however, be reduced by the amount of the vaccine damage payment.

Who can claim a vaccine damage payment?

Any person who has been severely damaged as a result of a vaccination (or more normally somebody acting on their behalf) may make a claim. The disablement must be at least 80 per cent under the rules governing severe disablement allowance (see p. 120). The vaccination must have been against one of the following diseases: diphtheria, tetanus, whooping cough, polio, measles, rubella, tuberculosis or smallpox. The vaccination must have been carried out in the UK or Isle of Man, after 5 July 1948, (and in the case of

124

smallpox, before 1 August 1971). It must have been carried out when the claimant was under 18 (with the exception of polio or rubella). The claimant must be at least 2 years old at the time of the application. If the person affected is now dead, they must have been at least 2 years old at the time of their death, which must have occurred since 9 May 1978.

In addition to the above, a person may also claim if they are the victim of a vaccination given to their mother whilst they were still in the womb, or if they had close contact with a person who was vaccinated with polio vaccine, subject to certain other conditions (see DSS Leaflet HB3).

How much is it?

A vaccine damage payment is £20 000.

Is a vaccine damage payment taxable?

The payment is tax-free. It will, however, be taken into account when assessing the claimant's eligibility for income support (see Chapter 8).

How is a vaccine damage payment claimed?

A claim should be made on DSS Form HB3. A claim may also be made in a letter. The claim must be made within 6 years of the vaccination, or by the time the claimant is 8 years old. The claim will be decided by the Secretary of State, who must state the grounds for the decision. They may, however, be very general.

An alternative forum in which the claimant may wish to establish the grounds of their claim is to ask for a vaccine damage tribunal to be set up to consider both the cause and the extent of the damage suffered. This tribunal will consist of a lawyer and two doctors. The claimant has the right to be represented before this tribunal. The tribunal will give written reasons for its decision.

Does an appeal lie against an adverse decision?

No. Both a vaccine damage tribunal and the Secretary of State make decisions which cannot be challenged, unless they erred in law, in which case their decision may be challenged in the High Court, with legal aid available. The Secretary of State may, however, review his or her decision should there be a change of circumstances, or if the original decision was based on a mistake of fact.

For further information on vaccine damage payments consult DSS leaflet HB3 *Payment for Severe Vaccine Damage*. There is also an Association of Parents of Vaccine Damaged Children, c/o 2 Church St, Shipston-on-Stour, Warwickshire CV36 4AP. It should be made clear to those concerned with the rights of the victims of vaccine damage that, in recent years, Vaccine Damage Payments Scheme apart, the law in the United Kingdom has been very reluctant to see a way to providing compensation in this field and test cases designed to expand legal rights have been largely unsuccessful.

EDUCATION

There are two major pieces of legislation that affect the legal rights of disabled children to receive special consideration regarding their education. The first is the Education Act 1981, which has introduced a complex series of procedures whereby the special educational needs of disabled children can be assessed, and provision made for meeting those needs. The second is the Act already referred to above, the Disabled Persons (Services, Consultation, and Representation) Act 1986.

Rights of disabled children under the Education Act 1981

The Education Act 1981 was intended to provide a new legal framework for the assessment and placement of children with disabilities in schools up to the age of 19 (though not if they are under 19 and in a college of further education). The Act focuses on children with 'special educational needs' which it defines as a 'learning difficulty which calls for special educational provision to be made'. A 'learning difficulty' means either 'having significantly greater difficulty in learning then the majority of children of the same age or

126

being hindered by a disability from using general educational facilities'. 'Special educational need' also includes a child under 5 who might have a learning difficulty if they do not have special help before they reach 5. The Act specifically excludes from this category children who have a learning difficulty because English is not the main language spoken in their home.

Children who have 'special educational needs' should be identified by the local education authority in which they reside and assessed as to how these needs can be met. The parent of any child aged between 2 and 19 can request that their child is assessed, and this request cannot be unreasonably refused. Assessment is a long and complex business involving reports from education, health, psychological and social services. It may take as long as a year. Assessment is followed by a complex procedure involving varying levels of responsibility on the part of the local authority and the parents. The most formal outcome of assessment will be the issuing of a Statement by the local education authority in which they will detail their findings as to the child's 'special educational needs' and their proposals for special educational provisions to meet those needs. Once a Statement has been made it must be reviewed annually. Any person who believes that an assessment is the appropriate course of action for a child should therefore consult one of the excellent specialist guides to the Education Act 1981, of which the following are particularly recommended:

The *ACE Special Education Handbook*, available from the Advisory Centre for Education, 18 Victoria Park Square, London E2 9PB (Tel: 01 980 4596).
RADAR Fact Sheets on the 1981 Education Act (Guide, Assessment, Appeals) available from RADAR (see below).

The Centre for Studies on Integration in Education (CSE) provides information and advice about educating children with special educational needs in ordinary schools and can be contacted at 1st Floor, 840 Brighton Road, Purley, Surrey CR2 2BH (Tel: 01 660 8552).
The Voluntary Council for the Handicapped Child, 8 Wakeley St, London EC1V 7QE (Tel: 01 278 9441) is concerned with all aspects of

127

disability and special needs in young people and provides a comprehensive advice service to parents and advisers.

Contact a Family, 16 Strutton Ground, London SW1P 2HP (Tel: 01 222 2695) is an organization that brings together families of children with special needs for mutual support and sharing of ideas.

Parents in Partnership, 25 Woodnook Road, London SW16 6TZ is a group campaigning to give more power to the parents of children with special educational needs to participate in the national decision making process.

Effects of the DPSCRA 1986 on rights under the Education Act 1981

As mentioned earlier in the chapter (see p. 89) the sections of this Act dealing with disabled children are now in force. The sections are designed to place greater responsibility on local authorities to ensure that the needs of disabled children leaving school are properly assessed. It is anticipated by the Minister for the Disabled that the first young people to benefit from these new provisions for statutory assessment before leaving school will be those reaching the statutory school leaving age in 1990. The Minister has, however, expressed the hope that the provisions will be applied by local authorities on a voluntary basis to as many as possible young people leaving school in 1989. The provisions are complex, but in summary they require the following:

- Each local education authority must find out from its local social services department whether a child on whom a Statement has been made following assessment under the Education Act 1981 (see p. 126) is disabled at the first annual review after their 14th birthday.
- Each local education authority must inform their local social services department of that person's presumed date of leaving full-time education (school or further education) 8 months before that date, so long as they are under 19 at the time.
- Once informed, the social services department must undertake an assessment of the person's needs for any of the services to

which the disabled are entitled and in particular to those set out under the CSDPA (see pp. 88–9). This assessment must be undertaken within 5 months of being informed, unless the person (or if under 16, the person's parent or guardian) asks them not to do so.

A useful manual providing employment ideas for disabled school leavers is *The Directory of Opportunities for School Leavers with Disabilities*, available from Queen Elizabeth's Foundation for Disabled People, Leatherhead, Surrey KT22 0BN (Tel: 0372 842204).

Anybody seeking further information on any of the above should contact the Advisory Centre for Education (ACE) (see p. 127 for address).

Special education grants for disabled students in higher education

Disabled students should also be aware that if they are in full-time higher education, and receiving a mandatory grant from their local authority, they can claim a special additional allowance as a supplement to their grant to cover the cost of any extra expenditure 'necessarily incurred' as a result of going on the course. Under this head disabled students have successfully claimed an allowance to cover such things as typewriters, paid helpers, tape recorders, additional heating, and special diets. Normally, extra travel costs are not included under this head. Students who receive only a discretionary grant can also claim this allowance, but in this case it will be entirely within the local authority's discretion, whether or not to pay the allowance.

For further information on these grants, contact the local education authority.

The National Bureau for Handicapped Students, 336 Brixton Rd, London SW9 7AA (Tel: 01 274 0565) is a charity specializing in the problems of handicapped and disabled students. They produce a useful leaflet on general financial help to disabled students, called *Financial Assistance for Students with Disabilities*.

For further information on the extra financial assistance available to disabled students seeking income support and to those seeking of income support with disabled dependants see Chapter 8, p. 262.

FURTHER ASSISTANCE

Throughout this chapter, reference has been made to sources of further information that can be obtained from government departments and from other specialist independent bodies. Where appropriate, addresses have also been provided. Two publications in particular have been repeatedly mentioned:

Child Poverty Action Group (CPAG) *Rights Guide to Non-Means-Tested Social Security Benefits*.
Disability Alliance *Disability Rights Handbook* (and *Hospital Patients' Handbook*).

Both these publications are inexpensive and contain highly accurate, reliable accounts of all the financial benefits referred to in this chapter. Both publications are updated annually. It is therefore important to obtain the latest edition. *The Disability Rights Handbook* also contains a range of further information on the wider rights of disabled people, going far beyond legal rights. It is an excellent general source of reference on these matters. It also contains a comprehensive list of addresses of agencies and organizations specializing in particular aspects of disability. The addresses where these 2 publications may be obtained are as follows:

- Child Poverty Action Group, 1–5 Bath St, London EC1V 9QA (Tel: 01 242 9149).
- Disability Alliance, 25 Denmark St, London WC2H 8NJ (Tel: 01 240 0806).

Leaflets on benefits for disabled people in Hindi, Punjabi, Urdu, Gujerati, and Bengali are available from ASRA, 155 Kennington Park Road, London SE11 4JJ (Tel: 01 820 0155).

For those in the London area there is an additional excellent source of information on sources of help for disabled people called *Information for Disabled People* and produced by GLAD and London Weekend Television. Copies are available from The Community Unit, London Weekend Television, South Bank, London SE1 9LT.

Further advice and assistance

The following agencies offer a free, specialized telephone advice service to disabled people or their advisers:

Disability Alliance (Tel: 01 240 0806).
Citizens' Rights Office (for advisers only; financial benefits only) (Tel: 01 242 9149).
Network (advice on legal action), 16 Princeton Street, London WC1R 4BB (Tel: 01 831 8031 or 837 7740).
Disablement Income Group (DIG), Millmead Business Centre, Millmead Road, London N17 9QU (Tel: 01 801 8013).
DIG Scotland, Ecas House, 28–30 Howden St, Edinburgh EH8 9HW (Tel: 031 667 0249).
RADAR (research, emphasis, campaigning body, some general advice) 25 Mortimer St, London W1N 8AB (Tel: 01 637 5400).

The British Council of Organizations of Disabled People, Greenlaw St, London, SE18 5AR (Tel: 01 854 7289) is a federation of 34 organizations of disabled people concerned to bring about the full integration of disabled people into society through self-help. It provides advice, information, training and counselling services to members.

Dial UK is a nationwide organization, with some 75 local information offices, that offers an information service to the disabled. Its national headquarters is at Dial House, 117 High St, Clay Cross, Derbyshire (Tel: 0246 864498).

Both the Child Poverty Action Group and Network are willing to provide legal support in cases of exceptional public importance.

In addition to the above national organizations, there are a number of regionally based organizations, that may be able to provide assistance. For information on local organizations consult the Disability Alliance, or the local Citizens' Advice Bureaux.

Finally, the Union of the Physically Impaired Against Segregation (UPIAS) is a group that aims to oppose all forms of segregation of disabled people and can be contacted at Flat 2, St Giles Court, Diane Road, Ealing W13 9AQ.

5

Legal Rights and Mental Disability*

INTRODUCTION

There are two distinct ways in which a social worker may become professionally involved with the problems of the mentally disabled. The first way is as an Approved Social Worker (ASW) exercising statutory powers to detain patients in a mental institution (usually referred to as a 'section'). Such work is complex, delicate and bound up in detailed legal procedures. There are a number of specialist books that deal with this area: (Gostin, L. *Mental Health Services: Law and Practice* (Shaw and Sons); Jones, R. *The Mental Health Act Manual* (Sweet and Maxwell) (2nd edn.); Gostin, L. *A Practical Guide to Mental Health Law* (MIND); Hoggett, B. *Mental Health Law* (Sweet and Maxwell); Gostin, L. *et al. The Mental Health Act 1983: a Guide for Social Workers* (BASW). A simple but accurate wallchart on the main procedures for detention under the Mental Health Act 1983 is available from MIND: *Compulsory Detention in Hospital under the Mental Health Act 1983*. A useful general list of the powers and duties of an ASW can be found in the *Social Work Law File on Mental Health* produced by the University of East Anglia in Norwich.

The second way is through the provision of general social work support – a task that may also be carried out by an ASW – to a client who is suffering from mental disability. This may involve a client in a mental institution, or in the community, or moving between both.

*Mental health law in Scotland and Northern Ireland is governed by different procedures and different legislation from England and Wales. The bulk of this chapter is devoted to the position in England and Wales. There is, however, at the end of the chapter, information on further sources of assistance regarding the position in Scotland and in Northern Ireland.

An ASW may often find themselves carrying out both statutory and general social work roles with the same client. This can be both uncomfortable and contradictory for the client, but inevitable in the circumstances. But whatever the difficulties, it is essential that the legal rights of the client are at all times safeguarded. This chapter will outline and explain the legal rights of those suffering from mental disability, and will assess the various procedures that exist with a view to safeguarding them. For detailed information on the legal powers and duties of ASWs with respect to detention, the adviser should consult one of the specialist works detailed above.

Definitions

One of the major problems facing anybody helping the mentally disabled is one of definition. What do we mean, when we talk of mental disability? The subject is sensitive, as our society all too readily stigmatizes victims of mental disability, with little regard for the additional problems such stigma may cause. The problem is compounded by the fact that whilst the law will grant or withhold a number of legal rights to those who fall within defined legal categories of mental disability, psychiatry is profoundly sceptical of this process of definition, and is frequently unable to agree a definition of a particular condition at all. The problem is further compounded by the desire of those who care for the *mentally handicapped* (i.e. those with some element of learning disability associated with damage to the brain or genetic malfunction) to distinguish these people quite clearly from the mentally ill. But this distinction also begs further questions about stigma. For by stressing the 'innocence' of the mentally handicapped, whose disability is usually the result of a congenital or an accidental injury, they are implicitly encouraging the assumption that the *mentally ill* are in some sense less deserving of care and sympathy than the mentally handicapped.

It would not be appropriate to enter into a discussion of the relative merits of these distinctions in this book. An excellent, short and sympathetic introduction to the whole problem of defining mental disability is John Payne's *All in the Mind* (OUP/Chameleon/Ikon), which can be recommended to the social worker interested in pursuing these themes further. For the purposes of this chapter, the term 'mental disability' will be used throughout to include both mental illness and mental handicap so long as the relevant legal rights are identical. Where the rights are affected by the distinction, the text will indicate accordingly.

A distinction that is of more consequence for our purposes, seeking as we are to identify legal rights, is whether a person is living in a mental institution as an in-patient, or alternatively is living in the community. A further distinction is necessary for in-patients, namely are they *voluntary patients* or are they *detained patients* (i.e. detained by compulsion under a section: see below)?

The in-patient client

In 1982 (the last time a major national survey was conducted) there were 65 000 people resident in mental illness hospitals or psychiatric units in general hospitals, 50 000 people (including 2500 children) in mental handicap hospitals, and 2000 people in high security *special hospitals* mainly for offenders and those thought to be a danger to the public. Half the mentally ill population was long-stay, with a large preponderance of elderly patients of whom half were 65 or over. For convenience sake, all the above institutions will be referred to throughout this section as mental institutions. A preliminary distinction has to be drawn between *detained patients* (approximately 6 per cent) and *voluntary patients*, i.e. those not detained under the Mental Health Act 1983 (approximately 94 per cent).

THE DETAINED PATIENT: THEIR RIGHTS IN A MENTAL INSTITUTION

A detained patient is a person resident in a mental institution who has been admitted, or remains in, the institution, by virtue of a section of the 1983 Mental Health Act which allows for such compulsory detention. The detention will either be for up to 72 hours as an emergency (s.4); for up to 28 days for assessment (which can include treatment) (s.2); for up to 6 months for assessment and treatment (s.4); by order of a criminal court (usually to a *special hospital*, see p. 137) (Part III); or on transfer from prison by Home Office warrant (usually to a special hospital) (Part III). Because the detention is by compulsion, it is essential that great care is exercised by those involved in their lives, to ensure that their legal rights are protected. The Mental Health Act 1983 supported by the (Draft) Code of Practice* sets out a number of important legal rights for patients in this category. The following section explains these rights, and outlines the procedures available to detained patients (or their advisers) to protect these rights.

General treatment

The (Draft) Code of Practice begins with the following important statement of principle:

> Mentally disordered people should be treated with the same respect for their dignity, personal needs, religious and philosophical beliefs, and accorded the same choices, as other people.

What must the patient be told on arrival?

It is the duty of the managers of the institution where the patient is detained to provide the following information to the patient, both orally and in writing, *as soon as is practicable* after their detention. Details of:

- the provisions under which they are detained;
- their rights concerning any censorship of their correspondence;
- their right to apply to a Mental Health Review Tribunal (MHRT) (see p. 155);
- how they might be discharged, either by the institution or by their *nearest relative* (see p. 152);
- their rights to refuse consent to certain types of treatment (see p. 140);
- the role of the Mental Health Act Commission (MHAC) (see p. 147);
- the Mental Health Act Code of Practice.

*At the time of writing the Code of Practice is still in draft form with no immediate prospect of progress to a more final form.

In addition to the above, unless the patient requests otherwise, the institution must take all practicable steps to supply the patient's nearest relative with a copy of the information supplied to the patient.

Some of the above rights require further clarification.

Can the patient's correspondence be censored in any way?

The answer will depend on whether the patient is in an NHS hospital or a *special hospital*. A special hospital is one with conditions of special security on account of its patients' 'dangerous violent or criminal propensities'. The major special hospitals in the UK are Broadmoor, Rampton, Moss Side and Park Lane hospitals.

Patients in special hospitals

Post sent by a patient may be withheld from the Post Office if either of the following apply:

- the addressee has so requested;
- the hospital managers consider it is likely to cause danger to any person, or distress to any person (excluding, in the latter case, members of the hospital staff).

These powers do not extend to 'privileged' correspondence (see below).

Post sent to a patient may be withheld if the hospital managers believe it is necessary in the interests of the safety of the patient, or of any other person.

It is clear from the above that the hospital managers have in practice very wide powers to censor the mail of patients in special hospitals, although there is little evidence of abuse of this power. They have the right to open any mail, in order to ascertain whether it should be withheld. If mail has been opened, the opener must, however, enclose a note in the packet or envelope stating that this has been done, and if the mail is to be withheld, inform the person who sent it of this decision within 7 days. The sender has 6 months in which to ask the Mental Health Act Commission to review this decision (for the full details see Mental Health Regulations 1983 No 893 Regs 17–18).

It should be further noted that none of the above restrictions apply to correspondence which can be described as *privileged*. In this category will be correspondence to or from a Minister, an MP, the Court of Protection or the Lord Chancellor's Visitors (see p. 171), the Ombudsman (see p. 146 and Chapters 2 and 3), an MHRT, a health or social services authority or Community Health Council (see Chapter 2), the hospital managers, any legally qualified person instructed by the patient, or the European Commission or Court of Human Rights (see Chapter 1).

Patients not in special hospitals

Post sent by a *detained person* can only be withheld if the addressee has specifically requested. Post sent to a detained person can never be withheld.

What are the patient's voting rights?

So long as a patient remains a detained patient it will be virtually impossible for them to vote. First, in order to vote they must be registered to vote in the constituency where they are resident. If this is a different address from that of the mental institution, and they are detained, they will not be in a position to go out to vote. Second, in order to vote they must be 'of sound mind' which means that at the time of voting, they must understand in broad terms that they are doing and the effect of doing it. To be detained a patient must be certified as suffering from a mental disorder. Even if they can get to the polling station where they are registered, they must convince the polling officer they are 'of sound mind'. The obstacles are thus formidable. The position once a detained patient becomes a *voluntary patient* is, however, very different (see p. 166).

Can the patient ask the institution for any money?

For details of welfare benefits available to patients see p. 174. In addition, it should be noted that the Secretary of State for Social Services does have power under s.122 of the Mental Health Act 1983 to provide hospitals with 'pocket money' for patients who would otherwise be without the resources to meet their personal expenses.

For a critical discussion of this whole issue see MIND Policy Paper No 1: *Money in Hospital*, October 1983 (MIND).

What powers of physical control do the hospital staff have over the patient in addition to the right to detain them for the prescribed period?

The terms of the order by which a patient is detained will prescribe the period for which such detention may last. This does not, however, give the institution the freedom to detain that person in whatever conditions they choose. The (Draft) Code of Practice states quite clearly that '*detained patients* do not necessarily need physical security. This is only needed for a small number'.

- It is a criminal offence for any member of the hospital staff to ill-treat or wilfully neglect any patient. Alleged criminal offences should always be reported to the police.
- It is the common law duty of any hospital to take all reasonable steps to offer patients the care and treatment they require, and to take reasonable steps to prevent them coming to any harm. In a mental hospital this will include caring for the patients' needs, both mental and physical.
- Solitary confinement (seclusion) should only be used as a 'necessary therapeutic tool' and not as a management and control exercise: see Royal College of Psychiatrists' *Guidelines on Isolation of Patients in Protected Rooms during Psychiatric Treatment 1980* obtainable from 17 Belgrave Square, London SW1 (Tel: 01 235 2351). The (Draft) Code of Practice also sets out detailed guidelines on the use of seclusion with the following preamble:

    Seclusion should only be used where the patient can no longer be managed on the ward and where there is the immediate risk of serious physical harm to self or others. . . . Hospitals using seclusion should have a clear policy and procedure document which seeks to balance safety factors with the dignity of the patient.

- Physical restraint of patients should only be used to prevent them doing harm to themselves or others or to prevent them from unreasonably disrupting the life of the hospital. According to the (Draft) Code of Practice '[restraint] should be used in accordance with *written hospital procedures*, always recorded in detail and reviewed by the multidisciplinary team in the context of the planned programme of care'.

Complaints of any abuse or alleged breaches of good practice should be directed through the complaints procedures outlined below. The (Draft) Code of Practice also prescribes what should be normal practice for behavioural methods used by staff in hospital wards.

Is a *detained patient* obliged to consent to any form of treatment?

The law on this subject is precise, but complex. As the patient may often be too befuddled to know what is really happening to them, it is essential that an independent adviser understands the legal position. The answer to the question will depend upon the type of treatment. In every case, however, a preliminary question has to be, what is the meaning of the word 'consent'? (see below).

Note first of all, that patients detained:

- on an 'emergency 72-hour admission' (under s.4 Mental Health Act 1983), *or*
- under ss. 135–6 Mental Health Act (which relates to the emergency 72-hour removal of mentally disordered people to mental institutions or other places of safety by the police: see p. 162).

are in the same position as voluntary patients regarding consent to treatment (see p. 163), unless their admission is subsequently extended beyond the 72-hour period.

For all other detained patients, the question of consent will depend upon the nature of the proposed treatment. But first of all, what is 'consent'?

What is 'consent'?

'Consent' in this context is simply agreeing to the particular type of treatment. The (Draft) Code of Practice makes a number of specific points:

- Detained status does not of itself imply inability to consent.
- Capacity to consent is variable in mental disorder and not everyone is equally capable of understanding the same explanation of a treatment plan.
- Wherever possible, treatment plans should be discussed with the patient both initially and also when changes in the plan are contemplated. A less able person is more likely to be capable of giving valid consent if the explanation offered is appropriate to his level of ability.
- Capacity to consent should be assessed in relationship to the particular treatment proposed.

Whilst these guidelines are clear and should be followed at every stage of a detained patient's treatment they still do not cover the situation where a patient's condition is so severe that they are quite incapable of giving any informed consent. A High Court judge has recently directed that in these rare circumstances the following principle applies:

in exceptional circumstances where there is no provision in law for consent (see below) and no one who can give consent (e.g. a parent) and where the patient is suffering such mental abnormality as to be unable ever to give consent then a medical adviser would be justified in taking such steps as good medical practice demands.

Psychosurgery and sex hormone implant treatment

The patient *must* consent (i.e. the above does not apply). The validity of the consent must be confirmed by a certificate signed by three people appointed by the MHAC. One of these three people must be a doctor. They must all certify that the patient has 'understood the nature, purpose and likely effects of the treatment'. The decision to use this form of treatment must be confirmed by a second opinion

141

from an independent doctor. This independent doctor must in turn have consulted two other people concerned with the patient's treatment, one a nurse and the other neither a nurse nor a doctor.

The reason for such stringent safeguards is the controversial nature of the treatment and its irreversibility. Although sex hormone implant treatment is very rare in the United Kingdom, psychosurgery is used in approximately 1–200 cases per year in England and Wales. (For comment on this form of treatment see Gostin, L. (1982) 'Psychosurgery; a Hazardous and Unestablished Treatment? A Case for the Importation of American Legal Safeguards to Great Britain', *Journal of Social Welfare Law*, no. 83).

Electro-convulsive therapy (ECT) *or* continuing to give medication after it has been administered for 3 months

There are two *alternative* circumstances in which the above treatment may be permitted.

First, the patient has consented, and the validity of the consent is confirmed by the Responsible Medical Officer (RMO) (i.e. the doctor in charge of the patient's treatment) or a doctor appointed by the MHAC. 'Consent' is the same as above.

Second, if the patient refuses to give their consent, or is incapable of doing so, but the doctor's opinion on the appropriateness of the treatment is supported by a second opinion from a doctor appointed by the MHAC (see p. 147). Before giving the second opinion, the doctor must consult other people as above. It is the view of one distinguished expert in the field that 'if the patient is competent and expressly refuses the treatment, it should only be imposed when there is substantial justification relating to the patient's health' (see Gostin, L. (1982) 'Compulsory Treatment in Psychiatry: Some Reflections on Self Determination, Patient Competency and Professional Expertise', *Poly Law Review*, no. 86.

Once consent has been given can the patient change their mind?

A patient may withdraw their consent at any time before or during the administration of the treatment. Once consent has been withdrawn, the procedures must start afresh as if the patient had never given consent. The only exception is that the RMO has power to continue with treatment even though consent has been withdrawn, if they consider that 'discontinuance would cause serious suffering to the patient'.

Can an open-ended second opinion be given to continue treatment indefinitely against the patient's wishes?

No. To guard against this possibility there is a duty on the RMO to provide the Secretary of State for Social Services with a report on the treatment and the patient's response if the treatment falls under either categories 1 or 2 above. This report must be furbished at 'regular intervals'. As the Secretary of State's supervisory tasks have been delegated to the MHAC, all enquiries and complaints in this respect should be addressed to the MHAC.

Can the provisions regarding consent or second opinions ever be disregarded?

Yes, but only where there is a case of extreme urgency. Urgent treatment is defined as treatment which is:

- immediately necessary to save the patient's life; *or*
- (not being irreversible) immediately necessary to prevent a serious deterioration in the patient's condition; *or*
- (not being irreversible or hazardous) immediately necessary to alleviate serious suffering by the patient; *or*
- (not being irreversible or hazardous) immediately necessary and represents the minimum interference necessary to prevent the patient from behaving violently or being a danger to themselves or others.

Any other treatment for mental disorder administered under the direction of the RMO

So long as the treatment is genuinely treatment for the *mental disorder*, such treatment can be administered without the patient's consent or a second opinion. Treatment for mental disorder includes nursing, occupational therapy, group therapy and so on, and in practice extends to virtually anything that a Responsible Medical Officer (RMO) deems to be helpful.

Whether the treatment is for the mental disorder or for a *physical disorder* associated with the mental condition may often be difficult to ascertain. This matter does, however, raise an important point of principle associated with the civil liberties and the basic dignity of a detained patient. For under the common law, nobody is obliged to consent to treatment for a physical disorder. The right to refuse treatment is a fundamental human right. (There may, however, be an exception to the consent rules where the patient is unconscious and delay would be dangerous, see Martin, C.R.A. (1979) *Law Relating to Medical Practice* (Pitman).) The bodies of the mentally disabled should not be considered less their property than those of the mentally well. At the same time it must be recognized that certain mental conditions lead patients to refuse treatment for unrelated physical ailments. What, for example, should be done about the schizophrenic person who refuses treatment for an abscess or the removal of an appendix, for reasons associated with their mental and not their physical state? Any doctor who carried out treatment in these circumstances would be stretching their legal powers of intervention in a person's life to the very limits, and could probably only justify in law action that alleviated a life-threatening condition. Thus a mental patient who refused treatment for an ulcer, for reasons associated with their mental state, could not have the treatment forced upon them, unless the ulcer became life-threatening, e.g. if septicaemia developed.

If a person is detained for treatment (under section 3 Mental Health Act 1983) can that treatment be administered to them anywhere other than in the hospital to which they are admitted?

No. An important court decision of 1985 decided that the practice of admitting a patient for treatment (under section 3) and then granting leave of absence (see p. 152) with the proviso that they should be treated in the community is unlawful, even if that treatment is to be under the auspices of the hospital doctor. If they are admitted for treatment under section 3 (which permits detention for 6 months) that treatment must be carried out in the hospital. Concern about the restraints of this ruling has led to a campaign by some activists to introduce a new order: the Community Treatment Order (see Gostin, L. (1986) *Mental Health Services Law and Practice* at 11:13).

PATIENTS' COMPLAINTS

If a person wants to complain that any of the rights set out above have been flaunted or ignored what do they do?

It is not enough to know a patient's rights. It is also essential to be familiar with the various procedures that a patient may invoke if they wish to register a complaint that one or more of their rights set out above has been violated. The main procedures for registering complaints by, or on behalf of, mental patients are therefore set out below. For a more detailed account of the procedures see the *Patients' Rights Handbook* produced by MIND (1983), or Gostin, L. (1984) *Mental Health Services and the Law* (5th edn.) (Shaw and Sons).

General complaints: using the internal complaints procedures

Both the DHSS and health authorities expect every mental institution to have some form of internal procedure for handling complaints by patients about staff. Thus the first avenue of complaint should always be to discover from the hospital or institution administrator how the internal complaints machinery operates. The normal procedure will be as follows:

Stage 1. The complaint should be directed to the person concerned either by the patient or by somebody acting on their behalf. If this is impossible or unsuccessful, the complaint should be made to a senior member of staff.

Stage 2. If Stage 1 does not resolve the matter, or the complaint is too serious or too delicate for Stage 1 to be the appropriate method, the complaint should be made in writing to the hospital, institution or district administrator. The matter will then be investigated either by the local health authority or by the MHAC. If the matter is considered to be very serious (e.g. allegations of brutality by staff, or systematic breaching of the mental health legislation) the health

145

authority or the MHAC can set up an independent inquiry, which may or may not publish its results.

Stage 3. The Secretary of State has the power to order a full-scale enquiry into the most serious allegations under s.84 National Health Service Act 1977 (limited to NHS hospitals) and under s.125 Mental Health Act 1983. As with Stage 2 enquiries, the running of the inquiry will normally be delegated to the MHAC.

Anybody considering invoking the formal inquiry procedures under Stages 2 and 3 above would be well advised to consult with the legal department of MIND before initiating the complaint. If there is no local branch, the central office can always help (for details see p. 174).

Complaints about clinical judgement: using the special procedure

This procedure is the same procedure that is used in other National Health hospitals and is described in detail in Chapter 2, p. 52.

Complaints of maladministration within the mental institution: using the Health Service Commissioner (Ombudsman)

The procedure for making complaints to an Ombudsman has already been explained in Chapters 2 and 3 (see pp. 54 and 76). In summary, the Ombudsman, who is completely independent of the health services, can investigate any complaint by, or on behalf of, a person who has suffered injustice or hardship caused by their health authority, through maladministration, inefficiency, or the failure to provide adequate services which they have a duty to provide. The procedure is initiated by a letter from the patient, or somebody acting on their behalf. The following are areas which the Ombudsman is, however, not empowered to investigate:

- matters which are to be the subject of inquiries set up by the Secretary of State (see above);
- matters relating to clinical judgement;
- matters which could be taken to a court or a MHRT (see p. 155) unless it would be unreasonable to expect the patient to do so. The question of unreasonableness will be decided by the Ombudsman;

- the merits of discretionary decisions unless actual maladministration is demonstrated.

For a fuller account of the general Ombudsman procedures, see
Chapter 2. A short leaflet introducing the powers and responsibilities
of the Ombudsman in this field entitled *Can the Health Service
Ombudsman Help You*? can be obtained together with any further
information from: The Health Service Commissioner for England,
Church House, Great Smith St, London SW1P 3BW (Tel: 01 212
6522); for Wales, 4th Floor, Pearl Assurance House, Greyfriars
Road, Cardiff CF1 3AG (Tel: 0222 394621) and for Scotland (but see
also p. 54) Second Floor, 11 Melville Crescent, Edinburgh EH3 7LU
(Tel: 031 225 7465).

Complaints of professional misconduct of staff

The various procedures for lodging complaints of professional
misconduct by doctors, nurses and other paramedical staff are set out
in Chapter 2, p. 52.

Complaints about detention itself: the lawfulness of detention?

This very important question is considered below in a separate
section (see p. 157).*

Using the Mental Health Act Commission (MHAC)

What is the role and function of the Mental Health Act Commission
(MHAC)?

One of the most important changes introduced in the Mental Health
Act 1983 was the introduction of the Mental Health Act Commission
for England and Wales.

What is the MHAC?

The MHAC is a body of approximately 92 people – doctors, nurses,
lawyers, social workers, academics, psychologists, psychiatrists, and
lay specialists – with responsibility for reviewing the effective

147

operation of the 1983 Mental Health Act. Most members of the Commission are part-time members. The Commission is principally concerned with the operation of the Act in respect of detained patients, although its jurisdiction may be extended by the Secretary of State to include informal patients.

What are the tasks of the MHAC?

Its principal tasks are as follows:

- To prepare and if necessary update a Code of Practice to stand alongside the Mental Health Act 1983. A (Draft) Code of Practice was circulated in December 1985 and a further (Draft) Code of Practice in August 1987.
- To keep under review the exercise of the compulsory powers and duties under the Act. This clearly gives the MHAC very wide general powers. The MHAC reports directly to the Secretary of State, who in turn has the power to order an enquiry, to declare a health authority in default, and even to dissolve a health authority and reconstitute it with different members. It will be important to monitor the extent to which the MHAC is prepared to use these powers.
- To exercise a number of specific duties as follows:
  a) To arrange for a Commission member to visit all detained patients and interview them in private. Over a 20-month period to 1986 members of the MHAC made 937 visits to 523 mental institutions. During these visits, the MHAC member has the power to inspect any records they wish, and can use the occasion to make probing enquiries.
  b) To review any decision to withhold correspondence (see p. 137) if requested to do so.
  c) To appoint the doctors who may provide second opinions and verify patients' consent to treatment (see p. 142). Also to provide the subsequent review reports on the treatment of such patients.
  d) To publish bi-annual reports on its activities.
  e) To deal with patients' complaints.

What complaints will the MHAC consider?

The MHAC will consider any complaint made by a detained patient relating to any matter which occurred during the period of their compulsory detention. This procedure exists in addition to the other procedures listed above, although in practice it is likely that the MHAC will make arrangements at a local level to avoid overlap, and double consideration of a complaint. This would be particularly likely in the case of complaints about clinical judgement where the special procedure applies (see p. 53), and complaints that fall within the jurisdiction of the Ombudsman (see p. 146) which must be made in the first instance to the hospital managers. If the patient remains dissatisfied a complaint to the MHAC may then be considered.

The MHAC will also consider a complaint about the exercise by a hospital of their compulsory powers in respect of a detained patient, made by any person.

The powers available to the MHAC member who is investigating a complaint are widely drawn, and are broadly similar to those of the Ombudsman. They include the right to visit and interview the patient in private, and to inspect the records relating to the patient's period of detention and treatment.

The addresses of the Mental Health Act Commission are as follows:

MHAC, Floors 1–2, Hepburn House, Marsham St, London SW1P 4HW (Tel: 01 217 6008).
MHAC, Cressington House, 249 St Mary's Rd, Garston, Liverpool L19 0NF (Tel: 051 427 2061).
MHAC, Spur A, Block 5, Government Buildings, Chalfont Drive, Western Boulevard, Nottingham NG8 3RZ (Tel: 0602 293409).

The detained patient's right to sue in the courts

It has been indicated at several points of the text that circumstances may arise where the above procedures are insufficient to satisfy the detained patient and they might wish to seek the alternative redress of a court action. This may be, for example, because they are seeking some financial compensation, or because they may wish to obtain a court declaration that a hospital or doctor has acted unlawfully (i.e.

149

beyond their legal powers). They may even wish to initiate a prosecution for a breach of the criminal law.

The use of the courts in any of the above circumstances is feasible but highly problematic. Unfortunately a patient in these circumstances faces formidable problems, related to the unwillingness of the legal system to allow a person with a mental disorder an unfettered right to apply to the courts, without preliminary examination of their state of mind. There is, in addition, a general statutory protection against litigation given to hospital staff in mental institutions who are acting 'with reasonable care and in good faith' (s.139 Mental Health Act 1983). Before being able to start proceedings, the patient will normally have first to satisfy the High Court (civil proceedings) or the Director of Public Prosecutions (criminal proceedings) that there are reasonable grounds for the action. For a wider discussion of this problems see Hoggett, B. (1983) *Mental Health Law* (p. 133) 338–346 and White, R. (1975) 'Mental Patients' Rights to Institute Criminal Proceedings', *Solicitors' Journal*, no. 119, 788.

It is important to be aware, however, that this preliminary hurdle imposed by s.139 does not apply to applications to the High Court for judicial review of a decision by a doctor, administrator, nearest relative or ASW on the grounds that their decision was either 'illegal' or 'irrational'. In other words, if a detained patient has been admitted to the institution without the correct procedures having been followed, or merely on the basis of a nearest relative's irrational fears, they have the right to apply immediately to the High Court for an order quashing their admission. This right is in addition to the rights of complaint outlined above, and the specific procedures requesting early discharge for detained patients described in the next sections. Legal aid is available for such actions; thus anybody with a client in this predicament should consult a specialist solicitor or the legal division of MIND (see below) at the earliest opportunity (see also an article by Gunn, M. (1986) 'Judicial Review of Hospital Admissions and Treatment in the Community under the Mental Health Act 1983' in *Journal of Social Welfare Law*, 290).

The procedures for judicial review are described in more detail in Chapter 2.

DETAINED PATIENTS: GETTING OUT

When a patient has been detained in England or Wales under the Mental Health Act 1983 (see p. 176 for relevant information on Scotland and Northern Ireland) it will have been as a result of a careful assessment of the patient's condition by a group of professionals, including in most cases an ASW. The (Draft) Code of Practice provides much detailed guidance for all parties involved in compulsory admissions, and deals in particular with ways of resolving disputes between the parties involved. It is always to be hoped that at least in the early stages, the detention, however traumatic, will be in the best interests of the patient. Despite this, it is nevertheless undoubtedly true that in the heat of the moment mistakes can be made, especially where relatives are pressurizing the professionals involved to take immediate action 'for their protection'. It is also possible that once a patient is detained a process of institutionalization sets in very quickly, and neither they, nor the staff caring for them, retain as urgent a sense of their rights to be released as the law allows and even, at times, encourages. In this section, the rights of the detained person to get out of the mental institution in which they are detained are examined.

When the prescribed period of detention has ended

Every compulsory admission to a mental institution will be for a prescribed period ranging from a minimum of 72 hours to a maximum of 6 months (see p. 135). Once that period has come to an end the patient is free to leave, unless an application for a further period of detention has been made and been granted which is a course of action open to the hospital managers if circumstances dictate. (Note, however, that a s. 2, [28-day] detention cannot be followed consecutively by a further s. 2. detention). There are two additional sets of circumstances in which the person may be detained for a further short period, which apply to *ex-detained* and *voluntary* patients alike (see p. 165).

Premature discharge by the RMO or hospital managers

At any time during the period of detention, the RMO or hospital managers have the power to discharge the patient if they feel it is no longer necessary to detain the patient.

Leave of absence granted by the RMO

The RMO has the power to grant a detained patient leave of absence from the mental institution at any time, either for a specified period or indefinitely (i.e. to the end of the period of the detention order). The RMO can place conditions on the leave such as the patient's place of residence, or the attendance by the patient at a hospital for treatment or at an MHRT hearing. Social workers (who do not need to be ASWs) can play an important part arranging and supervising such leave. A useful booklet on the housing of those discharged from mental institutions is Etherington, S. (1983) *Housing and Mental Health: a Guide for Housing Workers* (MIND/Circle 33).

It should, however, be appreciated that the RMO retains the power to recall the patient at any time so long as the patient is subject to a compulsory detention order, if the RMO feels recall is necessary for the 'patient's health or safety' or the 'protection of others'. There are time limits on this power, which should be checked by reference to one of the specialist works detailed above. The RMO cannot, however, recall the patient simply to renew the 'section'.

Discharge by the nearest relative

- Admissions under section 3 (6 months for treatment) are not permissible if the *nearest relative* objects, unless a successful application is made to the county court asking for that objection to be overruled on the grounds of its unreasonableness.

- In all cases of detention, other than those for up to 72 hours, the *nearest relative* has the power to discharge any patient who has been detained. The nearest relative must give the relevant hospital managers 72 hours' notice, preferably in writing, of their intention to discharge the patient. In addition, the nearest relative is entitled to instruct an independent doctor to visit the patient at any reasonable time to examine the patient in private, and to inspect the records relating to the patient's detention and treatment, in order to provide independent

advice on the question of early discharge. This entitlement is
guaranteed by statute and can be insisted upon by the relative.
Any refusal to allow this right amounts to a criminal offence.

- If, following an application to discharge by a nearest relative
the RMO raises no objection, the patient will then be
discharged after 72 hours. If, however, the RMO during the 72
hours provides the hospital managers with a report expressing
the opinion that the patient if discharged 'would be likely to act
in a manner dangerous to other persons or her/himself' (known
as a Barring Certificate) the nearest relative's 'discharge order'
will have no effect.

The *patient* can apply to be discharged by an MHRT within 14 days
of an admission for assessment (s. 2); the patient or the nearest
relative can apply for discharge of the patient by an MHRT within 28
days of the issue of a Barring Certificate if the admission was for
assessment and treatment (s. 3). If no application for discharge within
6 months of a s.3 admission for treatment is made, the hospital
managers should automatically refer the case to the MHRT for
review (see p. 154).

Who is the patient's nearest relative?

The law on this subject is a little complicated, and if in any doubt the
detailed answer can be found in one of the guides to the Mental
Health Act 1983, listed on p. 133. In summary, a patient's nearest
relative is the person who is highest on the list:

- Any relative with whom the patient normally resides, or who
normally cares for the patient. If there is more than one such
person priority will be given to the person highest on the list
below.
- Husband or wife (unless permanently or indefinitely separated; this does not have to be a *legal* separation); or cohabitee
of at least 6 months' cohabitation.
- Son or daughter. An adopted child is treated as if they are the
child of the adoptive parents. A child whose parents are
unmarried is treated as the son or daughter of the mother
alone. The child must be 18 or over. A step child is not

considered a son or daughter. In all these circumstances the oldest takes priority.

- Father or mother. Rules on adoptive, unmarried and step-parents are as above. Oldest takes priority.
- Brother or sister. Oldest takes priority.
- Grandparent. Oldest takes priority.
- Grandchild. Oldest takes priority.
- Uncle or aunt. Oldest takes priority.
- Nephew or niece. Oldest takes priority.
- Non-related house/flat sharers. This means any person, not related as above to the patient, but with whom the patient has resided for at least the past 5 years. Oldest takes priority.

If the nearest relative does not wish to exercise their powers under the Act, they may authorize somebody else to do so in writing (Regulation 14). This would be a useful precaution for a nearest relative to take, if they rarely see the patient or if they are anxious that their future relationship is not tainted by taking such action. It may be revoked at any time. If there is no nearest relative *or* the nearest relative is incapable of acting as such through mental or other illness *or* the nearest relative is unreasonably objecting to making an application for admission for treatment, an ASW, or any relative or person living with the patient at the time they were admitted to hospital, can apply to the local county court requesting the appointment of an alternative person as a nearest relative. Less than 12 cases per year are taken under this provision. It would, however, be a suitable course of action to take where a social worker is in strong disagreement with the nearest relative who has made the application, and wishes to ensure that a relative more in touch with the patient's needs is appointed in their place.

The (Draft) Code of Practice advises local authorities to have a policy on what they consider might amount to an unreasonable objection by a nearest relative to an application for admission for treatment.

Discharge by a Mental Health Act Review Tribunal (MHRT)

This section does not deal with the powers of the MHRT in relation to *guardianship*, as the chapter is limited to patients in mental institutions. The adviser who wishes to learn more about *Guardianship*, which is a procedure whereby a person can be given powers to control the daily activities of a mentally disordered person remaining in the community, (similar to the custody rights of a parent over a child), should consult one of the specialist books detailed above: of particular assistance is the *Social Work Law File on Mental Health*. The (Draft) Code of Practice also contains much guidance on the use of Guardianship. An article by Fisher, M. (1989) in the *Journal of Social Welfare Law* (1988) no. 5, provides the most recent overview.

What is a Mental Health Act Review Tribunal (MHRT)?

MHRTs are independent tribunals which were originally established under the 1959 Mental Health Act to hear appeals by or, on behalf of, detained patients seeking to be discharged. Since 1983 the powers of these tribunals have been considerably enhanced with a corresponding increase in the number of cases brought before them (1329 in 1982, 3888 in 1985). There is a MHRT for every region covered by a regional health authority in England and one for Wales. Four regional tribunal offices provide the tribunals with administrative support. These offices will provide patients, social workers and relatives with information concerning the location of the tribunal for their particular area. Their addresses are as follows:

Clerk to the Tribunal, Mental Health Review Tribunals, 15th Floor, Euston Tower, 286 Euston Rd, London NW1 (Tel: 01 388 1188). (Special Hospital in Region: Broadmoor.)
Clerk to the Tribunal, Mental Health Review Tribunals, 3rd Floor, Cressington House, 249 St Mary's Rd, Garston, Liverpool L19 0NF (Tel: 051 469 0095). (Special Hospitals in Region: Moss Side, Park Lane.)
Clerk to the Tribunal, Mental Health Review Tribunals, Spur A, Block 5, Government Buildings, Chalfont Drive, Western Boulevard, Nottingham NG8 3RZ (Tel: 0602 294222). (Special Hospital in Region: Rampton.)
Clerk to the Tribunal, Mental Health Review Tribunals, 2nd Floor, New Crown Buildings, Cathays Park, Cardiff CF1 3NQ (Tel: 0222 825798).

It has already been stressed earlier in this chapter that hospital managers have a duty to ensure that both patients and nearest relatives are informed at the earliest possible opportunity of the existence of these tribunals and the powers they possess. A useful article explaining the practical steps necessary in preparing a MHRT case is by Sander, A. (1989) in *Legal Action*, July at 11–13.

What powers do MHRTs possess?

The MHRT has broad powers to discharge detained patients. These powers vary according to the circumstances of the detention.

Patient detained with Restriction Order imposed by Court

The legal issues here are complex, as the patient will have committed a criminal offence, which may have been serious, and the MHRT will have a difficult task deciding whether it is safe to release the patient into the community. They have a number of options available to them, and the patient should, if possible, seek skilled legal advice and representation from the MIND/Law Society panel of specialists (see below) before an application to the MHRT is made. If time is pressing, however, it may be advisable to appeal anyway before legal advice can be obtained. For a summary of some recent important decisions on the limits on MHRT powers in restriction order cases see Harbour, T. in *Legal Action*, October 1988.

Patient Detained without a Restriction Order imposed by Court

Broadly speaking, the MHRT must discharge the patient if it is satisfied that the grounds for detaining them no longer exist. Again the legal issues are complex and will vary according to whether the patient is *detained for assessment* (s.2) or *detained for treatment* (s.3). The same advice applies as for Restriction Order patients – obtain expert legal advice before lodging the appeal.

Are there any helpful further sources of information?

Advisers may wish to refer to a useful handbook by Larry Gostin and

156

Elaine Rassaby (1980) *Representing the Mentally Ill and Handicapped: a Guide to Mental Health Review Tribunals* (Quartermaine House/MIND). This book should be treated with caution as it was written before the Mental Health Act 1983 came into force, and thus its chapters on substantive law are out of date. It does, however, still contain much valid and useful information on the representative's task. The heavyweight text which is useful and up to date is Gostin, Rassaby and Buchan (1984) *Mental Health: Tribunal Procedure* (Oyez/Longman). This is a detailed guide to effective representation at MHRTs which is an essential reference source for anybody who is planning an appeal.

Who sits on these tribunals?

Tribunal members are drawn from panels of lawyers (including circuit judges and recorders), medical practitioners and lay people with experience in administration and knowledge of social services, or other relevant qualifications or skills. All appointments are made by the Lord Chancellor. Most tribunals will be composed of three members: a lawyer (who will be the president), a medical practitioner, and a lay person. If the appeal concerns a patient subject to a Restriction Order (see above) the president will be a circuit judge or recorder. Research by Fennell suggests that the lawyer is normally the dominant figure on the tribunal (see Fennell (1977) 'The Mental Health Review Tribunal: a Question of Imbalance', *British Journal of Law and Society*, No. 4, 186). Anybody with a close knowledge of, or involvement with, the patient should not be a member of the tribunal.

How do you apply to a tribunal?

There are four ways in which matters can come before a tribunal:

- application by patient;
- application by nearest relative;
- automatic referral by hospital managers;
- referral by the Secretary of State for Social Services or (if Restricted Order patient) by Home Secretary.

Table 5.1

Category of admission etc	Application		Automatic reference by the hospital managers (s66)
	Patient	Nearest relative	
Admission for assessment (s2)	Within the first 14 days of admission	—	
Admission for treatment (s3)	Within the first 6 months of admission, during the next 6 months, and during each subsequent period of one year	Within 28 days after being informed that RMO has issued a report barring nearest relative from discharging patient	If MHRT has not reviewed case within the first 6 months of admission; thereafter, if MHRT has not considered case within period of 3 years (1 year for child under the age of 16)
Hospital order without restrictions (s37)	Between 6 and 12 months after the making of the order, and during each subsequent period of one year	Between 6 and 12 months after the making of the order, and during each subsequent period of one year	Reference by managers if a period of three years has elapsed since case was last considered by MHRT (1 year for child under the age of 16)
Patient with restriction order or restriction direction (defined s79) who is in hospital	Between 6 and 12 months after the making of the order or direction, and during each subsequent period of one year		Reference by Home Secretary in respect of any case not considered by MHRT within the last 3 years
Restricted patient who has been conditionally discharged and is recalled to hospital (s42, and see s75)	As if restriction order were made afresh on date of recall	As if restriction order were made afresh on date of recall	Reference by Home Secretary within 1 month after recall
Restricted patient who has been conditionally discharged and not recalled (s42, and see s75)	Between 1 and 2 years after conditional discharge, and during each subsequent period of two years	—	—

Reproduced from Gustin L (1983), A Practical Guide to the Mental Health Act 1983 (MIND)

Table 5.1 sets out the circumstances and time limits for these categories. Referrals by Government ministers in category four can in theory be made 'at any time if the minister thinks fit'. In practice, such applications are extremely rare and are only likely to be made in exceptional circumstances, where, for example, important new evidence has come to light since an earlier hearing.

The Rules of Procedure governing applications to MHRTs, and the subsequent conduct of the case, are the Mental Health Tribunal Rules 1983 SI 942. A useful, detailed analysis of these rules is contained in Gostin, L., Rassaby, E. and Buchan, A. (1984) *Mental Health Tribunal Procedure* (Oyez/Longman).

The procedure whereby a patient or nearest relative can make an application is relatively simple.

PROCEDURE FOR APPEALS AGAINST ADMISSION FOR ASSESSMENT (S. 2)

Only the patient can appeal against an admission for assessment (although a nearest relative can try to discharge the patient by writing to the hospital managers: see p. 152). The appeal must be initiated by the patient writing a letter to the offices of the tribunal serving the area of the institution where the patient is detained (see p. 155 for addresses). Anybody can write the letter on the patient's behalf. The letter should give the patient's name, the hospital address, the name, address and relationship of the nearest relative (if any), and the name and address of anybody authorized to represent them. As speed is of the essence, the letter should also stress that this is an admission for assessment case. Nothing else need be said in the letter. The letter should be sent by first-class post. A MHRT hearing should then be arranged for a date no later than 7 days after the office receives the application.

At the hearing the MHRT will have before it the patient's admission documents and medical recommendations, but little else, given the time available. The MHRT will endeavour to inform the nearest relative, the ASW involved in the 'section', and the hospital managers of the hearing, and request their attendance at the hearing.

PROCEDURE IN APPEALS AGAINST ADMISSION FOR TREATMENT (LONG-TERM CASES) (S. 3)

The procedure to initiate these appeals is the same as for the first category, except that the nearest relative may also appeal. The initiating letter should set out the section of the Mental Health Act 1983 under which the patient is detained (s. 3). All parties will be informed by the tribunal office of the application, and the hospital managers will be asked to provide the tribunal with a Rule 6 Statement within 3 weeks. The Rule 6 Statement will provide a number of formal details relating to the patient's detention. In addition, the hospital will provide an up to date medical report on the patient's condition (drawn up by the RMO), including the RMO's views on the patient's suitability for release and, where practicable, a report on the patient's social circumstances, drawn up either by a hospital social worker or by a social worker from the local social services department.

This latter report may have a lot of influence on the outcome of the hearing. It should cover the patient's home and family circumstances, the attitude of relatives to the release, opportunities to find employment, accommodation and other support within the community. Those writing the report should not forget that under s. 117 Mental Health Act 1983, both the district health authority and the social services department have a duty to provide, in cooperation with relevant voluntary agencies after-care services for patients who have been detained for treatment. This point should always be driven home, as tactfully as possible, to the relevant authorities in the patient's home area. At the same time, as the hospital social worker may not have the information or access to the information that the local fieldwork social worker may have, cooperation between the two social workers is an important part of the process of preparing the report. Eventually, once all the information has been obtained, a hearing date will be fixed. It is regrettably often several weeks before this can be done.

What happens at the hearing?

Whenever an application is made there must always be a hearing, unless the application is withdrawn. Before the hearing (normally, though not necessarily, on the same day) the medical member of the tribunal will examine the patient. The hearing will then take place, normally at the institution where the patient is detained. It will be in private, unless the patient requests that it be held in public. It is intended to be an informal hearing and it is not uncommon for the applicant to be addressed by a first name, to be allowed to smoke and so forth. Witnesses can be called to the hearing, and the tribunal may ask the patient to leave while others are giving evidence, although it must explain why. The writers of any written reports to the tribunal – e.g. medical reports, social work reports – have the right to request that their reports are not shown to the appellant. They must, however, give a reason for this request, and the tribunal has the right to overrule the request. The tribunal itself has the power to withhold any documents from the patient if it believes 'disclosure would adversely affect the health or welfare of the patient or others'. It cannot, however, withhold any documents from the patient's legal representative, or any other representative that the tribunal has deemed to be 'qualified' to represent them (e.g. a social worker, with the relevant skills). Once a report has been released to a patient it becomes the patient's property. At the end of the hearing the tribunal will give its decision, which may be a majority decision. This will subsequently be committed to writing, which will then be sent to the applicant. The decision must be set out clearly, with proper, intelligible and adequate reasons.

Is there an appeal procedure against a MHRT decision?

The only way of appealing against a decision of a MHRT is through the High Court and even then in very limited circumstances. This will certainly need the assistance of a lawyer. A MIND/or Law Society Panel solicitor should be approached for advice on this question.

Who can help the patient with the application?

MEDICAL SIDE

An applicant is entitled to instruct an independent doctor to visit the patient in the institution where they are detained (unless they are subject to a Restriction Order), to examine them in private, and to inspect any records relating to their detention. The MHAC or MIND can advise on appropriate doctors for this task.

LEGAL SIDE

Hospital managers should provide patients with as much help as they need in preparing their case. The DSS, MIND and MHRTs provide a series of helpful leaflets. It is, however, perhaps a little unrealistic to expect too much from a hospital in this respect, as they are presumably opposed to the application, and it is their judgement that is being brought into question. At the tribunal the patient can have a person of their choice to represent them at the hearing (so long as it is not another patient in their hospital) and also a friend to accompany them. If this person is a lawyer, the lawyer's fees can be paid for under the Legal Aid Scheme.

Self-advocacy

Patients and advisers interested in cooperative advocacy without resorting to legal representation should contact any of the following organizations:

The Campaign for People with Mental Handicaps, 12a Maddox St, London W1R 9PL (Tel: 01 491 0727) which campaigns for the rights of mentally handicapped people and monitors existing provision.
The Advocacy Alliance, c/o 115 Golden Lane, London EC17 0TJ (Tel: 01 253 3056). This group promotes self-advocacy in a number of areas, including mental disability.
National Citizens' Advocacy, 2 St Paul's Road, London N1 2QR (Tel: 01 253 2056). This organization promotes the development of citizen advocacy in England and Wales by providing information and advice on setting up and running citizen advocacy schemes and offices.

Discharge from emergency admissions following arrest by police in a public place

The police have a special power to remove a person from a public place to a *place of safety* if they consider that person to be suffering from a mental disorder and in immediate need of care or control. The police are advised that a *place of safety* under this section should

162

normally be a hospital. But a hospital is not legally obliged to admit a person detained in this way, and therefore it is normal practice for the police to take the person to the nearest police station and then seek the immediate assistance of an ASW who will probably attend the police station personally to assess the person's mental condition. The power of the police to detain a person in this way will lapse as soon as they have been examined and interviewed and, if necessary, suitable arrangements have been made for their care. In any event the police cannot detain a person in this way for more than 72 hours.

For further information and detailed research on the use made by police of this section consult Rogers, A. and Faulkner, A., *Place of Safety* (MIND).

THE VOLUNTARY PATIENT CLIENT IN A MENTAL INSTITUTION

Voluntary patients account for the vast majority (approximately 94 per cent) of the resident population of mental institutions in the United Kingdom. The (Draft) Code of Practice specifically states that informal (or voluntary) admission is preferred where possible. Social workers will come into contact with voluntary patients far more frequently than with detained patients. It is thus a matter of great importance that the patient client can be given good clear advice on their legal entitlements during the period of their residence in the institution, which may in some cases be for the rest of their lives.

Does a voluntary patient have to consent to treatment?

A voluntary patient in a mental institution is in exactly the same position as a patient in a general hospital: i.e. the administering of any form of treatment without their consent constitutes an assault or battery (trespass to the person) and is therefore unlawful. Consent can either be express, or inferred by the patient's action; e.g. offering an arm for an injection. The patient must, however, be given sufficient information about the nature of the treatment in order to make a reasoned decision whether to consent or not. Problems will clearly arise where the patient is frail, isolated, confused, or because of their condition simply unable to understand enough to be able to consent at all. In these circumstances, the law is at present very

163

unclear. A number of well publicized cases in recent years concerning the rights of parents to refuse consent for their children to receive contraceptive advice, or the rights of parents, doctors or courts to decide whether an abortion or a sterilization operation should be performed on a woman of severe mental handicap, deemed incapable of consenting, have failed to clarify the position. The law on this issue is currently very unsatisfactory (see discussion on p. 140 in the context of detained patients). What is clear is that, at all times, every effort should be made by medical staff to ensure that patients should be consulted and kept informed of the nature of their treatment to the fullest extent possible within the constraints imposed by their particular condition.

There is one situation where the need for consent can be dispensed with, namely that which the law defines as 'necessity'. 'Necessity' would include circumstances where treatment is necessary to save the patient's life, and they cannot give consent (because, for example, they are unconscious) and are not known to object to the treatment. It would also include the minimum treatment necessary to prevent a patient from injuring themselves, or those around them – e.g. to subdue a violent patient in an emergency. Such treatment should, however, only be administered under the supervision of a medical practitioner.

Can a voluntary patient leave the mental institution whenever they wish?

The answer to this question is a qualified 'yes'. As with consent to treatment, the voluntary patient is in exactly the same position as anybody who is not detained. They are free to leave the institution whenever they wish, and any attempt to restrain them, either physically, or by locking the doors, would amount to an unlawful imprisonment for which they could sue for financial compensation. What has to be recognized, however, is that it is always open to the hospital managers to convert the patient's voluntary status into that of a detained patient if they believe that the conditions necessary for detention have been satisfied. Furthermore, because the paperwork necessary to make an application for detention can take a little time, and the personnel involved in the application (supervising doctor, ASW or nearest relative) may not be readily available, the Mental

Health Act 1983 has introduced a system of 'holding powers' for both doctors and nurses, whilst the application is being prepared.

Doctor's holding power

If the medical practitioner in charge of a voluntary patient's treatment (or a medical practitioner on the hospital staff to whom they have delegated the task), forms the opinion that an application for the compulsory admission of the patient 'ought to be made', they should furnish a report to the hospital managers explaining why. Once the report is received, the hospital managers have the power to detain the patient for up to 72 hours. This power can also be used to detain an in-patient receiving treatment for a physical illness in a general hospital, provided the criteria for admission under the Mental Health Act 1983 are satisfied.

Nurse's holding power

Sometimes the relevant medical practitioner is not immediately available to make the application, and a nurse is faced with the problem of what to do about the voluntary patient who wishes to discharge themselves in circumstances where the nurse considers it dangerous to do so. The Mental Health Act 1983 has provided a limited holding power to nurses in this situation. The limitations are as follows:

- The nurse must be of the 'prescribed class' (a first-level nurse who is qualified in nursing mentally disabled patients as defined in the Mental Health (Nurses) Order 1983).
- The nurse must record in writing on a prescribed form her/his opinion that the patient is mentally disordered to such an extent that it is necessary for the patient's health or safety, or for the protection of others, for them to be immediately restrained from leaving the hospital and it is not practicable to secure the immediate attendance of the relevant medical practitioner.
- Compulsory detention is permitted only from the time the form is lodged with the hospital managers to the time the relevant medical practitioner arrives to assess the patient, and in any

165

event for no longer than 6 hours. Thereafter, unless the medical practitioner initiates procedures for further detention, the patient is free to leave.

- The power is limited to patients receiving in-patient treatment for a mental disorder; i.e. it cannot be used against non-psychiatric patients in general hospitals.

Additional powers under the general law

There is a general power under the common law for anybody to restrain physically a person who is clearly suffering from a mental disorder, and who presents an imminent danger to either themselves or others. This power is, however, severely limited and does not extend to the administering of medication or other treatment. It should only be exercised in an emergency, for as long as it is necessary to call the relevant member of the medical staff to consider the exercise of one of the special powers above.

Can a voluntary patient vote?

It is perfectly possible for a voluntary patient to vote so long as they are registered at their 'place of residence' as a voter. There are two alternative places which they might register as their 'place of residence':

1. The institution where they are in residence, so long as it is not 'maintained wholly or mainly for the reception and treatment of persons suffering from mental disorder'. Patients who can register under this category must not be mentally disordered and the category normally is limited to those who are living in the institution because they have nowhere else to go. The sorts of institution where registration would be appropriate are old peoples' homes, nursing homes, hostels and psychiatric wings of general hospitals. If in doubt as to the categorization of the institution or the patient, the second method of registration is likely to be more appropriate.
2. Either the address where they would be residing were they not currently residing in the mental institution or if this is not possible to provide, any address in the United Kingdom where they have

166

once resided. This address must be provided in an official Declaration on a special form available from HMSO. Hospital managers have a duty to inform any voluntary patient who is not already registered elsewhere as a voter of their right to make such a Declaration. The Declaration must be made annually, on or before the qualifying date for registration. It must be made 'without assistance' which means that the patient must be able to understand the information requested on the form even though they might need physical assistance in filling out the form. Once the Declaration has been completed, the patient has the right to vote either by post or in person.

The issues involved in the voting rights of the mentally disabled are complex and controversial. The Declaration system, for example, effectively prevents mental hospital in-patients from voting for a candidate who represents the constituency in which their hospital is situated, which may in reality be their permanent home. The form itself is written in formal, complex language. An interesting study of the voting rights of mental patients has been written by Linda Ward of the Campaign for People with Mental Handicaps. For those who wish to know more about the issues, this booklet is recommended: Ward (1987) *Talking Points No 6. The Right to Vote* (CMH address, p. 175).

For further official assistance see HC (83) 14 *Health Services Development – Representation of the People Act 1983: Electoral Registration in Mental Illness and Mental Handicap Hospitals* (statement of government policy) and DHSS Leaflet ER (MH) 1 *Voting in Elections* which can be obtained from DSS Store, Health Publication Unit, No. 2 Site, Manchester Rd, Heywood, Lancs OL10 2PZ.

Can a voluntary patient's mail be opened or withheld?

Neither the incoming or the outgoing mail of a voluntary patient may be opened or withheld.

Is a voluntary patient's right to sue in the courts subject to the same restrictions as those of a detained patient?

Although the Mental Health Act does not expressly exempt

167

voluntary patients from the provisions and restraints relating to legal action that affect detained patients (see p. 149) a court has held in one case, *R v. Runighian 1977, Criminal Law Review*, 361, that hospital staff do not have the same protection against legal actions by voluntary patients as they do against actions by detained patients. This means, for example, that a voluntary patient has every right to sue a member of the hospital staff who has wrongfully used force against them, or administered treatment without their consent, without recourse to s. 139 (see p. 149). In these circumstances legal advice from a sympathetic solicitor or MIND should be sought.

The right to initiate judicial review proceedings is also available to a voluntary patient (see p. 149 and Chapter 3).

Will the mental institution ever give a voluntary patient any financial assistance?

The powers of the Secretary of State to pay 'pocket money' to in-patients who would otherwise be without the resources to meet their personal expenses apply equally to voluntary and detained patients (see p. 138). Hospital managers should be approached on behalf of voluntary patients in appropriate cases.

See MIND Policy Paper 1 (1983) *Money in Hospital* (MIND).

What complaints procedures exist for voluntary patients?

With the one important exception of access to the MHAC, access to all the complaints procedures described on p. 145 for detained patients is available for voluntary patients, with like procedures and remedies as for detained patients. Whilst the Secretary of State for Social Services has, under the Mental Health Act 1983, the power to direct the MHAC to 'keep under review the care and treatment of informal patients', he has not yet directed them to do so. All voluntary patients should see their baseline as stated by Larry Gostin in the following way:

the rights of voluntary patients should be no different from those of any patient having treatment for a physical illness in a general hospital.

Any lowering of standards by hospitals and mental institutions below this norm should be challenged.

GENERAL POWERS OF OTHERS TO MANAGE THE PROPERTY AND AFFAIRS OF THE MENTALLY DISABLED

The majority of mentally disabled people are capable of managing their own affairs, sometimes with the assistance of caring relatives, friends or professionals. It is always desirable that so long as it remains feasible this should continue to be the case. There does come a time, however, in the lives of some mentally disabled people when they really cannot manage their affairs at all, and it is necessary to look to alternative solutions. The problem is particularly acute in the case of the very elderly, where the process of mental decline is slow but in some cases can be predicted. According to William Bingley, Legal Director of MIND, by the end of the century the number of people in the UK over 85 will have doubled to over 1 million. He estimates that 'at present more than 20 per cent of those over 80 suffer from some degree of dementia which to a greater or lesser degree renders them unable to make decisions on their own' (*Times*, 24 June 1987).

There are a number of possible remedies to this problem, the choice of which will depend upon the severity of the problem, of which the most extreme resolution is to vest control of all the person's affairs in the Court of Protection (see p. 171). Consistent with the principle of the minimum interference necessary to protect the individual, there is set out below a summary of the options, starting with the least level of interference.

Arranging for the person's income to be paid direct to another, who will manage their affairs for them

Social security benefits (see below and Chapters 8 and 9, p. 314) can be paid by the DSS directly to a 'suitable person' if the recipient's mental disability is such that they are unable to manage their property and affairs. The 'suitable person' will then be charged with the job of managing the person's affairs for them. Hospital 'pocket money' (see p. 168) can be paid in the same way. There are also provisions under s.142 Mental Health Act whereby the salary, pension or other benefits payable to the employee of a government department (and some other categories of employment) can be paid directly to the person who is managing their affairs.

Setting up a trust for the benefit of the mentally disabled person

Sometimes there are advantages in setting up a trust fund for the benefit of a mentally disabled person, whereby the trustees will administer all the money that is paid into the trust for the benefit of that person. This may well be the most suitable way of managing the affairs of a person suffering from severe mental handicap, or long-term mental disorder. There are a number of administrative and fiscal advantages in this method. A solicitor, MIND or MENCAP should be consulted before setting up such a trust.

Guardianship

It has already been mentioned earlier in the chapter that Guardianship is an alternative course of action to compulsory detention for dealing with people who are suffering from a mental disorder. If a person has been accepted as the Guardian of another who is suffering from mental disorder they have power to require the patient to reside at a particular place (not being a mental hospital), and to attend at places and times specified for medical treatment, occupation, training or education (for further information see p. 316).

Enduring Power of Attorney

Since the coming into force of the Enduring Power of Attorney Act 1985, any person anticipating a deterioration in their mental condition can appoint another person to have power of attorney on their behalf in the event of their subsequently becoming incapable of managing their own affairs. Certain formalities have to be observed when the power is first drawn up, and the power will only become effective if registered with the Court of Protection (see below), which must first be satisfied that the person is no longer mentally capable, i.e. by reason of mental disorder has become incapable of managing and administering their property and affairs. A solicitor's advice should always be sought before creating an Enduring Power of Attorney. For more information consult Cretney, S. (1989) *Enduring Power of Attorney* (2nd edn.) (Family Law: Jordan and Son).

Using the Court of Protection

The *Court of Protection* (which is an office of the High Court) exists to manage and administer the property and affairs of people who are incapable of doing so themselves by reason of their mental disorder. Its work is under the direction of judges and masters of the High Court, who delegate the work of visiting and interviewing those in its care to a panel of *Lord Chancellor's Visitors,* a body of lawyers, doctors and civil servants specially selected for this task. Approximately 220 people currently work for the Court of Protection. These people have to manage the affairs of some 23 000 people, which means that, with the best will in the world, their intervention is essentially passive.

Procedure

Anybody can apply to bring another into the Court of Protection: a friend, a relative, a social worker or even a creditor. The application must be supported by the evidence of one doctor, who can be the person's GP and need not be specialized in mental illness. The Court of Protection will supply the forms. The procedure to be followed is formal. The patient will be given notice of the application unless the court feels it to be unnecessary, as the patient will not be capable of understanding what is happening. The procedure is complex. For further information on the procedure and the consequences of the application consult Gostin, L. (1983) *The Court of Protection* (MIND). Once the application has been accepted, the Court has exclusive control over all the patient's property and affairs. This control will continue until the patient either recovers (which is rare) or dies. It is common for the Court to appoint a person close to the patient (often the person who made the application), as their receiver, with specific powers relating to the affairs of the patient, e.g. to receive their income, to pay certain bills, to effect a property sale. The receiver will, however, be closely monitored by the Court and will normally have to submit regular accounts of their activities in relation to the patient's affairs to the Court.

Other considerations

There are a number of factors that need to be borne in mind before considering an application to the Court of Protection. First, the Court charges fees for its services which are deducted from the patient's estate (but see below on the 'Short Order Procedure'). Second, there is no automatic review of the continuing need for the patient to be under the Court of Protection. An application has to be made for discharge, and only around 60 such applications are made annually. Third, the procedure of the Court is slow and impersonal. Fourth, the fact of the application with its consequential removal from the patient of the basic right to manage their own affairs may result in the further alienation of that person from those around them. Fifth, there may be no alternative.

It should be noted that there is a *Short Order Procedure* of the Court of Protection that is without fee that can be used to ensure 'fine tuning' of a patient's finances, as for example where they are not paying bills because they are under a fixed delusion that they are being paid by somebody else, despite evidence to the contrary. The address of the Court of Protection is as follows: Court of Protection, Stewart House, 24 Kingsway, London WC2B 6HD (Tel: 01 405 4300).

BACK IN THE COMMUNITY: LEGAL DUTIES OF THE LOCAL AUTHORITY

Once a mental patient has returned to the community the legal responsibility for their care shifts from the mental institution to the district health authority and the local social services department (see the *Griffiths Report* 1988 for some controversial perspectives on this issue). There are three major areas of statutory responsibility:

1. *Chronically Sick and Disabled Persons Act 1970*. This states that all the duties imposed on local authorities by this statute towards the physically disabled extend also to those who are 'substantially or permanently handicapped by illness, injury or congenital deformity' or suffering from mental disorder *of any description*

172

(my emphasis). Thus the scope of this Act is wider than those suffering from mental disorder under the Mental Health Act 1983 and will extend, for example to episodic disorder and the intervals between disorder. For a detailed account of the nature and extent of these duties see Chapter 4, p. 87.

2. *National Health Service Act 1977.* This imposes a duty on health authorities to provide facilities for prevention, care and after-care if appropriate, to those suffering from mental disorder within the Mental Health Act 1983. But this duty has been significantly extended by s.117 of the Mental Health Act 1983 in respect of patients released from hospital following a s.3 detention (i.e. detention for up to 6 months for treatment) whether their detention was in a mental institution, a 'special hospital' or a prison. Towards this category of ex-patient, both the district health authority and the social services department have a duty, in cooperation with relevant voluntary agencies, to provide after-care services until they are satisfied that the person no longer needs such a service.

3. *Disabled Persons (Services, Consultation and Representation) Act 1986.* This creates a new procedure* in respect of the discharge to the community of all patients who have been continuously receiving in-patient medical treatment for a mental disorder for at least 6 months. The treatment must have been continuous but periods in different hospitals can be aggregated together. The procedure applies to both detained and voluntary patients. Under the procedure, the health authority and social services departments where the patient is likely to reside must be informed of the proposed date of discharge (also the education authority if the patient is under 19), and they are then under a duty to assess the patient's needs for any of the services they are obliged to provide under the National Health Service Act 1977 (see above) and under the Chronically Sick and Disabled Persons' Act 1970 (see Chapter 4, p. 88). If possible this assessment should be carried out before the patient is discharged, although the patient has the right to ignore this provision, especially if they feel it might delay their departure. Once the assessment has been made, the relevant facilities for after-care should be set up.

*At time of writing this procedure is not yet in force.

SPECIAL FINANCIAL BENEFITS FOR THE MENTALLY DIS-ABLED

Welfare benefit advice for the mentally disabled is a specialized and complex business. Benefits will not be dealt with in any detail at this stage, as most of them are dealt with elsewhere in the book. These include attendance allowance, invalid care allowance (carers), mobility allowance, severe disablement allowance, vaccine damage payments, statutory sick pay, invalidity benefits, income support and housing benefit. For further information, consult the *MIND A–Z of Welfare Benefits for People with a Mental Illness* by Catherine Grimshaw, the two CPAG handbooks, and the *Disability Rights Handbook*. Particular attention should be paid to the chart in the CPAG handbook, setting out which benefits may continue while the claimant is in hospital, and for how long.

SOURCES OF FURTHER ASSISTANCE

Organizations

Mention has been made throughout this chapter of the use of Citizens' Advice Bureaux, and specialist solicitors whose names can be obtained from MIND and the Legal Aid Solicitors Referral Lists. There are also 3 specialist organizations that offer skilled advice and assistance.

MIND, 22 Harley St, London W1N 2ED (Tel: 01 637 0741) (National HQ)

North-west: 21 Ribblesdale Place, Preston PR1 3NA.
North: 158 Durham Rd, Gateshead NE8 4EL.
South-east: 4th Floor, 24–32 Stephenson Way, London NW1 2HD.
South-west: Bluecoat House, Saw Close, Bath BA1 1EY.
Trent and Yorkshire: The White Building, Fitzalan Square, Sheffield S1 2AY.
Wales: 23 St Mary St, Cardiff CF1 2AA.
West Midlands: Princess Chambers (3rd Floor), 52–54 Lichfield St, Wolverhampton WV1 1DG.

MIND is a campaigning body which seeks to promote the rights of people suffering from mental disability. MIND has a national headquarters, seven regional offices and nearly 200 affiliated local groups. It offers advice and information on all aspects of mental health, runs courses and conferences, and issues a wide range of publications. It has its own legal department which offers a MHRT representation service, and is occasionally willing to take test cases on issues of general importance in the higher courts. It will also offer advice, information and skilled specialist referral. If possible enquiries should be in writing because of the great pressure on the telephone service. All of the MIND publications referred to in this chapter can be obtained direct from the MIND Bookshop, 24–32 Stephenson Way, London NW1 2HD (Tel: 01 387 9126).

MENCAP, 123 Golden Lane, London EC1Y 0RT (Tel: 01 253 9433)

MENCAP offers an extensive range of services for mentally handicapped people and their families through its 12 regional offices, 500 local societies and central London office. It supports research into the causes of mental handicap, and runs a specialist bookshop.

Contact also the Campaign for People with Mental Handicaps, 12a Maddox St, London W1R 9PL (tel: 01 491 0727).

SCOTLAND AND NORTHERN IRELAND

Surprisingly little of the material in this chapter is of direct application to Scotland or Northern Ireland. The mental health legislation in each country is different in a number of key respects from that in England and Wales.

Scotland

In Scotland the relevant legislation is the Mental Health (Scotland) Act 1984. For a guide to the contents of this legislation and other related advice contact: The Scottish Association for Mental Health, Atlantic House, 38 Gardner's Crescent, Edinburgh EH3 8DQ (Tel: 031 229 9687). This association is an independent voluntary body devoted to broad issues of mental disability and mental health.

The statutory body in Scotland charged with responsibility for exercising 'protective functions in respect of persons who may be reason of *mental disorder* be incapable of adequately protecting their persons or their interests' is: The Mental Welfare Commission, 22 Melville St, Edinburgh EH3 (Tel: 031 225 7034).

Northern Ireland

In Northern Ireland the relevant legislation is contained in the Mental Health (Northern Ireland) Order 1986. A detailed guide to this legislation can be obtained from the Department of Mental Health, DSS, Dundonald House, Upper Newtonards Road, Belfast BT4 3SB (Tel: 0232 650111). A shorter summary of the law can be obtained from: The Northern Ireland Association for Mental Health, 84 University St, Belfast, BT7 1HE (Tel: 0232 228474). This organization is an independent voluntary body devoted to promoting mental health in the community through information and education and the work towards improvements in services for the psychiatric patient and ex-patient.

The rough equivalent body in Northern Ireland to the Scottish Mental Welfare Commission and the MHAC for England and Wales is: The Mental Health Commission, Elizabeth House, 116–18 Holywood Road, Belfast BT4 1MY (Tel: 0232 651157).

Finally, although a little out of date, the *MIND Mental Health Yearbook* of 1981–82 still provides a massive and unrivalled data bank of addresses and other sources of help and information on mental health issues throughout the United Kingdom.

6

Civil Rights and the Police

Relationships between clients and the police can be a critical element in the practice of many engaged in social work. There are of course a number of circumstances in which cooperation between social workers and the police is normal, and indeed essential, to the effective carrying out of the social worker's tasks, e.g. seeking place of safety orders, exchanging information regarding child abuse, seeking protection from violence in the course of daily work, etc. There are also, regrettably, but inevitably, a number of circumstances, where the social worker's client may be in conflict with the police. In these circumstances, it is essential that the social worker has a clear and accurate knowledge of the precise legal rights and duties both of themselves and of their client. As there will invariably be a sense of drama and urgency wherever there is police intervention, a vague and woolly notion of legal rights will be useless. Precise, accurate knowledge is essential to counter the tendency of some over-zealous police officers to ride roughshod over proper procedures, in their anxiety to obtain a conviction, and to give a client the detached, professional advice they need at such moments of crisis.

There are three particular sets of circumstances in which the social worker may be pulled into a situation of potential conflict with the police, in the interests of their client:

- A social worker may be asked in an emergency to advise a client, in conflict with the police, on their civil rights relating to such matters as search, arrest, or detention.
- A social worker may be called to a police station to sit in on an interview with a juvenile, or mentally ill or mentally handicapped suspect.

177

- A social worker may be asked to hand over to the police confidential records regarding a client.

In the course of this chapter, each of these three situations will be closely examined. The chapter will also examine a wide range of questions that may face the client or the social worker in those dramatic moments of conflict that characterize the early contacts between a police officer and a suspect. For those who wish to look in more detail at the legal relations between police and social workers, a good starting point is to read an article by Haley, M. and Swift, A. J. (1988) in *Journal of Social Welfare Law*, no. 6 (see p. 214).

The information contained in this chapter only relates to England and Wales. Police powers and responsibilities in both Scotland and Northern Ireland, whilst broadly similar, are also sufficiently different in detail for them to be regrettably excluded from the chapter.

SOURCES OF INFORMATION

Most of the law relating to police powers and duties is to be found in the Police and Criminal Evidence Act 1984 (commonly abbreviated to PACE). The Act is supplemented by a number of Codes of Practice which have been regularly amended since their introduction.*
In addition, there has also been in existence since 1988 a Code of Practice for Police Computer Systems (see Chapter 2, p. 33). The Codes can be obtained in full from HMSO for around £3. They are a very useful document in any social worker's library. Although a Code of Practice contains guidelines, and not law, a failure to follow any aspect of the Codes is treated by senior police officers as a serious matter that may lead to disciplinary proceedings. A failure to follow the Codes can in some circumstances provide a defendant with a defence against a charge of assaulting a police officer in the execution of his duty, and can lead to confession evidence being deemed inadmissible (see p. 000). This can lead to spectacular results, as in the case of the three juveniles charged with the murder of PC Keith Blakelock in the Broadwater Farm Riots. The cases against all three defendants were dropped in the course of the trial, exclusively

*The latest version of the Code of Practice should be in force in the Spring of 1990.

because of the number of serious and blatant failures on the part of the police to follow the 'Judges' Rules', (forerunners of the Codes of Practice), which rendered the juveniles alleged 'confessions' inadmissible.

This whole issue was exhaustively investigated by Amnesty International in their report entitled *Alleged Forced Admissions During Incommunicado Detention*. The report alleges that in this instance the police also violated the European Convention on Human Rights (see Chapter 1). The full report can be obtained from Amnesty International, 5 Roberts Place, Bowling Green Lane, London EC1.

Any defendant who believes that the police have failed to follow PACE or the Codes of Practice in any material detail should always inform their solicitor of the fact, as it might be relevant to their defence. In addition, there is a Complaints Procedure that allows an aggrieved person to lodge a complaint against a particular police officer (see Chapter 2).

An annotated list of sources for further information on police powers can be found at the end of this chapter.

N.B. All advisers should note that many of the rights and safeguards described below do *not* apply in cases where terrorist offences are suspected.

DETENTION BY THE POLICE

Does a person have to help police with their enquiries?

Technically speaking, nobody is under any duty to help police officers with their enquiries and refusal to do so cannot lead to any action or penalty, unless a person is guilty of wasting police time by giving them false or misleading information. A good citizen may, however, feel that as the main role of the police force is to assist in the prevention and detection of crime, cooperation with bona fide police enquiries is generally desirable, all other things being equal.

Can a person be arrested for refusing to cooperate with police enquiries?

It follows from the above that a person *cannot* be arrested for refusing to cooperate with the police. (But see p. 191 below on General Arrest Conditions.)

In what circumstance can a police officer detain a person?

There are only *two* general circumstances in which a police officer may detain a person:

1. limited detention to stop and search;
2. detention following arrest.

Both of these circumstances are carefully defined and limited by law, and are the subject of detailed treatment in the various Codes of Practice that govern police behaviour and practice (see p. 178). In addition to these two general circumstances, the police also have powers to order motor vehicles to stop for specific purposes (see p. 185).

LIMITED DETENTION TO STOP AND SEARCH A PERSON

If a police officer wishes to search a person it will clearly be necessary to detain them for the limited period of the search. A public search can be intimidating or humiliating. It amounts at face value to an infringement of the liberty of the individual, and is liable to abuse. Thus it is a matter of some importance that the boundaries between what is, and is not, permitted are clearly understood. The Code of Practice recognizes quite explicitly that the exercise of stop and search powers by police officers is a matter of some sensitivity. For example the original Code stated:

> There is strong evidence that on many occasions [stop and search] powers have been used where reasonable grounds to suspect the individual concerned of having the article in question on him did not in fact exist. There is also strong evidence that such misuse plays an important part in mistrust of the police among some sections of the community.

All those engaged in social work should ensure that the detail both of the Act and of the Codes of Practice are scrupulously observed in day to day practice. For if a police officer exceeds his or her powers, a citizen is entitled to resist these powers, and to register a subsequent complaint (see Chapter 2, p. 32). In addition, it is worth noting that any court has a discretion to exclude any evidence that has been obtained unlawfully (e.g. by police officers acting in excess of their powers), even though in practice it may sometimes be difficult to persuade a court to do so. See p. 201 on 'Inadmissible Evidence'.

Which police officers have power to stop and search?

Any police officer has the power to stop and search a person. The term 'police officer' includes all ordinary police officers (though not cadets), special constables, and police officers acting for a particular statutory body, e.g. Transport Police, Ministry of Defence Police, Harbour Police, Atomic Energy Authority Police, Civil Aviation and Airport Police etc. (For a full account of all the powers of special police forces see *Halsbury's Laws of England* , 36, paras. 211–19.)

What must the officer do before carrying out the search?

The police officer must inform the person about to be searched of:

- the officer's name, and the name of the station to which they are attached;
- the object of the search;
- the grounds for undertaking the search.

If the officer is not in uniform, identification in the form of a warrant card must be produced.

What happens if the suspect ignores the police officer, e.g. walks away?

Police officers have no power to force a person to stop in order to investigate an offence. It has, however, been established that the touching of a person in order to engage their attention is lawful. If, in addition, the police officer already has reasonable grounds for the search (see below) it would be lawful to use 'reasonable force' to detain the subject for the limited period for the search (see p. 185).

Must the police officer make a record of the search?

The police officer making the search must (unless it is impractical to do so at the time) make a written record of the search. The person to be searched must also be informed (unless it is impractical to do so) of their right to be given a copy of the record of the search if they request it within a year. This record must contain the following information:

- the object of the search;
- the grounds of the search;
- the name of the person searched, or if not known, a brief description of them;
- the date and time the search was made;
- the place the search was made;
- whether anything, and if so what, was found:
- whether, and if so, what injury to a person or damage to property appeared to the officer to have resulted from the search.

Where can a police officer stop and search a person?

A police officer can stop and search any person in a *public place,* which includes a place to which the public have ready access such as a pub car park, a cinema foyer or a shop (during opening times). It may also extend to a yard or garden that is actually private property, if the police believe that the person they wish to search has no lawful right to be in such a place. (On football match powers see p. 184.)

The power to stop and search does not otherwise extend to a person on private property (for police rights to enter private property see p. 196). The search should be carried out speedily. The Code of Practice states that 'it is an unusual search that cannot be completed within a minute or so'. A police officer may, however, ask the person to be searched to accompany them to a nearby police van or police station if they feel it appropriate that the search be carried out in a more private place. This might occur for example, if the police feel they must ask the suspect to remove more than outer clothing (see p. 186). The Code of Guidance states quite specifically on this point that 'every reasonable effort must be made to reduce to the minimum the embarrassment that a person being searched may experience'.

Can the police stop and search anybody they like?

No. The whole system of searching is underpinned by the concept of *reasonable grounds*. The Code of Practice accompanying the Act is intended to provide the safeguards to the Act's abuse by unscrupulous or heavy handed police activity in public. The Code of Practice contains the following broad philosophy:

- There is no power to stop and detain a person against his/her will in order to find grounds for a search.
- In some circumstances preparatory questioning may be unnecessary, but in general a brief conversation or exchange will be desirable as a means of avoiding unsuccessful searches.
- The fact that a person refuses to answer a question put to them in a public place is not, in itself, reasonable grounds for a search.

Reasonable grounds to suspect what?

The police can only stop and search a person they have reasonable grounds to suspect is carrying one or more of the following:

- *illegal drugs* (this power arises under the Misuse of Drugs Act 1971 s.23);
- *stolen goods*;
- *a prohibited article*. By this is meant an article made or adapted to commit burglary (e.g. a jemmy); deception (e.g. a false credit card) theft; or taking and driving away a car without the owner's permission (e.g. a master set of keys);
- *firearms or any other offensive weapon*. This category can include articles intended to be used as an offensive weapon such as kitchen knives, spanners or Stanley knives or articles that have been converted for use as offensive weapons, such as sharpened sticks or coins. The police may decide that the item is suspicious because of the circumstances in which the suspect is found to be carrying it and carry out a search accordingly;
- *items connected with terrorism*;
- *items linked to certain offences* in connection with game and wildlife.

In addition to the above, police have special statutory powers to stop and search people in proximity to certain 'statutory under-takings' e.g. nuclear power stations, military bases (see *Halsbury's Laws of England*, p. 181). They also have power to stop and search people, coaches and trains travelling to and inside certain designated football grounds, for intoxicating liquor.

'Reasonable grounds' are never defined as a matter of policy in statutes. The test, should, however, be an objective one. As the issue of police searches in a public place is a sensitive one, the first Code of Practice does, however, go out of its way to comment on what good police practice ought to be in this respect.

But even this first Code was so heavily criticized from a number of quarters that the revised Code has proposed an even more precise set of guidelines in this respect. There follows below an extract from the revised Code, proposed by the Home Office:

> Whether reasonable grounds for suspicion exist will depend on the circumstances in each case, but there must be some objective basis for it which would lead a careful officer to form the reasonable suspicion in question. . . . *Reasonable suspicion* can never be supported on the basis of personal factors alone. For example, a person's colour, age, hairstyle or manner of dress, or the fact that he is known to have a previous conviction for possession of an unlawful article, cannot be used alone or in combination with each other as the sole basis on which to search that person. Nor may it be founded on the basis of stereotyped images of certain persons or groups as more likely to be committing offences.

Can a police officer remove any of the suspect's clothing in the course of the search?

If the search takes place in a public place, the police officer carrying out the search has the power to request the removal of the suspect's jacket, gloves or outer coat. It is not permitted to request the removal of any other clothing, including head and footwear in public. The searching officer may, however, ask the suspect to go to a nearby police vehicle or station, or elsewhere, in order to carry out a fuller search which may require the removal of further clothing. This is only permissible if the search is intended to find an object whose presence has already been suspected. If the suspect refuses to remove the item of clothing voluntarily the police officer can remove it, using reasonable force.

Can a suspect be searched by a police officer of the opposite gender?

Any search involving the removal of more than an outer coat, jacket, gloves, headgear or footwear may only be made by an officer of the same gender as the person searched and may not be made in the presence of anyone of the opposite gender.

Can a police officer use force to carry out the search?

Force can be used by a police officer carrying out a search but only 'as a last resort'. Before force is used, the unwillingness of the suspect to cooperate voluntarily must first be established. The amount of force that can be used is the minimum that is reasonably necessary to complete the search.

What happens once the search has been completed?

Once the search has been completed the police powers of limited detention come to an end. The suspect must either be released or arrested.

STOP AND SEARCH: A VEHICLE

General powers to stop and search vehicles

General powers under the Road Traffic Act 1988

A police officer has a general power under the Road Traffic Act 1988 to require anybody driving a motor vehicle or riding a bicycle on a road to stop, if the officer making the request is *in uniform*. Failure to stop following such request is an offence. Once a vehicle has been stopped a police officer (including one not in uniform) may search that vehicle for the same general reasons that they may search a person, subject to the same preliminaries (p. 181).

Specific powers to mount road checks (as circumscribed by the Police and Criminal Evidence Act 1984)

In addition to the above powers, a police officer of the rank of superintendent or above (or in an emergency, any officer) can authorize the setting up of a special road check that can be maintained for up to 7 days for any of the following reasons:

- to discover whether there is an escaped prisoner in the vehicle;
- (if an officer has reasonable grounds for believing that a 'serious arrestable offence' (see below) has been committed in the area), to discover whether the person who committed the offence, or might have been witness to the offence is in the vehicle. This power extends to any suspicion on the part of the officer that there might be in the vehicle some person intending to commit such an offence.

In all the above cases, the grounds for suspicion must be reasonable enough to justify the road check, though once the check is justified, any vehicle may be checked, without needing to prove suspicion relating to that particular vehicle.

All the above procedures must be recorded, and any person stopped in a road check can apply for a written statement of the purpose of the check up to 12 months from the date of the check.

ARREST AND DETENTION FOLLOWING ARREST

Arrest

Arrest constitutes the second circumstance in which a person may be detained without their consent by a police officer. Again it is necessary to stress the distinction between voluntary attendance at a police station, to assist police officers with their investigations, and detention following arrest. According to the Code of Practice:

186

Any person attending a police station voluntarily for the purpose of assisting with an investigation may leave at will, unless placed under arrest.

What is an arrest?

An arrest is the taking of a person, if necessary by force, into custody. Every member of the public has the power to arrest another in certain very limited circumstances (e.g. if they have just seen that person commit a serious crime). Police officers have wider powers of arrest. If an arrest is unlawful (i.e. it is outside the officer's legal powers) the arrested person has a right to resist the arrest using reasonable force, and to take subsequent action in the civil courts for assault and wrongful imprisonment. There is an increase in the number of cases that are being taken against the police for assault and unlawful arrest. A very detailed and comprehensive book on the subject is Clayton, R. and Tomlinson, H. (1987) *Civil Actions Against the Police* which was also summarized in a five-part series in *Legal Action*, October 1987–February 1988. As a preliminary source of help the adviser might consult a short article by Peter Thornton, 'Suing the Police: Tactical Decisions' in *Legal Action*, March 1988.

Is physical contact with the arrested person necessary to constitute the arrest?

No. So long as the arrested person is informed that he or she is under the arrest, then the arrest has taken place, even without physical contact. The fact of the arrest must however be made clear to the arrested person. A court has decided, for example, that the words 'I shall have to ask you to come with me to the police station' are insufficient to amount to an arrest. A police officer may use such force as is reasonable to effect the arrest. It follows that serious attempts to resist arrest by force can be met by the arresting officer with equal force in return.

Must the arrested person be told why they have been arrested?

The arrested person must be made aware, in general terms, at the time of the arrest, of the reason for the arrest.

In what circumstances can a police officer carry out an arrest?

This question has to be answered in two parts as the circumstances will differ accordingly:

- arrest with a warrant;
- arrest without a warrant.

ARREST WITH A WARRANT

A warrant is a document that has to be issued by a Justice of the Peace on the basis of sworn evidence from a police officer. The arrest warrant will name the person to be arrested and specify in general terms the reasons for issuing the warrant. The sorts of offences for which arrest warrants will be issued are as follows:

- failure to pay money due under a maintenance order, fine or compensation order. (Note that a civilian enforcement officer, employed by the court to collect such sums due, does not have the same powers of arrest and entry as a police officer);
- failure to appear in court at the time and place specified in an earlier summons (limited to specified circumstances set out in Magistrates' Courts Act 1980);
- to arrest a bankrupt.

ARREST WITHOUT A WARRANT

There are a number of circumstances in which a police officer may arrest a person without an arrest warrant as follows:

- in connection with arrestable offences;
- to prevent breaches of the peace;
- under a specific statute;
- where the 'General Arrest Conditions' apply;
- to fingerprint a convicted person.

Arrest in connection with arrestable offences

A police officer may arrest any person whom they have reasonable grounds to suspect has committed, is committing, or is about to commit an arrestable offence.

188

WHAT IS AN ARRESTABLE OFFENCE?

An *arrestable offence* is one which carries a sentence of at least 5 years' imprisonment. Examples of arrestable offences are murder, manslaughter, rape, robbery, blackmail, theft, burglary, most offences of violence, criminal damage, causing death by dangerous driving, and many drugs offences; included here also are attempts or conspiracies to commit any of these offences. The important point is that the offence carries such a sentence, *not* that the sentence is likely to be imposed.

In addition to the above type of arrestable offence there are a number of other offences listed in PACE as arrestable offences even though they do not carry the possibility of long sentences. The most important of these are:

- taking a motor vehicle without authority, or being driven in such a vehicle;
- certain sexual offences;
- certain offences relating to official secrets and custom and excise;
- going equipped for burglary, theft or cheat.

(For the full list see s. 24 Police and Criminal Evidence Act.)

Although *juveniles* cannot be sent to prison, they can be arrested for arrestable offences.

Recent legislation has extended the power of arrest without a warrant to two new and important areas. First, in connection with certain sporting events (e.g. major football matches) police can arrest a person in possession of intoxicating liquor at the ground, or on certain vehicles travelling to the ground (Sporting Events [Control of Alcohol] Act 1985). Second, when public order is threatened, police can arrest for such offences as acting in a manner likely to stir up racial hatred, causing fear or provoking violence (Public Order Act 1986).

Arrest to prevent breaches of the peace

This is an ancient power given to the police to arrest any person they

189

believe to be breaking or about to break the peace in a public place. It is very general power and very hard to define. According to Professor Leigh of the London School of Economics:

> A (police officer) has power at common law to arrest without warrant any person whom he sees breaking the peace or who so conducts himself that he causes a breach of the peace to be reasonably apprehended. If no breach of the peace is imminent the most that a (police officer) can do is to admonish the persons concerned to keep the peace.

There have been a number of cases which have sought to define, extend or limit the concept of breach of the peace over many centuries. Fighting is clearly a breach of the peace. Threats that are not related to violence are probably not. Noisy demonstrations with no threat of violence would not constitute a breach of the peace. Demonstrations at which violence is anticipated would allow the police to justify arrests. The best recent judicial summary of the state of the law in this area is probably that of Lord Justice Watkins in 1982 as follows:

> We cannot accept that there can be a breach of the peace unless there has been an act done or threatened to be done which either actually harms a person, or in his presence his property, or is likely to cause such harm, or which puts someone in fear of such harm being done.

For further discussion of this subject consult St John Robillard and McEwan or Leigh (see pp. 213–14).

Arrest under a specific statute

A number of statutes grant police officers a specific power of arrest without warrant for that particular offence. The full list of such offences is contained in Schedule 2 of PACE. The most important of these offences relate to drunken driving, criminal trespass, persons unlawfully at large (on the run), immigration offences, and offences against animals.

190

Arrest where the General Arrest Conditions apply

Generally speaking, the police are encouraged to proceed by way of a summons rather than by arrest, in all minor alleged breaches of the criminal code. A summons is merely a court document ordering the suspected person to appear before a designated magistrates' court on a particular date, to answer the charges laid against them. Almost all driving offences, for example, proceed by way of a summons. There are some circumstances, however, where even though the offence would normally best be dealt with by summons, the police never-theless have the power to arrest the subject. These circumstances are as follows:

- the police officer believes the suspect to have committed, be committing or be about to commit *any* offence, however trivial; *and*
- the police officer has reasonable grounds for such belief. This means that a reasonable person acting without passion or prejudice, would fairly have suspected the suspect; *and*
- the police officer forms the view that service of a summons on the suspect is either impractical or inappropriate because one of the *General Arrest Conditions* applies.

WHAT ARE THE *GENERAL ARREST CONDITIONS*?

The *General Arrest Conditions* fall into three categories:

1. The police officer does not know the suspect's name or does not believe the name that has been given by the suspect or has not been given a satisfactory address at which to serve the subsequent summons. The address need not be the suspect's home: it can be that of a place of work or study, or that of a friend, social worker or solicitor, for example. As there is no power to detain the suspect, in order to check the address, a doubting police officer is left with the stark choice of believing the suspect or arresting them. The doubt must however be reasonable.
2. The police officer believes that an arrest is necessary to prevent the suspect from harming themselves or another, or from suffering an injury, or from causing loss or damage to property,

191

or from committing an offence against public decency or from causing an unlawful obstruction to the highway (if the unlawful obstructor has been asked to move and has refused). This could include the arrest of a helpless drunk, of an aggressive person, of people behaving in a sexually explicit way in public.
3. The police officer believes that arrest is necessary to protect a child or other vulnerable person from the arrested person. Protection here extends beyond physical protection, and could include protection from sexual abuse. A 'vulnerable person' is not defined, but according to a Home Office Minister it is:

> someone who is particularly susceptible to injury, somebody who is . . . particularly at risk. Someone in need of protection.

This power exists in addition to those already in existence under various mental health and child care provisions.

It is clear that the powers of arrest under this head are very wide indeed, and it is this width that has given civil liberties groups cause for much concern. At the same time it must be stressed that we are talking here about powers of arrest and not about new criminal offences. If arrests under these provisions do not lead to charges, the suspect must be released (see below).

Arrest for fingerprinting a convicted person

This power of arrest is very limited. It will only arise when:

* the person has been convicted of a 'recordable offence' (i.e. one which is kept on police records);
* the person was never detained in custody at a police station;
* the person's fingerprints were never taken at the time;
* within 1 month of the conviction the person was asked by a police officer to attend a police station for fingerprinting and after 7 days has failed to do so (on fingerprinting see p. 207).

What must happen to the suspect once they have been lawfully arrested?

After a person has been arrested (and any arrest that is not carried out in one of the above ways is unlawful) the police have to follow a very strict procedure. Although police statistics demonstrate the average time that a suspect remains in a police station following arrest is only 1½ hours, it is nevertheless important that the procedures are followed to the letter, however short the period of detention, if civil liberties are to be maintained. Evidence obtained in breach of any of these procedures may be subsequently deemed inadmissible evidence at a trial (see p. 201).

Detention at police station following arrest

- *Stage 1*. The suspect must be taken to a police station as soon as is practicable.
- *Stage 2*. The suspect must be cautioned before being asked any further questions. Nobody is ever obliged to answer any questions, either before or after arrest. The right of silence is absolute although at the time of writing the government is seeking to change this. If questions are put to a suspect after arrest, the suspect should be told: 'You do not have to say anything unless you wish to do so, but what you say may be given in evidence.'

    Failure to caution the suspect can render any statement inadmissible evidence (see p. 201).
- *Stage 3*. On arrival at the police station the suspect must be told both orally and in writing of their rights both to have someone informed of their detention and to see a solicitor. If the suspect is a juvenile (10–17) their parent or guardian must be informed as soon as possible of their presence at the police station.

    These two rights can only be denied a suspect in very exceptional circumstances and then only on the authority of a senior police officer. The exceptional circumstances would be that:

    a) the suspected offence is a serious arrestable offence (see p. 195);

    b) the senior police officer believes that the immediate exercise of the rights would either interfere with the evidence or alert other unarrested suspects or would hinder the recovery of stolen property.

In addition, it should be noted that the Court of Appeal has held that where a senior police officer denies access to a solicitor on one of the above grounds this is tantamount to believing that the solicitor is going to do something grossly unprofessional and almost certainly criminal. In the light of this decision it should be very rare indeed for a senior police officer to deny rights of access of a suspect to a solicitor. It is important to note however that in *any* case, a senior police officer may proceed with questioning before a solicitor arrives if 'awaiting the arrival of a solicitor would cause unreasonable delay to the processes of the investigation'. It is thus a good idea for social work advisers always to have open quick channels of access to a sympathetic solicitor. Given the existence of the nationwide Duty Solicitor Scheme (see p. 212) a decision to question a suspect in the absence of a solicitor on these grounds should always be challenged. If the person denied access is a solicitor's clerk the police may take a tougher line and remain intransigent.

- *Stage 4.* The suspected person must either be charged or released within 24 hours, unless the suspected offence is a serious arrestable offence in which case see Stage 5. The time begins to run from the moment of arrival at the police station.
- *Stage 5.* In the case of a serious arrestable offence a senior police officer may extend the period of detention to 36 hours, so long as s/he is satisfied of the following:
  a) The questioning is progressing diligently and speedily.
  b) Further time is necessary to secure or preserve evidence, or to obtain evidence from the suspect.
- *Stage 6.* After 36 hours have expired the suspect must either be released, charged or a further extension of the detention time obtained from a magistrate. The magistrate may extend the time to a maximum of 72 hours, but may choose to order a shorter extension, after which further applications can be made up to the 72 hours maximum. The magistrate is not allowed to hear the application to extend the detention unless the suspect has been given a copy of the documents applying for the

extension and is brought personally before the magistrate. The suspect is entitled to be legally represented. After this a suspect can only be detained a further 24 hours (up to a maximum of 96 hours, on the authority of a magistrates' court).

- *Stage 7.* If charged, the suspect must be brought before a magistrates' court at the earliest possible time, or bailed by the police to appear at a later date. Otherwise the suspect must be released.

What is a *serious arrestable offence*?

It will have been seen from the above that a distinction is made between an *arrestable offence* and a *serious arrestable offence*. If a suspect is being held in connection with the latter, the police have far greater powers. So what is a serious arrestable offence?

Essentially, it is an arrestable offence which was intended or likely to lead to any one of the following:

- serious harm to the security of the state or to public order;
- serious interference with the administration of justice or with the investigation of offences or a particular offence;
- the death of any person;
- substantial injury to any person;
- substantial financial gain to any person;
- serious financial loss to any person.

Some offences are always serious arrestable offences regardless of intention or outcome.

Who checks that the above procedures are followed?

By law every police station will have on duty at all times a police officer, not below the rank of sergeant, called the Custody Officer, whose sole responsibility will be to ensure that all these procedures are followed. The Custody Officer will not be involved in the suspect's case, will always be in uniform, and will have responsibility for keeping the custody record, the document that records every detail of the detention from the moment of the suspect's arrest. If there is a conflict between the Custody Officer and the officer who carried out the arrest, it must be referred to an independent senior officer. All suspects must be provided with a copy of their custody record, 'as soon as is practicable' after they leave the police station, if they so request.

Are there any other safeguards to protect the suspect?

The job of the Custody Officer, ensuring that correct procedures are followed, is supplemented by a further Review Procedure. If the suspect has been charged, the Review Procedure will be carried out by the Custody Officer. If the suspect has been arrested, but not yet charged, the Review Procedure will be carried out by an officer of at least the rank of inspector, who has not at any stage been involved in the investigation. The Review must take place at the following times:

- first Review not later than 6 hours after detention first authorized;
- subsequent Reviews at intervals of no more than 9 hours.

The purpose of the Review is to ensure that the procedures have all been followed, and to decide whether further detention of the suspect can be justified.

POLICE POWERS TO ENTER AND SEARCH PREMISES*

What exactly are premises?

The definition of premises is very broad and general. According to PACE, premises 'includes any place, and in particular includes any vehicle, vessel, aircraft, hovercraft, offshore installation, tent or movable object'. There are numerous reasons why a police officer might with to enter premises, e.g. to make enquiries, to look for a suspect, to carry out an arrest, to look for evidence of a crime, or in an emergency to protect somebody who is in some way at risk. But because the entering of private premises by police officers raises

*For a very detailed account of the law in this area consult Stone, R. (1989) *Entry, Search and Seizure* (2nd edn.) (Sweet and Maxwell). The most up to date account is to be found in Fairweather and Levenson (1990), (see p. 213)

fundamental questions about the privacy of the citizen and other civil rights, the law has laid down with great care the following.

In what circumstances can a police officer enter premises?

There are three alternative legal methods by which a police officer may enter premises. Whatever method is used the police must provide the occupier with a Notice of Powers setting out their rights.

Entering with the consent of the person able to grant permission to enter

Consent can only be given by the person with the immediate right of occupation, e.g. a landlord cannot consent to police officers entering and searching the premises of their tenant. The Code of Practice states:

> If it is proposed to search premises with the consent of a person entitled to grant entry to the premises the consent must be given in writing before the search begins. Before seeking consent the officer in charge shall state the purpose of the proposed search and inform the person concerned that s/he is not obliged to consent and that anything seized may be produced in evidence. If at the time, the person is not suspected of an offence, the officer shall tell them so when stating the purpose of the search.

If consent is subsequently withdrawn, even when the police are on the premises they must leave, or they will be trespassers.

Entering without consent and without a warrant

A police officer may only enter premises without consent and without a warrant, in the following circumstances:

- To arrest somebody or to recapture an escaped prisoner. Naturally, a power of arrest must also exist (see p. 188). The police officer must in these circumstances have reasonable grounds to suspect that the person they wish to arrest is on the premises.
- In an emergency to save life, limb, or prevent serious damage

to property. This power could therefore be used in domestic violence emergencies.

- They can also enter the premises controlled or occupied by a person they have arrested for an arrestable offence (see p. 189) if they have reasonable grounds to suspect they might find evidence related either to the offence for which the person was arrested, or evidence of a related or similar offence. The police cannot enter the premises of an arrested person for any other reason. It would, for example, be unlawful for the police to enter the premises of a person arrested for a public order offence, to search for stolen goods. When entering premises under this power the police officers must have with them a written authorization for the search from a police inspector (or above).

- There are a number of statutes that give the police specific powers of entry for particular offences, e.g. to execute an arrest warrant issued by a magistrate for non-payment of a fine (see p. 188); to look for drugs; under the gaming laws etc. The full list of such offences can be found in Fairweather and Levenson (see p. 213).

If a police officer does have lawful grounds to enter premises, and such entry is resisted, reasonable force may be used to secure entry.

IF THE POLICE ENTRY WAS UNLAWFUL CAN THEY USE ANY MATERIAL THEY SEIZE AS EVIDENCE IN A SUBSEQUENT TRIAL?

See p. 201 under 'Inadmissible Evidence'.

Entering without consent but with a warrant

If a police officer wishes to search premises, and none of the above conditions apply, it will be necessary to obtain a search warrant from a magistrate. The application will be made *ex parte*, i.e. there will be no access to the hearing for the person whose premises are to be searched. The application will be supported by sworn evidence given by a police officer. The magistrate must be satisfied that it is not possible or desirable to seek the owner's consent to the search (because, for example, the owner might try to conceal the evidence) and that it is likely that evidence of substantial value will be found on the premises. The warrant will only be issued if a serious arrestable offence (see p. 195) is believed to have been committed. The warrant can be used on one occasion only, a copy of the warrant must be given to the occupier of the premises to be searched, and once the search has been carried out, the warrant must be returned to the court that issued it.

Can a warrant be issued to search premises of somebody other than the suspect?

The premises to be searched under the warrant need not be those of the suspect. They may belong to any person. What matters is that the police believe they will find on the premises evidence relating to the particular offence. The warrant will however only relate to particular named premises.

What can a police officer seize once lawfully on the premises?

The answer to this question is particularly complex, and cannot be dealt with in any great detail in a chapter of this limited length. It is important, however, that the social work adviser has a general understanding of the general limits of police powers to seize material for two reasons:

1. In order to challenge any police officer who appears to be acting unlawfully at the time of the search.
2. Because there is always the possibility that evidence unlawfully obtained will not be admitted at any subsequent trial (see p. 201 under 'Inadmissible Evidence'). It is particularly important, therefore, that a social worker involved in a case at the time of the search keeps a record of exactly what is said by the police.

If a police officer has entered premises lawfully, by one of the above methods, it has already been made clear that he or she may seize any evidence of any offence, subject only to the exceptions set out below. This power extends to the lawful entry by a police officer of premises which have nothing to do with the suspect, but where the police hope to find evidence of crime. Thus the power may extend to a search of the premises of a social worker or social work adviser. It is for this reason that the following section is of particular importance to the social worker.

What evidence can a police officer *never* seize?

A police officer can *never* seize the following:

1. Any item subject to *legal privilege*. This basically means any correspondence with a solicitor, or other documents relating to some legal action, but the question is complex and advisers seeking more detailed information should consult Fairweather and Levenson, p. 213.
2. *Excluded material*. This is defined as any of the following:
    *   human tissue or fluid held confidentially for diagnosis or treatment;
    *   journalistic material in the form of documents, or records, and held confidentially;
    *   personal records of a trade, business or other profession or office, held confidentially. This will clearly extend to all client records held by social workers, and anybody engaged in social work, or holding office, e.g. as a councillor, so long as such records are genuinely confidential (see Chapter 3 on 'confidentiality of records').

Can a court give a police officer special authority to seize any evidence that could not normally be seized?

Yes. There are certain categories of potential evidence of which a circuit judge may authorize seizure after a special application by the police. Normally, but not always, the person in possession of the evidence has the right to appear at the hearing of the application. These categories are as follows:

*   Journalistic material not held confidentially. (For a comprehensive recent statement of the law on this issue see the case of *ex parte Bristol Press and Picture Agency* in the *Times*, 11 March 1986. In essence the court held that the material must be released to the police if the benefit to the course of justice

- If in care, the relevant care authority or organization. In these circumstances, if the suspect is living with their parents or foster parents, steps should also be taken to inform them, although this is not a legal obligation.
- Failing the above, another responsible adult who is not a police officer or employed by the police.

4. If the suspect is known to be the subject of a supervision order, reasonable steps must be taken to notify their supervisor of the detention.

5. Interviewing of the suspect should not normally begin until the appropriate adult has arrived. Nor should the suspect be asked to provide or sign any written statement in the absence of the appropriate adult. A senior police officer may however authorize that questioning may begin in the absence of an appropriate adult if they have a genuine belief that delay will involve an immediate risk of harm to persons or serious loss of or damage to property, or if they believe that awaiting the arrival of that person will cause 'unreasonable delay' in the investigation of the crime. Such delay is, however, only permissible where the suspect is suspected of committing a 'serious arrestable offence'.

6. The suspect should not be placed in a police cell, unless no other secure accommodation is available and the custody officer considers that it is not practicable to supervise them, if they are not placed in a police cell.

7. If either of the exceptional courses allowed at items 5 or 6 above are taken, the facts must be recorded in the custody record (see p. 195).

Suspect with mental handicap or physical or mental illness

The procedures concerning the treatment whilst in police custody of a suspect who is, or appears to be, suffering from some mental handicap or illness are very similar to that of the person appearing to be a juvenile. Failure to follow the correct procedures may lead to similar consequences as for juveniles. For suspects in this category the appropriate adult will be one of the following:

- a relative, guardian; *or*
- some other person who is responsible for their care or custody;
- another responsible person, who if possible is known and trusted by the suspect and if possible has experience in dealing with people with mental handicap or illness. This person cannot be a police officer or employed by the police, and must be 18 or over.

For further assistance see *Social Work Guidelines to the PACE* (BASW).

What is the appropriate adult supposed to do, once they arrive at the police station?

Once at the police station, the role of the appropriate adult is more than one of mere observer status. The appropriate adult is there to advise the suspect, to observe that the interview is conducted fairly, and to facilitate communication with the suspect. Advising the suspect, for example, to 'be careful what they say' is a perfectly legitimate role of the appropriate adult despite police views to the contrary. In the Broadwater Farm interrogations the police excluded social workers from witnessing interrogations for precisely this reason. The trial judge was extremely critical of police activity in this respect.

Are there special procedures for suspects who cannot understand what is being said to them for other reasons, e.g. they are deaf, or do not understand English?

Yes. The Code of Practice states as follows:

If the [suspect] does not understand English or appears to be deaf then the custody officer must as soon as is practicable call an interpreter and ask her/him to [help].

What happens if the suspect is, or appears to be, ill?

The Code of Practice states (in summary) that:

If a (suspect) appears to be suffering from physical or mental illness, or is injured, or is incoherent or somnolent, or is thought to be a drug addict or otherwise to need medical attention, or if [they] . . . become injured or ill the Custody Officer must immediately call the police surgeon, or in urgent cases send the person to hospital or call the nearest available medical practitioner. This applies even if the person makes no complaint and whether or not s/he has recently had medical treatment elsewhere.

Suspect's access to a solicitor

As stated above, all suspects have a right to consult a solicitor once they have been detained at a police station (subject to delays see p. 193). The right is to consult, if wished, a *specific* solicitor, in private. Alternatively, the suspect must be given the opportunity to consult either the duty solicitor (see p. 212) or to choose a solicitor from a list provided by the Custody Officer. As the right of access is only to a solicitor it may be denied to a solicitor's clerk, or a legal executive, but good reasons for denial must be communicated immediately to the solicitor.

Search of the suspect at the police station

We have already dealt with the general powers of the police to search a person in a public place (see p. 182). These same powers extend to a suspect who is voluntarily at a police station without having been arrested. Once a suspect has been arrested, wider powers of search arise. These are as follows, in order of extent:

1. *Basic search* to ascertain what possessions the suspect has with them. This will only become necessary if the arrested suspect refuses to submit voluntarily to a request of this nature. All items found on the suspect must be recorded in writing, which the suspect must then sign. The search may only be carried out by a police officer of the same sex as the suspect.
2. *Strip search*. This is a far more controversial power that has led to much criticism and bad feeling between the police and certain

205

categories of suspect. A strip search is 'a search involving the removal of more than outer clothing'. Such a search can only be carried out by a police officer of the same sex as the suspect, and should not be performed in the presence of a member of the opposite sex, unless that person is a doctor. Reasons for such a search must be given and recorded in the custody record. The reasons must be of a compelling kind – for example, the very reasonable suspicion that the suspect is concealing on their person evidence of the crime of which they are suspected. The courts have made some attempts to define the limits of such searches, the Court of Appeal finding for example that the removal of a suspect's brassiere would require 'considerable justification'. For, in the words of the Court of Appeal, 'strip searches involve an affront to the dignity and privacy of the individual'. It is 'the duty of the courts to be ever zealous to protect the personal freedom and dignity of all'. For a brief description of a successful action suing the police for an unlawful strip search near Greenham Common (£2000 damages) see *Legal Action*, September 1988.

3. *Intimate body search*. This is naturally the most controversial power of all, and is therefore the power subject to the closest regulation, and is dealt with in detail below.

Can a police officer ever retain a suspect's clothes or personal effects unrelated to the crime following the above types of search?

Yes, if the custody officer believes that the person from whom they have been removed would otherwise use them to cause physical injury either to themselves or to another person, to interfere with evidence, to damage property or to assist in their escape. Otherwise the police officer may only retain items that may be evidence of the crime suspected.

What is an *intimate body search*?

An intimate body search is a search of a suspect's body orifices, e.g. anus, rectum, vagina, nose, mouth or ear.

Who may authorize such a search?

A police officer of at least the rank of superintendent must authorize an intimate body search. If the authorization is verbal it must be translated into writing as soon as is practicable.

In what circumstances can such a search be authorized?

Only in one of two circumstances, namely that the authorizing officer has reasonable grounds to believe that the suspect has concealed in a body orifice *either*

- something which could cause physical injury *or*
- a Class A dangerous drug (e.g. heroin, cocaine).

Who may carry out such a search?

A drugs search *must* be carried out by a doctor or nurse either in a hospital, or at other suitable medical premises. The search for something that may cause physical injury (but is not a dangerous drug) *should* also be carried out by a similarly qualified person in similar circumstances. In an emergency, however, a senior police officer may authorize a police officer of the same gender as the suspect to carry out the latter type of search. Presumably, however, the suspicion that the suspect has a weapon concealed in a body orifice, creates by definition, an emergency.

Fingerprinting

It has already been explained earlier (see p. 192) that a police officer can arrest a person simply to take their fingerprints, but in very limited circumstances. A police officer may also take a suspect's fingerprints in the following circumstances:

- *At any time with the suspect's consent.* If the fingerprints are taken in the police station, the consent must be in writing and details will appear on the custody report. If the suspect is mentally ill, or mentally handicapped the consent is only valid if given in the presence of an appropriate adult (see above). If the suspect is aged between 14 and 17, the consent of a parent or guardian must be given in addition to the suspect's consent. If the suspect is between 10 and 14, the consent of a parent or guardian is sufficient.

- *Without consent* and using, if necessary, reasonable force. This may be authorized by a police officer of superintendent rank or above, who has reasonable grounds to believe that the suspect has committed an offence, and that the taking of finger-prints will tend to confirm or disprove their involvement in the offence. This power applies to any suspect over the age of 10.

What happens to fingerprints if the suspect is either not charged, or is charged and acquitted? (applies also to fingerprints of those not suspected e.g. the prints of the victim of a burglary).

All fingerprints of suspects in the above categories (and any copies of those prints) must subsequently be destroyed by the police. This must happen as soon as is practicable after the termination of the relevant proceedings or once they have fulfilled their purpose. If anyone asks to witness their destruction, they must be allowed to do so.

Taking of body samples

Body samples fall into two categories as follows:

1. *Non-intimate body samples.* These are defined as hair (except pubic hair); sample taken from a nail or under a nail; a swab taken from any part of a person's body; a footprint, or impression of any part of a person's body (including teeth) other than part of the hand.
2. *Intimate body samples.* These are defined as samples of blood, semen or other tissue fluid, urine, saliva, pubic hair, and a swab taken from a body orifice.

In what circumstances may a police officer take a non-intimate body sample?

The taking of such a sample will normally require the suspect's written consent. However, a police officer of at least the rank of superintendent can authorize the taking of such a sample, *without* the suspect's consent, and if necessary using reasonable force, if they believe:

- the suspect has committed a serious arrestable offence *and*
- the sample will tend to prove or disprove their involvement.

In what circumstances may a police officer take an intimate body sample?

An intimate body sample may *only* be taken from a suspect if they provide their written consent. The consent provisions for juveniles and the mentally ill or handicapped are the same as for fingerprinting (see p. 207). In addition, a sample can only be requested by a police officer of like rank and in like circumstances to those for the taking of non-intimate body samples *without* the suspect's consent. The difference is that if the suspect refuses permission to take an intimate body sample, the police have no power to take it.

There is, however, a powerful sanction which operates against the suspect who refuses an intimate body sample 'without good cause', e.g. religious grounds. The court in any subsequent trial will be told of the refusal, and will be allowed to 'draw such inferences as they think fit'.

Who takes the samples?

Only a registered medical practitioner may take intimate body samples, except urine or saliva. Failure to comply with this provision will render the taking of the sample unlawful. Non-intimate samples may be taken by police officers. If any clothing other than outer clothing is removed, there must be no officers of the opposite gender present.

Photographing a suspect

A suspect at a police station may only be photographed in one of two circumstances:

1. with their written consent *or*
2. in the *special circumstances* set out in the Code of Practice.

In either case the police *must* destroy the photographs together with any copies and negatives, if the suspect is either released without charge, or is tried for the offence and acquitted. The suspect must be allowed to witness the destruction of the photographic material, so long as they make such a request within 2 days of the decision not to proceed or the acquittal.

What are the *special circumstances*?

There are three categories of *special circumstances*:

- the suspect has been charged with or reported for a *recordable offence* (i.e. offences for which a conviction is recorded in national police records), and has not yet been released or brought before a court; *or*
- the suspect has been convicted of a recordable offence and no photograph has been taken of them already (there is no power of arrest for this purpose, as there is for fingerprinting) (see p. 192); *or*
- the suspect is arrested at the same time as other persons or at a time when it is likely that other persons will be arrested (e.g. at a demonstration), and a photograph is necessary to establish who has been arrested, at what time and at what place.

It is important to realize, however, that unlike the taking of a fingerprint, the mere taking of a photograph does not constitute an assault and therefore there is little that a person can do to prevent police officers from taking photographs in public places, where they are not generally subject to these tighter controls.

Identification parades

Identification parades must be held if identification evidence is disputed *and* if the suspect asks for one. They *may* also be held if the officer in charge of the case requests one, but then only with the suspect's consent. If the suspect refuses to participate, either in an identification parade, or in a controlled appearance with a more general group of people (e.g. outside a tube station), the police may decide to arrange for a direct confrontation between the suspect and the victim.

210

A suspect going before an identification parade must always be given a reasonable opportunity to have a friend or solicitor present.

The rules governing identification parades are very tightly drawn and are normally followed with scrupulous care by the police. Any social worker called to attend an identification parade as a 'friend' should consult Annexe A to PACE 1984 *Code of Practice D*.

Recording the interview

We have already looked at the procedure that a police officer must follow when interviewing a suspect, noting in particular that the interview should be recorded in writing, and signed by the suspect as a fair statement of what was said by all parties. Because of the risk of interviews being wrongfully conducted, a number of experiments are currently taking place in various parts of the country in the use of tape recorders to record interviews. There is not yet any consensus as to the advantage or success of the experiment. The experiments are, however, authorized by the Home Secretary and it seems likely that in future tape recordings of this nature will become more common. See Ian McKenzie and Barry Irving, 'Research on Police Interviewing', in *Policing*, April 1987; see also *Code of Practice (F)* 1988 HMSO.

Confession evidence

Any 'confession' that is obtained by *oppression* (defined as the use of actual or threatened violence, or indirect threats or inhuman treatment) will be considered inadmissible in any subsequent court hearing. This provision is a special provision relating to 'confessions' and is *in addition* to the provision on 'Inadmissible Evidence' (see p. 201). Examples of 'oppression' that has been considered sufficient to allow a court to render the evidence inadmissible have been 'confessions' made by a suspect held overnight merely because his story was disbelieved; by a suspect held for 50 hours without charge during which time 700 questions were asked; by a suspect kept alone in a cold cell for 4½ hours with no refreshments, no watch, and interspersed with 2 periods of rigorous questioning; and a suspect denied access to a solicitor and kept in custody for 7 days without charge.

The custody record

Mention has already been made of the custody record kept by the Custody Officer (see p. 195) and of the suspect's right to receive a copy. The record will contain details of the following:

- the grounds for the detention;
- the time of the detention;
- a record of any property taken from the suspect and the reason why it was taken;
- the suspect's signed acknowledgement that they were given written notice of their right to obtain legal advice, and to have a person of their choice informed of their detention;
- details of any complaints the suspect made about their treatment;
- details of any food or drink taken, of any visits, or messages received;
- details of any medical treatment given to the suspect, and any medical examinations or searches conducted on the suspect;
- details of any times that the suspect was not with the Custody Officer, e.g. because they were being questioned;
- records of all reviews of detention;
- records of fingerprinting, of any strip search or intimate body search;
- details of the time of release, of any applications to continue detention, and finally of any charges, and bail conditions.

The Duty Solicitor Scheme

There is now in existence in many police stations in the country a Duty Solicitor Scheme whereby local solicitors run a 24-hour rota to ensure that any suspect arriving at a police station has access to a solicitor should they request it. The Scheme is financed by the Government, and the suspect will not therefore have to pay for the service. The suspect is under no obligation to accept the solicitor offered by the Scheme. They are always at liberty to choose their own solicitor, providing that solicitor is willing to act for them. The Custody Officer ought to bring the Scheme to the attention of every detained suspect. The Criminal Law Committee of the Law Society have produced a useful leaflet called *Advising a Suspect at the Police Station*.

Complaints about the police

Throughout this chapter allusion has been made to the strict regulation of police powers both by the Police and Criminal Evidence Act 1984 and within the Codes of Practice. This chapter has not, however, dealt with the problem of what to do if a police officer does appear to the client or the adviser to have acted either unlawfully or in breach of the Codes of Practice. Essentially, there are two remedies:

- filing a complaint under the Police Complaints Procedure (see Chapter 2, p. 32).
- suing the police officer (but only if the victim has suffered some injury, e.g. as a result of assault or false imprisonment following wrongful arrest – see p. 187).

FURTHER SOURCES OF REFERENCE

Finally, some further reading on the subject of civil rights and the police. All these books will provide the reader with considerably more detail than is possible in this chapter. Where indicated they also include the full text of PACE and the Codes of Practice.

Detailed commentaries

Fairweather, F. and Levenson, H. (1990) *A Practitioner's Code to Police Powers* (Legal Action Group) (includes PACE and COP). (2nd edition)

Haley, M., Swift, A. J. (1988) 'PACE and the Social Worker' in *Journal of Social Welfare Law*, no. 6.

Leigh, L. (1985) *Police Powers in England and Wales* (2nd edn.) (Butterworths).

Robillard, St J. and McEwan, J. (1986) *Police Powers and the Individual* (Basil Blackwell).

Zander, M. (1985) *The Police and Criminal Evidence Act* (Sweet and Maxwell) (includes COP).

Practical handbooks

Hill, J. and Fletcher, Roger K. (1988) *A Practical Guide to PACE* (Waterlow).

Marston, L. and Nottridge, R. (1985) *Police Powers and Duties* (Fourmat Publishing).

Wegg, Prosser C. (1986) *The Police and the Law* (Longman).

On the police

Benyon, J. and Bourn, C. (1986) *The Police: Powers, Procedures and Proprieties* (Pergamon).

Southgate, P. (1988) *New Directions in Police Training* (HMSO).

On advising suspects at the police station

The Duty Solicitor's Handbook (Legal Action Group).

On the rights of prisoners

Treverton-Jones, G. (1989) *The Legal Status and Rights of Prisoners* (Sweet and Maxwell).

Note the most recent version of the *Code of Practice* is due for publication in Spring 1990. It should be consulted by all advisers for updating.

7

Legal Rights and the Workplace

This chapter will look at the legal rights of employees in their place of work. It would be impossible to cover the whole range of employment law in such a short space, and any adviser or client who wishes more detailed information on the law should consult one of the recommended reference works set out in the bibliography at the end of the chapter. What the chapter seeks to do is to identify a number of the most important areas in which disputes may arise and in which the adviser's assistance may be sought. The themes that the chapter will cover are as follows:

1. Getting a Job: Discrimination at the Hiring Stage.
2. Employment Contracts (Types and Contents).
3. Discrimination in Employment (on grounds of sex, race or trade union activity).
4. Maternity Rights.
5. Health and Safety at Work.
6. Losing Employment.
7. The Enforcement of Employment Rights.

In addition to the bibliography at the end of the chapter, there is a list of some of the most useful or important organizations where the adviser or their client can go for more detailed advice and assistance.

GETTING A JOB: DISCRIMINATION AT THE HIRING STAGE

This section does not deal with the problem of finding work but outlines the legal constraints imposed on employers at the hiring stage.

What matters must an employer ignore when deciding whether or not to employ somebody?

Ex-offenders

Normally the law does not require applicants to disclose facts about themselves which could hinder them in getting jobs, unless their silence amounts to fraud. Under the Rehabilitation of Offenders Act 1974 certain persons are relieved from the obligation to disclose 'spent' convictions to a prospective employer and it is unlawful for an employer to deny employment on the grounds that the applicant had a conviction which has 'spent'. However, this protection is not afforded to those applying for a whole range of jobs: for example, social workers, probation officers, teachers or nurses. (For the full list of jobs that are exempted from protection the Act should be consulted.)

WHAT IS A 'SPENT' CONVICTION?

Sentences of over 2½ years' imprisonment never become 'spent', otherwise convictions become 'spent' after periods which are related to the sentence imposed. Thus a sentence of imprisonment for a period of between 6 months and 2½ years is 'spent' after 10 years. Imprisonment for less than 6 months requires a 7-year rehabilitation period and fines and community service orders take 5 years to become 'spent'. A probation order, conditional discharge or binding over will be 'spent' after a year or when the order expires, whichever is the longer. Absolute discharges are 'spent' if 6 months has elapsed since sentence. Unfortunately the courts cannot compel an employer to engage a rehabilitated offender, they can only declare the exclusion of the applicant to be unlawful.

Disabled persons

The law relating to the employment of disabled people is set out in detail in Chapter 4, pp. 92–98.

Anti-discrimination legislation

It is not unlawful to refuse employment to someone on the ground that he or she either is, or is not a member of a trade union. Once a person has been employed, however, the law *will* protect them against discrimination on these grounds. The Sex Discrimination Act 1975 (SDA) and the Race Relations Act 1975 (RRA) make it unlawful to discriminate in any of the following ways when offering employment:

- in the arrangements made for the purpose of determining who should be offered employment;
- in the terms on which employment is offered;
- by refusing or deliberately omitting to offer employment.

It is equally unlawful to refuse to employ a person simply because they have given evidence in connection with proceedings, or have brought, or are about to bring, proceedings against a previous employer under the Equal Pay Act 1970 (EPA), the SDA or RRA.

VICTIMISATION

It is important to note that the titles of the SDA and the RRA do not fully reflect the matters that they cover. The SDA, for example, also outlaws discrimination against married persons on the grounds of marital status, while 'racial grounds' extend much wider than pure racial discrimination to include discrimination on grounds of colour, nationality, and ethnic or national origins.

Can discrimination on grounds of race or sex ever be lawful?

In certain limited circumstances sex or race discrimination at the recruitment stage is permitted by law, if there is a genuine occupational qualification (GOQ). In the case of discrimination on grounds of sex, there are several types of GOQ, of which the most important are as follows:

- The essential nature of the job demands a particular physiology (excluding physical strength): for example, when acting a particular role.
- The job needs to be held by a particular sex in order to preserve decency or privacy: for example, searching for security purposes.
- The nature of the establishment demands a person of a particular sex because it is an establishment for persons

217

requiring specialized care or attention: for example, in a single sex institution.

- The job holder provides personal services which can most effectively be provided by a person of a particular sex: for example, in a team of social workers providing specialized services.

The only GOQs allowed for under the RRA are:

- where discrimination is necessary in order to allow authenticity in the provision of food and drink, in entertainment or in modelling;
- where the job holder provides personal welfare services which can be most effectively provided by a person of a particular racial group.

Finally, it should be noted that an employer cannot rely on the existence of a GOQ if the organization already has sufficient workers capable of carrying out those duties whom it would be reasonable to employ in that way.

On the enforcement of rights under the SDA and RRA see p. 227.

EMPLOYMENT CONTRACTS (TYPES AND CONTENTS)

It is very important to be able to distinguish the type of contract that an employee has been given as many of their rights will depend upon this initial decision. It may often be the case that a contract is not in law what it is described to be by the employer.

What are the main types of contract found in the workplace?

Contracts of service and contracts for services

There are significant legal differences drawn between workers who are engaged under contracts of service (employees) and those who are engaged under contracts for services (self-employed or independent contractors). Employees gain the benefit of a number of

individual employment rights under employment protection legislation and are subject to the unwritten general obligations implied in
all contracts of employment (see p. 221). When employees, as
opposed to self-employed persons, are engaged, employers are
required to deduct social security contributions and tax.

Unfortunately, it is sometimes difficult to determine whether
someone works under a contract of service or for services. It is the
operation of the contract in practice rather than its appearance that is
crucial. Thus a person may be described as self-employed but be
treated by the law as an employee. If there is a dispute, it will
ultimately be for the court or tribunal to decide whether the person
was carrying on a business on his or her own account. The fact that
workers pay their own social security contributions and tax is not
conclusive. Indeed, people who work at home may be classed as
employees so long as there is a degree of mutual obligation to
continue the relationship with the person for whom they are working.
Although individuals engaged under special employment schemes
may not be categorized as employees, for certain purposes they are to
be treated as such, for example under health and safety regulations
(see p. 233).

Indefinite and fixed-term contracts

Employees may be hired for an indefinite period or for a fixed-term
(i.e. on a contract which has a defined beginning and a defined end).
Provided it is for a specified period, a fixed-term contract exists even
though it may be terminable by the giving of notice within that period
(see p. 237). From an employee's point of view the main disadvantage
of a fixed-term contract is that it is possible for the employer, by
means of an exclusion clause, to remove the right to claim unfair
dismissal (if the contract is for a year or more) or a redundancy
payment (if the contract is for 2 years or more).

Temporary and part-time employees

Since Parliament has not provided a definition of temporary status,
an employee *described* as 'temporary' who has satisfied any
necessary qualifying period of service and worked the requisite

219

number of hours (see below) will have exactly the same statutory rights as other employees.

'Part-time employment' is only indirectly defined by legislation and the statutory provisions are frequently at variance with the boundaries drawn in practice by employers and trade unions. The law stipulates that any person who has a contract of employment for more than 16 hours per week, or who has been continuously employed for the previous 5 years under a contract for more than 8 hours per week, can qualify for the full range of statutory protection.

The contractual rights of 'temporary' and 'part-time' workers will be determined by their individual contracts.

How can an employee work out their terms and conditions of employment if they have not been given them in a written contract?

Apart from apprentices, who can only be employed under written deeds, contracts of employment may be oral or in writing. In theory the parties to a contract of employment are free to negotiate the terms and conditions that suit them. However, in practice the vast majority of employees do not negotiate on an individual basis but are engaged on such terms and conditions as are laid down in currently operative collective agreements. Express terms are those which are expressly agreed as forming part of the contract. An express term takes precedence over an implied term (see p. 221). The exception is where the implied term derives from statute.

What information must be supplied to an employee about the terms and conditions of their employment?

If a written contract is not supplied, written particulars of the key terms of employment must be provided within 13 weeks of the job starting. The following information must either be given to employees personally, or must be contained in a document in which they are set out. An employee must be given a reasonable opportunity of reading them in the course of employment:

- The identity of the parties.

- The date on which the employee's period of continuous employment began.
- The scale or rate of pay, or the method of calculating remuneration, and the intervals at which remuneration is paid. Additionally, there is a right to receive an itemized pay statement.
- Any terms and conditions relating to hours of work and normal hours of work.
- Any terms and conditions relating to holidays and holiday pay.
- Any terms and conditions relating to incapacity for work owing to sickness or injury, including any provision for sick pay. The statutory sick pay scheme is outlined in Chapter 8.
- Any terms and conditions relating to pensions and a note stating whether a contracting-out certificate is in force (for further detail on pensions see Chapter 9, p. 301).
- The length of notice that the employee is entitled to receive and obliged to give (see p. 237).
- The title of the job.
- The name or description of the person to whom the employee can apply if they are dissatisfied with any disciplinary decision or wish to redress a grievance. This information does not have to be supplied where the employer has less than 20 employees.

Changes cannot be made to a contract of employment without the consent of the employee and where agreement is reached to alter the terms, the written statement must be amended to take account of the change within 1 month.

It is important to understand that the statement issued does not constitute a contract. It is merely the employer's version of what has been agreed. Nevertheless, if an employee confirms that what has been issued is an accurate summary of the main employment terms the statement will be treated as part of the contract.

Where there is no written statement, or an incomplete or inaccurate statement is issued, the employee can complain to an industrial tribunal (see p. 249).

What terms are implied into all contracts of employment?

Certain terms are regarded by the law as being inherent in all

221

contracts of employment. In the remainder of this section the major obligations which are imposed automatically on the parties to a contract of employment will be outlined.

The duties of the employer

THE DUTY TO PAY WAGES

This is the most basic obligation of the employer and is normally dealt with by an express term. However, in certain circumstances the law does not leave the parties entirely free to determine the amount of remuneration payable, for example, in a Wages Council industry or if an equality clause operates (see p. 228). The normal rule is that wages must be paid if an employee is available for work. Thus if employees voluntarily absent themselves from work (for example by taking strike action) an employer is entitled to withhold wages for the period of the absence. As regards deductions from wages for any other reason, the law provides that a deduction will be unlawful unless it is required by statute – for example, PAYE or social security contributions, or if the worker has agreed to it.

A useful organization to contact in connection with problems associated with low pay is the Low Pay Unit, a campaigning advice and research organization on the problems of low pay. The Unit runs a rights and advice service, and produces a large number of pamphlets relating to the issues of low pay. The address of the Low Pay Unit is as follows: Low Pay Unit, 9 Upper Berkeley St, London W1H 8BY (Tel: 01 262 7278).

THE DUTY TO PROVIDE WORK

Employers are not usually obliged to provide work and most employees who receive their full contractual remuneration cannot complain if they are left idle. Nevertheless, in exceptional circumstances the failure to provide work may amount to a breach of contract, as for example in the case of a pieceworker whose earnings depend on work being provided.

THE DUTY TO COOPERATE WITH THE EMPLOYEE

One effect of the unfair dismissal provisions (see p. 238) has been that the courts have frequently stated that employers must not destroy the mutual trust and confidence upon which cooperation in the workplace is built. Although each case depends on its particular set of facts, it may be interesting to note that employers have been held to be in breach of contract in the following situations:

- where an applicant for transfer had not been treated fairly;
- where there was a failure to investigate a genuine safety grievance;
- where there was a false accusation of theft on the basis of flimsy evidence;
- where an employer has persistently attempted to vary an employee's conditions of service.

THE DUTY TO TAKE REASONABLE CARE OF THE EMPLOYEE

This is detailed at p. 232.

The duties of the employee

THE DUTY TO COOPERATE WITH THE EMPLOYER

For convenience this can be divided into:

- The duty to obey lawful and reasonable orders.
- The duty not to impede the employer's business.

THE DUTY TO OBEY LAWFUL AND REASONABLE ORDERS

The obligation to carry out lawful orders has two distinct aspects. First, it means that employees are not required to obey an order if to do so would break the law, for example falsifying accounts. Second, it also means that employees are not obliged to obey orders which fall outside the scope of the contract. This is consistent with the view that, at least in theory, the terms of a contract cannot be unilaterally varied. Unfortunately, this does not prevent employees from being *fairly* dismissed for refusing to follow instructions which are outside their contractual obligations.

THE DUTY NOT TO IMPEDE THE EMPLOYER'S BUSINESS

Since the essence of the employment relationship is that the employee is ready and willing to work in exchange for remuneration,

223

it follows that going on strike breaches a fundamental term of the contract. Indeed, it would seem that even industrial action falling short of a strike is likely to be unlawful.

THE DUTY OF FIDELITY

Employees must avoid putting themselves in a position whereby their own interests conflict with those of their employer. Thus employees must not accept any reward for their work other than from their employer, for example a secret gift or commission. It is worth noting that there are three particular aspects to this duty: the obligation not to compete with the employer, the duty not to disclose confidential information and the law relating to inventions and copyright.

THE DUTY TO TAKE REASONABLE CARE

This is detailed at p. 235.

What can be done if either party breaks the contracts of employment?

The choices available to the innocent party will depend on whether the breach is of a minor or serious nature. An innocent party may choose to continue with the contract as if nothing had happened, they may sue for damages or, in the case of a serious breach, they may treat the contract as at an end. In most cases, however, employers will prefer to take disciplinary rather than legal action.

Traditionally the law has placed great emphasis on the personal nature of the contract of employment and courts have been reluctant to order a defaulting party to continue to perform the contract of employment. Thus, although an injunction (an order restraining a particular act) may sometimes be available, in most cases where there has been a breach of contract damages will be the normal remedy. Those who get damages will be compensated for the direct and likely consequences of the breach. This is a complicated legal formula that tries to take into account the loss to the innocent party that arises as a result of the breach of contract and express this in financial terms. Finally, it should be noted that ordinary breach of contract cases, for example failure to pay wages or holiday money that is due, are heard by the ordinary civil courts (in most cases the local county court) and not by industrial tribunals.

DISCRIMINATION IN EMPLOYMENT

Sex and race discrimination

These issues will be dealt with together since the relevant statutes are drafted in virtually identical terms. The definitions of sex and race discrimination were considered on p. 217.

What is the difference between direct and indirect discrimination?

Both the SDA and the RRA draw a distinction between direct and indirect discrimination. Direct discrimination occurs when a person is treated less favourably than a person of the opposite sex, a single person, or a person not of the same racial group would be treated. A person can complain of indirect discrimination where an employer applies a requirement or condition which would apply equally to a person of the opposite sex (single person or person not of the same racial group) but which is such that the proportion of the applicant's sex (marital status or racial group) who can comply with it is considerably smaller than the proportion of persons of the opposite sex (single people or persons not of the same racial group). For example, a height requirement might have a disproportionate impact. The applicant must also show that he or she suffered a detriment as a result of being unable to comply with the requirement or condition. Employers can avoid liability by demonstrating that the requirement or condition was justifiable irrespective or the sex (marital status or race) of the person to whom it is applied.

A number of points need to be made about the above definitions:

1. Both statutes stipulate that, when drawing comparisons, the relevant circumstances of the complainant and his or her comparator must be the same or not materially different.
2. The statutory definitions cover cases where the reason for the discrimination was a generalized assumption that people of a particular sex, marital status or race possess or lack certain characteristics, for example the assumption that married men rather than married women are the principal breadwinners.

225

3. The words 'requirement or condition' refer to something that has to be complied with.
4. The words 'can comply' have been interpreted to mean 'can in practice comply' rather than physically or theoretically comply.
5. The courts have ruled that a person only suffers detrimental treatment where its effect is such that a reasonable employee could justifiably complain about his or her working conditions or environment.
6. Indirect discrimination will only be justifiable if an industrial tribunal is satisfied that there were objectively justified grounds for the requirements or condition.

What would amount to unequal treatment in the course of employment?

It is unlawful for employers to discriminate:

- under the RRA, in the terms of employment afforded (terms which discriminate on the grounds of sex are covered by the EPA – see p. 228).
- in the way they afford access to opportunities for promotion, transfer or training, or access to any other benefits, facilities or services, or by refusing or deliberately omitting to afford access to them.

    However, special arrangements are permitted for the training of persons of a particular sex or racial group if it can be shown that within the previous 12 months only a small minority of that sex or racial group was performing a particular type of work in Great Britain.
- by dismissing·or subjecting the employee to any other detriment.

It should also be noted that dismissal on the grounds of pregnancy is capable of amounting to sex discrimination, although a woman who has been continuously employed for 2 years would be advised to claim unfair dismissal as an alternative (see p. 231).

How is the anti-discrimination legislation enforced?

If the provisions of the SDA or RRA are not complied with, both the employing body and named individuals can be sued. Individuals may be liable for instructing or putting pressure on someone to perform an unlawful act and for knowingly aiding another person to do an unlawful act. Employers will be liable for the acts of employees in the course of employment, whether or not they were done with the employer's knowledge or approval, unless it can be proved that the employer took such steps as were reasonably practicable to prevent the employee doing that act. Indirect discrimination is unlawful whether it is intentional or not, but no compensation can be awarded for indirect discrimination if employers can show that they did not intend to discriminate.

To whom should complaints be made?

Both statutes permit individuals to bring complaints before an industrial tribunal within 3 months of a discriminatory act occurring, although out-of-time claims can sometimes be heard. The Equal Opportunities Commission (EOC) and the Commission for Racial Equality (CRE) can provide financial support for complainants and, if they think it desirable, they can instigate formal investigations of anyone believed to be discriminating unlawfully. While the burden of proof is on the complainant to show unlawful discrimination, once a *prima facie* case of indirect discrimination has been established, the employer will have to satisfy the tribunal that the discriminatory requirement or condition was justifiable. Both statutes provide that customer or union prejudices cannot constitute a defence.

What remedies are available to the complainant?

If no settlement is reached and the complaint is upheld, three possible remedies are available. First, the tribunal can make a declaration of the complainant's rights, i.e. make a simple declaration that discrimination has occurred, which might be of sufficient symbolic importance to satisfy an applicant in some cases. Second, the person who has been sued (respondent) can be required to pay compensation, which may include an element to cover hurt feelings. The maximum that can currently be awarded is £8925. Finally, there may be a recommendation that the employer takes action within a specified period designed to reduce the effect of the discrimination that has taken place. It should be observed that where a discriminatory dismissal is alleged to have occurred the remedies available for unfair dismissal are likely to prove more attractive to the employee. Not only does the employer have to show a fair reason for dismissal but reinstatement or re-engagement can be ordered and greater financial compensation is available.

The two Commissions mentioned above can be contacted for further assistance as follows:

Commission for Racial Equality (CRE), Elliot House, 10–12 Allington St, London SW1 5EH (Tel: 01 828 7022).
Equal Opportunities Commission (EOC), Overseas House, Quay Street, Manchester, M3 3HM (Tel: 061 833 9244)

Equal pay

When is an employee entitled to equal pay?

An *equality clause* operates when a person is employed on any of the following:

- 'like work';
- 'work rated as equivalent';
- work of 'equal value' to that of a person of the opposite sex in the same employment.

The effect of the equality clause is that any term in a person's contract (whether concerned with pay or not) which is less favourable than in the contract of a person of the opposite sex must be modified so as to be not less favourable.

What is *like work*?

This concept focuses on the job rather than the person performing it.

Once a person has shown that her or his work is of the same or broadly similar nature as that of a person of the opposite sex, unless the employer can prove that any differences are of practical importance in relation to terms and conditions of employment – for example the performance of supervisory duties – that person is to be regarded as employed on *like work*. Attention must be paid to the frequency with which any differences occur in practice as well as to their nature and extent. Thus tribunals investigate the actual work done rather than rely on theoretical contractual obligations.

What is *work rated as equivalent*?

A person's work will only be regarded as rated as equivalent to that of a person of the opposite sex if it has been given equal value under a properly conducted job evaluation scheme. If the work has been rated as equivalent there is no need to show that a similar job is performed.

When can an *equal value* claim be brought?

Because of the complexities involved in bringing an *equal value* claim it is likely that this procedure will only be invoked where it cannot be shown that like work or work rated as equivalent is being performed. Indeed, where work has been given different ratings under a job evaluation study, an equal value claim cannot proceed unless a tribunal is satisfied that there are reasonable grounds for concluding that the evaluation study was discriminatory.

What defence is available to the employer?

An employer can defeat a claim for equal pay by proving that the variation between the woman's and the man's contract was 'genuinely due to a material factor which is not the difference of sex'. For example, the variation is due to differences in length of service or geographical location. However, the burden of proof will only be discharged if the employer can demonstrate objectively justified grounds for any difference in pay.

How is the equal pay legislation enforced?

Employees can apply to an industrial tribunal and claim arrears of pay. However, a tribunal cannot make an award in respect of any employment earlier than 2 years before the date on which the proceedings were commenced.

Complainants must identify a comparable person of the opposite sex in the same employment, i.e. a person employed at the same establishment or at another of the employer's establishments where broadly similar terms and conditions are observed. Although comparisons cannot be made with a hypothetical person, a complainant can compare her/himself with a previous job incumbent.

Victimization on trade union grounds

Action short of dismissal

This is a negative right. Employees have the right not to have action short of dismissal taken against them as individuals by their employer for the purpose of:

either
- preventing or deterring them from being, or seeking to become, a member of any independent trade union or penalizing them for doing so;

or
- preventing or deterring them from taking part in the activities of an independent trade union at any appropriate time, or penalizing them for doing so;

or
- compelling them to become a member of any trade union or of a particular trade union or of one of a number of particular trade unions.

Several points must be made about the nature of this protection.

1. 'Action' is defined as including omissions. Thus a *failure to promote,* as well as more positive acts, like segregation, are covered.

2. Tribunals have the task of determining what are 'activities of an independent trade union'. The following have been accepted as such:
    - attempting to recruit new members or form a workplace union branch.
    - taking part in union meetings and consulting a union official.
3. 'Appropriate time' is defined as being outside working hours or within working hours in accordance with arrangements agreed with the employer. The employer's consent may be express, for example in a collective agreement, or it may be implied from the conduct of the parties.

Dismissal on trade union grounds is dealt with below on p. 242.

MATERNITY RIGHTS

Since the law is both detailed and complicated this section will merely list the maternity rights that exist. The reader seeking more detailed information is advised to refer to the specialist publications listed at the end of this chapter.

1. It is unfair to dismiss a woman because she is pregnant, or for any other reason connected with her pregnancy, unless her employer can prove that she was, as a result of the pregnancy, incapable of adequately doing the work that she was employed to do or that she could not continue to work without contravening a statutory provision, for example regulations prohibiting the exposure of pregnant women to certain substances. Thus in selecting for redundancy an employer must disregard the fact that a female employee is pregnant.
2. A pregnant woman who, on the advice of a registered medical practitioner, midwife or health visitor, has made an appointment to receive ante-natal care, has the statutory right not to be unreasonably refused time-off during working hours to keep the appointment.
3. Women who are absent from work wholly or partly because of pregnancy or confinement are entitled to either statutory

maternity pay or maternity allowance depending on their length of service and level of earnings.

4. A woman has been absent from work wholly or partly because of pregnancy has the right to return to work with her employer at any time before the end of 29 weeks, beginning with the week in which the confinement occurred.

For further information on the range of benefits available to expectant and new mothers see DSS Leaflet FB 8 *Babies and Benefits* and the *TUC Guide to Maternity Benefits and Rights*.

HEALTH AND SAFETY AT WORK

What precautions must an employer take to ensure that an employee is reasonably safe from injury?

Recognizing that employers cannot guarantee that no employee will be injured at work, the standard of care which the law demands is that which 'an ordinary prudent employer would take in the circumstances'. Thus it is accepted that employers should only be held liable if they fail to safeguard against something which was reasonably foreseeable. Employers are entitled to follow recognized practices in their industry, unless they are obviously unsafe, but must make arrangements to ensure that they are kept abreast of current developments. Once an employer knows of a source of danger, or could have been expected to know of it, it is necessary to take all reasonable steps to protect employees from risks which hitherto have been unforeseeable. The duty is to assess the likelihood of injury and to weigh the risk against the cost and inconvenience of taking effective precautions to eliminate it. The duty is owed to each individual employee. Thus employers will be expected to take special precautions in respect of disabled, untrained or inexperienced workers, together with those who have language difficulties.

The duty of care may be divided into the following headings:

- Safe premises, for example non-slippery floors.

- Safe plant, equipment and tools.
- Safe system of working. Under this heading are all the matters which relate to the manner in which the work is performed, job design, working methods, the provision of protective clothing, training and supervision. There is no reason in law why this should not apply equally to the proper protection of social workers from violence from clients or health workers from illness and disease.
- Safe and competent colleagues. This means that employers must engage competent staff, instruct employees in safe working methods and then provide adequate supervision to check that these methods are being adhered to.

What has been the effect of the Health and Safety at Work Act 1974 (HASAW)?

With the exception of domestic workers, all employed persons are covered by the HASAW. The Act also seeks to protect persons *other than those at work*, i.e. members of the general public, against risks to their health and safety arising out of, or in connection with, work activities.

The general duties under HASAW

It is the duty of every employer to 'ensure, so far as is reasonably practicable, the health, safety and welfare at work of all his employees'. The matters to which this duty extends include:

- The provision and maintenance of plant and systems of work that are, so far as is reasonably practicable, safe and without risks to health.
- Arrangements for ensuring, so far as is reasonably practicable, safety and absence from risks to health in connection with the use, handling, storage and transport of articles and substances.
- The provision of such information, instruction, training and supervision as is necessary to ensure, so far as is reasonably practicable, the health and safety at work of employees.
- So far as is reasonably practicable as regards any place of work

233

under the employer's control, to maintain it in a condition which is safe and without risks to health and to provide and maintain means of access to and egress from it that are safe and without such risks.

- The provision and maintenance of a working environment for employees that is, so far as is reasonably practicable, safe, without risks to health and adequate as regards facilities and arrangements for their welfare at work.

What does *so far as is reasonably practicable* mean?

While the standard of care owed is similar to that imposed by the implied duty to take reasonable care (see p. 232) the defendant in any legal proceedings for a failure to comply with the HASAW has to prove that it was not reasonably practicable to do more than was in fact done.

Do employers have to have safety policies?

Except where less than 5 employees are employed at any one time in an undertaking, every employer must: 'prepare and as often as may be appropriate revise a written statement of his general policy with respect to the health and safety at work of his employees, and the organisation and arrangements for the time being in force for carrying out that policy, and to bring the statement and any revision of it to the notice of all of his employees'.

What are the functions of safety representatives and safety committees?

The HASAW provides for the appointment by recognized trade unions of safety representatives from amongst the employees. Where such representatives are appointed, employers have a duty to consult with them with a view to the making and maintenance of arrangements which will enable the employer and employees to cooperate effectively in promoting and developing measures to ensure the health and safety at work of the employees, and in checking the effectiveness of such measures.

Where at least two safety representatives submit a written request employers must establish a safety committee. Before doing so they must consult with the safety representatives who made the request and with the representatives of recognized trade unions. The function of safety committees is to keep under review the measures taken to ensure the health and safety at work of employees.

What are the responsibilities of employees under HASAW?

Two general duties are imposed on employees while they are at work:

1. to take reasonable care of the health and safety of themselves and of others who may be affected by their acts or omissions;
2. to cooperate with employers to enable them to fulfil their statutory duties.

Clearly it could be argued that employees who refuse to wear protective clothing or fail to observe safety procedures are in breach of this statutory duty. Finally, it is stated that nobody should intentionally or recklessly interfere with or misuse anything provided in the interests of health, safety or welfare in pursuance of any statutory provision.

How is the HASAW enforced?

While a breach of the HASAW or Regulations issued under it amounts to a criminal offence, civil liability only arises if there is a failure to comply with Regulations. A failure to observe any provision of an approved Code of Practice does not of itself render a person liable to any proceedings, but such a Code is admissible in evidence and proof of a failure to meet its requirements will be sufficient to establish a contravention of a statutory provision unless a court is satisfied that the provision was complied with in some other way.

Apart from the Crown, and most of the National Health Service, any person or corporate body can be prosecuted for an offence under the HASAW. However, if an offence is proved to have been committed with the consent or connivance of, or to have been

235

attributable to neglect on the part of, any director, manager, secretary or other similar officer, that person as well as the corporate body may be found guilty of an offence. Where the commission of an offence by any person is due to the act or default of some other person, that other person may be charged whether or not proceedings are taken against the first mentioned person. Thus Crown servants may be prosecuted despite the immunity of the Crown itself. If people are convicted of offences in respect of any matters which appear to the court to be within their power to remedy, the court may, in addition to, or instead of, imposing any punishment, order them to take such steps as may be specified to remedy those matters.

Except for the enforcement responsibilities of local authorities, (the Regulations impose certain inspection duties on local authorities), the HASAW is enforced by the Health and Safety Executive (HSE). Where an inspector from the HSE is of the opinion that a person is contravening (or has contravened) a statutory provision in circumstances that make it likely that the contravention will be repeated, he or she may issue an *improvement notice* stating that opinion. If an inspector believes that activities are being carried on (or are about to be carried on) which will involve a risk of serious personal injury, the inspector may issue a *prohibition notice*. If the risk of serious personal injury is imminent a prohibition notice may take effect immediately, although ordinarily such a notice will take effect at the end of the period specified in the notice. A person on whom an enforcement notice (whether an improvement or a prohibition notice) is served may appeal to an industrial tribunal, which has the power to cancel, affirm or modify the notice. Failure to comply with a notice is an offence.

How often does the HSE take action through the courts?

The number of recorded convictions as a result of HSE prosecutions in 1985 was 1853 with an average penalty of £425. The number of enforcement notices issued was 14 324 of which 10 888 were improvement notices, 2996 were *immediate* prohibition notices and 440 were *deferred* prohibition notices.

The address of the Health and Safety Executive is: HSE, Baynards

House, 1–13 Chepstow Place, London W2 4TF (Tel: 01 229 3456). The inquiry point of the HSE is able to deal with urgent questions.

LOSING EMPLOYMENT

Although the bulk of this section deals with the statutory rights to claim unfair dismissal and redundancy payments it might be helpful to begin by outlining the basis on which an action for breach of contract can be brought.

Dismissal in breach of contract

The first distinction to be made is that between dismissal without notice and dismissal with notice.

Dismissal without notice

Where the employer terminates the contract without giving notice the employee is said to be summarily dismissed. In order to justify a summary dismissal the employee must be in breach of an important express or implied term of the contract, i.e. guilty of gross misconduct. Although certain terms are always regarded as important, for example the duty not to steal or damage the employer's property, the significance of other terms will depend on the nature of the employer's business and the employee's position in it. If employers do not invoke the right to summarily dismiss within a reasonable period of the conduct occurring it will be assumed that they have waived this right (although they may be able to dismiss fairly *with* notice, see below). What is a reasonable period will depend on the facts of the particular case.

Dismissal with notice

Usually either party is entitled to terminate a contract of employment by giving notice and once notice has been given it cannot be unilaterally withdrawn. For notice to be effective it must be possible to ascertain the date of termination and not infrequently employees

237

have confused an advance warning of closure with notice of dismissal. The length of notice will be determined by the express or implied terms of the contract. Apart from the situation where the employee is guilty of gross misconduct, the law provides that certain minimum periods of notice must be given. After a month's service an employee is entitled to a week's notice and this applies until the employment has lasted for 2 years. At this point 2 weeks' notice is owed and from then on the employee must receive an extra week's notice for each year of service up to a maximum of 12 weeks. An employee with a month's service or more need only give 1 week's notice to terminate, but there is nothing to prevent the parties agreeing that both should receive more than the statutory minimum.

What are the remedies for wrongful dismissal?

Basically a wrongful dismissal is one without notice or with in-adequate notice in circumstances where proper notice should have been given. The expression also covers dismissals which are in breach of agreed procedures. Thus where there is a contractual disciplinary procedure an employee may be able to obtain an injunction or declaration from the courts to prevent a dismissal or declare a dismissal void if the procedure has not been followed. However, in the vast majority of cases the employee's remedy will be damages for breach of contract. Since damages are not available for hurt feelings or the manner in which the dismissal took place, an employee will normally only recover the amount of wages lost.

Unfair dismissal

Who can claim unfair dismissal?

Whilst the law grants many employees the right not to be unfairly dismissed, and the right to seek reinstatement and compensation if they are unfairly dismissed, there are nevertheless a number of general exclusions from and qualifications upon this right. First, no claim can be made if on or before the effective date of termination the individual had attained the normal retiring age for an employee in his or her position or, if there is no normal retiring age, was 65 years old.

238

Second, 2 years' continuous service is required before the right arises. However, neither the age limit nor the service qualification apply if the reason for dismissal is related to trade union membership. Third, while Crown employees are covered by the legislation those who ordinarily work outside Great Britain are excluded.

What is a dismissal?

For both unfair dismissal and redundancy purposes an employee is to be treated as dismissed if:

1. The contract under which he or she is employed is terminated by the employer with or without notice. It should be noted that where an employer has given notice to terminate, an employee who gives counter-notice indicating that he or she wishes to leave before the employer's notice has expired is still to be regarded as dismissed. Obviously if people resign of their own volition there is no dismissal at law, although if pressure has been applied the situation will be different, for example where the employee is given the choice of resigning or being dismissed. A mutually agreed termination does not amount to a dismissal.
2. A fixed-term contract expires without being renewed under the same contract (see p. 219 for exclusion clauses in fixed-term contracts.)
3. The employee terminates the contract with or without notice in circumstances such that he or she is entitled to terminate it without notice by reason of the employer's conduct. This is commonly referred to as a *constructive dismissal*. Employees are only entitled to treat themselves as constructively dismissed if the employer is guilty of conduct which is a fundamental breach of contract, for example where the employee is demoted or given a significant change of job duties without their consent. If employees continue for a lengthy period after such a breach without leaving, they will be regarded as having elected to affirm the contract and will lose the right to treat themselves as discharged.

239

Must an employer give a reason for a dismissal?

Yes, and if not the employee can apply to an industrial tribunal (see p. 249). Once an employee has proved that there has been a dismissal the tribunal will require the employer to show the reason, or if there was more than one, the principal reason for dismissal and that it falls within one of the following categories:

1. It related to the capability or qualifications of the employee for performing work of the kind which he or she was employed to do.
2. It related to the conduct of the employee.
3. The employee was redundant.
4. The employee could not continue to work in the position held without contravention of a duty or restriction imposed by statute. – for example, where a person loses a driving licence.
5. There was some other substantial reason of a kind such as to justify the dismissal of an employee holding his or her particular position.

In all the above cases the reason for dismissal must have existed and been known to the employer at the time of dismissal. This makes it impossible for an employer to rely on subsequently discovered misconduct.

Must the employer put the reasons for the dismissal in writing?

A person who has been continuously employed for 2 years and has been dismissed has the right to be supplied with a written statement giving particulars of the reason for dismissal. The employer must provide the statement within 14 days of a request being made. If it is alleged that the employer unreasonably refused to provide such a statement, or that the particulars given were inadequate or untrue, a claim may be presented to an industrial tribunal (see p. 249). If the complaint is well founded the tribunal may make a declaration as to what it finds the employer's reasons for dismissing were, and must order that the employee receive 2 weeks' pay from the employer.

What reasons for dismissal are potentially fair?

CAPABILITY OR QUALIFICATIONS

Capability is to be assessed by reference to 'skill, aptitude, health or any other physical or mental quality' (on *incapability* arising from pregnancy see p. 231). *Qualifications* means 'any degree, diploma or other academic, technical or professional qualification relevant to the position which the employee held'. For our purposes it is convenient to consider capability in terms of competence and ill health.

As regards incompetence, unless it can be shown that a warning would have been 'utterly useless', for example where the inadequacy of the employee's performance is extreme or the actual or potential consequences of a mistake are grave, employees should not be dismissed unless warnings have been issued.

In relation to ill health, it should be emphasized that the decision to dismiss is not a medical one but a matter to be determined by employers in the light of the medical evidence available. The basic question is whether in all the circumstances the employer could have been expected to wait any longer for the employer to recover. Clearly, where there has been long-term absence owing to illness a discussion of the position with the employee will be more appropriate than a warning.

CONDUCT

In this context *conduct* means behaviour of such a nature, whether done inside or outside the course of employment, which has an impact in some way on the employer/employee relationship. It is not the function of tribunals to decide whether misconduct is gross or criminal but whether the employer has, in the circumstances of the case, acted reasonably in dismissing.

REDUNDANCY

It is well established that employers have a duty to consider the alternatives to compulsory redundancy and the ACAS Code of Practice (see p. 244 on the legal status of the Code) suggests methods of avoiding such redundancies. If compulsory redundancies cannot be avoided, in the absence of an agreed procedure or customary

241

arrangement, the personal circumstances of employees must be taken into account. While an employer will be expected to show some special reason for not consulting it should be observed that the absence of consultation does not render a dismissal automatically unfair.

See p. 245 on the circumstances in which an employee is redundant and see below on automatically unfair dismissals).

Some other substantial reason (sosr)

This was included in the legislation so as to give tribunals the discretion to accept as a fair reason for dismissal something that would not conveniently fit into any of the other categories. It covers such diverse matters as dismissal for failing to obtain a fidelity bond, refusing to sign an undertaking not to compete and personality clashes between employees. SOSR has frequently provided a convenient peg where employees have been dismissed as a result of a reorganization of the business.

Will a dismissal ever be automatically unfair?

A dismissal will be automatically unfair if the reason for it (or if more than one, the principal reason) was that the employee:

1. was or proposed to become a member of an independent trade union;

or

2. had taken, or proposed to take part in the activities of an independent trade union at any appropriate time (see p. 231);

or

3. was not a member of any trade union or of a particular trade union, or had refused or proposed to refuse to become or remain a member.

If the reason a person was selected for redundancy related to trade union membership or if a person was selected in contravention of a customary arrangement or agreed procedure and there were no special reasons justifying a departure from that arrangement or

242

procedure, dismissal will also be unfair. Selection because of pregnancy will also be unfair (see p. 231).

Where the transfer of an undertaking (or a reason connected with it) is the reason or principal reason for dismissal then the dismissal is to be treated as unfair, unless there is an economic, technical or organizational reason entailing changes in the workforce. For these purposes an 'undertaking' includes a trade or business but excludes those which are not commercial ventures.

N.B. Where at the date of dismissal the employee was locked out or taking part in a strike or other industrial action, a tribunal has no jurisdiction to determine whether a dismissal was fair or unfair *unless* it can be shown that one or more 'relevant' employees of the same employer were not dismissed in the circumstances or that, within 3 months of the complainant's dismissal, any such employee has been offered re-engagement and the complainant has not.

In what circumstances will a dismissal be reasonable?

Where the employer has given a valid reason for dismissal the determination of the question whether the dismissal was fair or unfair depends on:

whether in the circumstances (including the size and administrative resources of the employer's undertaking), the employer acted reasonably or unreasonably in treating it as a sufficient reason for dismissing the employee; that question shall be determined in accordance with equity and the substantial merits of the case.

Thus, at this stage, tribunals must take account of the wider circumstances. In addition to the employer's business needs, attention must be paid to the personal attributes of the employee, for example seniority and previous work record. The words 'equity and the substantial merits' also allow tribunals to apply their knowledge of good industrial relations practice and to ensure that there has been procedural fairness. However, it is not the function of tribunals to ask themselves whether they would have done what the employer did in the circumstances; their function is merely to assess the employer's decision to dismiss to see if it falls within a range of responses which a reasonable employer could have taken. Finally, it should be noted that the ACAS Code of Practice does not have the force of law and therefore a failure to comply with it does not make a dismissal automatically unfair.

What are the remedies for unfair dismissal?

RE-EMPLOYMENT

When applicants are found to be unfairly dismissed tribunals must explain their powers to order *reinstatement* or *re-engagement* and ask employees if they wish such an order to be made. Only if such a wish is expressed can an order be made and if no order is made the tribunal must turn to the question of compensation.

Where re-employment is sought a tribunal must first consider whether reinstatement is appropriate, i.e. should the complainant be treated in all respects as if he or she had not been dismissed. If reinstatement is not ordered the tribunal must then decide whether to order re-engagement and, if so, on what terms.

Where a person is re-employed following a tribunal order but the terms are not fully complied with, if the matter is referred again to the tribunal the employee can be compensated for the loss caused by the non-compliance. If a complainant is not re-employed in accordance with such an order compensation will be awarded, together with an additional or special award, unless the employer satisfies the tribunal that it was not practicable to comply with the order.

AWARDS OF COMPENSATION

Compensation will be calculated in accordance with the following formula.

Basic award. Normally this will be calculated in the same way as a redundancy payment and will be reduced by the amount of any redundancy payment received. Where the reason or principal reason for dismissal related to union membership there is a current minimum award of £2520. The basic award can be reduced by such proportion as the tribunal considers just and equitable on 2 grounds: the complainant unreasonably refused an offer of reinstatement; any conduct of the complainant before the dismissal.

244

Compensatory award. The amount of this award is that which a tribunal 'considers just and equitable in all the circumstances having regard to the loss sustained by the complainant in consequence of the dismissal in so far as that loss is attributable to action taken by the employer'. However, it should be noted that a complainant cannot be reimbursed for the cost of pursuing an unfair dismissal claim.

The compensatory award can be reduced where the employee's action caused or contributed to the dismissal and where the employee failed to mitigate his or her loss. The maximum compensatory award is currently £8925.

The legislation aims to reimburse the employee rather than to punish the employer. Thus employees who appear to have lost nothing, for example where it can be said that irrespective of the procedural unfairness that occurred they would have been dismissed anyway, may not qualify for a compensatory award.

Redundancy

In what circumstances is an employee redundant?

Employees are redundant if their dismissals are attributable to:

1. the fact that the employer has ceased, or intends to cease, to carry on the business for the purposes for which the employees were employed, or to carry on that business in the place where the employees were so employed;
2. the fact that the requirements of that business for employees to carry out work of a particular kind, or for employees to carry out work of a particular kind in the place where they were so employed, have ceased or diminished or are expected to cease or diminish.

In this context 'cease' or 'diminish' mean either permanently or temporarily and from whatever cause. Thus employees will be entitled to a payment notwithstanding that it could be seen from the commencement of the contract that they would be dismissed for redundancy. It is also important to note that dismissed employees are presumed to have been dismissed by reason of redundancy unless the contrary is proved.

What is the effect of an offer of alternative employment?

If before the ending of a person's employment an employer makes an offer to renew the contract or to re-engage under a new contract which is to take effect either on the ending of the old one or within 4 weeks afterwards, the law states as follows:

1. if the provisions of the new or renewed contract as to the capacity and place in which the person will be employed, together with the other terms and conditions, do not differ from the corresponding terms of the previous contract;

or

2. the terms and conditions differ but the offer constitutes an offer of suitable employment (for example, work at another location);

and

3. in either case the employee unreasonably refuses that offer,

he or she will *not* be entitled to a redundancy payment.

The burden is on the employer to prove both the suitability of the offer and the unreasonableness of the employee's refusal.

If there is a change in the ownership of a business (or part of it) and the new owner offers to renew the employee's contract or re-engage under a new contract, such an offer is to be treated as if it had emanated from the previous owner.

Where the terms and conditions will differ from those of the previous contract a *trial period* may be invoked. This will last for 4 calendar weeks unless a longer period has been agreed for the purpose of retraining. If during the trial period the employee for any reason terminates the contract, or the employer terminates the contract for a reason connected with or arising out of the change (as for example when the employer terminates the contract because the employee is incapable of doing the new job) the employee is to be treated for redundancy purposes as having been dismissed on the date the previous contract ended.

Who can claim a redundancy payment?

Employees who have 2 years' continuous service over the age of 18 qualify for a payment. Certain categories are specifically excluded, for example civil servants and National Health Service employees. Also ineligible are employees who ordinarily work outside Great Britain and those who are 65 years old. On exclusion clauses in fixed-term contracts, see p. 219.

Workers will normally only be entitled to make a claim if within 6 months of their employment terminating they have:

either
- given notice to the employer that they want a payment;

or
- referred a question as to their right to a payment, or its amount, to a tribunal;

or
- presented a complaint of unfair dismissal to a tribunal.

How is a redundancy payment calculated?

Redundancy payments are calculated according to the following formula, with a maximum of 20 years being taken into account. Starting at the end of the employee's period of continuous service and reckoning backwards:

- $1\frac{1}{2}$ weeks' pay is allowed for each year of employment in which the employee was between the ages of 41 and 64. Those who are aged 64 have their entitlement reduced by $\frac{1}{12}$ in respect of each month they remain in employment.
- A week's pay for each year of employment in which the employee was between the ages of 22 and 40.
- Half a week's pay for each year of employment between the ages of 18 and 21. A week's pay is calculated on a gross basis but the reckonable maximum is currently £172 per week.

Can an employee get time-off to look for work when facing redundancy?

A person who has been continuously employed for 2 years or more and is under notice of dismissal by reason of redundancy is entitled to

247

reasonable time-off during working hours to look for new employment or to make arrangements for training. Such an employee should be paid at the normal hourly rate throughout the period of absence.

A complaint that an employer has unreasonably refused time-off, or has failed to pay the whole or part of any amount to which the employee is entitled, must be presented to an industrial tribunal within 3 months of the day on which it is alleged that the time-off should have been allowed. If the complaint is well founded the tribunal must make a declaration to that effect and order the employer to pay the amount which it finds due to the employee. However, the maximum that can be awarded is two-fifths of a week's pay.

THE ENFORCEMENT OF EMPLOYMENT RIGHTS

Having dealt with a number of the most important issues in the workplace where the employee has legal rights this chapter will conclude by reference to the various methods whereby an employee can seek to enforce these rights, and will also suggest sources of further advice and assistance.

Where to get specialist advice and assistance

Apart from general advice agencies like CABs and law centres and specialist bodies like the Equal Opportunities Commission, Commission for Racial Equality and the Health and Safety Executive, (see above at pp. 228, 236) there are two main sources of employment advice and assistance.

Trade unions

Those who are members of a trade union should approach their local union representative for assistance. Most employment problems can be resolved without recourse to the law but if legal proceedings are necessary trade unionists are often entitled to representation and financial support.

Advisory, Conciliation and Arbitration Service (ACAS)

ACAS is an independent body with the general duty of promoting the improvement of industrial relations. One of its functions is to provide advice without charge to workers, trade unions and employers on any matter concerned with employment.

In addition, ACAS has the task of conciliating in industrial tribunal cases (other than claims for redundancy payments). When a claim is received by an industrial tribunal a copy of it will be sent to a conciliation officer who has the duty to promote, if possible, a settlement without the matter having to go to a tribunal hearing. Conciliation officers can intervene if requested to do so by the employee or employer or where they believe they could act with a reasonable prospect of success. Most importantly, the conciliation officer can act before a complaint has been made to the tribunal if there is a dispute which could be the subject of tribunal proceedings. Where a settlement is reached after the involvement of a conciliation officer the employee is prevented from taking the case to a tribunal hearing.

What are industrial tribunals?

Although ordinary breach of contract cases are heard in the county court or High Court, (see Chapter 1) most employment protection rights are enforced at industrial tribunals. Usually tribunal cases are heard by legally qualified chairpersons and two other persons, known as lay members, who are nominated by organizations of workers and employers. Hearings at industrial tribunals are relatively informal. The parties can represent themselves or be represented by a lawyer, trade union official or any other person. While legal aid is not available for tribunal hearings it is possible to obtain advice and assistance in preparing a case under the Legal Aid Scheme.

Complaints, known as originating applications, must normally arrive at an industrial tribunal within 3 months of the action complained about – for example, the date of the employment terminating in a claim for unfair dismissal. Each party has to bear their own costs unless it can be shown that the other party behaved frivolously, vexatiously or otherwise unreasonably in bringing or conducting the proceedings.

249

SOME USEFUL ADDRESSES

ACAS (central office), 27 Wilton Street, London, SW1X 7AZ (Tel: 01 245 6105). ACAS also has a number of regional addresses situated in London (including SE: Tel: 01 388 3041) Birmingham, Nottingham, Newcastle upon Tyne, Manchester, Liverpool, Bristol, Leeds, Glasgow and Cardiff.

The addresses of the central offices of the industrial tribunals in the United Kingdom are as follows:

England and Wales: 93 Ebury Bridge Rd, London SW1W 8RE (Tel: 01 730 9161).
Scotland: St Andrews House, 141 West Nile St, Glasgow G1 2RU (Tel: 041 331 1601).
Northern Ireland: 2nd Floor, Bedford House, Bedford St, Belfast BT2 7NR (Tel: 0232 327666).

Industrial tribunals are located in London, Ashford (Kent), Birmingham, Bristol, Bury St Edmunds, Cardiff, Leeds, Liverpool, Manchester, Newcastle upon Tyne, Nottingham, Sheffield, Southampton, Aberdeen, Dundee, Edinburgh and Glasgow. Applicants should contact the nearest office to their home or place of work. For the full address consult the local telephone directory or local CAB.

The Employment Appeal Tribunal (EAT) has a central office in London but can sit anywhere in England, Wales or Scotland. It hears appeals on points of law from industrial tribunals, and consists of High Court judges and a panel of lay members nominated by employers' and workers' organizations. Its decisions are binding on industrial tribunals.

Legal aid is available for representation before the EAT. The address of the Employment Appeal Tribunal is as follows: EAT, 4 St James Square, London SW1 4JU (Tel: 01 210 3000).

The Trades' Union Congress (TUC) can also be contacted by anybody who wishes either to join a trade union or is seeking information as to which unions cover their particular workplace. The address is: TUC, Congress House, Great Russell St, London WC1B 3LS (Tel: 01 636 4030).

BIBLIOGRAPHY

Angel, J. (1985) *Industrial Tribunals: Preparing and Presenting your Case* (Tolleys).
This is a fully referenced and highly practical guide for anyone who may be involved in an industrial tribunal case.

Bowers, J. (1989) *Bowers on Employment Law* (Blackstone).
In this book employment rights are explained without recourse to legal jargon and its discussion of everyday problems gives an insight into how the law works in practice.

Hastings, M. (ed.) *The Health and Safety Directory 1987–8* (Kluwer).
This book contains the addresses and telephone numbers of several organizations active in the field of occupational health and safety.

Hepple, R. and Fredman, S. (1986) *Labour Law and Industrial Relations in Great Britain* (Kluwer).
This book provides an introduction to employment law in its industrial relations context. It assumes no prior knowledge of law and is aimed primarily at students.

Lewis, D. (1990) *Essentials of Employment Law* (3rd edn.) (IPM).
A practical guide for managers and a textbook for students of personnel management.

McMullen, J. (1983) *Rights at Work: a Workers' Guide to Employment Law* (Pluto).
Although now slightly out of date this is the only comprehensive work specifically designed for trade union activists and staff representatives.

Selwyn, A. J. (1988) *Law of Employment* (Butterworths).
A detailed handbook for someone dealing with employment law on a daily basis.

Smith, I. and Wood, J. (1989) *Industrial Law* (Butterworths).
A well-written textbook for students of employment law.

TUC Guide to Maternity Benefits and Rights (TUC Publications).
Provides details of state maternity benefits and assesses their impact.

Wedderburn, Lord (1986) *The Worker and the Law* (Pelican).
Discusses the present state of employment law in terms which the intelligent non-lawyer will be able to appreciate and also explains the social, economic and political background.

The Labour Research Department regularly publishes inexpensive guides to changes in employment legislation. For details of full publication list contact: Labour Research Department, 78 Blackfriars Rd, London SE1 8HF (Tel: 01 928 3649).

The Department of Employment produces a number of guides to employment law which are available free of charge from local offices. The central office is at Caxton House, Tothill St, London SW1H 9NF (Tel: 01 213 3000). The Department has eight regional offices.

8

Welfare Benefits

The need for those engaged in social work and advice work to have a basic working knowledge of welfare benefits cannot be overstressed. Most social work clients are entitled to some form of welfare benefit, and the statistics confirming low take-up rates are truly alarming. Furthermore the links between low take up and other forms of social stress and deprivation are well documented. For example the Social Security Advisory Committee Research Paper No. 1 (HMSO) (1989) has recently demonstrated the parallel (and interlinked) sharp rises in serious debt, mortgage repossession and homelessness (see Chapter 10). It is unfortunately the case that the initial assessments by the DSS of client entitlements are frequently defective: the 1987 *Annual Report of the Chief Adjudication Officer* suggesting that as many as one-third of social security decisions are wrong! A report entitled *Quality of Service to the Public at DHSS Offices*, HC 491 (HMSO 1988) published at the same time found that DSS offices were widely failing to provide the public with sufficient information on benefit entitlement. In these circumstances advisers have a duty to be accurate and vigilant in the advice they give to their clients.

In a book of this length it is only possible to provide an outline of the system of welfare benefits that is currently in operation in this country. (For the purposes of this chapter we are talking about the unified system that operates throughout England, Wales and Scotland, though not Northern Ireland, which has its own social security system.) There are, however, a number of excellent guides to welfare benefits of which the Child Poverty Action Group (CPAG) guides are the most detailed and value for money. No adviser should be without these guides published annually under the titles *Rights Guide to Non-Means Tested Benefits* and *National Welfare Benefits Handbook*. There is in addition a plethora of further guides of which some of the most helpful are listed under 'Further Reading' at the end of the chapter. All relevant DSS leaflets are referred to individually in the appropriate section of the chapter. Note that although the DHSS has been split since 1989 into two sections, the Department of Health (DOH) and the Department of Social Security (DSS) many of the leaflets currently in circulation still emanate from the DHSS, having been published before the division was made. For the real specialist, the definitive annotated guide to all the means tested social security legislation is Mesher, J. (1989) *CPAG's Income Support, Social Fund and Family Credit* (CPAG).

The chapter is divided into two sections to reflect the two basic categories of benefit. The first section deals with benefits to which claimants who satisfy the relevant criteria will be entitled *as of right,* i.e. without a means test. The second section deals with benefits that are *subject to a means test.* The two CPAG guides also reflect this same broad division.

Two further general points should be made to welfare rights advisers. First, always claim as early as possible. Many benefits can only be backdated for a limited period unless 'good cause' can be shown for the delay. For detailed advice on this issue, consult Partington, M. (1989) *Claim in Time* (2nd edn.) (Legal Action Group). Second, advisers should familiarize themselves with the concept of 'passporting' i.e. entitlement to one benefit e.g. income support, will often give the claimant access to further benefits, so it is worth claiming the first benefit, however small the amount. The latest edition (third) of Ogus and Barendt (1988): *Law of Social Security* (Butterworths) provides detailed assistance in this area, but most welfare rights guides address the problem in outline.

NON-MEANS TESTED WELFARE BENEFITS

Benefits for people incapable of work

What does *incapable of work* mean?

This means that the claimant is unable to go to work either because they are ill or convalescing after illness, or because they may be the carrier of an infectious disease. Evidence from the claimant alone is normally sufficient for the first week of incapacity, after which a medical certificate should be obtained from the claimant's GP. Any disputes as to whether the claimant is in fact incapable of work as a result of their condition can be referred by the DSS to the DSS Regional Medical Service.

The benefits that may be claimed in these circumstances will depend upon the length of the incapacity and the cause of the incapacity. A claimant in receipt of any of these benefits may also 'top up' their income with income support if their means are sufficiently low (see p.262). The sequence of entitlements is broadly as follows:

1. statutory sick pay or sickness benefit for first 28 weeks of incapacity during period of entitlement (see p. 256);
2. invalidity benefit (pension and allowance) thereafter (see p. 256).
3. severe disablement allowance (for severely disabled claimants: see Chapter 4, p. 118);
4. industrial injuries benefits if the incapacity is the result of a work induced accident or illness; see Chapter 4, p. 107 and DHSS Leaflet FB 15 *Injured at Work?* A more detailed source of reference is *Compensation for Industrial Injury* (Professional Books).

For specialists, the definitive annotated guide to non-means tested social security legislation is Bonner, D. (1989) *Non-Means Tested Benefits: the Legislation* (CPAG).

STATUTORY SICK PAY (SSP)

Most employees who are incapable of work will be entitled to receive SSP from their employees after 4 days' incapacity. The maximum amount of SSP payable is 28 times the current weekly rate in any one *period of entitlement* after which time the employee will claim invalidity benefit if still incapable of work. Periods of incapacity of 4 or more consecutive days are joined in one period of entitlement if there is less than 8 weeks between them. So long as the employee informs their employer of their incapacity they will automatically receive SSP without having to claim it. Many employees will find that in their contract of employment (see Chapter 7, p. 221) their employer has agreed to pay them *more* than the current rate of SSP during a period of incapacity. There are two rates of SSP which are related to the earnings of the claimant at the time of the incapacity. PAYE tax and NI contributions will be deducted from SSP. A few categories of employee are excluded from the scheme in which case they will have to rely upon sickness benefit.

For further information see: DSS Leaflet NI 244 *Statutory Sick Pay*.

SICKNESS BENEFIT (SB)

A person who is incapable of work but is not entitled to receive SSP (see above) can claim sickness benefit (SB) if they have paid sufficient NI contributions (see Chapter 9, p. 301 on how to find out how many NI contributions that you have paid). SB may thus be an alternative benefit to people who are incapable of work but are in an excluded SSP category (see above) or are unemployed or self-employed but have paid sufficient NI contributions. It should be noted however that even the lower rate of SSP (see above) is higher than the current rate of SB. SB is not taxable. It has to be claimed on DSS Form SC1.

For further information see: DSS Leaflet NI 16 *Sickness Benefit*.

INVALIDITY BENEFIT (IB)

If a claimant is still incapable of work after 28 weeks in receipt of either SSP or SB they will normally automatically receive *invalidity benefit* (IB). IB is made up of a basic invalidity pension, which is higher than the SB rate but lower than the higher rate of SSP and, if the claimant was under 55 (women) or 60 (men) when their incapacity began, an additional invalidity allowance. The amount of the invalidity allowance will depend upon the age at which the incapacity began. In both cases there will be additional payments for any adult or child dependants of the claimant. An additional payment will be made to reflect any contribution by the claimant to SERPS (see Chapter 9, p. 306). IB is not taxable. Subject to means testing, receipt of invalidity benefit provides a 'passport' to a disability premium to the claimant in receipt of income support (p. 265).

For further information see: DSS Leaflet NI 16A *Invalidity Benefit*.

Unemployment Benefit (UB)

This is a benefit paid to people who are available to work but have no job. It is payable for a period of up to 1 year in fortnightly payments. To claim UB a claimant must have paid the appropriate number of NI contributions (see p. 301), they must be *available for work* (see below) and must not be *disqualified*. UB is not payable for the first 3 days of interruption of employment, and is taxable.

What does *available for work* mean?

A claimant of UB has to be actively seeking work, and available and ready for any suitable work that is offered to them. This does *not* mean:

- that they must accept work that involves self-employment;
- that they must accept work that it would be unreasonable to expect them to do, i.e. a claimant can restrict their availability to work requiring their particular skills or in a particular place at reasonable hours or at a certain level of pay. This power to restrict the range of suitable work becomes more limited after a certain period has lapsed during which no work has been found. Eventually, a claimant will have to be willing to accept work at a lower rate, and agree to attend 'restart interviews' for different types of employment to maintain their continuing eligibility for this benefit.

There are a number of special rules regarding studying and the taking of holidays whilst receiving UB, and doing part-time or seasonal work. On part-time work see DSS Leaflet FB 26 and on seasonal work see DSS Leaflet NI 55. For details on the position regarding those affected directly or indirectly by a strike or other industrial action consult *The Strikers' Moneyguide* (1985) (CAITS).

What does *disqualified* mean?

A claimant may be disqualified from receiving UB for up to 26 weeks if:

either

- They lost their previous job through misconduct. Whether this is the case is often a matter of dispute between the claimant and their ex-employer. A claimant has the right to appeal to a social security appeal tribunal against any decision regarding misconduct (see p. 259).

or

- They voluntarily left their previous employment *without just cause*. The precise meaning of this phrase has been the subject of many cases before appeal tribunals and its interpretation will ultimately depend upon the facts of each particular case. The general rule is that an employee should not voluntarily give up their employment without first securing another job, no matter how unsuitable their current employment may be. A person who volunteers for redundancy will not, however, be disqualified. If a job is vacated in order that the employee can live with a relative who lives in another area, a period of disqualification may be imposed unless that relative is the employee's spouse, in which case disqualification is unlikely.

A claimant who feels that they have been unfairly disqualified from claiming UB, even for a short period, should seek advice on the possibility of an appeal to the SSAT (see p. 259).

UB is claimed by 'signing on' for work at the local Unemployment Benefit Office. When 'signing on' a claimant should take with them their NI Numbercard and their P45 form from their previous employer, if they have one. The claim is made on Forms UB 461 and UB 671.

For further information on UB see DSS Leaflet NI 12 *Unemployment Benefit* or a useful article by Wikeley, N. (1988) 'Unemployment Benefit', *Legal Action*, September. People doing voluntary or part-time work should consult DSS Leaflet FB 26 *Voluntary and Part-Time Workers*.

Those who have been made redundant should consult DHSS Leaflet NI 231 *Made Redundant*? Specialist advisers should refer to *The Adjudication Officers' Guide*, Chapter 10 which contains useful summaries of relevant case law.

Social security appeals tribunals (SSATs)

All the decisions regarding claims for the welfare benefits listed above are made by adjudication officers working for the DSS. Adjudication officers are human and can make mistakes. If a claimant or their adviser believes that a mistake has been made they should consider an appeal to the local *social security appeal tribunal* (SSAT).

It is a simple procedure to lodge an appeal. The claimant, or a person acting on their behalf, merely writes a letter to their local SSAT within 3 months of receiving written notification of the adjudication officer's decision, explaining the reasons why they wish to appeal against the decision. In exceptional circumstances a chairperson may allow an appeal outside the 3-month period. The addresses of the SSAT offices are listed at the end of the chapter. The letter of appeal should be as detailed as possible as it is normally this letter that will form the basis of the arguments when the appeal is heard. If the grounds for the appeal are strong, the adjudication officer may review the matter in the claimant's favour before the appeal is heard, otherwise a date will be fixed for the hearing which will normally be some weeks after the application for appeal is first filed.

The hearing

A SSAT hearing is relatively informal. The SSAT will consist of three (or occasionally two) members of whom the chairperson will be a lawyer with experience in the area of social security law. Hearings often take place in such informal venues as church or town halls. A claimant has the right to be represented by a person of their choice and research suggests that representation increases their chance of success. Legal aid is not however available for representation, although a solicitor can give the claimant general advice under the Green Form scheme, prior to the hearing (see Chapter 1) and any relatively articulate person with a sound knowledge of welfare rights should be perfectly able to put a claimant's case for them, if they are unable or anxious about doing it themselves. Particular organizations which specialize in the provision of free advice and representation to claimants in this situation are the Free Representation Unit (FRU),

259

the Claimants and Unemployed Workers Union and local claimants' unions (addresses from the Federation of Claimants' Unions). For details on all these see p. 261. In addition a local CAB may be able to advise on any independent advice service that operates in their area.

At the hearing the presenting officer will rely upon the written statement that will have been circulated to the claimant prior to the hearing date. The claimant or their representative will be given the opportunity to question the presenting officer on any part of the statement with which they disagree. The claimant will also be given the chance to put their case to the tribunal. When all the evidence has been heard the members of the tribunal will discuss the appeal in private. They will normally give their decision to the claimant that day and will send the claimant a more detailed written account of their reasons for reaching this decision.

If the decision against which the claimant is appealing was made by a Medical Board rather than by an adjudication officer (as in the case of the medical aspects of claims for industrial injuries benefits, severe disablement allowance and mobility allowance) the appropriate appeal tribunal is called a *medical appeal tribunal* (MAT). The MAT operates in an almost identical manner to the SSAT with similar time limits on applications and rules of procedure. The members of the MAT will normally be two doctors in addition to a lawyer chair-person.

Is there any further appeal?

It is possible in some circumstances for a claimant to appeal against an unfavourable decision by a SSAT or a MAT. These circumstances are limited to where it is alleged by the claimant that the tribunal made an *error of law*. This means in broad terms that the tribunal did one or more of the following:

- It made a decision based on a misunderstanding of the relevant law.
- It failed to give an adequate statement of the facts on which it reached its decision and the reasons for that decision.
- It had no evidence on which it could have reached its decision.
- It broke the rules of natural justice (see Chapter 3, p. 83).

An appeal in these circumstances is to the Social Security Commissioners who are professional judges with specialist knowledge in the area of social security law. Again legal aid is not available, but the local CAB will be able to advise a claimant if there are any specialist agencies in their area who are willing to take up such cases. Anybody considering an appeal against a tribunal decision must write to the clerk to the tribunal within 3 months of that decision requesting 'leave' (permission) to appeal and explaining the reasons why they wish to do so.

In some circumstances, and especially in London and South-east England a claimant might be able to use the free services of an organization called the Free Representation Unit (FRU) a group of young barristers and solicitors who offer free representation in a number of tribunals. They can be contacted at 3 Middle Temple Lane, London EC4 (Tel: 01 353 3697). Other possible sources of free representation are The Claimants and Unemployed Workers Union, 120 Standhill Crescent, Barnsley, South Yorkshire S71 1SP (Tel: 0226 28776) and a local claimants' union. Addresses of the latter can be obtained from The Federation of Claimants' Unions whose regional contact points are as follows:

National: 296 Bethnal Green Road, London E2.
Scotland: 2 Cranston St, Edinburgh EH8.
Wales: 37a Regent Street, Swindon, Wilts.
Eastern England: St Ann's Cottage, 14 St Ann's Lane, Norwich.
South-west England: Kingdom House, Pym St, Tavistock, Devon.
Northern England: Flat 1, 158 Hyde Park Road, Leeds LS6 1AG.
North-west England: 3 Stonehope St, Ashton, Tameside.
London and South-east England: 72 West Green Road, London N15.

The addresses of the Social Security Commissioners are listed at the end of this chapter. For further information on reviews and appeals consult *DHSS Guide to Reviews and Appeals* NI 260. See also (1988) *Social Security Appeal Tribunals* (2nd edn.) (HMSO).

Further information

Those seeking more detailed information on any of the above non-means tested benefits should consult any one of the following reference sources:

Rowland, R. (1988–89) *Rights Guide to Non-Means-Tested Social Security Benefits* (CPAG).
Ogus, D. and Barendt, P. (1988) *The Law of Social Security* (3rd edn.) (Butterworths).
Bonner, Hooker, Smith and White (1988) *Non-Means-Tested Benefits: the Legislation* (3rd edn.) (Sweet and Maxwell).

MEANS TESTED BENEFITS

Since the reorganization of the system of means tested benefits introduced in April 1988 there are now three principal categories of benefit: income support, family credit and housing benefit. In addition, there is a discretionary fund of money available to give out loans and occasionally grants to meet exceptional difficulties and emergency needs which is called the Social Fund. Housing benefit, which is a subsidy towards the cost of rent and rates (community charge) is dealt with in Chapter 11, p. 407). The other means tested benefits are dealt with below.

Income support (IS)

Income support (IS) is a welfare benefit to help people who do not have enough to live on. The minimum amount of money that a person requires to live on is however defined by law. It is only if a person's means do not reach this minimum amount that they may become entitled to claim IS. IS is administered by adjudication officers and DSS staff operating from the local DHSS office. It is paid either by girocheque or through a weekly benefit book.

Who is eligible for IS?

To be eligible for IS a claimant must meet *all* the following conditions:

- They must be aged 18 or over. Between 16 and 18, to receive a small benefit a young person has to enrol on a government sponsored Youth Training Scheme (YTS). There are only a very few limited exceptions to this rule.

- They must be resident in Great Britain (although temporary periods abroad for up to 4 weeks can be ignored).
- Their capital must not exceed £6000. Some capital items are however ignored, of which the most important are the value of the claimant's home (and the capital they hold as a result of selling the home if it is to be used to purchase a new home in the next 6 months); the whole of the surrender value of a life insurance policy; and the value of a trust fund arising from a personal injury claim payment for a period of at least 2 years (For full details see *The National Welfare Benefits Handbook*.)
- Their income must not exceed the relevant applicable amount (see p. 264).
- Neither the claimant nor their cohabitee (see p. 264) must be engaged in full-time remunerative work (see p. 266).
- The claimant must be available for work (see p. 257) unless they are exempted from these provisions (see p. 267).
- If the claimant is aged under 19 they must not be in relevant education. This provision is complex. It excludes most students under 19 who are attending courses of study of 12 or more hours per week from claiming IS. For details of the exceptions to this rule see *The National Welfare Benefits Handbook*.
- If the claimant is a student aged 19 or over, they will not normally be eligible to claim IS if their course is a full-time course (single parents and disabled students can be exempted from this provision). A student in these circumstances should approach their local education authority for an education grant. For a useful article on the social security system as it affects students see Brown, B. in *Legal Action* 1988.

Can a claim be made on behalf of more than one person?

If a claimant is living with a partner, whether married or unmarried, with whom they share a common household, the claim is considered to be made by the 'family'. An unmarried couple is treated as a 'family' where the two are 'cohabiting', i.e. living together as man and wife. A gay or lesbian couple would not, therefore, be treated as a 'family'. This concept of 'family' extends to include any child or young person who is a member of that household for whom the claimant and/or their partner are responsible.

A couple can choose which partner makes the claim for both of them, but this is of little economic consequence as the income and capital of the whole 'family' are generally treated as belonging to the claimant.

The term 'household' is not defined by law, but it is generally expected that in order to establish a separate 'household' whilst living under the same roof as the claimant (and thereby not be relevant to the calculation of their claim) it will be necessary to demonstrate considerable independence from the claimant in such matters as financial arrangements, eating and cooking arrangements, responsibility for individual housing costs, and some separate living quarters within the property.

The phrase 'living together as man and wife' or 'cohabitee' has caused an immense amount of debate, and generated much case law. Gone are the days of the social security snooper counting the number of shoes under the bed, but the general approach is set out in the *DHSS Supplementary Benefits Handbook* and a Commissioner's decision R(SB)17/81. The decision will derive from the answers to the following collection of questions, which will not necessarily be put directly to the claimant, but which might be deduced by the adjudication officer from circumstantial evidence. The questions will be:

- Are the couple living in the same 'household'?
- Is the relationship stable?
- How are money matters handled in the relationship?
- Is there a sexual relationship?
- Are there any children?
- Do the people 'behave like a couple' in public?

What is the claimant's *applicable amount*?

This is the key concept for the calculation of IS. Each claimant's *applicable amount* is made up of three components:

1. *Their personal allowance* plus (if relevant) the personal allowance of their partner (cohabitee). The amount of the personal allowance is fixed annually by the Secretary of State for

Social Services (see latest edition of *The National Welfare Benefits Handbook* or DHSS Leaflet NI 196 *Social Security Benefit Rates* for current rates. The amount of the personal allowance will differ according to the age of the claimant and the number (if any) of their dependent children.
plus

2. Any premium to which they might be entitled in addition to their personal allowance. Premiums are payable to a claimant in any of the following categories:

    *   A *family premium* and *lone family premium* both of which are paid if the claimant has a child for whom they are responsible and who is a member of their household. 'Child' includes a person under 16 and a person under 19 who is in full-time education.
    *   A *pensioner premium* (Rate 1: aged 60–74, Rate 2: aged 75–79) and a higher pensioner premium (over 80, or over 60 and in receipt of a disability benefit or blind).
    *   A *disability premium* for the long-term invalid or disabled claimant under 60 (see also Invalidity Benefit at p. 256).
    *   A *disabled child premium* in respect of any dependent child in receipt of attendance allowance, mobility allowance or who is blind.
    *   A *severe disability premium* which is available to a single claimant living alone in receipt of attendance allowance where nobody is receiving invalid care allowance in respect of their care, or to a couple when they *both* satisfy this condition. (For details on attendance allowance and invalid care allowance see Chapter 4, pp. 110, 122). For fuller details of these premiums see *The National Welfare Benefits Handbook* or the *Disability Rights Handbook*.

    If a claimant qualifies for more than one premium they will normally be entitled to claim only one such premium, whichever is the highest. There are three exceptions to this rule:

    *   The *family premium* is awarded in addition to any other premium.
    *   The *disabled child premium* is awarded to each child who qualifies and in addition to any other premium.
    *   The *severe disability premium* is awarded in addition to

either the disability premium or the higher pensioner premium.

plus

3. Any eligible housing costs. Most housing costs, e.g. rent and rates will be met through housing benefit. But most people in receipt of IS will be expected to pay 20 per cent of their community charge. In theory, this sum will be notionally included in the amount of IS they receive. If the claimant owns their own home, however, certain housing costs are an eligible addition to their applicable amount. The following are the principal housing costs that are eligible, wholly or in part, as an addition to the applicable amount (for fuller details see *The National Welfare Benefits Handbook*).

- Mortgage interest payments. But if the claimant or their partner is under 60 the DSS will pay only 50 per cent of the interest payments for the first 16 weeks.
- Interest on a home repairs or improvements loan.
- Rent or ground rent on a lease in excess of 21 years.
- Any payments under a co-ownership scheme.
- Service charges (though deductions will be made from the eligible service charge should it include any amounts for heating, hot water, cooking or lighting as these are supposed to be paid for out of IS).

N.B. A claimant is expected to pay their water rates out of their IS.

What is *full-time* remunerative work?

IS cannot be claimed if either the claimant or (if claiming as a couple) their spouse or cohabitee is working for 24 hours or more each week. The work must be work for payment or in expectation of payment. If the hours fluctuate from week to week the adjudicating officer can average them over a 'recognizable cycle'. Certain claimants will not be treated as being in *full-time remunerative work* for the purposes of IS even though they may be working in excess of 24 hours. They are:

- Disabled people whose disability has reduced their earning capacity by 25 per cent or more.

- Childminders working at home.
- Claimants on certain government training schemes.
- Claimants involved in a trade dispute after the first seven days of the dispute have passed. But there are numerous restrictions on claiming welfare benefits during a trade dispute (see *The Striker's Moneyguide* (CAIT), *The National Welfare Benefits Handbook* and Webb, J. (1988) 'Income support and the trade dispute disqualification' in *Legal Action*, December).
- Voluntary workers receiving expenses only.
- Carers looking after a person in receipt of attendance allowance or someone who has claimed attendance allowance and is awaiting the decision.

Who is exempted from the need to be available for work?

The following categories of claimant are exempted from the need to be available for work. Any claimant who is:

- aged 60 or over;
- a lone parent or lone foster parent caring for a child under 16;
- incapable of work through disease or mental or physical disablement;
- suffering a mental or physical disability that has reduced their earning capacity by 25 per cent or more;
- registered as blind;
- in receipt of invalid care allowance;
- pregnant, in the period 11 weeks before birth to 7 weeks after birth and incapable of work through pregnancy;
- caring for an invalid receiving attendance allowance or who has applied for attendance allowance in the last 6 months;
- engaged in temporary child care because the parent or normal carer is ill or temporarily absent;
- receiving a government training allowance.

These are the main exemptions. For complete list see Social Security Act 1986, Schedule 1.

Any claimant who is not in an exempted category must be available for work in order to be eligible to claim IS.

If a person believes they may be eligible to claim income support how do they work out how much they will receive?

The formula for calculating IS is relatively straightforward:

Applicable amount minus *Income* = IS.

What is meant by *income* for these purposes?

Income for these purposes is worked out in the following way:

- Total net weekly income of claimant and, if relevant, of their cohabitee/spouse (i.e. income after stoppages such as tax and national insurance). If the claimant and/or their cohabitee/spouse pay anything towards an occupational or personal pension scheme, only 50 per cent of that payment will be deductible from their gross income.

plus
- If the claimant has any capital in excess of £3000 every £250 of that capital in excess of £3000 is deemed to generate £1 of income per week.

plus
- A claimant may also be treated as having further 'notional' income if they have deprived themselves of income in order to claim or increase their benefit or if they are working without claiming the going rate for the job, unless the work is genuinely voluntary.

All the following sources of income are ignored:

(In full)
- mobility allowance and attendance allowance (see Chapter 4, pp. 110–114);
- education maintenance allowance;
- any grant for non-advanced education;
- any fostering allowance;
- payments by social services under s. 1 Child Care Act 1980.
- payments from a local authority, health authority or voluntary organization for looking after somebody on a temporary basis;

- the Pensioners' Christmas Bonus (DSS);
- Housing benefit (see Chapter 11, p. 407).
- Payments under the Social Fund (see p. 276).

(In part)
- earnings (called the *earnings disregard*, the level of which is fixed each year by the Secretary of State for Social Services). Some categories of claimant e.g. lone parents, are allowed a higher level of earnings disregard: for full details see *The National Welfare Benefits Handbook*;
- two-thirds of any earnings from childminding;
- the first part of any of the following sources of income: weekly payments from boarders and sub-tenants; regular charitable or voluntary payments (unless from the McFarlane Trust in which case they are ignored); war disablement pension or war widow's pension. For precise details on the ways in which deductions are calculated see *The National Welfare Benefits Handbook*.

Special rules on income support for people living in *special accommodation*

This section deals with a claimant who lives in any of the following types of accommodation (*special accommodation*):

- residential care or nursing homes (see also Chapter 9, p. 289);
- board and lodging accommodation (e.g. bed and breakfast hotels, guest houses, lodging houses or any accommodation which includes payment for cooked meals).

A claimant will not be treated as a boarder in any of the above places unless the arrangement is on a commercial basis. If the landlord or person running the accommodation is a close relative, IS will not be payable. Since October 1989 claimants living in hostels are eligible for normal rates of IS and can also claim housing benefit (see p. 407).

The applicable amount for any claimant in this category is calculated in a wholly different way from other claimants and is made up of two components:

- An amount for personal expenses (which is fixed annually by the Secretary of State for Social Services and will vary according to the type of accommodation) plus extra sums for dependants.
- An allowance towards the cost of the accommodation. The DSS sets a maximum ceiling for the allowance in each type of property which is published annually and which will vary according to the part of the country in which the accommodation is situated. There are provisions to allow claimants to receive payments in excess of the maximum in exceptional circumstances. They are complex. For full details consult *The National Welfare Benefits Handbook*. There are no extra premiums payable to claimants in special accommodation.

Special provisions for young people under 25 in *special accommodation*

Subject to certain exceptions (see below), time limits are placed upon the length of time that a young person in special accommodation can be treated in this separate way for the purposes of IS. Once the time limits have expired the young person will only be entitled to the ordinary personal allowance for IS (see p. 265) and will not be able to claim housing benefit so long as they remain in special accommodation. The time limits are complex and vary according to the area in which the claimant is living. The initial time period will be 2, 4 or 8 weeks depending upon the area, after which time the special payment will cease. It is this system of time limitation that has provoked the phenomenon of 'moving on' as a new time limit will come into effect once the claimant moves to another area.

The list of those who are exempted from the time limit/'moving on' restrictions is long. It includes a claimant where they or their partner fall into any of the following categories: they have a child, are pregnant, are chronically sick, have a physical or mental disability, have been in the care of a local authority within the previous 12 months, or have been placed in the accommodation as part of a programme of rehabilitation or resettlement. It also includes a young

270

person living in a hostel if the premises provide board or cooking facilities, are not self-contained and are managed either by a registered housing association or are run on a non-commercial basis by a charity, a voluntary association or with assistance from public funds. For reports on what has happened to some young people, made homeless by these regulations, see (1988) *Disappeared: the Effects of the 1985 Board and Lodgings Regulations* (CHAR), (1988) *Unsecured Futures* (The Young Homelessness Group) and Randall G (1988) *No Way Home* (Centrepoint Soho, 33 Longacre, London WC2 9LA).

For detailed list of exempted claimants under this head consult *The National Welfare Benefits Handbook or Benefits* (CHAR) (see p. 330).

How is IS claimed?

IS is claimed by filling out DSS Form SB1 which can be obtained from any post office or filling out an Income Support leaflet obtainable from any DSS office. Some people can claim IS through an interview without having to fill in the form themselves.

How is IS paid?

People who are unemployed are usually paid IS by girocheque at the end of each 2-week period of the claim. The giros are usually sent out by the Unemployment Benefit Office and they can be cashed at a post office. Other claimants are normally paid by an order book that can be cashed every week at a post office.

Can a claim for IS be backdated?

IS is normally paid from the date the claim is first received although it can be backdated if the claimant shows continuing 'good cause' why they failed to claim earlier (see Partington, ref. above at p. 254).

If a claimant is paid too much IS do they have to repay the overpayment?

The answer to this question will depend upon the reason for the overpayment. If the claimant revealed all material facts in their claim and the overpayment was an office error the claimant is under no obligation to repay it. If the claimant failed to reveal a material fact in their claim form they can be ordered to repay the overpayment even if their failure to disclose the fact was completely innocent and not intended to deceive.

Is there an appeal against any decision regarding IS?

The same procedure for appealing against IS decisions is available as for the non-means tested benefits outlined above on p. 259.

Further assistance

In addition to *The National Welfare Benefits Handbook* (CPAG) advisers can obtain further information from the *DHSS Guide to Income Support* SB 20. The IS and family credit (FC) laws are available in a looseleaf manual called *The Law Relating to Social Security* (The Blue Book) which can also be obtained for use by the specialist. The DSS produces its own *Adjudication Officers Guide* which contains a mass of information and guidance about the law in this area.

Single people without a permanent home should consult *Benefits* which is a detailed manual explaining how to claim IS and housing benefit (see Chapter 11) when living in a nightshelter, bed and breakfast accommodation, a lodgings house, a bedsit, a hotel, a hostel, a resettlement unit, a women's refuge, or with a relative or squatting. It is available from CHAR, Room 11, 5–15 Cromer Street, London WC1H 8LS (Tel: 01 833 2071).

Family credit (FC)

This is a means tested benefit for claimants who are employed or self-employed and who have at least one child. It is designed to help low-earning families where at least one member of the family is in full-time work. Its principal purpose is to keep low-earning families out of the poverty trap whereby the move from unemployment to employment results in a decrease in income. For a broad and general guide to welfare benefit for families with a young child see Rowe, T. and Trelogan-Dunn, C. *Social Security Benefits for Families with a Young Child* available from Voluntary Organizations Liaison Council for Under Fives, 77 Holloway Road, London, N7 8JZ.

Who is eligible for FC?

To be eligible for FC a claimant must meet the following conditions:

- They must be resident in Great Britain.
- They must support at least one child who normally lives with them, whether as part of a married couple, with a cohabitee or as a lone parent.
- Their capital must not exceed £6000 (see p. 263).
- They must be *engaged and normally engaged in remunerative work*, i.e. not less than 24 hours per week of work that is paid or is done in the expectation of payment, e.g. on a commission basis: for more detail see p. 266. *Work* includes self-employment.

Where the claimant is living as part of a couple (see p. 263) the claim must normally be by the woman, although both partners must sign the claim form.

How is FC claimed?

FC is claimed by filling out DHSS Form FC1 which can be obtained from a post office or a DSS office. Once filled out the form has to be despatched to the DSS central office that administers FC. The claim will be treated as made on the day it is received by that office. The claim can be backdated for up to a year so long as there is 'good cause' for the delay, e.g. the claimant was ill, preoccupied by other major concerns and so forth. Mere ignorance of the right to claim FC is not 'good cause' for backdating. For the address of FC Central Office (known as the Family Credit Unit) see p. 275.

How is entitlement to FC calculated?

The following formula will be applied when calculating the claimant's entitlement – if any – to FC.

Stage One: Calculate the claimant's maximum payable FC according to the rates currently fixed by the DSS (these will vary according to the number and ages of dependent children).

Stage Two: Calculate the claimant's income. The same general principles apply for calculating income as for IS (see p. 268), i.e. it is net joint income that is used, including estimated income from capital between £3000 and £6000 and notional income. Any income will be averaged out over 5 weeks before the date of the claim or 2 months if the claimant is paid monthly. If self-employed the calculation will be based upon the claimant's average net profit over the preceding 6 months. There are also a number of categories of income that are ignored either in full or in part. Some of these are the same as for IS; others differ. For a full list of these categories consult *The National Welfare Benefits Handbook*.

Stage Three: Compare the claimant's income with the applicable amount for FC (otherwise known as the *threshold level*). This is fixed each year by the Secretary of State for Social Services. Unlike the applicable amount for IS, the threshold level does not vary according to the size of the claimant's family.

- If the claimant's income is *below* the threshold level they will be entitled to maximum FC.
- If the claimant's income is *above* the threshold level the following formula will be applied in calculating their entitlement:

Maximum FC minus 70 per cent difference between Claimant's Income and Threshold Level = Claimant's FC.

How is FC paid?

Once the DHSS has processed the claimant's application it will inform them in writing of its decision. If favourable, FC will be paid to the claimant for 26 weeks regardless of any change in their circumstances. It can be paid *either* directly into a bank or building society account every 4 weeks *or* by order book that can be cashed weekly in a post office. If the claimant wishes to continue receiving FC after 26 weeks they should make a fresh claim within the last 4 weeks of the period. If a claimant is dissatisfied with the decision regarding their claim they may appeal to a social security appeal tribunal (SSAT) (see p. 259).

Does receipt of FC entitle the claimant to any further benefits?

A person in receipt of FC will not have to pay for any of the following either for themselves or for their partner or child/ren:

- NHS prescriptions;
- NHS dental treatment;
- travel to hospital for NHS treatment;
- part of the cost of purchasing glasses.

For further information on FC consult *The National Welfare Benefits Handbook* or DHSS Leaflet NI 261 *A Guide to Family Credit: FB4 Help While You Are Working* and FB 27 *Bringing Up Children*.

The Family Credit Unit can be contacted directly at DSS, Government Buildings, Warbreck Hill, Blackpool FY2 0YF (Tel: 0253 500050 or 0253 856123).

Addresses of SSAT/MATs and Social Security Commissioners

SSAT/MATS

London North: Whittington House, 19–30 Alfred Place, London WC1 7LW (Tel: 01 580 3941).
London South: Copthall House, 9 The Pavement, Grove Row, Sutton, Surrey SM1 1DA (Tel: 01 642 2226).
Midlands: Chaddersden House, 77 Talbot Street, Nottingham NG1 5JU (Tel: 0602 472942).
North-east: York House, York Place, Leeds LS1 2ED (Tel: 0532 451246).
North-west: The Triad, Stanley Road, Bootle, Merseyside, Lancs L69 9BN (Tel: 051 922 6767).

Scotland: 28–30 Thistle Street, Edinburgh EH2 1LN (Tel: 031 225 9313).
Wales and South-west: Oxford House, The Hayes, Cardiff CF1 2DR (Tel: 0222 378071).

SOCIAL SECURITY COMMISSIONERS

England and Wales: Harp House, 83 Farringdon Street, London EC4A 4DH (Tel: 01 353 5145).
Scotland: 23 Melville Street, Edinburgh EH3 7PW (Tel: 031 225 2201).

The Social Fund

The Social Fund is described by the DSS as 'a scheme' to help people with exceptional expenses which are difficult for them to pay from their regular weekly income'. The Social Fund is 'cash limited' which means that no local DSS office will be able to spend more than its annual allocation from central government. The national allocation for the first year of the Discretionary Scheme within the Social Fund (see below) was set at £200m, of which only £60m was available in grants (the rest being in the form of loans). This figure compared with the £350m paid out in single payments in 1986, the system that the Social Fund has replaced. It seems thus inevitable that many claimants will not receive the help they require from the state and will be obliged to seek alternative forms of financial assistance. For further analysis of this problem see *The Social Fund and Voluntary Organisations: How Do You Respond?* (1988) which can be obtained from the Social Security Consortium c/o NCVO, 26 Bedford Square, London WC1B 3HU. *The Social Fund Budget* (1988) lists the allocation and distribution of the SF budget in England, Wales and Scotland and compares them with previous payments and is obtainable from London Welfare Benefits, PO Box 1119, London W3 6NJ.

The Social Fund is operated by local DSS offices in two parts:

1. *The Regulated Scheme:* which provides legal entitlement to payments for maternity needs, funeral expenses and fuel costs in cold weather.

276

2. *The Discretionary Scheme:* which provides the possibility of loans and grants to cover certain defined crises.

What follows below is merely a summary of the two schemes to provide advisers with a preliminary idea of the circumstances in which an application to the Social Fund might be considered and a sense of the severe constraints that operate upon the Social Fund. Those seeking a more detailed appraisal of the detail and scope of the Social Fund should consult Becker, S., Hannam, J. and Hyde, D. (1988) *Guide to the Social Fund Manual* (Nottingham Welfare Rights Service) which can be obtained from County Hall, West Bridgford, Nottingham NG2 7QP, or the latest edition of *The National Welfare Benefits Handbook* (CPAG). The *Guide to the Social Fund Manual* does not contain reference to the regulated scheme but it provides a detailed and compact technical summary of the *Social Fund Manual* which is the official handbook of DSS staff in this matter. The Association of Metropolitan Authorities, 35 Great Smith Street, London SW1P 3BJ has produced its own *Social Fund Position Statement and Practice Guide for Local Authority Associations* and BASW has produced advice to members in *Social Fund Guidelines*. The DSS produce, free of charge, their own *Guide to the Social Fund* SB16 which can be obtained from any DSS office.

How does the Social Fund operate?

Payments made under the Social Fund are based on guidelines issued by the Secretary of State, which are summarized in the *Guide to the Social Fund Manual* (see above). Decisions are made by special DSS officials called Social Fund Officers (SFOs). The Social Fund is divided into two segments: the Regulated Scheme and the Discretionary Scheme.

The Regulated Scheme (i.e. non-discretionary)

MATERNITY EXPENSES PAYMENT

A flat rate maternity expenses payment is payable to a person, if they or their partner is in receipt of income support or family credit (see pp. 262, 272) for each baby expected, born or adopted. The payment will be reduced by the amount of any capital that the claimant has in excess of £500 unless the capital was in the form of a widow's payment

277

(see Chapter 9, p. 308) in which case it is ignored. For further advice and claim form see DHSS Leaflet NI 17A.

FUNERAL EXPENSES PAYMENT

A graduated funeral expenses payment is payable to a person if they or their partner are in receipt of income support or family credit (see pp. 262, 272) and they, or a member of their family, take responsibility for the cost of a funeral. A 'member of the family' means partner or child of claimant (or partner) for whom they have responsibility and who is a member of their household. The same rule regarding capital applies as for a maternity expenses payment (see above). The payment should cover most of the costs of the funeral. For full details of amount see *The National Welfare Benefits Handbook*. For further advice and claim form see DSS Leaflet D49 and Form SF 200.

FUEL COSTS IN COLD WEATHER

In certain circumstances a person in receipt of income support may be able to claim a grant from the Social Fund to help towards the cost of extra fuel used during a period of exceptionally cold weather. For further details on this contact the local DSS office.

IS THERE ANY APPEAL AGAINST DECISIONS UNDER THE REGULATED SCHEME?

An appeal against a decision of an adjudication officer to a SSAT lies in the same way as for any other social security benefit (see p. 259).

The Discretionary Scheme (budgeting loans, crisis loans and community care grants)

BUDGETING LOANS

These loans are designed to help a claimant spread the cost of exceptional expenses over a longer period. To be eligible a claimant (or their partner) must have been in receipt of income support (see p. 262) for at least 6 months. The loan is interest free but it has to be repaid by weekly deductions from income support. Regulations describe the various normal rates of repayment. Each applicant will be required to sign and return an acknowledgement of the terms of the loan and agree that, should benefit cease, repayments will continue. Loans can be recovered from the benefit of a claimant's partner. If the claimant has capital in excess of £500 will be deducted from the amount of the loan.

For what items or services can a budgeting loan be given?

The guidance to SFOs (which is not binding but which will normally be followed) sets three categories of applications described as *high priority, medium priority* and *low priority*. There is also a long list of matters for which a budgeting loan is not payable, which includes school uniforms or sports clothing, travelling expenses to and from school, school meals, work related expenses and any educational or training need including clothing and tools. Local education authorities (LEAs) do however meet a number of the costs connected with education outlined above and should be approached directly.

A high priority must be given to an application where refusal could cause 'hardship or damage or risk to the health or safety of the applicant or the family'. In addition, applications for any of the following items or services are to be considered high priority: essential items of furniture or household equipment, bedclothes, essential home repairs and maintenance for owner occupiers if a bank loan or mortgage is not available, fuel meter installation and reconnection charges and non-mains fuel costs, e.g. oil, paraffin or bottled gas. Examples of medium priority items and services are non-essential items of furniture and household equipment, redecoration where the applicant is responsible, HP and other debts, and clothing. Examples of low priority items and services are rent in advance where the applicant already has secure accommodation and a move is not essential (but see *crisis loans* on p. 280) and leisure items.

All decisions regarding budgeting loans are made by the Social Fund Officer (SFO) operating from the local DSS office. The SFO cannot exceed their local budget. Each payment will be stored and monitored on an office microcomputer. SFOs are instructed to 'take care to identify circumstances which might give the application a higher priority' but they must always look at the least expensive means of meeting a need, such as repair rather than replacement or whether the need can be better or partly met from another source.

This provision has great implications for local authority social workers as the SFO may feel that the local social services department (or indeed a charity) is the most appropriate source of assistance. Claims should normally be decided within 28 days (see p. 284).

For more detail on the amount and extent of budgeting loans consult *The Guide to the Social Fund Manual* or *The National Welfare Benefits Handbook* (see p. 277). A claim for a budgeting loan should be made on DSS Form SF300 but if sufficient information is contained in a letter this can be accepted instead.

CRISIS LOANS

Any person aged 16 or over can apply to the DSS for a *crisis loan* (i.e. they do not need to be in receipt of income support) if they are without sufficient resources to meet the immediate short-term needs of their family or themselves and they are involved in an emergency or a disaster (e.g. fire or flood; emergency travel expenses; emergency board and lodging expenses; down payments for rented accommodation if the claimant is leaving institutional or residential care). The list is illustrative and is not exhaustive, which means that the SFO must consider any circumstances that are alleged to constitute a crisis. In addition, unless the loan is a down payment of rent (see above) it must be shown that the loan is the 'only means by which serious damage to the health or safety of the claimant or a member of their family can be prevented'. The SFO guidance states that when deciding whether a crisis loan claimant has 'sufficient resources' a wide range of resources should be considered including credit facilities, money available through bank and building society facilities and other loan sources. A number of the claimant's 'resources' will, however, be disregarded, including housing benefit, the assets of any business owned by the claimant, and the value of their home. For full list see the *Guide to the Social Fund Manual or the National Welfare Benefits Handbook*. A person on IS should not be required to use credit facilities.

The need for help will normally be for a specific item or service or for immediate living expenses for a period not normally exceeding 14 days. Loans are interest-free but will have to be repaid at a rate agreed in advance. The same items and services are excluded as for *budgeting loans* (see p. 279) and in addition a number of other items

are excluded, including installation, rental and call charges for a
telephone; mobility needs; holidays; TV licence, rental or aerial
charges; and housing costs. Crisis loans cannot be paid to people in
Part III Residential Accommodation (see Chapter 9), nursing
homes, residential care homes, hospital, or prison.

Consult handbooks for more detail on the amount and extent of
crisis loans. An application for a crisis loan should be made in writing
on DHSS Form SF400 either at an office interview or, exceptionally,
in the course of a home visit.

COMMUNITY CARE GRANTS (CCGs)

CCGs form the only payments in the discretionary sector of the Social
Fund that are not repayable. They are intended to help promote
community care by complementing health and personal social
services provision to eligible applicants.

Who is eligible for a CCG?

To be eligible for a CCG a claimant must be:

1. *Either* in receipt of income support (see p. 262) *or* be hoping to
   be discharged from an institution within 6 weeks and then to
   claim income support;
and
2. seeking assistance with expenses in connection with one of the 4
   specified 'community care needs' as follows:
   - *Situation A*: help to re-establish themselves in the community
     following a stay in institutional or residential care.
   - *Situation B*: help to remain in the community rather than
     enter institutional or residential care.
   - *Situation C*: help in easing 'exceptional pressures' on
     themselves and their family.
   - *Situation D*: help to provide assistance with expenses of
     travel within the UK in order to visit someone who is ill, or
     attend a relative's funeral, or ease a domestic crisis, or visit a
     child who is with the other parent pending a custody decision,
     or move to suitable accommodation.

Exceptionally, a CCG may be considered for an ineligible applicant in considerable need if there is a serious risk to health or safety. The same rules regarding capital apply as for the Social Fund loans (see above).

Priority groups

The DSS has identified 10 groups of potential eligible applicant to whom priority for CCGs may be given as follows:

1. elderly people – in particular those with restricted mobility or having difficulty performing personal tasks;
2. mentally handicapped people;
3. mentally ill people;
4. physically disabled people – this includes those with sensory impairment;
5. chronically sick people – in particular the terminally ill;
6. people who have misused alcohol or drugs;
7. ex-offenders requiring resettlement;
8. people without a settled way of life undergoing resettlement;
9. families under stress;
10. young people leaving local authority care.

The regulations make it clear that there may be applicants who do not exactly match a priority group but whose personal circumstances nevertheless require that they be treated as a priority applicant. SFOs should meet the highest priority need first wherever it arises. These are specifically described as:

- people setting up home in the community after a stay in residential or institutional care;
- people who are likely to go into institutional or residential care unless they receive a CCG;
- children being boarded out for a short period prior to adoption.

For what expenses might assistance be given where an eligible applicant applies for a CCG?

The SFO guidance makes it clear that the nature of the assistance that might be funded by a CCG will vary depending upon which of the situations (see p. 281) is relevant to the application. In addition, it makes it clear that within each of the four situations consideration will be given primarily to claimants in the relevant priority groups for that particular situation.

The types of assistance (grants) available in the form of CCGs are as follows:

1. Start-up grants.
2. Cost of one change of clothing, sufficient protective clothing and footwear.
3. Removal expenses when travelling to take up a new tenancy (lower of two estimates) and if necessary cost of furniture storage.
4. Fares when moving home: normally the cheapest means available.
5. Connection charges, including where reasonable, disconnection and reconnection of domestic appliances.
6. Furniture and furnishings, although this is subject to rigorous and detailed guidelines and only covers such extreme situations as, for example, where previous furniture has been damaged by the prevailing housing conditions, such as damp.
7. Minor structural repairs and maintenance costs, where the claimant is the person responsible for the repairs and the property does not belong to a local authority or a housing association.
8. Internal redecoration and refurbishment if the claimant is the person responsible for the work. The grant normally only covers the cost of materials.
9. Bedding, washing machines and heaters, but only in exceptional circumstances, e.g. where the claimant is bedridden and incontinent or chronically sick.
10. Fuel costs, which are limited to reconnection charges if the supply has been disconnected and the claimant is going on to fuel direct payments; re-siting meters if a disabled person needs easier access; and installation of prepayment meters for claimants who have difficulty in budgeting for quarterly bills.
11. Heavy laundry needs, limited to the incontinent.

12. Furniture: this only covers very limited circumstances as follows: where an elderly person needs special furniture which the local authority have no duty to provide; where a claimant has a chronic medical condition requiring them to sleep in a separate bed from their partner; and where a claimant or their partner has damaged existing furniture as a result of a behavioural condition. All other claims should be treated as application for a budgeting loan (see p. 278).

13. Excessive wear and tear of clothing and footwear caused by a particular condition or illness.

14. Boarding-out fees if a claimant's child is being placed for a short and limited period with specialist foster parents while adoption is arranged and is not in local authority care and boarded out by them.

15. Other circumstances: not defined but described as 'low priority'.

How to work out which types of assistance might be relevant to which applicants

The chart in Table 8.1, which is based on a more detailed summary available in the *Guide to the Social Fund Manual*, provides a quick reference for any adviser who is considering advising a client to apply for a CCG. The numbers in brackets refer to the priority groups and the grants: types of assistance are as set out on pp. 282, 283.

Is it possible to challenge a decision of a SFO regarding payments under the Social Fund?

There is no appeal procedure for challenging the decision of an SFO as there is to challenge the decision of an adjudication officer regarding other benefits. There is, however, an internal review procedure. Applications requesting that an SFO decision be internally reviewed must normally be made within 28 days from the date the challenged decision was issued or posted. A detailed formal procedure must then be followed, at the end of which the decision will either be altered or confirmed. At this stage a dissatisfied claimant can request a further review by a Social Fund Inspector (SFI) (all currently based in the DSS regional office in Birmingham). Again this request must be made within 28 days of the SFO decision. If the

Table 8.1

Situation A	Situation B	Situation C	Situation D
Setting up home (priority 1–6; grants 1–5)	*People moving to more suitable accommodation* (priority 1–5; grants, 3, 4, 5, 6)	*Breakdown of the relationship* (priority 9, especially where domestic violence; grants 1, 2, 3, 5)	Fares to visit patient in hospital or home
Discharge from hospital (priority 1–6; grants 1–5)	*Applicants moving nearer relatives close friends who will provide support (includes applicants moving into another household)* (priority 1–5; grants 3, 4. 5, 6)	*Reconciliation of the relationship* (priority 9; grants 3)	Fares to visit critically ill relatives
People leaving homes or hospitals (part of a planned programme) (priority 1–8; grants 1–5)	*Applicants moving nearer to or into the house of vulnerable groups to provide greater support* (priority 1–5; grants 3,4,5,6)	*High washing costs because of a disabled child* (priority 9 – with disabled child; grants 5, 11 – washing and drying machine)	Fares to attend funerals or cremations
Discharge from prison and youth centres (priority 1–7 and young people unable to live with parents; grants 1–5)	*Applicants moving within the community to set up home for the first time* (priority 1–5; grants 1, 3, 4, 5)	*Families needing to move house* (priority 9; grants 3, 5, essential furniture (12))	Domestic Crisis
Home leave for prisoners and young offenders (priority – NA; grants – living expenses)	*Vulnerable groups (other than families) improving living conditions* (priority 1–5; grants 7, 8, 9, 10, 11, furniture)	*Repair/replacement of items damaged by behavioural problems within the family* (priority 9 – with mentally handicapped ill child; grants 2, 8, essential household items, security items)	Custody proceedings
Young people (16 plus) leaving Local Authority Care (priority 10 and young people who left care in last 12 months; grants 1, 4, 5)		*Minor structural repair to keep home habitable or for safety of child* (priority 9 – with disabled child; grants 3, 7)	Fares when moving house
Moving house to look after a person moving from institutional care (priority 1–8; grants 3, 4, 5, 6)		*Excessive wear and tear on clothing* (priority 9, grants 2)	
Child or young person rejoining the household after a period in care or special residential school (priority – children under 16 and young people 16–19 returning to their families; grants 2, essential furniture (12))		*Short term boarding out prior to adoption* (priority 9; grants 14, boarding out fees for up to 8 weeks)	
		Fuel costs (priority 9 – child disabled or under 5; grants 5, 10 – installation of prepayment meter)	

Reproduced with the permission of Benefits Research Unit (Service) Ltd, from *Guide to the Social Fund Manual* (Nottinghamshire Welfare Rights Service) claimant is still dissatisfied they can complain to the Social Fund Commissioner (SFC), whose task it is to monitor the quality of decisions of SFIs and help them to improve the standard of their decision making by giving any appropriate advice and assistance. The SFC can be contacted at New Court, Carey Street, London WC2. In very limited circumstances (see Chapter 3, pp. 81–84) it may be possible to apply to the High Court for *judicial review* of the SFO/I decision. For further detail on how to challenge Social Fund decisions see Luba, J. (1988) 'Challenging Social Fund Decisions' in *Legal Action*, May 1988.

Further assistance

The best sources of information on the Social Fund are *The National Welfare Benefits Handbook* and The *Guide to the Social Fund* Manual detailed on p. 277. The adviser who has regular dealings with the Social Fund should also obtain from the DSS the more detailed (and more expensive) *Social Fund Manual* (DSS). The DSS also produce a *Social Fund Factsheet: Fig 4* which is only an outline and the more substantial *Guide to the Social Fund* SB 16. Those who prefer to seek alternative help from charities should consult *The Directory of Charities* (1988) (Charities Aid Foundation) which provides details of a wide range of charities, and the types of applicants for which they cater.

9

Law and Elderly People

This chapter examines the needs of elderly people by looking at various ways in which the law entitles them to special assistance over and above that provided to the rest of the population. For a large variety of reasons, the number of elderly people in the United Kingdom is rising rapidly, both in absolute terms and as a proportion of the population as a whole. Official government projections suggest that there will be a million more elderly people in 30 years' time than today. What is of particular significance for social work is the increase in the number of elderly aged 75 and over, which is likely to rise from 32 per cent of those of pensionable age in 1981 to 38 per cent in 2011. Whilst many of the themes dealt with elsewhere in this book may also be relevant to elderly people, with like rights and entitlements, this chapter will focus on three areas where special provision is available for them: housing, state benefits, and the management of personal affairs.

HOUSING AND ELDERLY PEOPLE

Elderly people at home

According to the Centre for Policy on Ageing 'over 90 per cent of old people stay in their own homes until they die'. The ideological movement away from residential care towards community care for elderly people over the past 2 decades has guaranteed that this figure will remain fairly constant, even though there is convincing evidence that the ideological shift from residential care towards community care has not been accompanied by any consequential shift in resources by either central or local government. For a damning analysis of this unsatisfactory situation see Jack, R. (1987) 'Last Chance for the Last Refuge', *Social Policy and Administration*, Vol. 21, No. 2, 147–156. Jack concludes from a detailed study of the evidence that 'there is no evidence of any redistribution to or real increase in community care services and no unequivocal comparative evidence in relation to either its cost effectiveness, or its beneficial effects on recipients'. See generally also the *Griffiths Report* (1988).

Whatever the political arguments in favour of or against caring for elderly people in their own homes, the fact remains that this is where the majority of them will remain for the foreseeable future and it is therefore important to see the alternative possibility of accommodation in a residential home in its correct perspective. The bulk of social work carried out with elderly clients will be with those who are still living in their own homes, whether they be owner occupiers, renting, or living on an informal basis with relatives. There is ample evidence that elderly people living at home suffer disproportionately from bad housing conditions (see in particular Karen Smith (1986) *I'm Not Complaining: the Housing Conditions of Elderly Private Tenants* (SHAC) and Hedley Taylor (1987) *Growing Old Together: Elderly Owner-Occupiers and their Housing* (Centre for Policy on Ageing)). Other chapters in this book address the specific issues relating to legal rights and housing. These chapters should be consulted in addition to this chapter, in relation to the housing problems of elderly people at home, as follows:

- Detail on ways in which the law might assist elderly people to improve the conditions of their homes, see Chapter 11.
- Detail on the rights of the elderly homeless, see Chapter 10.
- Detail on security from eviction for both private and public tenants, licensees and defaulting mortgages, see Chapter 10.
- Detail on rent registration and assistance in paying rents and rates (Community Charge) see Chapters 8 and 11.
- Detail on the rights of chronically sick and disabled elderly people to receive special assistance from their local authority in adapting their homes for their more convenient use, see Chapter 4 and see also: *Care and Repair: a Guide to Setting Up Care and Repair Agency Services for Elderly People* (1988) (Shelter).

288

Age Concern produce several very useful publications which may also be of interest and assistance to the elderly person who wishes to remain in their home:

Bookbinder, D. (1987) *Housing Options for Older People* considers a number of options, include special housing schemes, special mortgage schemes for elderly people, financial help with improvements and repairs, and home income plans.

Hinton, C. (1987) *Using Your Home as Capital* is a practical guide to ways in which elderly people can free the capital tied up in their home to produce income but remain living there.

Owning Your Home in Retirement provides advice on routine maintenance, alterations and extensions, labour saving fixtures and adaptations and home security measures.

A Buyer's Guide to Sheltered Housing provides comprehensive practical advice on the purchase of a flat or bungalow in a sheltered scheme.

All these publications are obtainable from Age Concern (for address see p. 318). Another publication of interest in this respect is Ferndale, *A Study of Special Caring Services for the Elderly* (Shelter). *Not Rich, Not Poor* is a guide to housing options for elderly people on middle incomes produced by SHAC/Anchor Housing Trust.

Residential accommodation for elderly people

We shall define the accommodation that is provided for those who do not live in their own homes as *residential accommodation*. Residential accommodation for elderly people is provided from three different sectors of society: local authorities, voluntary (non profit-making) organizations and the private sector. Although the sources of funding of each category of home will clearly differ, there is considerable overlap in practice between the three sectors, with each sector being subject to statutory regulation, and many elderly people being placed by local authorities in one of the other two sectors, either because there is no available space in any local authority home, or because the home in question is more suitable to the needs and wishes of the elderly person.

Which department in the local authority should be approached for assistance in finding residential accommodation for elderly people?

If the person is homeless or threatened with homelessness (for explanation of these terms see Chapter 10) the local housing department should be contacted. Most housing departments have special units to deal with applications from homeless people. In all other cases, it is the responsibility of the social services department.

Does a local authority have a duty to provide or find residential accommodation for every elderly person who requests it?

In general, a local authority cannot be forced to find or provide residential accommodation for an elderly person who requests it: in other words the provision of residential accommodation for elderly people is a power and not a duty. This remains the case despite some rather confusing suggestions in past years from the DSS that the power should in fact be seen as a duty. Such statements seem to be remarkably unrealistic, given the fact that in 1983 there was an estimated shortfall in residential accommodation for elderly people in the United Kingdom of some 52 000 places (for further commentary on the real relationship between supply and demand in this sector see Jack, R. (1987). 'Last Chance for the Last Refuge'. *Social Policy and Administration*, Vol. 21, No. 2 (also quoted on p. 288). If the elderly person seeking residential accommodation is actually homeless or threatened with homelessness, this is an entirely different matter and the procedures described in Chapter 10 must be followed.

Are there any circumstances in which an elderly person can be forced into residential accommodation (including a hospital) against their will?

There are three circumstances in which action may be taken to compel an elderly person to enter residential accommodation (which can include a hospital) without their consent. The first is where the elderly person is deemed to be suffering from a mental disability or disorder under the Mental Health Act 1983, and one of the procedures for committing a mentally disabled person to a mental institution is followed (see Chapter 5).

The second is where an elderly person is considered by a local authority to be in the above category, but the alternative of Guardianship Proceedings is chosen, and the local authority as guardian wishes to place the elderly person in a particular home (see Chapter 5 on Guardianship). This procedure is currently rarely used (less than 200 cases per year) but may become a more attractive option if the current rhetorical emphasis on 'community care' becomes a reality through financial support.

The third is a procedure under section 47 of the National Assistance Act 1948 (used in practice in only about 200 cases per year) whereby a magistrate can make an order to remove an elderly person to a residential home (or hospital) for up to 3 months at a time if s/he is satisfied, on the evidence of the District Community Physician, that the elderly person is:

- suffering from grave chronic illness;

and

- living in insanitary conditions;

and

- not receiving proper care and attention;

and

- it is in the interests of that person to be detained either for their own good, or because they are a serious nuisance to other people.

Seven days' notice of the application must be given either to the elderly person direct or to some person in charge of them, unless the District Community Physician and one other doctor certify that removal of the person without delay is necessary, in their own interests, in which case *written notice is not required*. If written notice is not given, however, an order can only be made with a maximum duration of 3 weeks, although it is open to the local authority to apply, on notice, to extend that order to 3 months during that period. In addition, the person managing the premises to which it is intended to remove the elderly person must be given 7 days' notice of the hearing to give them the opportunity to explain their position to the magistrate and express any objections that they may have to receiving the person – objections which may influence the decision.

After the 3 months have expired the local authority can apply to extend the detention for further 3-month periods. Legal aid is not available to a person who wishes to contest the application (see Chapter 1).

The British Geriatric Society (BGS) and the British Association of Social Workers (BASW) have produced guidelines for the use of Section 47 applications which can be obtained from either organization (*Services for Elderly People* Guidelines issued by BASW). There is also a useful discussion on the issues involved, with case histories in Age Concern (1986) *The Law and the Vulnerable Elderly* (see below). Use of the section remains controversial and there is wide regional variation in its use: some local authorities never use the section as a matter of policy. Only 15 per cent of those admitted under Section 47 ever return to their homes, and the average survival rate once admitted is only 2 years.

For further information contact the British Geriatric Society, 1 St Andrew's Place, London NW1 4LB (Tel: 01 935 4004) or BASW, 16 Kent St, Birmingham B5 6RD (Tel: 021 622 3911).

What sort of people will a local authority consider eligible for a place in residential accommodation for the elderly (Part III accommodation)?

The circumstances in which a local authority may grant residential accommodation to the elderly are broadly set out in Part III of the National Assistance Act 1948. The primary test is one of need. The Act states that such accommodation may be provided to those who are in need of care or attention by reason of age, infirmity or any other circumstances and for whom such care or attention is not otherwise available. It is thus not strictly necessary for the applicant to have reached retirement age.

There is continuing controversy over the adequacy of current assessment procedures prior to the acceptance of elderly people into Part III accommodation. There are no standard procedures, although there is a basic approach that the Government believes should be universal and which is described in a document produced by the DHSS Social Services Inspectorate Development Group (1985) *Assessment Procedures for Elderly People Referred for Local Authority Residential Care* (DHSS).

Must the applicant satisfy any residence requirements before the local authority will consider the application?

Yes. Applicants must fall within one of the following categories:

- They are ordinarily resident in the area of the local authority.
- They are in that area and have no settled residence anywhere.
- They are ordinarily resident elsewhere but are nevertheless in the area at present and in urgent need of residential care.
- Any other persons provided that the local authority in whose area they normally reside consents (it seems unlikely that many local authorities would be likely to refuse such an offer).

If the local authority decides to offer the applicant residential accommodation does it have to be in one of its own homes?

No. The accommodation may be in a home run by the local authority in its own area, or in another area. It may even be in a home run by a voluntary organization but under the general management responsibility of the local authority. If the local authority has no such accommodation it can assist the applicant to find a place in the private sector. If that is the case, the applicant will want to canvass the widest possible number of options.

Information on particular homes can be obtained from Counsel and Care for the Elderly (CCE) (previously known as Elderly Invalids Fund) 131 Middlesex St, London E1 7JF (Tel: 01 621 1624). CCE themselves visit all the private and most of the residential care homes in the Greater London Area. Another organization, Elderly Accommodation Counsel Ltd., 182–4 Campden Hill Rd, London W8 (Tel: 01 621 1624) operates a computer register of all forms of accommodation for elderly people but does not visit. GRACE LINK, Upper Chambers, 7 Derby St, Leek, Staffordshire ST13 6HN (Tel: 0345 023330) is an organization which visits and provides advice about private residential or nursing home accommodation to applicants and seeks to match them with their needs, for a reasonable fee.

If a place is available and offered in a particular home how can its suitability be assessed?

This is clearly a question of critical importance as the home is likely to be that person's home for the rest of their life. A number of helpful publications are available to assist in making this choice:

1. Young, P. (1988) *At Home in a Home* (Age Concern) is a cheap and practical guide to what to think about and investigate when choosing a home.
2. *Home Life: a Code of Practice for Residential Care* (1986) (Centre for Policy on Ageing). This is a cheap, widely available, definitive work that is essential reading for all those running, or selecting a home for an elderly person. It covers every type of residential care home, and sets standards for physical and social care, covering such things as admission procedures, privacy, medical care, financial affairs, diet, environment, and management and training of staff. It is available, together with all other Centre for Policy on Ageing publications from Bailey Bros & Swinfen Ltd (see p. 319).
3. Kellaher, L., Peace, S. and Willcocks, D. *Living in Homes: a Consumer Guide to Residential Homes* (Centre for Environmental and Social Studies) is available from Polytechnic of North London, 62–66 Highbury Grove, London N5 2AD (Tel: 01 606 2789).
4. A series of pamphlet checklists for people inspecting homes is available from the Consumers' Association, Castlemead, Gascoyne Way, Hertford SG14 1LH (Tel: 0992 589031).
5. Wilson, M. (1984) *The College of Health Guide to Homes for Elderly People* is available from the College of Health, 18 Victoria Park Square, London E2 9PB (Tel: 01 980 6263).
6. The major reference work (though not advised for individual purchase as it is expensive) on private homes is the *Handbook on the Registration and Inspection of Nursing Homes* produced by the National Association of Health Authorities (NAHA) and available in a good public library. For address of NAHA see Chapter 2, p. 55.

Who pays for the accommodation?

Here we come to what may often be the most critical and complex question: who is going to pay for the accommodation? The resolution of this difficult question can cause severe emotional stress to any elderly person or their family and it is thus essential that the position is understood before any final decision is made.

PART III ACCOMMODATION

The basic position is that each resident is liable to pay for the accommodation and care with which they are provided if they are placed in residential care by a local authority under Part III of the National Assistance Act 1948. The rate of payment, known as the 'standard rate' is fixed by the local authority managing the premises in question. According to the DHSS *Memorandum of Guidance to Local Authorities* the 'standard rate' should represent 'as closely as possible the true economic cost of providing the accommodation'. If the elderly person has been placed by the local authority in a voluntary home the rate will be that which is charged by that home to the authority for accommodating and providing care to that person.

Are there any circumstances in which local authorities might reduce or waive the fees?

If the person in question can satisfy the local authority that they are unable to pay the rates described above the local authority has the power to reduce the rate to the level they consider that person to be able to afford. There is, however, always a basic *minimum* charge fixed by law, below which a local authority cannot go. This minimum is fixed annually by the Secretary of State and is normally around 80 per cent of the single person's state pension (the remaining 20 per cent supposedly being available to the resident for 'pocket money'). Exceptionally, and only if the home is a local authority home, and the resident is assisting in its running, the local authority can reduce the payment below the 'standard rate' for that individual but it can never waive the payment entirely.

What factors will the local authority take into account in deciding whether the resident is unable to pay the 'standard rate'?

The formula that the local authority will use in determining whether the resident will be relieved from paying the whole of the 'standard rate' is complex, and is linked also to Social Security provisions that are dealt with separately in Chapter 8, p. 269. In short, the local authority will carry out a detailed investigation into the means of the person before it offers the accommodation, both as to income and capital. A few (very few!) items are disregarded, for example up to £1200 capital, but most are included. In calculating income from capital (and the capital calculation includes the market value of the person's home, if one is owned at the time of the application, less a standard 10 per cent reduction), the authority assumes that the applicant has a weekly income of 25p for every £50 of their capital above £1200, whether or not this is actually realized. The value of the house may, however be disregarded, if *either* the applicant's spouse or child (if under 16) *or* any other person who has been looking after the applicant, is still living in the house and has nowhere else to go.

It is not possible for an elderly person who anticipates going into residential accommodation to avoid this charge on their capital by transferring the house to another person shortly before moving into the residential accommodation. For the law allows the local authority to recover payment from anyone to whom a person in residential accommodation has transferred assets (including a house) less than 6 months before entering the home if they did so 'knowingly and with the intention of avoiding charges for the residential accommodation'.

Whilst a local authority cannot force a person to sell their home in order to meet the charge that is levied by the local authority to cover the cost of the residential accommodation, it can protect its interest by insisting that a legal charge is placed on the property. This legal charge will enable it to recover any unpaid fees at a later date, when the property is transferred either by will, or on intestacy or sale. This factor is one of great importance to consider, if an elderly person wishes to leave their home to a relative, as a long, accumulating debt expressed as a charge on that property will substantially reduce the value of the legacy to the relative.

Most residents will also be in receipt of some form of social security assistance from the state to help them with their costs. For details on this see p. 300 and Chapter 8.

What methods can the local authority use to recover the residential accommodation charges if the resident does not pay?

It has already been explained that the local authority can place a charge on the resident's house to protect its financial position in the event of non-payment of the fees. In addition, the local authority can issue proceedings in any court for the recovery of any outstanding debts (but see page 171 on the role of the Court of Protection and at page 316 on the Enduring Power of Attorney). It may also issue proceedings against the resident's spouse, but not against any other member of their family.

PRIVATE SECTOR ACCOMMODATION

Again the responsibility for paying will be with the applicant and the rates will be those negotiated between the parties.

Can a resident ever be evicted from the residential home in which they are living?

PART III ACCOMMODATION

There are a number of safeguards to the security of tenure of a Part III resident:

1. The elderly person will have the status of a secure tenant even though they only hold a licence to occupy (see Chapter 10, p. 337). In these circumstances they can only be evicted if the managers of the home can establish grounds for possession as set out in Chapter 10, p. 338.
2. The National Assistance Act 1948 allows the Secretary of State to intervene in any situation where s/he thinks fit to do so, if satisfied that the local authority has failed to carry out its responsibilities to provide Part III accommodation. Whilst this power is rarely used, it is a useful fallback position for a dissatisfied person to adopt, if they feel they have been wrongfully deprived of their residential accommodation. Even if this formal power is not used, a complaint to the DSS can always be considered in cases of serious concern about the conduct in question. The right to complain to the DSS has the effect however of precluding any right to complain to the courts.

3. The Local Government Ombudsman can always be brought in where maladministration or bias is suspected (for details on this procedure see Chapter 3).

PRIVATE SECTOR ACCOMMODATION

As the status of the resident will almost invariably be that of a licensee and not a tenant (see Chapter 10) it will always be legally possible for the owners or managers of the home to evict the resident, although it will be necessary to do so through court proceedings (see Chapter 10, p. 350).

Can an elderly occupant of residential accommodation be locked in their room against their will?

The only circumstances in which the managers of a residential home can deprive an occupant of freedom of movement by locking them in their room is where the occupant is the subject of a compulsory detention order under the Mental Health Act 1983 (a 'section'), in which case they are subject to the same laws as any other person committed under that Act (see Chapter 5, p. 139). Otherwise, any attempt to regulate the freedom of movement of residents within the parts of the premises to which they have legal access will amount to an infringement of their civil liberties and should be resisted.

What controls operate on residential homes to ensure that they are properly run?

PART III ACCOMMODATION

Part III residential accommodation is the responsibility of the local authority social services department and thus any controls that operate on these homes are those which the local authority itself imposes. This also means that all the complaints procedures outlined in connection with eviction and also those procedures outlined in Chapter 3, p. 72 are available in connection with Part III accommodation. If the complaint amounts, however, to an allegation by a member of staff about patient care, and the home is part of the National Health Service, there is a procedure available that has been devised by the National Association of Health Authorities (NAHA) and is contained in a 1985 publication called *Protecting Patients: Guidelines for Handling Staff Complaints about Patients' Care* (see Chapter 2, p. 55).

PRIVATE SECTOR ACCOMMODATION

Most of these homes are regulated by the Registered Homes Act 1984 which is a long, complex, but comprehensive piece of legislation. Anybody who is engaged in social work with the elderly in residential settings would be well advised to familiarize themselves with its general provisions. For a detailed, but readily comprehensible social work legal textbook on the Act and related matters consult Freeman, M. and Lyon, C. (1984) *The Law of Residential Homes and Day Care Establishments* (Sweet and Maxwell).

In summary, the Act provides a system of registration for a whole range of residential homes, including any home providing 'residential accommodation with both board and personal care for persons in need of personal care by reason of old age'. The important exception to this very broad definition is an establishment providing board and care for fewer than four persons (not including the managers, staff and any of their relatives living on the premises). If the residential home also provides either physical or mental nursing care, it will be subject to a further set of detailed regulations governing the conduct of the institution. Guidance on the Act is provided by DHSS Circulars Nos. LAC (84)15, HC(84)21,LAC(86)6 and HC(86)5.

Any home covered by the Act cannot operate unless it has been registered. Operating a residential home covered by the Act without registration is a criminal offence. Applications for registration are considered by the social services department of the local authority in which the home is situated. An application may be refused, accepted, or accepted with conditions. There is a right of appeal to a registered homes tribunal. Detailed information regarding registration can be found in *Home Life: Code of Practice for Residential Care* referred to on p. 294. Registration officers should also consult the BASW *Practice Notes for Social Workers and Residential Officers Working with the Private and Voluntary Residential Sector*.

The registers of a registration authority must be made available to the public for inspection at all reasonable times, and members of the public are entitled to take copies of entries on payment of an

299

appropriate fee. Any complaints about a particular home should be addressed in the first instance to the registration authority, and if the complainant alleges maladministration by the registration authority in its registration, then the Local Government Ombudsman (see Chapter 3, p. 76).

Much on-going research is currently in progress on the impact and effectiveness of the Registered Homes Act 1984 and a useful summary of this research, together with an account of monitoring projects on the Act within one local authority area, can be found in *Insight*, Vol. 3, No. 15 at 16. The author of this article writes that 'seldom can any new piece of legislation have generated so much activity, ranging from new national associations being formed, new journals being published, major developments in local authority practice, the registered homes tribunal hearing at least 70 appeals, to the first million pound homes being sold'. For information on the limited research carried out in the United Kingdom on abuse of the elderly in the domestic setting, see Cloke, C. (1983) *Old Age Abuse in the Domestic Setting: a Review* produced by Age Concern and see also *The Impact of the 1984 Registered Homes Act* published in 1986 by BASW. A very recent piece of detailed research into tribunal hearings is Harman, H. and Harman, S. (1989) *No Place like Home* (NALGO).

Are there any special social security benefits to assist people living in residential accommodation?

Any person in receipt of income support (see Chapter 8, p. 269) will be entitled to financial support to cover all or some of the fees. The figure is worked out on a board and lodging basis, and will vary according to the type of home. It is subject to a statutory maximum.

STATE BENEFITS FOR ELDERLY PEOPLE

State benefits for elderly people are complex and many involve making careful choices which should be based on sound advice. This section will summarize the most important benefits. For more detailed information advisers should consult two excellent manuals produced by Age Concern: *Your Rights: a Guide to Money Benefits for Retired People* and *Your Taxes and Savings*. New editions of each of these manuals appear annually. For quick advice on a particular state benefit ring DSS Freephone: 0800 666555.

State benefits for elderly people can be divided into two categories: those to which an elderly person is entitled as of right, and those which are discretionary, that is to say they are subject to need, to means, or to both. This section will consequently be divided into two parts to reflect these two general categories.

Benefits as of right

Pensions

Rights to pensions are closely linked to the number of national insurance contributions that a person, or their spouse, has paid during their working life. Every employee and employer have a duty to pay national insurance contributions if the employee's earnings are above the legal 'lower earnings limit' (see DSS Leaflet NI 208). The amount of the contribution will be a percentage of the employee's wage.

Pensions can be divided into two broad categories, the basic state *retirement pension* and the *additional pension*, of which there are several categories.

THE RETIREMENT PENSION

Who can claim a retirement pension?

Any person of *pensionable age* (see below), who has paid a sufficient number of national insurance contributions during their working life is entitled to claim a retirement pension. To achieve a 'sufficient number' the person must have paid or been credited with national insurance contributions during approximately 90 per cent of their working life. (Working people should therefore take care to ensure that they are credited with national insurance contributions during periods of unemployment, sickness, or child/elderly person care: see p. 308 on how to check your national insurance contribution record). Some married women may have paid national insurance contributions at a reduced rate, which will affect their entitlement to a full retirement pension. Anybody in these circumstances should consult DSS Leaflet *Married Women – Your National Insurance Position*

NI 1. Divorced or separated women should consult DSS Leaflet NI 95 *Divorced Women National Insurance Guide*.

Whether or not a person chooses to claim their retirement pension from the moment they become entitled to it (see below) will require a careful assessment of their overall financial position, including in particular an assessment of the level of their future earnings upon which expert financial advice from a CAB or other adviser might well be sought. A retirement pension can normally be backdated for only 3 months, though claims can in fact be made up to 4 months in advance of eligibility. Once a claim has been processed, and the level of payment agreed (see below) the claimant will either be sent a book of money orders, to be cashed weekly in advance, or if preferred, arrangements can be made with the DSS for the person to be paid monthly or quarterly in arrears (for further information see DSS Leaflet NI 105).

Does everybody in receipt of a retirement pension receive the same amount?

No. The amount will depend upon the category into which the claimant falls (see below).

Does the claimant have to have 'retired' in order to claim a retirement pension?

This is a complex matter. There are two sets of ages to consider as follows:

- *pensionable age* (65 for men, 60 for women)
- *retirement age* (70 for men, 65 for women).

In summary the position is as follows:

1. A claimant must be of pensionable age in order to claim a retirement pension.
2. A claimant who has reached pensionable age but not reached retirement age must also have 'retired' (i.e. ceased regular full-time employment) in order to claim a retirement pension (unless they are a category B retirement pension widow: see below). In this category 'retired' includes the following:

- A person who is not doing any paid work.
- A person who works only occasionally, or for not more than an average of approximately 12 hours per week.
- A person who does light, casual work (different from the work being done before retirement) 'of the sort that a pensioner might often do'. This is deliberately left open and vague to allow for discretion. (N.B. see below on 'earnings rule'.)

3. A claimant who has reached retirement age will be automatically entitled to a retirement pension irrespective of earnings or income (but see below on the 'earnings rule').

The 'earnings rule'

In the case of a man under 70 and woman under 65 any earnings above a certain level affect the basic pension (and certain other state benefits: see Chapter 8) to which such a retired person would otherwise be entitled. There is an obligation on the part of a pensioner to inform the DSS when earnings exceed the current level of the 'earnings rule' (for current level consult any social security handbook). Certain sums can, however, be excluded from earnings, e.g. fares to work. For the full list contact the local social security office.

'The earnings rule' does not apply to or affect the amount of any graduated retirement pension (see NI 92), or additional pension (see p.306).

Are there any financial advantages in deferring the date on which a claimant decides to claim retirement pension?

This will obviously depend upon the particular circumstances of the individual. The following two factors might influence any decision:

1. Retirement pensions are taxable and count in full as income resources for the purposes of income support (see Chapter 8). This also applies to additional pensions (see p. 306).
2. If a claimant in Category A or B (see below) defers claiming retirement pension for at least 7 weeks, the retirement pension ultimately payable will be increased at the approximate rate of 7½ per cent of pension for every full year of deferred retirement;

thus, for example, 2 years' deferment will give rise to a pension enhancement of 15 per cent. The claimant does not have to pay national insurance contributions during the deferred period. The claimant will, however, require a Certificate of Age Exception (CF 384) which they should obtain from the local social security office and give to their employer.

N.B. All retirement pensions are automatically increased by an age addition when the pensioner reaches 80 (see DSS Leaflets NI 92 and NP 32).

What are the various categories of retirement pension?

The amount of the retirement pension that a claimant will receive will depend upon which of the following categories the claimant falls into. The higher the category the larger the pension. The current rates of payment are given in DSS Leaflet NI 184.

Category A. This pension will be payable if the claimant has satisfied the national insurance contribution requirement on the basis of their own record (for full details see CPAG *Rights Guide to Non-Means-Tested Social Security Benefits* or DSS Leaflets NP 32, NI 42 and NI 48) or Age Concern *Factsheets* see p. 306). For details on how to obtain information on national insurance contributions see p. 308.

This pension may also be supplemented by further amounts to reflect:

- any adult or child dependant of the pensioner (unless the adult dependant is claiming a Category B pension, which amounts to the same sum: see below).
- any contributions made by the claimant to the graduated retirement benefit scheme between 1961 and 1975 (for further information on this see DSS Leaflet NI 92, contact the Leaflets Unit, PO Box 21, Stanmore, Middlesex HA7 1AY or ring DHSS Freephone 0800 666555);
- any additional pension (see below);
- income support, although this is means tested (see Chapter 8).

N.B. In addition to the above, it should be noted that certain widows and widowers are also entitled to receive Category A pensions, although the claim is not based on their own contributions. The rules for such claims are complex. For full details consult CPAG *Rights Guide* (see p. 306).

Category B. This pension will be payable to married women over pensionable age whose husbands are entitled to Category A retirement pensions, who are not themselves entitled to Category A pensions. (For further information see DSS Leaflet *Retirement Benefits for Married Women NP 32*).

Category B (Widow or Widower). This pension will be payable to the widow or widower of a person who was entitled to receive a Category A pension. This pension is subject to a number of qualifications regarding the age and entitlements of both the claimant and the deceased (see CPAG *Rights Guide* and DSS Leaflet *Your Retirement Pension If You Are Widowed or Divorced NP 32A*. Although this is called a Category B pension it is paid at the Category A rate!

Category C and Category D. These pensions are non-contributory retirement pensions and are rare. They are only available to the very elderly, or to the widow or widower of the very elderly (see CPAG *Rights Guide* and DSS Leaflet 184).

Is a retirement pension reduced if the recipient is in hospital?

Retirement pensions are reduced after the pensioner has spent 6 weeks in hospital for 'in-patient' treatment on the National Health Service, and are reduced still further if the recipient remains in hospital for over a year (see DSS Leaflets NI 9 and SF 300). The pension is reduced immediately if the recipient was living in residential accommodation at the time of their admission to hospital. Sometimes part of the reduced amount can be set aside as 'resettlement money' but this will not be the case if the recipient remains in hospital for 2 years. It is worth noting that some hospitals and some social work departments have befriending schemes for volunteers to visit and advise pensioners who are in hospital for a long time.

Can a person who cannot work regularly because of home care responsibilities protect their retirement pension rights?

Since 1978 there has been a scheme in operation to protect the pension rights of a person who has been unable to work regularly because they have had to stay at home to care for an elderly or disabled person or children. It is called Home Responsibilities Protection (HRP). The effect of eligibility is to reduce the number of 'working years' that person will have to establish in order to be eligible for a retirement pension. A person who is looking after:

- a child for whom they receive child benefit;

or

- someone who is getting attendance allowance (see p. 110) or constant attendance allowance and who is not in receipt of invalid care allowance (see p. 122)

must claim HRP to protect their future pension rights on DSS Leaflet and Form NP 27.

Further sources of information on retirement pensions

1. DHSS Pamphlet *Your Retirement Pension* NP 32.
2. CPAG *Rights Guide to Non-Means-Tested Benefits* (latest edition) published annually in April.
3. Consumer Association booklet *What will my pension be?*
4. Age Concern Factsheets: *National Insurance Contributions and Retirement Pensions (up to 1948)*; *National Insurance Contributions and Retirement Pensions (1948–75)*; *National Insurance Contributions and Basic Retirement Pensions 1975 onwards*. Help the Aged also produce a free information sheet on pensions.
5. A free leaflet on state provision in 8 languages (Greek, Turkish, Bengali, Hindi, Punjabi, Gujerati, Urdu and Chinese) is provided by Pensioners Link, 19 Balfe St, London N1 9EB (Tel: 01 278 5501).
6. *Your Rights* and *Your Taxes and Savings* (see p. 311).

ADDITIONAL PENSION (see DSS Leaflet NP 38)

SERPS

Many employees are entitled to an additional pension to supplement their state retirement pension. The first of these is administered by the DSS and is earnings related. It is commonly known as SERPS. Under SERPS the DSS calculate an earnings factor for every year that the claimant has worked since 1978, based on the claimant's income which is then adjusted upwards to take account of inflation. On retirement an additional pension is paid to the pensioner on the basis of this figure. Anybody in this scheme and of pre-retirement age can obtain from the DSS a statement of the current value of their additional pension by filling out a form contained in DSS Leaflet *Your Future Pension* NP 38.

Occupational pensions and personal pensions

All employees have the right to opt out of the SERPS pension scheme, and take the alternative of an *occupational pension scheme* (if one is operated by their employer) or a *personal pension*. The options may be complex, and the choice critical. All employees are strongly advised to seek independent advice on this issue before deciding which scheme to choose, as once a decision has been made it will be difficult, if not impossible, to switch. Detailed information packs on the pension choices can be obtained from the Leaflets Unit, PO Box 21, Stanmore, Middlesex.

A number of private insurance companies are also now offering a range of alternative personal pension schemes in a bid to encourage people away from the occupational pensions. They should be considered with great care and on their merits, having taken independent advice.

For further specialist advice on occupational pensions contact: The Occupational Pensions Advisory Service (OPAS), 8A Bloomsbury Square, London WC1A 2LP (Tel: 01 831 5511).

Widows' benefits

Although this chapter is primarily designed to provide advice on the legal rights of elderly people, it seems the most appropriate place to include details of widows' benefits. It is of course possible that a woman may be widowed before she becomes elderly, in which case she may be entitled to further benefits which are not available to the older widow. Any woman who is widowed before the age of 40, or whilst she still has dependent children should consult the CPAG

Rights Guide to Non-Means Tested Social Security Benefits for full details on any available extra entitlements, or obtain DSS Leaflets NP 29 *Help When Someone Dies*, and NP 45 *A Guide to Widow's Benefits*.

A NOTE ON NATIONAL INSURANCE CONTRIBUTIONS

All the benefits below depend upon accurate information concerning national insurance contributions. In order to obtain this information a letter should be sent to the local office of the DSS enclosing the national insurance number of the deceased and if appropriate the widow, requesting a written statement of their national insurance contribution record (see DSS Leaflets NI 42 and NI 48).

If the woman was still married to her husband (not cohabitee) at the time of his death (even if they were separated, or were in the process of obtaining a divorce which had not yet been finalized) she is able to claim the following widow's benefits:

1. *Widow's payment*, a one-off tax free sum of £1000 payable if:
    - either she was under 60 when he died *or* he was under 65 *or* he was 65 or over and was not receiving a state retirement pension *and*
    - he has paid a sufficient number of national insurance contributions.

2. *Widow's pension,* a weekly, taxable benefit which will continue until she is entitled to receive a retirement pension (see p. 301) or until she remarries, which is payable so long as the woman was 45 or over when her husband died. The amount will depend upon the level of national insurance contributions paid by her husband. In limited circumstances women between 40 and 45 on their husband's death can apply; on changes in the law in this respect, consult the local CAB.

Claims for either or both of the above benefits should be made within 12 months of the death on Form BW1, which can be obtained from any DHSS office. Widow's payment is paid by girocheque. Widow's pension can be paid either in a order book cashable weekly in a post office, or by credit transfer into a bank account, every 4 or 13 weeks.

N.B. All pensions can be topped up by the means tested income support (described in detail in Chapter 8) where the person's means are less than their legally defined needs.

For further information on retirement pension for widows consult DHSS Leaflet *Your Retirement Pension if You are Widowed or Divorced* NP 32A. For further advice, information and friendly support, widows can contact The National Association of Widows, 1st Floor, Neville House, 14 Waterloo St, Birmingham, B2 5TX (Tel: 021 643 8348).

Benefits payable on proof of need

These benefits can be grouped into two distinct categories: those which are subject to proof of special disability but are not means tested, and those which are subject to proof of special need and are in addition means tested.

Special needs benefits which are not means tested

The four most important benefits in this category are *attendance allowance*, *invalid care allowance* (payable to the carers of those with attendance allowance), *mobility allowance* and benefits arising from *injury, illness or disablement at work*. As none of these benefits relate exclusively to elderly people, they are all dealt with in detail in other parts of the book as indicated. In summary, however, the benefits relate to the following circumstances:

- Attendance allowance is payable to a severely disabled person who needs very frequent attention either in connection with their bodily functions or to prevent them from injuring themselves. For full details of this benefit (which is payable to anybody aged 2 or over) see Chapter 4, p. 110 and DSS Leaflet NI 205.
- Invalid care allowance is payable to a person of working age who is unable to work because they are engaged in the full-time home care of a severely disabled person. For full details of this benefit see Chapter 4, p. 122 and DSS Leaflet NI 212.
- Mobility allowance is payable to a person aged between 5 and

75 (if they were already receiving it at 70) who is so severely disabled that they are virtually unable to walk. For full details of this benefit see Chapter 4, p. 114 and DSS Leaflet NI 211.

- Benefits arising from injury, illness or disablement at work. These benefits are all dealt with in Chapter 4, p. 116 and Chapter 8, p. 255. They cover circumstances where a person is no longer able to work through illness, industrial accident or industrial disease, or where their capacity to work has been removed or limited as a result of disablement caused by an accident at work.

Means tested special needs benefits for elderly people

All the benefits in this category, relating to such things as extra heating, warm clothing, special diets, fares to hospital and so forth are covered by the Social Security Act 1986 and are mostly only available to a person in receipt of income support. For full details on the income support system and the Social Fund from which special payments are drawn see Chapter 8. Those who do not get income support may still get free dental treatment (DSS Leaflet D11); free eye treatment and help towards the cost of glasses (DSS Leaflet G11). All people of pensionable age receive free prescriptions. Applications for assistance in the cost of travel to and from hospital for treatment can be made on a hospital claim form AG1. The form can be obtained from a hospital or social security office. Once filled out it should be sent to Agency Benefit Unit, Longbenton, Newcastle upon Tyne.

FUEL COSTS

There is a special code of conduct regarding the disconnection of the gas or electricity supply to a house in which there are elderly or sick residents which is described in detail in Chapter 2, pp. 17–19. The Electricity Council (see Chapter 2 for address) has produced a special leaflet for elderly people called *Electricity and You: Advice for Elderly People*. Guides on keeping down heating costs are available from the Department of Energy (Room 1312, Thames House South,

Millbank, London SW1 4AJ Tel: 01 211 3000) in particular *A Guide to Home Heating Costs* and *Handy Hints to Save Energy*: *Help with your Winter Heating*. For details on insulation grants see Chapter 4, p. 101. For information on draughtproofing grants (only available in certain parts of the country) contact Neighbourhood Energy Action, 2–4 Bigg Market, Newcastle upon Tyne, NE1 1UW (Tel: 091 261 5677). The most comprehensive general guide on all questions relating to fuel cost management is *The Fuel Rights Handbook* (SHAC). Finally, Shelter (1988) produce some very useful *Hard to Heat Packs* written by the Nottingham Heating Project.

If the local DSS office declares it to be a period of *Exceptionally Severe Weather (ESW)*, a person in receipt of income support in a house containing a person over 65, or a child under 2, or a chronically sick or disabled occupant can claim an ESW payment. Savings in excess of £500 will be taken into account.

Tax planning

It is clear from the complex range of benefits set out above that elderly people may need specialist advice on their tax planning. The first source of assistance should be the Inland Revenue leaflet: *Income Tax and Pensioners*: Inland Revenue Leaflet IR4 which is available from any local tax office. Elderly people should also be aware that if their total income is below a certain level, they may be entitled to a higher personal allowance against tax which is known as the 'age allowance'. Information on this can be found in *Income Tax, Age Allowance*, Inland Revenue Leaflet IR4A.

Other useful sources of advice are as follows:

1. The most up to date and comprehensive specialist guide on the market at present is the Age Concern booklet *Your Taxes and Savings* which is produced annually. It explains in simple terms the complexities of the tax system, how to work out a tax bill and how to minimize tax payments. It also advises on the great range of investment opportunities that are of special interest to elderly people.
2. *Income Tax and Widows:* Inland Revenue Booklet IR 23.
3. *Approaching Retirement, What will my pension be?, Which Tax*

Savings Guide (all published by the Consumers' Association).
4. Free Information Sheets provided by Help the Aged.
5. Botting, L. and Duggleby, V., *Making the Most of Your Money* (Orbis).

THE MANAGEMENT OF PERSONAL AFFAIRS

The majority of elderly people are perfectly capable of continuing to manage their personal affairs right up to the time of their death, with perhaps little more than the occasional assistance of a relative, friend or trusted family adviser, like the family solicitor. Sometimes, however, the onset of old age brings with it a real or perceived anxiety in the minds of elderly people that they may no longer be able to manage their own affairs. This section looks at some of the commonest problems facing elderly people who are feeling unable to manage their affairs and sets out the possible courses of action that are available.

Making a will

A person who makes a will is described as a testator. Everybody should make a will regardless of their age, but many do not contemplate such matters until they are elderly. There are good reasons for making a will, the most obvious being that a will enables a person to decide to whom they would like their property to pass on their death. If a person dies without making a will (intestate) the law takes over and applies a series of rules which determine to whom any property will pass, which may not be what the deceased person would have wished.

It is advisable to consult a solicitor before making a will. The legalities of will writing are complicated and precise, and it is better that any problems are sorted out in the testator's lifetime rather than after death. A solicitor will charge a fee for this assistance, which should be discussed in advance. It is almost certainly a worthwhile investment.

Is the legality of a will affected by the testator's mental state at the time when the will is made?

A will is not valid if at the time of making it the testator was incapable of understanding what they were doing, or the nature and effect of the will. If any relatives or dependants, on the death of the testator, are aggrieved by the testator's failure to leave them anything, the law permits them in certain defined circumstances to apply to the court for the will to be rewritten. In practice, this is rarely done and legal advice should be sought before any such action is contemplated. Even if a person's affairs are under the general supervision of the Court of Protection (see p. 171), they can still make a valid will, although the Court of Protection does have the power to override that will at a later date, on proof that the testator was incapable of knowing what they were doing.

For further information and advice on the making of wills consult the Consumers Association booklet *Wills and Probate*. A will form can be obtained from any large stationers.

How can a person leave instructions concerning funeral arrangements and other personal matters following their death?

It is perfectly in order to leave any instructions in a will in the hope and expectation that the executors will carry them out. Alternatively, there are more private ways of dealing with such matters, which may be more appropriate in some circumstances. Age Concern produces a useful form called *Instructions for my Next of Kin and Executors Upon my Death* which can be used to sort out these personal details. The form is not a will, and can be kept separate and private from the will.

Giving legal power to another to manage your affairs

There are a number of ways in which elderly people may grant legal powers to allow others to manage some or all of their affairs for them during their lifetime.

Agency

An elderly person may nominate or instruct another to act on their behalf as their *agent*. This procedure is commonly used by an elderly person who wishes somebody else to collect their pension or other benefits from the post office for them, because they are unable to go there themselves. The DSS have a standard procedure whereby such a nomination may be made. If the practice is to continue for a long time, it is advisable to obtain an 'agency card' from the DSS which the agent can produce as authority for the payment to be made to them. If the elderly person is in Part III residential accommodation (see p. 292) they can alternatively nominate an official of the local authority as their *'signing agent'* who will cash all their benefits for them on their behalf. It seems that in 80 per cent of local authority homes it is official policy to use this procedure as a way of ensuring that the 'standard payment' is made. This clearly has certain quite disturbing civil liberty implications and advisers should be alert to detect any abuse of this power by over-zealous officials, particularly where the elderly person might also be mentally disordered. (For further information see the report by the Social Services Inspectorate of the DHSS of 1985 entitled *Inspection of Local Authority Care for Elderly Mentally Disordered People* (DSS).)

Finally, if the elderly person is too ill to be disturbed or to understand what is happening, and an agent has not previously been appointed, there is a special procedure whereby the DSS can take a statement of the circumstances from any 'responsible person' and appoint a temporary agent who may well be that same 'responsible person' who will be empowered to cash benefits as the elderly person's agent until they are well enough to issue instructions personally.

Appointee

An alternative to agency is to appoint another person who will not only collect a benefit on the elderly person's behalf but will also be entitled to spend it. This person is described as an *appointee*. This power only relates to social security benefits, but it does therefore include pensions. An appointee has to be appointed by the DSS who will only make such an appointment where it is satisfied that the claimant is unable to act personally and is not under the Court of Protection (see p. 171). About 45 000 such appointments are made each year (they are by no means limited to the elderly). The DSS has a detailed checking procedure that must be followed to confirm the suitability of a prospective appointee. Generally, the ideal appointee would be a close relative who lives with the claimant. If the elderly person is in a residential home or hospital, a member of the staff of that institution will normally be made an appointee. The DSS stipulates that when an appointee is appointed 'any benefit received must be used in the interests of the claimant'. If the claimant is in hospital, the appointee should ensure that, from the amount of benefit granted, a sufficient weekly sum is provided to the claimant to meet personal needs.

In an emergency, and only if there is no appointee the DSS does have the power to pay a claimant's benefit to any person it thinks fit, e.g. to a public utility or landlord, if it believes that the claimant is incapable of budgeting, or wilfully refusing to budget for any item of normal, additional or household requirements applicable to them.

Power of Attorney

It is always open to any adult person to grant a Power of Attorney to another adult person to act on their behalf in the management of all their personal affairs if, for example, they are going abroad for a substantial period or are going into hospital. The Power of Attorney is granted by filling out a simple form (with the help of a solicitor if necessary). A Power of Attorney ceases, however, if the grantor ceases to be mentally capable of knowing what they are doing. This is because a Power of Attorney implies a continuing clear and conscious awareness on the part of the grantor of what the grantee is doing. In reality however, it is likely that Powers of Attorney continue to be used long after the grantor remains mentally capable, despite the fact that this is in effect an illegal use of the Power. In order to combat this problem, there has been in existence since 1985 an alternative Power of Attorney known as the Enduring Power of Attorney.

Enduring Power of Attorney

If a person has the ability to grant a Power of Attorney, and is worried that at some time in the future they may lose their mental capabilities there is the alternative choice of granting an Enduring Power of Attorney. The mental capacity to grant such a power is the same as that for making a will (see p. 313). The procedure for granting such a power is similar to the ordinary Power of Attorney. The difference is that if the grantor loses mental capability the grantee can continue to exercise the Power of Attorney but only if the Court of Protection subsequently registers the Enduring Power of Attorney, on the application of the grantee. Notice of any application to the Court of Protection to register the Enduring Power of Attorney must be given to specified relatives. The Court of Protection will only register the Enduring Power of Attorney if it is satisfied with the evidence of the donor's mental incapability, and if all the procedures regarding notice etc. have been followed. For more detailed information consult Cretney, S. (1989) *Enduring Power of Attorney* (2nd edn.) (Family Law, Jordan and Son).

Having the power to manage your own affairs taken away

There is a considerable overlap here with the information contained in Chapter 5 regarding those suffering with mental disability. If it becomes necessary to take away an elderly person's legal powers to manage their own affairs it is not because of their age but because of their mental capacity (see Chapter 5, p. 169). The two possible procedures are to put the elderly person's affairs under the Control of the Court of Protection (see p. 171) or to make them the subject of Guardianship Proceedings (see p. 170). Whilst the powers conferred by the Court of Protection are very wide indeed, those conferred by Guardianship are far more limited and confined to three, namely the power to require the person to reside at a specified place, the power to require the person to attend at any given time for treatment, and the power to insist that the person provides access to named individuals, e.g. a doctor or a social worker. Guardianship is only likely to be a success, however, if local authorities are prepared to use it, and more importantly to commit the necessary resources to make it work.

For full details on procedures regarding both the Court of Protection and guardianship see Brenda Hoggett (1984) *Mental Health Law* (2nd edn.) (Sweet and Maxwell), Larry Gostin (1983) *The Court of Protection* (MIND) and *The Law and Vulnerable Elderly People* (Age Concern).

N.B. The equivalent of the Court of Protection in Scotland is the Curator Bonis, where a person is nominated to take over the affairs of a mentally incapacitated person. A Scottish lawyer should be consulted in the drawing up of the relevant documentation. In Northern Ireland the Office of Care and Protection has similar powers to those of the Court of Protection, for citizens of Northern Ireland.

What to do when someone dies

It is an unfortunate fact that in addition to coping with the pain and stress of losing a close relative, there also remain many formalities that have to be complied with, normally the responsibility of the nearest surviving relative. There is set out below a checklist of the matters that will have to be dealt with. For a more detailed account of what has to be done consult the relevant section of the *Penguin Guide to the Law* by John Pritchard.

- The death must be registered with the local Registrar of Births, Marriages and Deaths within 5 days of the death. The Registrar's address will be in the local telephone book. In order to register the death the Registrar will require a death certificate from a doctor (or if the matter was reported to the coroner, a coroner's form), and basic details of the time annd place of death. The Registrar will then issue a certificate of registration of death (necessary in order to claim widow's benefit: see p. 307), and a certificate to enable disposal of the body to take place.
- The funeral must be arranged. This can be done by an undertaker (funeral director). If possible, a funeral director who is a member of the National Association of Funeral Directors (NAFD) should be used, as their members are bound by a Code of Practice agreed with the Office of Fair

317

Trading. (On the status of Codes of Practice generally see Chapter 2.) An NAFD undertaker must give a full estimate of the cost of the funeral in advance. Advice on the choice of burial or cremation, and the location can also be obtained from the funeral director.

- All persons or agencies with whom the deceased held current accounts or investments must be notified of the death by the executors (or the administrators if no will has been written) so that, where appropriate, accounts can be closed or transferred to the names of the executors or administrators or the relevant beneficiaries.

- Where the deceased has left a will it is the duty of the executors, if appointed by the will, to carry out the terms of the will. Where the assets are substantial, the executors will need to obtain Probate of the will from the Probate Registry. This can be done personally by the executors but a solicitor should be consulted in case of difficulty. Where the deceased has not left a will the distribution of the assets is the responsibility of the nearest relative (called the administrator) according to the law of intestacy. It is necessary to apply for Letters of Administration from the Probate Registry where the assets are considerable. For further information on the procedures to follow consult the Consumers' Association booklet *Wills and Probate* or the *Penguin Guide to the Law*.

The address of the Probate Registry is South Wing, Somerset House, Strand, London WC2 (Tel: 01 936 6000) or for personal applications 5th Floor, Golden Cross House, Duncannon St, London WC2.

SOURCES OF FURTHER ASSISTANCE

Much prominence has been given in this chapter to a leading charity that is devoted to assisting the elderly, Age Concern. Age Concern has a large number of local offices, but its national headquarters are as follows:

Age Concern England, Bernard Sunley House, 60 Pitcairn Rd, Mitcham, Surrey CR4 3LL (Tel: 01 640 5431).

Age Concern Northern Ireland, 6 Lower Crescent, Belfast, BT7 1NR
(Tel: 0232 2454729).
Age Concern Scotland, 33 Castle St, Edinburgh EH2 3DN (Tel: 031
225 5000).
Age Concern Wales, 1 Park Grove, Cardiff CF1 3FJ (Tel: 0222 371
821 and 0222 371 566).

An organization with a research and policy making role with
reference to the needs of the elderly is:

The Centre for Policy on Ageing, 25–31 Ironmonger Row, London
EC1V 3QP (Tel: 01 253 1787).

In addition to a large publications list, the Centre provides advice and
information to professionals working with the elderly. The Centre
has a substantial reference library and is actively engaged in
initiatives aimed at the integration of all elderly people into the
community.
   For the publications of the Centre for Policy on Ageing write to
Bailey Bros & Swinfen Ltd., Warner House, Folkestone, Kent CT19
6PH (Tel: 0303 56501).
   A further organization that is London based but is an excellent
source of referral information on a wide range of problems affecting
the elderly is Help The Aged, whose address is as follows:

Help The Aged, St James's Walk, London EC1 (Tel: 01 253 0253).

This organization provides a telephone advice and referral service, a
range of free pamphlets giving advice to the elderly, and a number of
reasonably priced guides on specific areas of concern, including some
of those mentioned in this chapter.
   There are two excellent sources of further information on a whole
range of issues relating to the elderly:

1. The Longman Self Help Guide by Gill Manthorpe (1986) *Elderly
    People – Rights and Opportunities*, which sets out in clear terms
    the rights of elderly people in a range of areas including
    retirement, money, housing, health, families, local and legal
    services, and holidays, and provides a mass of information on
    further sources of assistance.

2. The Age Concern publication (1986) *The Law and Vulnerable Elderly People*, which combines an accurate account of the law relating to accommodation, money management, consent to treatment, and compulsion of the elderly, with many ideas for reform well backed up with informed comment and statistics.
3. *Daily Mail Retirement Guide* is a concise, cheap, readable guide covering a wide range of problems.

Finally, Citizens' Advice Bureaux are excellent sources of advice and information on all these matters and are particularly good at dealing with the problems of the elderly.

10

Finding and Keeping a Home[*]

This chapter will take a look at the various ways in which the law can be used as a tool to assist in finding or keeping a home. Wherever there is a problem demanding social work intervention, there is a high probability that the absence of a decent home, or a state of uncertainty concerning the client's existing home, will form a direct or indirect part of that problem. Many legal rights and responsibilities will operate upon such problems. This chapter will illuminate the most important of these. It is arranged in the following way:

1. Getting Council Accommodation (whether homeless/or already housed).
2. Buying Council Accommodation from the Council.
3. Retaining Council Accommodation as a Tenant.
4. Rights to Housing Association Accommodation.
5. Seeking and Keeping Privately Rented Accommodation.
6. Retaining Mortgaged Accommodation.
7. The Criminal Law and the Protection of Accommodation Rights.

GETTING COUNCIL ACCOMMODATION

The rights of an individual to obtain council accommodation will

[*]The chapter will deal only with the position in England and Wales. Housing rights in both Scotland and Northern Ireland, whilst broadly similar to those in England and Wales, do differ in significant points of detail and anybody advising clients in those countries should take local advice to clarify exactly where those differences lie. (For a summary of the content of the recent Housing (Scotland) Act 1988, see *Roof*, January–February 1989)

depend upon whether, at the time of their application, they are homeless.

Rights to council accommodation if homeless

Homelessness is a problem of major proportions in the United Kingdom. Estimates of the numbers of homeless people at present in the United Kingdom rise as high as 200 000. Official figures acknowledge that in 1987 over 100 000 people were accepted by local authorities as 'officially homeless' (compared to around 53 000 in 1978) and the numbers are rising. According to the London Housing Unit there were 64 500 single homeless people living in London in 1988. Most of these people would not figure in any official statistics. In these circumstances it is easy to understand how hard pressed council housing departments have adopted very rigorous procedures to try to ensure that priority is given to the most deserving cases. Not only is the pressure on resources immense, but it is disproportionately directed towards inner city councils with large, fluid populations. In 1987 the London Borough of Camden, claimed that it was spending 10 per cent of its total annual budget, (some £20m) on providing temporary accommodation to homeless families. Government figures stated that in June 1987 £45m was being spent by local authorities in England and Wales to keep 11 000 families in temporary hotel accommodation. By June 1988 this figure had risen to 11 270 families in England alone. In these stressful circumstances it is clearly a matter of considerable importance that the adviser has a good understanding of the legal obligations that lie with councils to provide accommodation to those who request it. (For a dramatic account of the health consequences for families living in bed and breakfast accommodation see Conway, J. (1988) *Prescription for Poor Health: The Crisis For Homeless Families* (Shelter).)

What duties do councils have to provide accommodation to homeless persons?

The answer to this question is to be found in an important piece of legislation that began its life in 1977 as the Housing (Homeless Persons) Act and is now Part III of the Housing Act 1985. This Act is supplemented by a *Code of Guidance*. All Homeless Persons Units attached to councils in England and Wales are supposed to operate strictly according to the terms of the Act. The Act has in turn been much scrutinized and modified by a number of important cases. What follows is a summary of the position. Those seeking more detailed information should consult Arden, A. (1986) *The Homeless Persons Handbook* (Allison and Busby) or Arden, A. (1988) *Homeless Persons: The Housing Act 1985 Part III* (3rd edn.) (Legal Action Group). Local authorities have themselves drawn up a document called the Local Authority Agreement, which attempts to set out the model policy they try to follow.

The basic position under this legislation is that a council has a legal duty to provide permanent accommodation to certain categories of people who are either homeless or threatened with homelessness and to provide temporary accommodation or advice and assistance to certain other categories. As would be expected, each one of these words has been exhaustively analysed and defined by the courts. In addition, official reports demonstrate that the ways in which local authorities in practice interpret their responsibilities differ widely; see *Responding to Homelessness: Local Authority Policy and Practice* (HMSO, 1988).

What does *homeless* mean?

The law considers a person to be *homeless* if they have 'no accommodation' in England, Wales or Scotland. 'They' extends to any person who might normally be expected to live with the homeless person as a member of their family, for example a caring relative, a child or a spouse. The phrase 'no accommodation' is a legal term and means something different from a 'roof over your head'. It means accommodation that the occupier has a *legal* right to occupy, i.e. which they own, rent, occupy under a trust, have a licence to occupy, or which they have a special legal right to occupy, for example as a result of a post-divorce settlement or pending a court possession order hearing. It also extends to accommodation that is legally available to the homeless person to occupy but which they are prevented from occupying through fear of domestic violence or because the landlord has illegally locked them out. There are special rules about owners of mobile homes and houseboats with nowhere to install them. See Letall, M. (1988) *Mobile Homes: An Occupier's Guide* (Shelter).

A person is 'threatened with homelessness', if they are likely to become homeless within 28 days. Thus a person who has received a possession order, or a person in temporary hostel accommodation with a maximum stay period of less than 28 days is 'threatened with homelessness'.

Must the accommodation be of a certain standard?

The accommodation must be 'available' to live in, but must it be of any particular standard?

In the past few years there have been a number of important cases that have tried to set down some coherent answer to this question, without much success. In 1986 Parliament amended the relevant section of the 1985 Housing Act in an effort to clarify the position. The law now states that a person will be treated as having 'no accommodation' unless they are in accommodation *which it is reasonable to expect them to continue to occupy*. But in deciding what is 'reasonable', a council can take into account the general standard of accommodation in their area, i.e. if housing is generally bad in the area, the standard of the accommodation need be no better than the prevailing standard. This amendment therefore does nothing to assist the development of uniform housing standards, which is unfortunate, as it is in the areas of the poorest housing conditions that the highest levels of homelessness are also to be found: 70 per cent of the local authority expenditure on bed and breakfast accommodation for homeless families is in London. Case law in this respect is not encouraging, as it is only in the most extreme cases that the courts have accepted arguments of 'unreasonableness' (as in one case where it was deemed unreasonable to describe as 'accommodation' a rat-infested hut 10 ft by 20 ft, with no mains services, inhabited by a couple with three children, including a young baby.)

Is a person homeless if they are in temporary accommodation?

The answer to this question will depend on how 'temporary' the accommodation is. A woman given temporary accommodation in a women's refuge is certainly homeless. Similarly, a person given temporary accommodation in a night shelter is homeless. If the legal rights of the occupant are slightly more strong, e.g. they have a temporary licence to be there, they will not be homeless, but they may well be 'threatened with homelessness' if the notice period necessary to remove them is less than 28 days.

What happens if the homeless person has accommodation outside England, Wales or Scotland?

The fact that an applicant may have accommodation in another country is not a relevant consideration in deciding whether they are homeless although it may be a relevant factor in deciding if they are *intentionally homeless* which will enable the local authority to refuse to house them: (see p. 331) This factor is of particular importance to new immigrants and refugees. Some particularly hard pressed local authorities have recently been refusing to house applicants precisely because they have accommodation in another country that in the view of the council they should not have left. In a particular series of cases concerning homeless families in Tower Hamlets, the court was prepared to hold that inadequate accommodation in Bangladesh was available to the applicants as it had in fact provided them with occasional homes in the previous 18 months, so by giving it up they were consequently intentionally homeless.

What happens when a person claiming to be homeless presents themselves to a council?

Councils have differing responsibilities towards different categories of homeless people. A council has a legal responsibility towards any person who presents themselves to the council as 'homeless' or 'threatened with homelessness' to make any necessary enquiries to establish whether this is true. The enquiries do not have to be 'CID type', but they must be sufficient to come to a rapid and fair decision. If in addition to claiming homelessness the applicant appears to be in 'priority need' (see below) the council must provide the applicant(s) with temporary accommodation pending the outcome of their enquiries. In hard pressed inner city areas this will normally be 'bed and breakfast' accommodation.

If after initial enquiries the council accepts that the applicant is homeless or threatened with homelessness, what happens next?

The answer to this question will depend upon whether the applicant is 'homeless' or 'threatened with homelessness'.

Homeless

If the applicant is homeless the council officers must then carry out a number of further enquiries to establish the following:

- Does the applicant have a *priority need*?
- Did the applicant become homeless *intentionally*?
- Does the applicant have a *local connection* with another housing authority in England, Wales or Scotland? (They will only make this third enquiry if the applicant appears to have *no* local connection with them, and even then, they are not obliged to follow this third procedure.)

What is priority need?

The law defines *priority need* as a person in any one or more of the following categories:

- A pregnant woman, or a person with dependant children either living with them or who ought reasonably to be living with them, e.g. the children are in voluntary care because the parent/s are unable to accommodate them. Grandchildren, foster children and adopted children all come in this category, but dependency is normally deemed to end at 16 (19 if child is in full-time education or training and not otherwise able to support his or herself).
- Anybody who ought reasonably to be living with the above people, e.g. spouse, cohabitee or dependant children.
- A person who is homeless through flood, fire or other disaster.
- A person who is vulnerable *either* as a result of old age (near or over normal retirement age) *or* for some other special reason such as physical or mental disability (including illness). Councils are not normally willing to include what they term self-imposed disabilities, e.g. alcoholism and drug addiction, unless other disabilities are also manifested.

What is intentional homelessness?

This is the part of the legislation that has caused the most difficulty and controversy. The idea behind this part of the legislation is to disqualify from eligibility for immediate accommodation anybody who has deliberately given up their existing accommodation. Sadly, many councils have exploited this loophole in the legislation as a way of avoiding responsibility to house people who are often in a desperate plight. Case law has tended to come out on the side of councils in this area and a line of restrictive decisions has resulted in many homeless people never getting beyond this hurdle.

In claiming 'intentional homelessness' and thereby avoiding the need to provide permanent accommodation, councils may rely upon either the applicant's deliberate acts or the applicant's failure to do something. Thus not only is an applicant intentionally homeless if they deliberately give up accommodation they have a right to occupy, they are also intentionally homeless if they fail to do whatever is necessary to keep their existing accommodation, e.g. wilfully refuse to pay rent, fail to keep their family or lodgers under control or illegally sublet, resulting in their own eviction. The case law in this area is prolific, and legal advice from an expert should always be sought if there is any suggestion by the council of 'intentional homelessness'. The Code of Guidance to the Act is also very important because although it is not legally binding it should normally be followed. The Code emphasizes the fact that the disqualifying conduct of the applicant, whether by an act or a failure to act, must be shown to have been in *bad faith* and not just the result of a genuine lack of understanding. Thus non-payment of rent in ignorance of the availability of housing benefit (see Chapter 11) or the acceptance of temporary accommodation in the belief it was permanent would be examples of behaviour that may lead to homelessness, but would be unlikely to give rise to a successful allegation of 'intentional homelessness'.

Some further points need to be made regarding 'intentional homelessness'.

- The deliberate giving up of accommodation that remains available to occupy in another country has been construed as 'intentional homelessness'.

- The giving up of accommodation that cannot accommodate those with whom the applicant reasonably expects to share the accommodation, e.g. his or her children, does not amount to 'intentional homelessness' even though the accommodation may remain available to the applicant if living alone.
- Councils may look beyond the immediate cause of the applicant's homelessness for an earlier act that amounted to 'intentional homelessness' and thereby avoid any liability to provide accommodation. This is called the 'chain of causation, which is best illustrated by an example. A and B voluntarily move out of their accommodation to live in a squat when A becomes pregnant. They did not have to move, although the accommodation they had been living in was squalid and inappropriate for a young baby. After several more squats they are finally evicted and they present themselves at the local council as homeless. Although they are clearly homeless and in priority need, the council will be able to argue that they are 'intentionally homeless' because they voluntarily left the first accommodation. Once a person is thus 'tainted' with 'intentional homelessness' it is very difficult for them to break the causation chain. It can only be done if they manage to secure for themselves some 'settled accommodation' in which they spend a period of time. This will have the effect of breaking the chain so that if they have the misfortune to become homeless at some date in the future the council will no longer be able to refer back to the earlier act of 'intentional homelessness'. 'Settled accommodation' means accommodation in which the occupant has a 'reasonable degree of security' and will not therefore be established by a period in temporary hostel accommodation, or a holiday let.
- Where homeless applicants were previously living with relatives but were asked to leave by those relatives it is sufficient for the relatives to have given the applicant written notice to leave within a reasonable period, and for that period to have passed for the applicant to be deemed homeless. Despite statements by some councils to the contrary, it is not necessary for the relatives to take court proceedings to avoid the charge of intentionality. A number of decisions by Ombudsmen in recent years have put this matter beyond any doubt. Once the relatives have ended their guest's licence to remain, the guest is homeless.

What happens if the applicant has a local connection with another housing authority?

In some circumstances the local authority will also inquire whether the applicant has a 'local connection' with another housing authority in England, Wales or Scotland, in order to pass the responsibility to house the applicant to that authority. But this can only be done in very limited circumstances. The local authority can only invoke this line of enquiry if neither the applicant, nor anybody who might reasonably be expected live with them, has any 'local connection' with them.

By 'local connection' is meant a connection with the local authority because of one or more factors: employment in the area; past or present voluntary residence in the area; family associations in the area or for any other special reason. Thus if a person gets off a train in London and presents themselves as 'homeless' and they have no 'local connection' with that authority it is legitimate for that local authority to contact an area with which they do have a 'local connection', providing one exists. There is a Local Authority Agreement which states that a period of residence of less than 6 months in the 12 months immediately prior to the application will not normally be sufficient to establish a 'local connection'. This Agreement is *policy*, however, and not law and if an applicant has established a 'local connection' after a shorter period the policy need not be applied, particularly where a local connection is argued also on the basis of, say, family associations.

If a local authority does use the 'local connection' provision and that other authority accepts responsibility for the applicant the first authority must provide them with temporary accommodation whilst their transport back to the other authority is being negotiated. It follows from the above that if the applicant has no 'local connection' with any other authority in England, Wales or Scotland, e.g. they are a political refugee from another country, or they have just got off a boat from Belfast or Dublin, the provisions are of no relevance. (But, note the alternative possibility of an argument of 'intentional homelessness', see p. 327).

The 'local connection' provisions will also not apply if the applicant runs the risk of domestic violence should they be returned to the housing authority with which they have a 'local connection' and which area they have presumably left because of this risk.

What are the council's duties once it has carried out all the above enquiries?

The enquries may take anything from a few days to many weeks, depending on their complexity. The applicant should cooperate with the council as far as they are able (giving false information is a criminal offence – see p. 334) but should also seek the help and support of an experienced adviser, particularly before signing any forms or statements. The help of a social worker could be very significant at this stage. The applicant should be given copies of any forms that they sign (On access to personal files see Chapter 3, pp. 70–71). Once the decision has been taken it must be communicated to the applicant in writing. It has already been stated that if the applicant is homeless and in priority need the council must provide them with temporary accommodation pending the completion of any other enquiries. The following is a list of the council's duties to the homeless applicant once the enquiries are completed:

1. If it finds that the applicant is homeless but without priority need the council's duty is limited to providing 'such advice and assistance as the council considers appropriate'. This may in practice mean no more than a list of accommodation agencies, hostels and bed and breakfast hotels. For assistance in the London area consult the *London Hostels Directory* (1989–90) (Resource Information Service). The applicant should always check whether the council has any special schemes offering accommodation to people like themselves. There are also a number of charities and pressure groups that try to provide advice and assistance to homeless people who fall in this category: e.g. Campaign for the Homeless and Rootless (CHAR) (Tel: 01 833 2071); IYSH, 19–29 Woburn Place, London WC1H 0LY (Tel: 01 837 7151); see also Saunders, B. (1987) *Homeless Young People in Britain: the Contribution of the Voluntary Sector*. (Bedford Square Press/NCVO) and O'Mahony, B. (1988) *A Capital Offence* (Routledge) on the plight of the young single homeless in London.

2. If it finds that the applicant is homeless, has priority need but is intentionally homeless, its duty is to provide the applicant with temporary accommodation for a reasonable period to enable them to find accommodation of their own. There is no fixed period, and it will depend upon the facts of the individual case

but the applicant cannot expect to be allowed more than a few weeks as a maximum.

3. If it finds that the applicant is homeless, has priority need and is *not intentionally homeless*, it has a duty to ensure that the applicant, together with those reasonably expected to live with the applicant, are provided with 'suitable accommodation'. This can be provided by themselves or somebody else, e.g. a housing association. The deliberate insertion of the word 'suitable' is an explicit recognition by Parliament that the particular needs of the applicant, and if necessary their family unit, must be taken into account.

Can the applicant appeal against the council's decision?

There are three possible ways in which an applicant might appeal against an unfavourable decision:

1. Use any appeals procedure that exists within the council itself (see Chapter 3, p. 72). Alternatively, appeal to a senior officer, to a councillor or to the relevant sub-committee (see Chapter 3, p. 76).

2. Complain to the Local Government Ombudsman (see Chapter 3, p. 76). This will only be possible if the applicant is alleging bias or maladministration. There have been a number of complaints upheld by Ombudsmen in connection with the administration of homelessness applications. For example, when a Homeless Persons Unit failed to make adequate enquiries in the case of applicants being made homeless by their own housing department; or when a council provided inadequate temporary accommodation pending the outcome of their enquiries; or when councils insist that relatives evict their families through the courts before the council will accept them as homeless.

3. Apply for *judicial review* of the decision. This is a complicated and lengthy procedure that involves making an application to the High Court, and will inevitably require the use of lawyers. Legal aid would be available for such an application (see Chapter 1). For further details on judicial review see Chapter 3, p. 81. Successes for applicants under this procedure are not very common. It is thus of the greatest importance for the applicant to be sure that their original application argues their case as strongly as possible. It is at this early stage that social work intervention could prove invaluable.

Threatened with homelessness

If the applicant is not homeless, but is threatened with homelessness the duties of the council officers are more straightforward. First, they must establish whether the applicant and/or their dependants are in *priority need*. If they are not in priority need the council's duty rests at 1 above. If, on the other hand, the applicant and/or their dependants are in priority need the council has a duty to take steps to try to prevent the threatened homelessness coming about. This could mean, for example, advising the person on their rights to obtain housing benefit and other welfare rights if the homelessness is threatened as a result of rent arrears. Or it could mean taking action against a landlord who is threatening illegal action to evict a tenant.

Are there any criminal offences associated with homelessness?

It is a criminal offence for an applicant to lie to the council about their circumstances in an attempt to be classified as eligible for housing as homeless. It is also a criminal offence for an applicant to withhold from the council any changes in their circumstances that occur before the application is determined that might affect the council's decision. It is a criminal offence for anybody else to lie to the council to try to help the applicant obtain housing. Lying includes making statements without any idea whether or not they are true, e.g. saying that the applicant has always lived in the area, or that they have children without knowing one way or another. All these offences are triable in the magistrate's court and are punishable with a fine.

Will the council look after the applicant's property while their application is being examined?

The council will have a duty to take reasonable steps to protect the property of an applicant who is homeless or threatened with homelessness while they are processing the application, if they believe it is in danger of being lost or damaged, that no other suitable arrangements to protect it are being made and the applicant is unable to look after it.

Rights to council accommodation if not homeless

Despite the fact that there are approximately 1.3m people on the waiting lists for council housing in the United Kingdom, government policy in the past decade has concentrated on the deliberate attrition of the council housing stock as part of its wider philosophy of privatization. This attrition has been stimulated in two ways. First, the introduction in 1980 of the right of a council tenant to buy their home from the council which has resulted in the sale of over 1 million council homes into the private sector since 1981. Second, in the steep decline in the number of new council houses built each year falling from 159 000 in 1976 to 53 000 in 1982 to only 16 317 in 1986. The percentage of the housing stock that is now council housing has fallen to its lowest level since the war. Further decline is inevitable in the wake of the Housing Act 1988 with the extension of the Right to Buy provisions, the facilitation by the Government of the voluntary disposal by local authority of their housing stock to the private sector, the creation of Housing Action Trusts, and the introduction of the right of council tenants to vote for a private landlord takeover. For further information on the new choices available to council tenants read Franey, R. (1988) *Tenants Choice: A Guide for Council Tenants*, obtainable from TPAS , The Crescent, Salford, M5 4NY.

Despite the developments outlined in the previous paragraph, the allocation of council houses to new tenants still continues, albeit on a far more limited scale than in the past. This section will examine the legal framework within which the allocation of council homes operates.

Is a council obliged to inform the public of its council house allocations policy?

Yes. Every council housing department is obliged by law to publish a summary of the rules and procedures they adopt in allocating their housing stock to tenants. This summary will normally be in the form of a short pamphlet available in housing offices and the Town Hall. It must be free of charge. It will describe the system that the council uses in establishing its priorities but it does not have to state how long an applicant will normally have to wait before being offered a home. A more detailed description of the rules and procedures must also be made available to anybody on request, normally for a small charge. In addition, anybody who has actually applied for council accommodation (e.g. by putting their name on the waiting list) is entitled to a free copy of their application form, in order to check that the details are correct.

Is a council obliged by law to adopt any particular type of allocations policy?

There are very few legal constraints on the type of allocations policy that a council must adopt. The law makes the general statement that a council must give 'reasonable preference to applicants who are occupying insanitary or overcrowded houses, have large families or are living in unsatisfactory housing conditions' but it is very difficult in practice to make much use of this statement to further the claim of a particular individual. In practice, a council is likely to adopt one of three different types of scheme: a *date order scheme* whereby tenancies are allocated to the person who is top of the waiting list on a 'first come first served' basis; a *merit scheme* whereby tenancies are allocated according to the views of councillors as to the merit of each particular case; or a *points scheme* whereby points are allocated to each applicant on a complicated scale of need and tenancies are granted to those who achieve the highest number of points. The third scheme has become the most widely used in recent years, but the factors for which points are awarded vary considerably between councils. They may include such factors as length of time on the waiting list, existing housing conditions, age, number of children, overcrowding in current accommodation and health factors. Any council adopting a points scheme should explain its rules and procedures for allocation in the information pamphlet that it makes available to the public.

There are two circumstances where a council *must* provide a person with accommodation regardless of their own procedures:

1. If they have a legal obligation under the homelessness legislation (see p. 331).
2. If they have displaced that person from their existing home by a *compulsory purchase order*, a *closing order*, a *clearance or demolition order*, or the service of an *improvement notice* (see Chapter 11, p. 390).

What kind of council allocation policy might be unlawful?

There are certain things which a council cannot do lawfully in connection with its housing allocations policy:

- A council cannot impose a blanket condition that prevents it from considering the merits of a particular case. For example, a council cannot impose a policy condition that it will *never* offer accommodation to a person who still has the joint tenancy of another home, but who needs new accommodation because of domestic breakdown.

- A council cannot discriminate either directly or indirectly against an applicant on the grounds of their colour, race, nationality, sex or ethnic origins. This means that any policy to encourage a reasonable black/white balance on council estates is unlawful, whatever the merits of its intentions. The Commission for Racial Equality (CRE) has, however, approved the practice adopted by many housing authorities of recording the ethnic origin of all applicants for their housing so long as this is used constructively to improve the circumstances of ethnic communities and not in order to bring in discriminatory policies (for further information see Chapter 3, pp. 80–1).

Examples of indirect discrimination (see Chapter 3, p. 81 and Chapter 7) might be a requirement that housing points can only be given for children actually living with their parents, as this might discriminate against an immigrant applicant whose family is waiting to join him; or even a residence requirement as many members of new immigrant communities might be disadvantaged by such a requirement. For further information on this particular problem see Bindman, G. (1979) 'Indirect Discrimination and the Race Relations Act'. *New Law Journal* no. 129, 408 and Harrison, P. (1984) 'How Race Affects Councils Housing', *New Society,* 12 January at 43.

What can an applicant do to complain about the way in which their application has been handled?

The procedures for complaining about a council service, or lack of it, are fully explained in Chapter 3, p. 72. An applicant who alleges maladministration in the handling of their application can lodge a complaint with the Ombudsman (see Chapter 3, p. 76).

If there is a serious possibility of discrimination on the grounds of race or sex, the applicant should contact the Commission for Racial Equality (CRE) or the Equal Opportunities Commission (EOC) for further advice or assistance. For further information see Chapter 3, pp. 80–81.

BUYING ACCOMMODATION FROM THE COUNCIL

Since 1980 it has been possible for *secure tenants*, i.e. council tenants with security of tenure (see p. 337) and certain types of housing association tenants (see below) to buy their home from the council on very favourable terms. Not surprisingly, this right has proved very popular and over a million tenants have taken advantage of it. The law governing the right to buy is complex, as is the general law governing the purchase of property. A tenant is strongly advised to consult a solicitor or licensed conveyancer before embarking upon the purchase of their council home. The general principles governing the purchase of a council home are set out in Arden (1986) *Public Tenant's Handbook* (see bibliography). A summary of these principles is set out below:

- The tenants must have been a *public sector tenant* for at least 2 years before they can claim the right to buy. The 2 years need not have been continuous, nor in the same property.
- The property can be a house or a flat but it must not be in one of the list of exempted categories. (The council will soon inform the applicant if their property is exempted!) The list includes sheltered accommodation for the frail or elderly.*
- The purchase may be of a freehold or a long leasehold, depending upon the nature of the property.
- The tenant will be entitled to a discount off the market value of the property, depending on the length of time they have been a 'public tenant'. It will vary from 32 per cent for 2 years to a maximum of 60 per cent for 30 years or more if the property is a house and from 44 per cent to 70 per cent if the property is a flat. The maximum discount is now £50 000.
- If having purchased the property the tenant (now owner) resells it within 3 years they will have to pay back the discount less 20 per cent for each full year of occupation since the purchase. There are limited exceptions to this rule, e.g. where

*S. 123 Housing Act 1988 extends the right to buy the properties designed, built or converted for disabled people.

the resale is a 'family transaction' such as a transfer on death or divorce (for full details see Arden, *Public Tenants' Handbook* (see 'Further Sources of Reference', p. 369)).

RETAINING COUNCIL ACCOMMODATION AS A TENANT

How secure from eviction is a council tenant?

Since 1980 most council tenants have had security of tenure, which means that they cannot be evicted unless the council takes them to court and proves legal grounds for the eviction. The legal term used to describe such tenants is a logical one: they are described as *secure tenants*. The term 'secure tenant' extends wider than tenants, however, to include amongst others, council licensees (for the distinction between a licensee and a tenant see p. 347). The only exception is a licensee who entered the property initially as a trespasser (or squatter) to whom the council has subsequently granted a licence to remain in occupation. A person in this situation cannot become a secure tenant.

Some council tenancies are specifically excluded from being secure tenancies. The most important of these exceptions are service tenancies (i.e. where the tenant is required to occupy the premises for the better performance of their duties, as in the case of a resident caretaker), and various forms of temporary accommodation, e.g. temporary accommodation given to homeless people unless they have occupied it for more than a year from the date the council informed them they would only be given temporary accommodation; temporary accommodation given to a person for up to a year when they have been offered employment in the area of the council and are looking for accommodation in the area; and temporary accommodation given to a person by a council whilst repairs are being carried out on their main home. If there is any doubt as to the status of the tenancy a letter to the council requesting clarification should be sufficient to resolve the problem. For a full list of the exemptions see Arden's *Public Tenants' Handbook*.

Must the council have grounds to evict a secure tenant?

A council cannot evict a secure tenant unless it can prove one of the *grounds for eviction* set out in Group A, B or C below.

337

Group A (Grounds 1–8)

In addition to proving one or more of these grounds the council must also satisfy the judge that it would be *reasonable* to evict the tenant i.e. the judge retains a discretion not to evict the tenant, despite the existence of grounds for possession because he or she believes that it would be an unjust decision to make.

Group B (Grounds 9–10)

In addition to proving one or more of these grounds the council must satisfy the judge that *suitable alternative accommodation* will be provided to the secure tenant if they are evicted. Suitable alternative accommodation is accommodation which is reasonably suited to the needs of the tenant bearing in mind:

- their income;
- their existing accommodation;
- the size of their family;
- the proximity of the accommodation to their work and to any schools or relatives whom they might need to visit regularly.

If the secure tenant does not feel that the accommodation being offered *is* suitable, they should defend the court action on this basis.

Group C (Grounds 12, 13, 15 and 16)*

In addition to proving one or more of these grounds the council must also prove both that it is reasonable to evict the secure tenant (see A) and that suitable alternative accommodation is available (see B).

The Grounds (the numbers relate to those used in the Housing Act 1985)

Grounds 1–4: These are identical to the Discretionary Grounds for Possession against Protected Private Tenants (see p. 338). They relate broadly to circumstances in which the secure tenant has either

*Grounds 11 and 14 only apply to charities and housing associations)

breached a term in the tenancy agreement, e.g. by falling into arrears of rent, or been in some other way at fault, e.g. by causing a nuisance to neighbours. In the recent past some progressive councils have been using these grounds in an attempt to evict tenants who engage in systematic racial harassment of other tenants on their estate, with some success. For a detailed guide to the ways in which councils can take action against tenants who indulge in racial harassment see Forbes, D. (1988) *Action on Racial Harassment* (Legal Action Group).

Ground 5: The tenant obtained the tenancy by making a false statement.

Ground 6: The tenant obtained the tenancy by an exchange during which money passed hands.

Ground 7: The tenancy was tied to a particular job and the tenant has been guilty of unacceptable behaviour making it impossible for them to remain on the premises (for further details see Arden's *Public Tenants' Handbook*).

Ground 8: The tenant is the secure tenant of 'other premises' but was granted temporary accommodation in these premises whilst repair work was carried out on the 'other premises'. The work is finished but the tenant refuses to move back.

Ground 9: The premises are illegally overcrowded. This is a legal phrase that is very carefully defined either by reference to the ratio between the total number of occupants and the total room size, or by the fact that two or more people of the opposite sex, aged 10 or over, who are not living together as man and wife, are obliged to sleep in the same room. The local Environmental Health Officer will confirm whether or not premises are illegally overcrowded.

Ground 10: The council needs to move the tenant in order to demolish, or carry out major structural alterations on the property. The council must, however, prove both that it intends to carry out works *and* that the works could not be reasonably carried out without first obtaining possession, i.e. it would not be possible to move the tenant to temporary accommodation pending completion of the works. This ground will also operate if the premises form part of an official Redevelopment Scheme. (The council will provide details of what this is.)

Ground 11: Only applies to tenants of a charity.

Ground 12: This relates to certain types of tenancy tied to employ-

339

ment when the employee's replacement needs to move into the premises (for full details see Arden, *Public Tenants' Handbook*).

Ground 13: The premises are specially adapted for a physically disabled person and there is no longer such a person residing on the premises.

Ground 15: The premises form part of a group of dwellings for people with special needs (e.g. the mentally ill or elderly) with special facilities nearby (e.g. resident wardens or social services day centres) and there is no longer anybody living on the premises with special needs.

Ground 16: The tenant became a secure tenant of the premises by succeeding to the tenancy on the death of a family member, and the council considers that the property is too large for them.

If the council have grounds to evict a secure tenant what procedure must it follow?

If a council wishes to evict a secure tenant it has to follow a set procedure. First, in the case of the majority of secure tenancies it has to serve on the secure tenant a document called a Notice of Intention to Seek Possession (NISP). This document will set out the grounds on which the council is intending to seek possession against the tenant (e.g. rent arrears, nuisance, demolition of property and so forth). It will also state the earliest date on which it might commence court proceedings against the tenant to put its intentions into effect. If a secure tenant receives a NISP it is always advisable for them to seek immediate specialist advice from a law centre, a solicitor or a housing aid centre.

At the second stage of the procedure, once the date specified in the NISP has passed, the council can apply to the local county court for a possession summons to be issued against the secure tenant. This summons will inform the secure tenant of the date set for the hearing of the summons and will provide more detail of the grounds upon which possession is being sought. If they have not done so already, at this stage, the secure tenant should certainly consult a housing specialist law centre, housing aid centre or solicitor. A solicitor may decide to apply for legal aid on behalf of the secure tenant to represent them at the hearing (see Chapter 1).

The third stage of the procedure takes place at the county court on the day of the hearing. The council will have to prove its case to the court. To do this it must provide evidence of one or more of the legal grounds described above.

What will happen to the secure tenant if the council wins the case?

If the council proves its case to the satisfaction of the judge an order for possession will be made. Unless the grounds fall in Group B above, however, the court will have a wide discretion as to what sort of order to make and it is important for the tenant to try to persuade the judge to make the most lenient order possible. If, for example, the grounds for possession are rent arrears, the court may suspend execution of the order indefinitely so long as the tenant pays back the arrears at a regular agreed rate. Alternatively, if the tenant has breached some other term of the agreement, the court may accept an undertaking by the tenant to make good any damage, and will suspend the order accordingly. If the court makes an absolute order for possession, because they consider the grounds to be sufficiently serious, the judge can still order that it should not be executed until a date fixed some weeks ahead. The tenant will, however, remain liable for rent throughout that period. Only a court bailiff (or sheriff if the hearing was in the High Court) has the power to carry out the eviction. It is a criminal offence to resist the eviction by force.

Will the council rehouse the tenant after the eviction?

It is extremely unlikely that a council will offer to rehouse a tenant whom they have evicted. However, if the tenant or any other people evicted from the property qualify as homeless people to whom the council has a legal obligation (see p. 330) they will be given further accommodation, although it is likely to be inferior to the accommodation from which they have been evicted. It should be noted that it is open to councils to treat as *intentionally homeless* tenants who are evicted for rent arrears that they could and should have paid, or for unacceptably anti-social behaviour.

What effect will the Housing Act 1988 have upon the rights of council tenants?

The Housing Act 1988 has not affected the security of tenure of council tenants, although it has opened up the possibility for council tenants to find themselves with new landlords in the form of a Housing Action Trust (HAT), a housing association or a private landlord/company. A HAT is a temporary organization set up by the government to take over selected estates which are particularly dilapidated and run down for a temporary period. (For further information see the DOE booklet *Housing Action Trusts* (June 1988) from HPS Division, DOE Room N11/20, 2 Marsham St, London SW1P 3EB). Complex procedures have also been introduced giving secure tenants the opportunity, with or without the support of their council, to opt out of the council sector and pick a new landlord, subject to a ballot. These procedures are beyond the scope of this book. For a detailed analysis of the procedures see Rodgers, C. (1989) *Housing – The New Law* (Butterworths).

RIGHTS TO HOUSING ASSOCIATION ACCOMMODATION AND COOPERATIVE HOUSING

Housing associations are organizations that provide subsidized housing for rent in very similar ways to councils. They receive grants from both central and local government to purchase, administer and maintain their properties. Although they employ full- time officials, each one is under the general control of its elected management committee which will often include tenant representatives. Housing associations are either registered with the Housing Corporation, or unregistered. It is only registered housing associations that fall in the public sector. A simple telephone call to the Housing Corporation (Tel: 01 387 9466) will ascertain whether or not a particular association is registered. If the housing association is *not* registered, the position of the tenant is exactly the same as if they were tenants of a private landlord (see Licence in the Private Sector below).

How do housing associations allocate their houses?

Every housing association has to have an allocations policy, the details of which it must provide to anybody who asks to see it. The policy will vary widely according to the particular area and purposes of the association. Many associations have been set up to cater for a specific target group, e.g. the elderly, the disabled or the single homeless, in which case these people will form the basis of their allocations policy. Details of a particular policy can be obtained from the registered address of each association, details of which may be obtained from the Housing Corporation, 149 Tottenham Court Road, London W1P OBN (Tel; 01 387 9466).

What security of tenure do tenants of registered housing associations have?

Tenants of registered housing associations are considered by law to be secure tenants, with all like consequences (see p. 337). The exception to this rule is a registered housing association *which is also a cooperative* in which case there is no right of secure tenancy. All the Grounds for Possession set out for council tenants (see above) apply to secure housing association tenants with an additional Ground 14 as follows:

> The landlord is a housing association or trust which lets dwellings to persons whose non-financial circumstances make it difficult for them to satisfy their housing need, and either there is no longer such a person residing in the dwelling or the tenant has received an offer of a secure dwelling from a local authority and the landlord requires the dwelling for occupation by a person with special needs.

For a possession order to be made under Ground 14 the court must also be satisfied that it would be reasonable to make the order and that suitable alternative accommodation will be available to the tenant after eviction (see p. 338).

Does a housing association tenant have the same right to buy their property as a council tenant?

Although the right to buy (see p. 336) is granted by legislation to secure tenants which definition, as we have seen, includes some housing association tenants, it should be noted that the major exemptions from this right are:

343

- secure tenants of a housing association which is a charity;
- secure tenants of specially adapted property see p. 336 and footnote.

Anybody wishing to buy their housing association property from their landlord is therefore advised to approach the association directly and request whether they do in fact have a right to buy. A number of housing associations operate a range of alternative schemes to assist tenants in the purchase of their own or another flat, details of which can be obtained from the relevant management officer within the association.

Housing association law is complex and changing and cannot be dealt with in any depth in this chapter. Those seeking a definitive account of housing association law should consult Alder, J. and Handy, C. (1987) *Housing Association Law* (Sweet and Maxwell.) Another useful source of information of how housing associations operate is the National Federation of Housing Associations' *Committee Members' Handbook* which can be obtained from 175 Gray's Inn Road, London WC1X 8UP (01 278 6571). On the consequences for housing associations of the Housing Act 1988, see Rodgers, C. (1989) *Housing: The New Law* (Butterworths)

Housing cooperatives

The idea of the housing cooperative (or co-op) in which a group of people share the expense and organization of obtaining, and running a property or group of properties is fast gaining in popularity, particularly amongst younger people living in the big cities. The subject is complex, with a wide range of possibilities. Those interested in setting up a co-op should write to the Housing Corporation (see p. 343) which produces a series of helpful booklets explaining exactly what is involved. Those interested in buying co-operatively (as compared to renting should read Treanor, D. (1988) *Buying Your Home with Other People* (Shelter Publications). For further information generally about Housing co-ops contact The National Federation of Housing Cooperatives, 88 Old Street, London EC1V 9AX (Tel: 01 608 2494).

SEEKING AND KEEPING PRIVATELY RENTED PRIVATE ACCOMMODATION

Although private renting has seen a steep decline since the beginning of the century from 90 per cent of the housing stock to around 12 per cent in 1987 it remains an important source of accommodation for certain types of people such as young house sharers, recently divorced or separated couples, and new immigrants to Britain. It is part of the policy of the current Government to seek to restimulate the private rented sector by deregulating private rents and easing the restrictions on eviction of certain private tenants (see pp. 406, 367). To this end it has introduced a range of new measures designed to encourage an increase in private renting which affect all tenancies in the private sector which commenced on or after 15 January 1989.

There are a large number of legal problems associated with private renting that seem out of all proportion to the relative size of the private rented sector in the housing market. This section will concentrate on the most common legal problems facing tenants of rented property in the search for a property to rent and in the struggle to remain in that property if the landlord wants to evict the tenant.

How much can an accommodation agency legally charge a prospective tenant for its services?

There is a law which controls the way in which accommodation agencies may ask for commission for their services from prospective tenants. It is part of the criminal law, which means that in theory any accommodation agency that breaks this law can be reported to the police and be prosecuted. In practice this is very rare, although it is possible for the Director of Fair Trading to prohibit estate agents convicted of this offence from further carrying out such work, and the threat of such a loss of livelihood can be effective in resolving any disputes of this nature. Prosecution aside, it is clearly a matter of some importance to people who use accommodation agencies in their search for privately rented accommodation to know how much the agency can legally charge them for their services. Any illegal charge will not have to be paid by the client.

In summary the position regarding accommodation agency charges is as follows:

- The agency cannot charge the client for registering the client's name and requirements on their lists, nor can they charge for providing the client with particulars of a place that is available for renting.
- The agency can charge for other services for which they have genuinely incurred cost, providing this was made clear to the client at the outset. This means, for example, that they can charge for the work involved in matching available accommodation to the client's needs, letters, telephone calls, introductions and so forth so long as the charge does not include any of the work for which they are prohibited from charging. (For a short but useful article on this subject see Partington, M. (1975) 'Accomodation Agencies and the Law' *New Law Journal* no. 125, 148).

In what circumstances can a landlord or outgoing tenant charge a premium in exchange for the grant of a tenancy?

If the tenancy is a *Rent Act protected tenancy* (see p. 351) it is illegal for anyone (i.e. landlord or outgoing tenant) to charge the incoming tenant a premium in exchange for the tenancy. Any such premium can therefore be recovered by an action in the local county court. It is also a criminal offence. This rule does not, however, apply to a tenancy which is not protected (see p. 358).

What is the law governing deposits demanded by landlords at the beginning of a tenancy?

It is normal practice for a landlord to request an incoming tenant to pay a deposit repayable at the end of the tenancy as a security against arrears of rent, damage and breakages. The deposit must however be reasonable and in any event must not exceed the equivalent of 2 months' rent.

LICENCES IN THE PRIVATE SECTOR

For many years it was common practice for a landlord letting property to offer prospective tenants an agreement called a *licence* rather than a *tenancy*. Whereas a tenant may have all sorts of legal rights such as the right not to be evicted without legal grounds being established, or the right to register a fair rent (see Chapter 11, p. 401) a licensee will have no such protection. In recent years, however, it has become considerably harder for landlords to offer a licence as a legitimate alternative to a tenancy, following two important decisions of the House of Lords (*Street v. Mountford 1985* and *Antoniades v. Villiers 1988*). In both these cases the House of Lords decided that what a landlord *calls* the letting should be treated as of little importance. What matters is what it actually *is*. And they said that when deciding what the letting actually is 'a court should be astute to detect and frustrate sham devices whose only object is to disguise the grant of a tenancy'. In other words, since these decisions we can safely say that if a letting amounts to the grant of a tenancy it matters little that the parties to the agreement have signed a document *calling* it a licence. This will apply regardless of whether there is a single tenant or two or more people sharing. What a tenancy actually *is* can be discovered on p. 349.

These two cases should *not*, however, be taken to mean that it is no longer possible for a genuine licence to be created. There will still exist situations in which a licence rather than a tenancy is created: The following are some examples:

- If two or more people are sharing accommodation in which they each occupy some part of the premises that is their own, e.g. bedroom, but share the use of other rooms, e.g. living room, kitchen and bathroom *and* the landlord has made it clear that a) they are each only liable for a proportion of the rent and b) should one occupant leave, the landlord reserves the right to choose their replacement, then the occupants are licensees. The reason for this is that the occupants cannot be said to exercise exclusive possession of the premises against the landlord (see p. 349).
- If the arrangement is one of extreme informality, as for example where a member of one's family, or a close friend is given accommodation to help them through a difficult period, it is likely that a court will also describe such accommodation as a licence.

- Most hostel and hotel arrangements.

What are the consequences of having a licence and not a tenancy?

A licence is a contract granting the licensee permission to live in the premises for the period set out in the licence, in the same way that a theatre ticket is a contract allowing the holder to remain in the theatre for the duration of the play in exchange for money. But whereas the theatre owner normally reserves the right to end the contract prematurely, as for example in the case where the ticketholder is drunk or misbehaves, the legal position of a residential licensee is a little stronger. For most residential licensees (but see the note below. below) cannot be legally evicted unless the landlord obtains a court order in the local county court. Any eviction that does not follow this procedure is almost certainly unlawful and could lead to the prosecution of the landlord under s. 6 Criminal Law Act 1977 and an action for compensation by the tenant for illegal eviction.

N.B. The position of *some* licensees ('excluded licensees') whose licence was created on or after 15 January 1989 is not as secure, as the need for a landlord to obtain a court order does not apply in some circumstances (including where the licence was granted to a person previously squatting the premises; where the landlord is resident, it is his only or principal home, and s/he is sharing with the licensee more than just the common parts or storage areas; and where the premises are a hostel). If in any doubt as to whether a licence is excluded from protection in this way consult a solicitor. It should further be noted that if a landlord threatens violence in the absence of a court order it is likely that they are is committing a criminal offence under s. 6 of the 1977 Criminal Law Act. The police should be called.

How can a licensee be evicted?

Licences created before 15 January 1988

A very simple procedure exists whereby a landlord can seek a court order against a licensee. All the landlord needs to do is give the licensee 4 weeks' notice in writing to vacate the premises by a certain date. The notice can be written or verbal. If it is given in the form of a *notice to quit* it must be in the form of a proper legal document (see p. 356). The landlord need not give any reason for the notice. If the licensee has not vacated by the given date, the landlord can immediately apply to the court for a possession order, and also ask that the licensee pay the costs of the application. In practice the pressures of time on county courts mean that it may be some weeks, or even months, before the matter comes before the court although procedures are being streamlined for this type of application. At court the licensee will have no defence to the action unless it can be established *either* that the notice period was inadequate *or* that the letting was not a licence at all but a tenancy (see below). If the licensee loses the case, they can be ordered to pay the costs of the hearing including a contribution to the landlord's legal costs. A possession order will be issued which will enable the court bailiff to evict the licensee within a fairly short period.

Licences created on or after 15 January 1988

The only circumstance in which the same procedure as above need *not* be followed is if the licensee is an 'excluded licensee' (see p. 367 and note on s.6. Criminal Law Act 1977 p. 348).

TENANCIES

What is a tenancy?

There are three features of a tenancy, namely *exclusive possession*, a *fixed or periodic term* and *rent*. Let us examine each of these features in turn.

Exclusive possession

This simply means that the tenant is granted the right to exclude all others from the premises including the landlord. If the tenant is a sole tenant this right is personal to the tenant. If the tenant holds the tenancy jointly with others it is their collective right. Whether or not exclusive possession had been granted is often hard to establish. The sort of question to ask is: Do the parties act as if (for the duration of the letting) the tenant owns the property with all the formal responsibilities that entails, or is the arrangment somehow more informal, with the landlord coming and going at will? The former tends to suggest exclusive possession, the latter not. The fact that a landlord may visit the premises by arrangement to collect rent, carry out repairs and so forth does not mean there is no exclusive possession vested in the tenant. But if the letting genuinely allows the landlord to shift the tenant(s) from room to room, as in the hostel arrangement, exclusive possession cannot be said to exist.

Fixed or periodic term

This refers to the necessity that the letting is for an identified period of time such as a week, a month or a year. The letting may also allow for automatic renewal of that period by use of such words as 'weekly' or 'monthly' in which case the tenancy is called a 'periodic tenancy'.

Rent.

This is defined as money, or quantifiable goods or services and will extend to rent that is deducted from wages if the letting comes with a particular job.

In what circumstances can a landlord evict a tenant?

The answer to this question is complicated by the fact that there are a number of different categories of tenancy with differing consequences. A tenant's rights will differ according to the category of the tenancy. In the event of any threatened eviction proceedings it is therefore always sensible to seek expert advice from an adviser trained in housing law, in for example a law centre, a housing aid centre, or a solicitor's office. A summary of the position is set out below.

Position for tenancies created before 15 January 1989

If the letting is a tenancy and not a licence (see above) the next question to decide is whether the tenancy is protected by the Rent Act 1977 (as amended) because such a tenant has far more extensive rights than one who is not protected.

Tenancies fully protected by the Rent Act (protected tenancies)

A tenancy is fully protected by the Rent Act if it is a tenancy of residential premises (which may be no more than a room in a house) and it does not fall into the stated list of exceptions of which the following are the most common:

- The landlord lives in the same building as the tenant and has lived there continuously since the tenancy began. This exception will apply even if the part of the building that the landlord occupies is an entirely separate dwelling, e.g. a self-contained flat, but will not apply if the building is a purpose-built block of flats. The landlord must genuinely reside there as a 'home' although s/he may own another home. There are complicated provisions covering the situation where a resident landlord dies, on which further advice should be sought.
- The letting is for a holiday so long as this is a genuine holiday and not a sham.
- The letting includes the provision of 'board' which was a genuine part of the agreement between the landlord and the tenant when the tenancy was first created. 'Board' is not clearly defined, but basically amounts to the regular provision of some meals which have been prepared for the tenant on behalf of the landlord, e.g. a substantial daily breakfast or evening meal would amount to 'board'.
- The cost of the letting includes a substantial proportion to cover the provision by the landlord of personal services to the tenant, e.g. room cleaning and linen change.
- The letting amounts to college accommodation provided to a student by a university, polytechnic or other college of further or higher education.
- The tenant uses the property for business purposes instead of or in addition to a residence. This covers the situation where a tenant works from home, or starts to run a business involving the property, e.g. taking in lodgers for profit. The exception will not be established if the business use is very trivial or marginal.
- The rent is very low, i.e. less than two-thirds of the rateable value of the property. This exception is normally limited to tenancies of long leases where the tenant pays a large capital sum to acquire the lease and a small annual ground rent

thereafter. Such tenancies are not intended to come within the protection of the Rent Act.

- The rateable value of the property is exceptionally high (this relates to luxury lets and is unlikely to be of concern to most social work clients).

WHAT IS THE ADVANTAGE TO THE TENANT OF A FULLY PROTECTED TENANCY?

There are two outstanding advantages that the fully protected tenancy has over other tenancies. First, the tenant can register a fair rent at the local Rent Officer Service which will be binding on the property for the next 2 years (see Chapter 11, p. 401). Second, the tenant cannot be evicted from their tenancy unless the landlord proves grounds for eviction to the satisfaction of the local county court. These grounds are limited and are set out in various pieces of legislation. In summary the grounds are as follows.

Grounds where, if the facts are proved to the court, the judge must make a possession order, i.e. there is no discretion (the mandatory grounds)

Protected shorthold tenancies. The tenancy is a protected shorthold Tenancy, the period of the Shorthold has come to an end, and the landlord has served the correct notice indicating an intention not to continue the tenancy any longer. A protected shorthold tenancy was a new type of protected tenancy introduced by the Conservative Government in 1980. The aim of this provision was to encourage landlords to let empty properties to tenants for a fixed period of between 1 and 5 years in the knowledge that the landlord has the absolute statutory right to regain the property at the end of the period, regardless of the tenant's wishes and without needing to prove any grounds for possession. For a number of reasons that are beyond the scope of this book, protected shorthold tenancies have not had the impact that the Government would have wished. DOE figures in 1981 suggested that there were around 3500 Shorthold lettings, and 50 000 empty 'lettable' properties. In any event, since 15 January 1989 such tenancies have been supplanted by *assured shorthold tenancies* (see p. 362).

Returning owner occupier. The tenancy is of a property that the owner once lived in (as a freeholder or a tenant) and the owner now wants it back:

352

either

- as a home for themselves or a member of their family so long as that person has also previously lived there. The need must be 'genuine' though it does not have to be 'reasonable'. The intention may only be to live there intermittently. That will be sufficient to gain possession.

or

- to sell in order to purchase another home more suited to the owner's work needs (e.g. closer to a new job).

These grounds will typically cover the situation of the homeowner who wants to rent out their home for a period while they are working abroad but at the same time wants to be sure that they can regain their home on their return. Normally the court will only allow possession if the owner made it quite clear in writing before the tenancy began that this was the situation. These grounds can also be used by people who inherit homes and want to live in them or sell them with vacant possession and by mortgage companies who want to sell the house with vacant possession because the mortgagor has defaulted on the mortgage payments. This latter provision only applies, however, if the mortgage was in existence before the tenancy began. It can thus be seen that the grounds are potentially very extensive and can be abused. The equivalent provisions for tenancies created *after* 15 January 1989 are different and less complex (see p. 360).

Where there are joint owners of the property it will be sufficient to demonstrate that the grounds apply to at least one of the owners; i.e they do not all need to demonstrate a desire to live there.

Retirement homes. Sometimes people buy themselves a retirement home some way in advance of their projected retirement date and in the interim wish to rent it out to a tenant. So long as they inform the tenant in writing at the beginning of the tenancy that they will be wishing to repossess the home as their retirement home they will have grounds for possession against the tenant when that time arrives. Should they die before that date, or should they default on a mortgage in force on the property at the outset of the tenancy, similar provisions apply regarding repossession as for properties let by owner occupiers (see above). Likewise, the same provisions apply regarding the 'genuine' (though not 'reasonable') need of the landlord, and regarding joint owners of the property.

In the case of *returning owner occupiers* and *retirement homes* it

353

seems to be the case that a court will sometimes be willing to grant possession even if the tenant was not given full notice of the intention to repossess at the time the tenancy began. There would have to be special reasons for this oversight, however, such as the failure of a letter to arrive or the belief on the landlord's part that verbal oral notice was sufficient.

Miscellaneous grounds. There are a number of other miscellaneous mandatory grounds for possession that are unusual and are therefore not treated here in any detail. Further information on these grounds can be found in Martin, J. (1986) *Security of Tenure under the Rent Act* (Sweet and Maxwell) or Arden, A. (1989) *Manual of Housing Law* (4th edn.) (Sweet and Maxwell) (and see Further Sources of Reference, p. 369). They cover such situations as out of season lettings of holiday homes or student lettings, lettings by servicemen abroad, and lettings to certain types of agricultural worker.

Grounds where the judge retains the discretion whether or not to grant a possession order (the discretionary grounds)

There are a number of situations where a landlord wishes to regain possession of a fully protected tenancy but the mandatory grounds set out above do not exist. In these circumstances, the landlord first has to prove one or more of the discretionary grounds set out below and second has to satisfy the judge that it would be reasonable to make the order for possession. Even then the judge has wide discretionary powers to suspend the execution of the order on condition that, for example, the tenant clears outstanding rent arrears within a reasonable time, or to give the tenant a lengthy period to find alternative accommodation before the landlord can execute the order. The discretionary grounds are as follows:

- *Suitable alternative accommodation* is available to the tenant. There have been a number of cases which have tried to define exactly what amounts to suitable alternative accommodation. Essentially the accommodation must be roughly the same size, same price and in an area that is reasonably suitable to the needs of the tenant. The 'character' of the area is a factor that can be taken into account in rejecting the accommodation as unsuitable, if it differs significantly from the area where the tenant currently lives. The courts have held that 'character' does not extend to ethnic character or the proximity of friends.

- The tenant has breached a term of the tenancy agreement, e.g. non-payment of rent.*
- The tenant has allowed the property or furniture in the property to become seriously damaged or neglected.*
- The tenant or any other occupier has been found guilty of using the premises for illegal or immoral purposes or has caused serious annoyance or nuisance to nearby residents, e.g. by persistent noise at anti-social hours.*
- The tenant has sublet the whole of the premises without the landlord's consent.
- The tenant has given the landlord notice to quit the tenancy as a result of which the landlord has made a commitment to sell the property to another person with vacant possession.
- The tenancy was originally a service tenancy, i.e. it came with a full-time job offered by the landlord, the tenant is no longer employed to do that job and the landlord needs the property for another full-time employee of the landlord.
- The landlord needs the property as a residence for him/herself, or any son or daughter over 18 years of age, or his/her mother or father, or a father-in-law or mother-in-law. This particular ground will be defeated if the tenant can show that they, or anybody living with them will suffer greater hardship by losing the tenancy than the landlord/relative will suffer by not acquiring the property.

  If a landlord successfully obtains possession under either of the above two grounds and it subsequently transpires that this was under false pretences, the tenant has a right to sue the landlord in the same court for financial compensation for the loss of the tenancy.

- The tenant has sublet part of the property at a rent which is in excess of any registered rent operating on the property (see Chapter 11, p. 401).

WHAT PROCEDURE MUST A LANDLORD FOLLOW IN ORDER TO OBTAIN POSSESSION UNDER ANY OF THE ABOVE GROUNDS?

Possession proceedings against fully protected tenants are subject to

*see footnote on p. 338.

rigorous procedures that must be followed to the letter. The adviser who needs a detailed account of every aspect of these procedures should consult Luba, J., Madge, N. and McConnell, D. (1989) *Defending Possession Proceedings* 2nd Edn (Legal Action Group). The procedure is the same whether grounds are mandatory or subject to the judge's discretion. In summary it is as follows.

The landlord must begin the procedure by bringing the contractual tenancy to an end. This means either waiting for the lease to expire, if the tenancy was for a fixed term, or serving the tenant with a detailed legal document that is either a *forfeiture notice* or a *notice to quit*. If the contractual tenancy has not been brought to an end by one of the above methods any possession proceedings will be struck out as null and void. It is always worth asking a housing expert to scrutinize the document to check that is has been correctly drafted. For example a notice to quit must give the tenant at least 4 weeks notice, and the notice must end on a day when rent is due. It must also contain certain information about a tenant's rights, once the notice to quit has been served. A letter from a landlord merely giving the tenant a month's notice is *not* a notice to quit.

Once the contractual tenancy has ended, the landlord has to serve the tenant with a possession summons which will be issued from the local county court. This summons will set out the details of the grounds on which the landlord is seeking possession and fix a date for the hearing. At this stage the tenant should consult a solicitor or other housing adviser in order to consider the drafting of a defence, which must normally be submitted to the court within 14 days and certainly in advance of the hearing date. Legal aid is available to a tenant to defend possession proceedings subject to a means test (see Chapter 1) provided the legal adviser believes that the tenant has an arguable defence. It should be noted that where certain of the mandatory grounds are being argued (returning owner occupier, retirement home, servicemen lettings) a special quick procedure is available to landlords to bring the matter more rapidly before the courts.

Assuming that no settlement is reached between the parties the matter will have to be heard by a judge sitting in the county court where the summons was issued. Some county courts nowadays have a duty advocate who will be prepared to assist unrepresented parties, but it is strongly advisable to obtain legal advice and representation in advance of the hearing. At the hearing the judge will listen to evidence from both sides, plus any witnesses either side wishes to call and will then make a decision. If s/he decides that *mandatory* grounds for possession have been proved an order for possession to take effect in 14 days will be made. It is also possible that the tenant will be ordered to contribute towards the landlord's costs. In cases of grave hardship the 14 days can be extended to 6 weeks. If s/he decides that *discretionary* grounds have been proved, s/he has a further discretion as to what action if any to take. The normal order, however, is for possession to be granted in 28 days, and it is unusual for a judge to exercise a wider discretion than this except in case of rent arrears where there are mitigating factors to be taken into account, and it seems likely that the tenant will be able to pay off the arrears over an extended period.

Tenancies partially protected by the Rent Act

Some tenancies may not be fully protected by the Rent Act despite their being tenancies and not licences, because they are expressly exempted from such protection (see p. 351), e.g. where there is a resident landlord. A few of these tenancies do, however, qualify for very limited protection as *restricted contracts*. A restricted contract is a private tenancy or licence that is not fully protected but which includes the payment of rent and the provision by the landlord of furniture or services. It will thus extend to most lettings by resident landlords (unless unfurnished), educational establishments, lettings providing some board or substantial personal services, and many licences. Certain tenancies are expressly excluded from being restricted contracts, in particular holiday lettings and those where board is substantial (such as half/full-board hotels/hostels).

An occupier (whether tenant or licensee) who has a restricted contract has certain limited rights not available to an occupier who does not have a restricted contract. These rights relate to the length of time for which a judge may suspend any possession order that is made in the county court. In the case of a restricted contract, if entered into after 28 November 1980, the court may suspend the order for up to 3 months. Before this stage is reached however, the landlord must go through exactly the same process as for an action against a fully protected tenant (see p. 356) first bringing to an end the contractual tenancy, then serving a possession summons. The only difference is that the landlord will not have to prove any grounds for possession.

Tenancies without any Rent Act protection

It follows from the above that there remains a small residue of private tenancies that are completely unprotected by the Rent Act. These will principally be genuine holiday lettings and lettings where substantial board is provided. The position of the tenant in these circumstances is exactly the same as that of a licensee (see p. 348). The law states that it is unlawful to evict *any* tenant or residential licensee without a court order. Any such eviction can lead to prosecution with the possibility of a substantial fine, compensation order and even imprisonment (see p. 366). Any threats suggesting eviction without a court order should be reported to the local authority legal department or the police. Unreasonable refusal to leave the premises will, however, increase the likelihood of the tenant being ordered to contribute towards the landlord's costs at the court hearing.

Position for tenancies coming into existence after 15 January 1989

The Housing Act 1988 introduced two new types of tenancy. It is no longer possible to create a protected tenancy of the type described above. The two new types of tenancy are the *assured tenancy* and the *assured shorthold tenancy*. Both types of tenancy are regulated by the Housing Act 1988. They have less security of tenure than enjoyed by previous protected tenancies and little regulation by law of the rent.

Assured tenancies

Assured tenancies are lettings at market rents with some security of tenure. There is no control over the rent at which an assured tenancy is initially let and subsequent rent regulation is minimal (see Chapter 11, p. 406). The security of tenure provided is different to that granted to Rent Act tenants (see below) and the grounds for possession are more widely drafted.

What is an assured tenancy?

An assured tenancy is one in which the tenant is an individual tenant (or tenants), i.e. not a company, of residential premises (which may be just a room) occupying the premises as their only or principal home and the tenancy does not fall within one of stated exceptions. The most important exceptions are as follows:

- The tenancy is an *assured shorthold tenancy* (see p. 362).
- The landlord is a resident landlord (see p. 351 but note that in addition, the home must be the landlord's *only or principal home* for this exemption to apply).
- College letting (see p. 351).
- Tenant uses the property for business purposes in addition to or instead of as a residence (see p. 351)
- The rent is very low (see p. 351) or the rateable value of the premises is very high (see p. 352).
- The letting is for a holiday (so long as it is a *genuine* holiday and not a sham).

If the tenancy falls within one of the above exemptions it is unprotected except that in most cases (see p. 366) the landlord will have to obtain an order of the court to evict the tenant. There is no 'halfway house' equivalent to the restricted contract under the 1977 Rent Act (see p. 357).

How can an assured tenant be evicted?

A landlord can only evict an *assured tenant* by following the detailed procedure laid down in the Housing Act 1988. It is complex and what is set out below is no more than an outline. Advisers seeking more detailed information should consult a specialist work, e.g. Rodgers, Arden, A. and Hunter, C., Driscoll (p. 370)

The landlord must first serve on the tenant a notice in prescribed form (similar to the NISP for secure tenants: see p. 340) which must set out the grounds for possession (see below) and specify the detail of those grounds, e.g. the precise amount of arrears, the detail of any alleged tenant's misbehaviour and so forth. An old style notice to quit (see p. 356) is of no effect on an assured tenancy. The period of the notice will depend upon the grounds. Advice should always be sought as to whether sufficient notice has been granted. The court does have power to dispense with the need to serve a notice if it considers that it would be 'just and equitable' to do so. It *cannot* dispense with the need to serve a notice, however, where the grounds for possession are that the tenant has three months arrears of rent (see p. 361). Once a notice has been served the landlord has 1 year in which to commence possession proceedings against the tenant.

If possession proceedings are served a date for a court hearing will be fixed. The procedure thereafter is very similar to the procedure for Rent Act possession actions (see p. 356). At court the landlord will have to satisfy the judge that grounds for possession exist against the tenant. In summary the grounds are as follows:

Grounds where if the facts are proved to the court, the judge must make a possession order, i.e. the judge has no discretion (The Mandatory Grounds)

Ground 1: returning owner occupier. The landlord must prove that before the tenancy began, written notice was served on the tenant(s) stating that possession might be recovered under this ground, although the court has power to dispense with the notice requirement if it feels that it would be 'just and equitable' to do so, for example where it is proved that a notice was sent by post and did not arrive. In addition, the landlord must prove that *either* at some time before the tenancy began they occupied the dwelling as their 'only or principal home' *or* that they now require the premises to become the 'only or principal residence' for themselves or their spouse. A landlord cannot use the latter case if they became landlord by purchasing the property after the tenancy had already begun.

Ground 2 applies where the property was mortgaged at the time the Ground 1 tenancy was created, and the morgagee wishes to exercise their power of sale over the property (e.g. because the mortgagor has defaulted on the mortgage) and sell the property with vacant possession. This ground is subject to the same provisions concerning notice as Ground 1.

Ground 3 applies to 'holiday property' let out of season by landlords for a period of up to 8 months. For this ground to be used the landlord *must* have served notice of intent not later than the beginning of the tenancy.

Ground 4 applies to 'college property' let out of term. The same notice provisions apply as for Ground 3.

Ground 5 applies to residences for ministers of religion.

Ground 6 applies where the landlord intends to demolish or reconstruct the whole or a substantial part of the dwelling house or carry out substantial works. Reconstruction means 'a substantial interference with the structure of the premises and then a rebuilding in probably a different form, of such part of the premises as has been demolished by reason of interference with the structure'. In addition the landlord must satisfy the court that the work cannot reasonably be carried out without the tenant giving up possession and must pay the tenant's reasonable removal expenses. Like Ground 1, this ground cannot be used by a landlord who bought the property after the tenancy had begun.

Ground 7 allows a landlord to obtain possession against a person who inherits the tenancy from the deceased tenant unless they are a spouse succeeding to the tenancy (see p. 364). Proceedings must commence within 12 months of the landlord becoming aware of the death.

Ground 8 allows a landlord to obtain possession where 3 months' rent arrears (13 weeks if a weekly tenancy) both at the time notice is served and at the date of the court hearing. Delays in paying housing benefit on the part of the DSS or local authority provide no defence.

Grounds where once the facts are proved to the court the judge still retains a discretion not to make a possession order (the Discretionary Grounds)

Ground 9. Suitable alternative accommodation is available to the tenant. For what constitutes SAA see Driscoll (1989) (p. 370).

Ground 10. Rent arrears both at the time of the notice and the date of the hearing.

Ground 11. Persistent delay in paying rent, whether or not there are arrears at the date proceedings are commenced.

Ground 12. Breach of any other term of the tenancy.

Grounds 13–14 are similar to Rent Act 1977 grounds (see p. 355) regarding nuisance to neighbours, illegal or immoral use of the premises, and allowing the premises or the furniture to fall into significant neglect.

Ground 16. The premises were let to the tenant by the landlord (or previous landlord) in consequence of the tenant's employment which has now come to an end.

Once a judge has made an order for possession the power to suspend the order and the time limits for making an order are the same as for Rent Act tenants (see p. 357).

Assured shorthold tenancies

The *assured shorthold tenancy* replaces the *protected shorthold tenancy* under the Rent Act 1977 (see p. 352) and provides a tenant with no long-term security of tenure. It is also subject to minimal rent-control (see Chapter 11, p. 406). For an assured shorthold tenancy to come into effect:

- The tenancy must be for a fixed term of not less than 6 months.
- The tenancy must not contain any provision enabling the landlord to terminate the tenancy within 6 months of the beginning of the tenancy.
- Notice in the prescribed form must have been served on the tenant prior to the commencement of the tenancy. The court has *no* power to dispense with this provision.
- The tenancy would have been an assured tenancy, had the above three conditions not been met.

WHAT IS THE SECURITY OF TENURE OF AN ASSURED SHORTHOLD TENANT?

During the fixed term of an assured shorthold tenancy a landlord can recover possession against the tenant in the same way as against a fixed-term assured tenant under Grounds, 2, 8, 19, 11, 12, 13, 14 or 15. At the end of the fixed term the landlord has the right to obtain possession through a court order subject to the need to give at least 2 months' notice to the tenant. Notice can be given before the tenancy comes to an end so long as the expiry date is not earlier than the end of the fixed term. For the position regarding rent regulation under an assured shorthold tenancy see Chapter 11, p. 406.

Other ways to end a tenancy

There are a number of other ways in which a tenancy can be ended which are listed below in summary form. For further information consult Arden or Martin (see Further Sources of Reference, p. 369).

1. *Surrender by the tenant.* This occurs when the tenant and landlord come to an agreement that the tenancy will end and the tenant leaves the property and returns the key. This sometimes occurs in exchange for a lump sum of money paid by the landlord to the tenant to vacate the property without court proceedings and is a perfectly legitimate and legal practice. If a landlord offers a tenant a lump sum in exchange for vacant possession, however, the tenant should always take advice before accepting the money and also must be certain that they have new accommodation available. They will not be rehoused by the council as they will be considered as 'intentionally homeless' see p. 327). As a general rule, a tenant in this situation should be seeking to negotiate a sum that represents the difference to the landlord between the value of the tenanted property and its value with vacant possession. This often amounts to several thousand pounds or more.

2. *Declaration as unfit.* If a local authority declares a house to be unfit for human habitation (see Chapter 11, p. 387) they may place a closing order on the property at which stage they are obliged by law to provide the occupants with alternative accommodation and the tenancy of the property will end. The occupants may also be entitled to financial compensation (see Chapter 11, pp. 398–9).

3. *Overcrowding.* If the tenanted property is overcrowded, the landlord can seek possession against the tenant. Overcrowding exists if the number of people sleeping in the premises exceeds levels set down in Part IX of the Housing Act 1985, or if two people of different sex over 10 (not married or cohabiting) are sleeping in the same bedroom. For further information see Luba, Madge and McConnell, *Defending Possession Proceedings* or Arden, *Manual of Housing Law* (see p. 369).

4. *Transfer to another tenant.* Unless there is something written in the tenancy agreement expressly forbidding transfer (known technically as *assignment*) it is possible for a tenant to end their tenancy by transferring it in writing to another tenant. This should never be done however without first consulting a solicitor

or expert housing adviser, as there are a number of possible complications, depending upon the type of tenancy. For further information on this consult Arden, *The Private Tenant's Handbook*. (see p. 369)

5. *Succession to another family member on death of tenant*. On the death of a *Rent Act protected* tenant (see above) the tenancy will pass automatically to their spouse providing the spouse was living with them at their death. The spouse will become the new tenant of the landlord on the same terms. This right also applies to a cohabitee who was living with the tenant in a stable relationship at the time of the tenant's death. If there is no spouse or cohabitee in this position the right of succession passes to any member of the deceased tenant's family who had been living with them for at least 2 years at the time of the death. There is no fixed rule as to who qualifies as a 'member of the tenant's family' for these purposes and any dispute, if unresolved, will ultimately have to be resolved by the local county court. If succession is to a member of the deceased tenant's family (and only one such succession is permitted) the new tenancy will be an *assured tenancy*.

On the death of an *assured tenant* (unless they became the tenant by succession) who was living in the premises as their only or principal home, any spouse or cohabitee living with them at the time of the death will succeed to the tenancy as the new assured tenant.

If the tenancy was an unprotected tenancy, whilst the tenant may make provision in their will to leave their tenancy to a named person – and if not it will pass to their next of kin –the inheritor will remain as vulnerable to eviction proceedings as their predecessor (see p. 358). For further detail on this complex area of law consult a specialist manual or seek the advice of a solicitor.

RETAINING MORTGAGED ACCOMMODATION

What is the effect of a mortgage?

When a building society or finance company lends money to a home owner either to help buy or to help improve property it will invariably

364

enter into a parallel agreement with the borrower, setting out the terms for the repayment of the loan. By far the commonest arrangement is a scheme whereby the borrower agrees to make a monthly payment to the lender over a period of many years. It is not uncommon for these schemes to be linked to life or endowment insurance policies. The general term to describe such arrangements is a *mortgage*. So long as the borrower keeps up the payments there should be no problems. (If the borrower is in receipt of income support it may also possible for them to receive assistance in repaying the interest on the loan: see Chapter 8, p. 266.)

Naturally, the lender (the *mortgagee*) will seek more security from the borrower (the *mortgagor*) in the event of the *mortgagor* failing to keep up the repayments. This security will normally take the form of a *charge* on the property. A charge has two effects. First it gives the *mortgagee* the right to sell the property in the event of the *mortgagor* failing to keep up the payments; and second, it ensures that any prospective purchaser of the property is aware of the existence of the loan, which will have to be repaid before they can acquire the property.

What will the mortgagee do if the mortgagor fails to keep up with their repayments?

If a mortgagor falls behind on their payments, the following procedure will probably be adopted by the mortgagee.

- *Stage One:* the mortgagee will write a letter asking the mortgagor to make arrangements to get the payments up to date.
- *Stage Two*: if the payments are not restored the mortgagor will write threatening legal proceedings, and will pass the matter to their solicitor. Eventually, a summons may be issued in the local county court setting out the details of the arrears in a document headed Particulars of Claim. The mortgagor will be asked to return a form to the court stating whether the details of the claim are correct. A date will be fixed for the hearing of the case.
- *Stage Three*: if the matter has still not settled, the court hearing will take place. If the mortgagor makes a satisfactory proposal to the court for clearing the arrears, this will probably end the matter. If they fail to do this, the court can make an order allowing the mortgagee to repossess the property, and sell it, in order to recover the loan. Even at this stage however, the court

can suspend the execution of the order to allow the mortgagor time to find the money to pay off the loan, in which case no eviction will occur.

Legal aid will normally be available to help the mortgagor defend the proceedings (See Chapter 1). For further information both on the above and also on various ways in which a mortgagor in this position can obtain financial assistance, consult an excellent handbook produced by SHAC and CPAG called *Rights Guide for Home Owners*. See also Meadowcroft, C. (1987) *The Homeowner's Guide to the Law* (Fourmat) and (1989) *Owning your own Flat: a Practical Guide to Problems with your Lease and Landlord* (SHAC)

THE CRIMINAL LAW AND THE PROTECTION OF ACCOM-MODATION RIGHTS

There are a number of criminal offences that a landlord can commit. If a tenant believes that their landlord has committed or is about to commit any of these offences they should seek the assistance of the Tenancy Relations Officer in their local council, whose job it is to try to ensure these offences are not committed, and to consider prosecution of offenders. In the case of the most serious of these offences, illegal eviction, the police should be immediately involved, as they are more likely to be able to influence a landlord to restore the tenant immediately, and if not, may proceed to prosecute. It is possible for a landlord to be sent to prison if found guilty of a serious illegal eviction, even for a first offence.

What are the criminal offences associated with accommodation rights?

Illegal eviction

It is a criminal offence for anybody to evict either a tenant or a licensee from their home, without a court order. This applies whether or not the tenancy is protected. The *only exception* to this provision is where the letting is an 'excluded letting' under the Housing Act 1988, in which case no court order is necessary to evict the occupant once their contractual right of occupation has been terminated. There is every chance, however, that in carrying out an eviction without a court order the landlord may commit an offence under s.6 of the Criminal Law Act which makes it an offence to use or threaten violence to enter any premises on which there is a person opposed to the entry. 'Excluded lettings' are as follows:

- Where the tenant/licensee shares accommodation with the landlord and it is the landlord's only or principal home. This exclusion does not apply if the shared accommodation consists only of storage areas or means of access such as staircases or corridors.
- Where the tenant/licensee lives in the same building as the landlord and shares accommodation with a member of the landlord's family (which includes spouse, parents, grandparents, children, grandchildren, siblings, uncles and aunts). The same restricted definition applies to accommodation as for the previous exclusion.

Neither of the above two exclusions apply where the building in question is a purpose-built block of flats.

- Where the tenancy/licence was granted as a temporary expedient to a person who was at that time a squatter.
- Where the tenancy/licence had been a genuine holiday let, which has now expired.
- Where the tenancy/licence was provided free of any charge.
- Where it is hostel accommodation provided by any of the list of organizations set out in the Housing Act 1988 s.31 (includes, local authorities, housing trusts, the Housing Corporation, housing action trusts and so on).

WHAT IS AN ILLEGAL EVICTION?

Any act that prevents the tenant/licensee from entering their home, e.g. by changing the locks, removing their belongings, will amount to an illegal eviction. A landlord who has carried out an illegal eviction can be prosecuted in either the magistrate's or the crown court, and can be fined or imprisoned. In addition, the evicted person can apply *immediately* to the local county court to be reinstated, and can seek damages. In the past 2 years, damages awards of up to £5000 have been recorded in a number of instances. In future, awards are likely to be much higher, as the 1988 Housing Act allows victims of both illegal eviction and harassment (see below) to sue the landlord for damages that reflect the difference in value to the landlord of the tenanted property and with vacant possession. This figure may well be very substantial. Such actions are likely to be in the High Court owing to the magnitude of the damages claims. Legal aid will be available to the tenant (see Chapter 1).

HARASSMENT

If a landlord, or somebody acting on their behalf, does things likely to intimidate a tenant and encourage them to leave the premises (for example, by making threats, disconnecting services, sabotaging the property, or generally making life difficult or unpleasant) they may be guilty of the criminal offence of harassment. In these circumstances, the local Tenancy Relations Officer should always be consulted. If they believe harassment is taking place they should take steps to prevent its continuance. If they are unsuccessful the tenant can apply to the county court as above under Illegal Eviction for similar remedies and the Tenancy Relations Officer may prosecute the landlord. If the harassment amounts to racial harassment consult (CRE) (p. 228). Advisers should also obtain a copy of the CRE *Race Relations Code of Practice* (private renting) which will eventually become part of the housing legislation.

Failure to Provide name and address of landlord

Every tenant has the right to know the name and address of their landlord. If they do not have this information, they should make a written request to the person who last collected any rent from them for it. If the rent collector fails to provide the information, the Tenancy Relations Officer has the power to prosecute them in the local magistrate's court, where they can be ordered to provide the information and can be fined.

Failure to provide a rent book

Every tenant with a *weekly tenancy* is entitled to a rent book, unless their tenancy includes substantial board (all or most meals). If a landlord refuses to provide a rent book, the tenancy relations officer can prosecute them as above. The rent book must contain details of the name and address of the landlord and agent (if any), of the rent payable, and of the tenant's rights to have a fair rent fixed, to claim housing benefit, and of their protection from eviction without a court order. Newsagents frequently stock rent books.

FURTHER SOURCES OF REFERENCE

There are a number of useful guides and manuals on housing law that could be used by advisers to provide more detailed information. There are three Handbooks written by Andrew Arden and published by Sphere with non-lawyer advisers in mind: *The Homeless Person's Handbook, The Private Tenant's Handbook* and *The Public Tenant's Handbook*. SHAC manages to include everything in outline in a single manual *The Housing Rights Guide* which is reissued annually. Together with CPAG they also produce a *Rights Guide to Home-owners*. Another straightforward guide for homeowners is Meadowcroft, C. (1987) *The Homeowner's Guide to the Law* (Fourmat Books). Specifically for flatowners SHAC have produced (1989) *Owning your own Flat: a Practical Guide to Problems with your Lease and Landlord*. Those living in bedsits should consult *Bedsit Rights* (1989) produced by the Campaign for Bedsit Rights, 5–15 Cromer St, London WC1H 8LS.

For more detailed information advisers with some knowledge of the law should use the following (the title in each case indicates with precision the scope of the work):

Arden, A. (1989) *Manual of Housing Law* (3rd edn.) (Sweet and Maxwell).

Hughes, D. (1987) *Public Sector Housing Law* (2nd edn.) (Butterworths).

Martin, J. (1986) *Security of Tenure under the Rent Act* (Sweet and Maxwell).

Luba, J., Madge, N. and McConnell, D. (1989) *Defending Possession Proceedings* (2nd edn.) (Legal Action Group).

Arden, A. (1986) *Homeless Persons: The Housing Act 1985 Part III* (Legal Action Group).

Letall, M. (1988) *Mobile Homes: an Occupier's Guide* (Shelter).

Resource Information Service (1988) *Women's Housing Handbook*

All the following deal with the 1988 Housing Act:

Arden, A. and Hunter, C. (1989) *The Housing Act 1988* (Sweet and Maxwell).
Rodgers, C. (1989) *Housing: The New Law* (Butterworths).
Driscoll, J. (1989) *A Guide to the Housing Act 1988* (Fourmat).
Burrows, L. (1989) *The Housing Act 1988* (Shelter), Outline only.
Bowden, G. (1989) *Housing Act 1988* (Shaw and Sons).
Bridge, S. (1989) *Guide to the Housing Act 1988* (Blackstone Press).
Institute of Housing (1989) *The 1988 Housing Act Explained* (Institute of Housing).

The following organizations may also be of assistance:

Association of Housing Aid, Peggy Middleton House, 50 Woolwich New Road, London SE18 (Tel: 01 854 0055). Produces a bi-annual directory of housing aids and advice agencies, publishes training manuals. Membership open to housing advisers.

Federation of Black Housing Organizations, 374 Gray's Inn Road, London WC1X 8BB (01 837 8288). Voluntary organization whose aim is to highlight the housing needs of black people and to campaign against racism in housing. Provides practical advice and information on setting up housing associations and co-ops (see p. 344) and undertakes campaigns and lobbying. Publishes national directory of black housing and advice groups.

Federation of Private Residents' Associations Ltd., 11 Dartmouth Street, London SW1H 9BL (01 222 0037). Federation of voluntary groups representing the interests of private tenants. Provides free legal advice to its members.

Housing Aid Trust, 88 Old Street, London EC1V 9HU (01 253 0202). Provides independent housing advice and aid to individuals and communities on all aspects of housing. Provides regional services, bi-monthly magazine, training courses, wall charts, and many other resources to use to advisers.

National Tenant's Organization 44 Wensley Gardens, Sheffield S4 8JP (0742 426177). Federation of tenants' organizations across the country. Lobbying, publication, training etc. Has 13 regional branches. Scottish equivalent is Scottish Tenant's Organization, 20–4 St Andrew's St, Glasgow G1 5PD (Tel: 041 880 6444).

Tenants' Participation Advisory Service (TPAS) works with tenants, councils and housing associations to try to increase tenant involvement in housing management. Provides information, advice and training. Offices as follows:
(England) 48 The Crescent, Salford, M5 4NY (Tel: 061 745 7903).
(Wales) Welsh Consumer Council, Castle Buildings, Womanby St, Cardiff CF1 2BN (Tel: 0222 396056).
(Scotland) 20–4 St Andrew's Street, Glasgow G1 5PD (Tel: 041 552 3633).
(Northern Ireland) 127–31 Ormeau Road, Belfast BT7 1SH (Tel: 0232 321224).

SHAC, 189a Old Brompton Road, London SW5 OAR (Tel: 01 373 7276) is a housing aid and advice centre for those living in Greater London. Produces a number of key guides.

Shelter campaigns against homelessness and bad housing in Britain. Produces numerous publications and spearheads many campaigns. Addresses as follows:
(England) 88 Old Street, London EC1V 9HU (Tel: 01 253 0202).
(Wales) 57 Walter Road, Swansea SA1 5PZ (Tel: 0792 469400).
(Scotland) 66 Cockburn St, Edinburgh EH1 1BU (Tel: 031 2266347).

Noise Abatement Society, PO Box 8, Bromley, Kent BR2 0UH (Tel: 01 460 3146) campaigns to reduce noise from all sources including those connected with housing e.g. neighbours, traffic. For further information on what to do about noisy neighbours consult DOE Leaflet: Bothered by Noise? What can you do about it?

371

11

Using Legal Rights to Improve a Home*

Many hundreds of thousands of people, perhaps even millions of people in the United Kingdom live in sub-standard accommodation. Social workers do not need to be told that poor accommodation is one of the major sources of family stress and breakdown. But the law is not entirely passive when it comes to improving housing conditions. It is the purpose of this chapter to outline in some detail the various ways in which people living in sub-standard accommodation, or accommodation that has not been kept in a proper state of repair can use the law to improve their housing conditions. The chapter will also indicate the procedures whereby a tenant, living in accommodation where they consider the rent to be too high, can apply to have it reduced to a level that is fair, or if the rent is not reduced can seek financial assistance to meet the payment. Because the law provides little by way of extra assistance to owner occupiers in sub-standard accommodation (with the exception of accommodation in which a disabled person is living: see Chapter 4), this chapter will focus primarily upon the rights of tenants. Some of the rights described in the chapter relate only to private tenants, others relate to all types of tenant regardless of the status of the landlord. The best guide for homeowners is Meadowcroft (see p. 369). A simple guide on disrepair and how to spot it is Morris, I. (1989) *Bazaar Property Doctor* (BBC).

*With the exception of 'Housing Benefit' p. 407, which also extends to Scotland, the provisions in this chapter only apply to England and Wales.

GETTING THE LANDLORD TO DO REPAIRS: THE DIRECT APPROACH

What repairs is a landlord liable to carry out under contract law?

A landlord's liability to carry out the repairs set out below applies regardless to the type of tenancy. It therefore applies equally to private tenancies, council tenancies, and housing association tenancies. The liability does not apply if the letting is only a licence (see Chapter 10).

Whenever there is a tenancy for which the initial term is less than 7 years (it does not matter if the tenant in fact lives in the premises for more than 7 years), and the tenancy commenced later than 24 October, 1961, the landlord has a legal duty under section 11 of the landlord and Tenant Act 1985 to *keep in repair* (which includes a duty to *put in repair*) the following parts of the dwelling:

- The structure and exterior of the house, including drains, drainpipes and guttering. This will therefore include roofs walls, floors, ceilings, doors, window frames, sills, sashes and glass (unless broken by the tenant). It will also extend to outside walls if they form an integral design feature and are actually fixed to the house, and will include the essential means of access to the property, and common parts. It will not however extend to damage caused by design defects, e.g. condensation caused by a lack of proper insulation, unless the condensation actually caused damage to the structure or the exterior of the property (but see p. 392), nor will it extend to damage caused by the tenant acting in an 'un-tenantlike' manner.
- All installations for supplying or making use of water, gas and electricity, e.g. pipes, wiring, water tanks, toilets, basins. This does not extend to appliances which are not firmly fixed to the premises, and therefore excludes such things as cookers, plug-in electrical equipment and plumbed-in washing machines.
- All installations for space or water heating e.g. radiators, water heaters, and boilers. For tenacies which began after January, 1989 installations include those directly serving the tenant's property, though not part of it, so long as they belong to the landlord.

373

The landlord's responsibility to keep all the above in repair is absolute, i.e. the landlord cannot contract out of the responsibility in the letting agreement. But this is also subject to the following conditions.

- Liability to repair (and also to provide compensation for the effects of living with disrepair) only begins at the moment that the landlord has, or is deemed to have (i.e. through an agent), notice of any disrepair. It is for this reason that it is essential for a tenant to ensure that their landlord (or the landlord's agent) is always informed of any defect or disrepair as soon as it is discovered, preferably in writing. If the landlord or agent ever visit the premises, the tenant should always record the details of the visit in writing.

- Liability to repair does not, however, extend to repairing property that has been destroyed or damaged by fire, storm, flood or other natural disaster or to keep in repair such of the tenant's belongings as he or she is entitled to remove from the premises at the end of the tenancy, e.g. fitted kitchens and heating systems installed by the tenant, unless the damage arises as a consequence of other disrepair for which the landlord *is* liable (e.g. the leaking roof that damages the heating system).

- The standard of repair that is expected by law is no higher than the general standard of repair in the area. Thus the standard of repair expected in a slum area is lower than in a well-kept area.

- The landlord's liability is only to *repair* not to *improve* the property, unless the only way that the repair can be effected is by replacing an obsolete or out of date part with a more modern equivalent. The way in which the courts interpret this provision depends very much on the age of the property in question and the cost of the 'improvements' compared with the cost of the 'repair'. If the property in disrepair is relatively modern and the defect in question is caused by a design or construction defect, the courts *can* order repairing work that amounts to the use of a new and improved construction method, e.g. by using better methods of underpinning or expansion joints. This discretion is, however, used sparingly. If the property is older, the courts may authorize more extensive use of 'improvements' as the basis for repairing work, but in these circumstances they will always take account of the cost of the work, and will not order work that amounts to the virtual reconstruction of the property.

How can a tenant make a landlord do these repairs?

As soon as a tenant becomes aware of any disrepairs in the above categories they should immediately inform their landlord. The landlord then acquires the right to enter the premises at a reasonable time to inspect the disrepair, subject to giving 24 hours' notice. With luck, the repairs will then be carried out by the landlord, and all will be well. If the landlord fails to do anything, the tenant has the right to issue proceedings in the local county court asking that the landlord be ordered to carry out the repairs, and also, if appropriate, for compensation for the inconvenience and discomfort caused to the tenant by the disrepair. Legal aid is available for such an action (see Chapter 1) and a solicitor should be consulted before any proceedings are initiated. It is essential to check the tenant's security of tenure (see Chapter 10) before taking action. For if a tenant has no security of tenure it will be open to the landlord to respond to the disrepair proceedings by eviction.

Can a court make a landlord do the repairs?

If the landlord does not agree to do the repairs, despite the tenant's summmons, there will be a full hearing before the local county court. If the judge is satisfied that the disrepair exists, and that it is the landlord's responsibility to do the repairs, s/he will make an order setting out a schedule of work to be done by the landlord and a time scale. Compensation can also be ordered (see p. 376).

Can the tenant do the repairs themselves and deduct the cost from future rent?

Yes, so long as the tenant first gives notice in writing to the landlord that this is their intention and gives the landlord one final opportunity to do the repairs. Also the cost of the repairs can only be deducted from that part of the rent that is actually 'rent', i.e. it cannot be deducted from any part of the rent that goes towards paying the rates (community charge) regardless of the disrepair.

Local authority tenants and most housing association tenants also have the right to receive grant aid to carry out these repairs (see p. 400).

How does the court work out the amount of compensation for disrepair?

Recent years have witnessed a considerable increase in the amount of money that courts are prepared to order landlords to pay in compensation to tenants who have been obliged to endure living in unrepaired premises. The first principle underlying the amount of compensation ordered is to return to the tenant a sum of money that represents the difference in value to the tenant between the premises in their repaired state and the premises in their disrepaired state. This sum should cover the entire period that the premises remain unrepaired from the moment that the landlord has notice of the disrepair. Thus, if half the premises are uninhabitable due to disrepair, the landlord should be ordered to pay back half the rent for the whole period they remain in disrepair. The second principle is that there should be added to this figure a sum that reflects any general suffering, inconvenience or distress occasioned to the tenant by the disrepair (known as *general damages*). This figure is often a lump sum of several hundred pounds, depending upon the degree of distress. The third principle is that the tenant should also be compensated for any specific damage to their property caused by disrepair (known as *special damages*). Thus the 'replacement cost' of furniture, clothes, bedding and other personal items damaged as a result of the disrepair (e.g. through water penetration) can also be claimed. 'Replacement cost' means the estimated cost of replacing the item in the state it was when damaged, not the cost of a brand new replacement. Since 1988, courts have been prepared to make awards well in excess of £1000 for serious disrepair. The leading case, setting out the guidelines is *Chiodi v. De Marney* (1988), *Estates Gazette 41* at 80.

How long does it take to process a claim against a landlord through the courts?

The least satisfactory aspect of this procedure is the time it takes to process the action. Proceedings should never be initiated until the landlord has been given written notice of *each* defect, a reasonable amount of time in which to carry out the necessary repairs and has failed to do so. The preparatory work necessary to issue a summons, obtain reports and so on may take a further few weeks. If the landlord defends the action, it can take up to a year before a date is set for the court hearing. At the very least, a period of months is likely to pass before a date is set. Thus, a tenant should be under no illusion of the frustrations that lie ahead if they choose to take this type of action. It should however be made clear that the threat of such action is often sufficient to persuade a defaulting landlord to carry out the necessary repairs. For the truly resilient tenant, it is possible to conduct the action without using a lawyer. But take care! See *Taking your Own Case to Court or Tribunal* (1985) (Consumer Association).

Can anybody other than a tenant exercise these repairing rights?

No. These rights arise exclusively by virtue of the status of a tenant, and are not available to licensees, squatters, sub-tenants, or family and friends of the tenant who are living with them.

What can somebody who is not a tenant but who suffers injury or damage whilst on the disrepaired premises do?

If a person is not a tenant they cannot use contract law. The law of tort states, however, that if a person is not the tenant of premises in disrepair, but they nevertheless suffer personal injury or damage to their property whilst on the disrepaired premises they may still, in certain circumstances, be able to sue the landlord for the damage or injury that they have suffered. The circumstances are as follows:

- They are a lawful visitor of the tenant (e.g. the tenant invited them to be there, either to live or as a visitor).
- The damage or personal injury was caused by a defect in the

premises of which the landlord knew or *ought to have known*. In other words, if the damage or injury was caused by a defect (e.g. falling plaster) of which the landlord had no knowledge because of a failure to inspect the property at reasonable intervals, the visitor may still be able to sue the landlord.

- The defect that caused the damage or injury to the visitor must be a defect that the landlord has a legal obligation to put right (see p. 373).

What happens if the damage or injury is the result of the defective work of a third party e.g. a builder?

Anyone who carries out work of construction, repair, maintenance, enlargement, conversion, demolition or any other work in relation to premises owes a duty of care to all those who might reasonably be expected to be affected by resulting defects in that work. This means that they will be liable for any injury or damage suffered by anyone so long as the injury or damage was reasonably foreseeable. The injured person does not have to be on the premises in order to be able to sue for damages. They may, for example, be a neighbour or a passer by, injured by falling debris. A landlord may also be liable for the negligent work of a contractor if reasonable care was not taken in the selection of a competent person for the particular job.

Most structural building work is now covered by the Building Regulations. If a person is injured or their property harmed as a result of a failure by a builder to comply with the Building Regulations, that person can take legal action against both the builder and the owner for compensation unless the breach of the Building Regulations was actually condoned by the local authority in which case they are the best party to sue. For further information on Building Regulations contact the local authority Building Control Department. For further information consult *Which: Getting Work Done on Your House.* (Hodder and Stoughton).

GETTING THE COUNCIL TO HELP: THE POSITION OF THE PRIVATE TENANT

There are a number of ways in which the local council can intervene in cases of serious disrepair to privately rented property. The extent to which a private tenant living in accommodation which is in a bad state of repair can enlist the assistance of their local council will depend upon three things:

- Is the accommodation in a *special category*, i.e. a House in Multiple Occupation (HMO) or a Common Lodging House (CLH)?
- How *extensive* is the disrepair?
- What are the *policies* of the local authority concerning the exercise of its discretionary powers?

In addition the general point should once again be made that before taking any action regarding disrepair a tenant should *always* begin by checking their security of tenure (see Chapter 10). There is little point in asserting legal rights to have repairs carried out, only to be subsequently evicted.

SPECIAL CATEGORIES OF ACCOMMODATION

There are certain types of private accommodation to which special laws apply, namely Houses in Multiple Occupation (HMOs) and Common Lodging Houses (CLHs). This section will look at the special provisions which apply to these two types of accommodation.

Houses in Multiple Occupation (HMOs)

If the building in which the tenant is housed is a House in Multiple Occupation (HMO) local authorities have available to them a whole range of special powers of intervention in the running of the house. Whether they exercise these powers is a political and a financial question: for most of these powers need extra financial resources to back them up, otherwise they are of little value.

An HMO is a house which is occupied by persons who do not form a single household. This description covers accommodation where separate households are sharing bathrooms, toilets, cooking facilities, common living areas and the like, but does not extend to buildings in which there may be a number of self-contained flats, the only common parts being entrance halls and stairs. The description therefore covers such arrangements as houses divided into bedsits, hostels and hotels housing homeless families.

Some of the worst housing conditions in the country are to be found in HMOs. There is controversy surrounding the number of HMOs in the United Kingdom. There have been two recent surveys of HMOs, one carried out by the DOE to cover the whole of England and Wales (1986) and the other limited to the Greater London Area (1987). The official DOE estimate of the number of HMOs in England and Wales of 334 000 is almost certainly an underestimate. (For further information contact Campaign for Bedsit Rights see p. 386.)

It has been estimated that 77 per cent of HMOs contain households who are living in sub-standard accommodation (and sub-standard means merely households who share or lack basic sanitary amenities such as baths or inside toilets). This figure of 77 per cent is a national average and rises to 90 per cent in parts of Greater Manchester, Sheffield, Bradford, Leeds and certain London boroughs. The Government's own survey of conditions in hostels and lodging houses carried out in 1976 revealed that 85 per cent of hostels were built before 1914, and that 78 per cent of the hostels were in buildings that fell below the Government's minimum standards for toilets, wash basins and baths. By 1986 the Department of the Environment estimated that the 334 000 HMOs, contained in excess of 2 million people. Of these, 110 000 needed major repairs, 96 000 were lacking basic amenities, 53 000 were overcrowded, 77 000 were managed unsatisfactorily and 127 000 lacked legal fire hazard precautions. It is against these deeply depressing statistics that all that is written below on legal powers has to be read. For it must be accepted that enforcing these powers will be an uphill task for anybody.

Despite numerous attempts at private members legislation to improve the conditions in HMOs, little improvement has been seen in the past 20 years. The problem is compounded by the fact that inhabitants of HMOs may be highly vulnerable both legally (because they may not have the status of tenancy: see Chapter 10) and emotionally (because their occupation of an HMO has been forced upon them by a crisis such as divorce, homelessness, lack of money, eviction, or personal problems like drug or alcohol addiction). It is however anticipated that some changes in the law regarding HMOs may be introduced by the Government in the course of 1990.

Despite these difficulties, there are a number of powers available to councils to improve the conditions and safety of those living in HMOs. These powers relate to the following:

- fire precautions;
- overcrowding;
- execution of works to improve the conditions within the HMO.

Fire precautions in HMOs

By their very nature, HMOs carry high fire risks (see above for Government estimates). Between 1979 and 1981 431 people died in fires in HMOs. The relative risk of death by fire for the occupant of an HMO is *nine times greater* than that for a person living elsewhere. Although many of these fires are simply the result of excessive strain being placed upon archaic electrical systems, there is clear evidence that many are also preventable by the installation of proper fire precautions within the HMO.

Local authorities do have strong legal powers relating to fire precautions in HMOs which they should be encouraged to utilize.

- Any HMO comprising three or more storeys (excluding a storey below the floor level of the principal entrance to the house), whose total floor space exceeds 500 square metres, *must* comply with fire precautions drawn up for that building by the local authority after consultation with the fire authority. These precautions will vary according to the conditions of the house and may include the addition of fire doors, smoke screens, fire detectors or proper means of escape. The local authority can serve notices on the person having control of the premises (see p. 383) setting out the work that should be done, and can do the work in default, if it is not done. It is clear from the evidence that there is widespread failure by local authorities to enforce these powers which is a matter for deep regret. It would also appear that these provisions apply to less than 10 per cent of all HMO's.
- If the HMO is smaller than described above, the local authority does have powers to insist upon fire precautions but they are all

discretionary. These powers relate principally to the installation of proper means of escape from fire. For details consult the local Fire Authority or the local authority Environmental Health Department.

Overcrowding in HMOs

A local authority has the power to determine the maximum number of people who are allowed to live in a particular HMO including the maximum number who are to sleep in each room in the house. These maximums can be age and sex related. This is a discretionary power, but local authorities should be encouraged to use the power in HMOs where overcrowding is creating insanitary, or dangerous conditions for the inhabitants.

Once fixed, a 'maximum numbers order' is served on the 'person having control of the house' (see p. 383) in the form of a notice. If there are more people in occupation that the maximum numbers, the notice does not require the reduction of the numbers by eviction, but merely forbids the replacement of departing occupants in excess of the maximum numbers contained in the notice.

It is a criminal offence to fail to comply with an overcrowding notice, although in practice, prosecutions under these provisions are very rare.

Execution of works to improve the conditions within the HMO

The living conditions within an HMO are often of a very poor quality. The fact that complete strangers have to share many facilities often means that there is no clear agreement as to who is responsible for what duties, which means that little gets done by way of cleaning or repair. (This is notwithstanding the fact that each individual occupant of an HMO – provided they are a tenant and not a licensee (see Chapter 10) – has the same repairing rights as tenants of other accommodation: see p. 373). Many HMOs are large impersonal edifices, crammed too full with lonely isolated people with little money, and a limited sense of their rights to have improvements done to their home.

The following description of a large hostel for single men in Tower Hamlets (an HMO) by an independent Environmental Health

Inspector provides a chilling though accurate picture of much hostel accommodation:

The room I was allocated was little larger than the bed it contained. Its thin wooden walls meant that I could hear everything in adjoining rooms. The bed linen was filthy and stained with excrement. The nearest toilets were damp and filthy and some were broken. The walls, floors and surfaces were dirty. The wiring to the electric light was perished, exposing live wires. Every fire door in the corridor was wedged open and the fire precautions were inadequate.

But local authorities *do* have legal powers to do something about such conditions if they can exercise the political will to produce the resources to use these powers. If an HMO is in a bad condition, in respect of one or more of the list of matters set out below, a local authority has power to serve notices on the 'person in control' (see below of the HMO requiring them to carry out specified works on the property to render it reasonably suitable for its existing inhabitants to continue living there. These works may relate to any of the following:

- Natural and artificial lighting, ventilation, water supply, personal washing facilities, drainage and sanitary conveniences, facilities for the preparation, cooking and storage of food, facilities for the disposal of water, and installations for space heating, or the use of space heating appliances (e.g. plug-in electric fires).

It will be seen that the list is very extensive and the local authority has power to carry out the works in default if they are not done. In practice, however, local authorities do not make much use of these powers.

Person in control of HMO

It will have been seen that many of the notices concerning HMOs have to be served on the 'person in control' of the premises. The law defines the 'person in control' as the person receiving the *rack-rent* on the premises, whether as landlord or as the landlord's agent or

383

trustee. The *rack-rent* is rent amounting to at least two-thirds of the rateable value of the property.

Can a local authority take over the running of an HMO if its owners or landlords persistently fail to manage it to a satisfactory standard?

The law provides local authorities with two special procedures to take over the running of HMOs when they consider they are being inadequately run. Both these procedures are discretionary and involve the local authority in extra management work that it may feel it has inadequate resources to provide. As the appalling conditions in many HMOs become more apparent however there has been a discernible increase in the use of these powers by local authorities. The two powers are *Management Orders* and *Control Orders*.

MANAGEMENT ORDERS

If a local authority considers that an HMO is in an unsatisfactory state, due to a failure to maintain adequate standards of management, they may serve a notice on the person who directly or indirectly receives the rent on the premises ordering them to comply with the Management Regulations, a series of Regulations prescribed by the Secretary of State for the Environment in SI 1962 No. 668 HMSO. A copy of the notice must be posted in a prominent position in the house in order that all occupants are made aware of its existence.

The Management Regulations cover a wide range of management functions not all of which may be relevant to the particular property. They include:

- general repair, water supplies, cleaning of rooms and common parts, drainage, safety of the occupants, tidiness of any garden, fire escapes, good ventilation, proper space and water heating, refuse disposal, and proper electricity supplies.

A failure to comply with the Management Regulations, once served, amounts to a criminal offence. Local authorities have wide powers to carry out any works in default.

In 1987 there were approximately 4000 Management Orders in

force, an entirely inadequate figure when set against the 77 000 households living in HMOs that are poorly managed (p. 380).

CONTROL ORDERS

The greatest power of all that a local authority possesses to intervene in the running of an HMO is the Control Order. If a local authority makes a Control Order over an HMO it may immediately enter into possession of the property and take such steps as it feels necessary to protect the safety, health or welfare of the inhabitants of the HMO. The local authority is entitled to collect and keep the rent payable on the property for the period of the Control Order, and must in return pay the owner an annual sum of money by way of 'compensation'. The local authority must also prepare within 8 weeks a scheme of work designed to remedy the problems that brought about the Control Order. The Control Order can last up to 5 years after which time it will automatically lapse.

It can be seen that the dual effect of a Control Order is:

- that the owner loses all control over their property for the period of the order; and
- that the local authority takes upon itself the full legal and financial burden of being a landlord of a property that by definition is likely to need a lot of money spent on it.

It is therefore not suprising to learn that Control Orders are rare, running at present time at around 40 per year, across the entire country.

A Control Order can only be made on an HMO if there is already in existence on that HMO either a Management Order, or a notice concerning fire precautions, overcrowding, or the execution of works to improve conditions within the HMO, and that order or notice has not been effective.

Is there any appeal against the imposition of the above notices and orders?

Every one of the notices and orders that are outlined above

concerning HMOs can be appealed against by the person on whom it is made, i.e. the person normally in 'control of the property' (see p. 383). This creates yet more hurdles for the occupant of an HMO, as they will then have to await the outcome of the appeal, which may take several months, during which time both they and the local authority are powerless to do anything.

Further information

It is clear from the above that the conditions of those living in HMOs are a source for very serious concern. For those who wish to find out more about conditions in HMOs the results of the two surveys mentioned above are essential reading. See Kirby, K. and Sopp, L. (1986) *Houses in Multiple Occupation in England and Wales: Report of a Postal Survey of Local Authorities* (HMSO) and Thomas, A. (1987)
Greater London Houses in Multiple Occupation Survey (Association of Metropolitan Authorities).

The main organization campaigning for an improvement in the prevailing conditions in HMOs and a strengthening of the legal rights of those who occupy HMOs is called the Campaign for Bedsit Rights and can be contacted at 5–10 Cromer St, London WC1 H8CS (Tel: 01 278 0598).

Common Lodging Houses (CLHs)

In some large cities in the United Kingdom there exist large HMOs, mostly of a dour Victorian red brick that have the special function of providing basic accommodation to people who would otherwise be likely to find themselves on the streets. The law describes these premises as Common Lodging Houses (CLHs). They are defined as follows:

A CLH is a house provided for the purpose of accommodating by night poor people who are not members of the same family and who are allowed to occupy one common room for the purpose of sleeping or eating.

If an HMO fits this description (and the 'common room' can be can be divided into cubicles) it has to be registered as such with the local authority, which has the power to restrict the number of people who may sleep there on any one night. The local authority also has a number of powers relating to health controls within the CLH, and can close the CLH if it appears that the CLH is unfit because of inadequate sanitation, water supply, or means of escape from fire, or the keeper is unfit to be responsible for the CLH.

It is clear from the evidence obtained by the DOE and GLC reports on HMOs, and the evidence obtained by the Campaign for Bedsit Rights, that very many CLHs fail to reach reasonable standards of care in respect of these duties, and yet their registration is not withdrawn. Advisers who are concerned about the standards in a particular HMO should put pressure on their local authority to reconsider the registration which in any event has to be reconsidered every 13 months or should contact the Campaign for Bedsit Rights (see p. 386).

HOW EXTENSIVE IS THE DISREPAIR?

The above section has detailed certain special categories of private sector rented accommodation which have special problems that local authorities have special powers to help resolve. This section will look at the general powers vested in local authorities to intervene in cases of serious disrepair in all privately rented accommodation. In each case the power to intervene is determined by:

- the extent of the disrepair *and*
- the attitudes and policies of the council.

Houses which are unfit for human habitation

The 1981 House Condition Survey found that of the 18.1 million dwellings in England and Wales approximately 1.1 million (6 per cent) were unfit to live in. A further 900 000 lacked basic amenities. In both these circumstances there are legal procedures available to local authorities to help towards the improvement of this unacceptable state of affairs.

387

What does *unfit for human habitation* mean?

The law states that a home is *unfit for human habitation* (UHH) if it is so far defective in one or more of the list of matters set out below that it is unsuitable for reasonable occupation. This includes a home in such a state of disrepair that there is a real danger to the life, limb or health of the occupants. The list of matters is as follows:*

- repair; stability; freedom from damp; internal arrangement (i.e. planning defects that result in such features as toilets leading off kitchens, steep or dangerous stairs, dangerous, hidden steps and so forth); natural lighting; ventilation; water supply; drainage and sanitary conveniences; facilities for the preparation and cooking of food, and disposal of waste water.

The test is applied to the occupant's integral home whether it be a whole house, a flat or simply a room in a house (as in the case of the inhabitant of an HMO).

Who decides if a home is UHH?

It is the duty of the local authority Environmental Health Department to inspect its area for homes that are UHH and it is the local authority alone that has the power to determine the issue of unfitness. If, however, a local authority refuses to inspect a particular home for unfitness, despite a request by the occupant that it does so, it is open to the occupant to go to their local magistrate's court and ask a JP to order the local authority to carry out an inspection. The JP will only do this, if the applicant can provide them with sufficient initial evidence that the home appears to be unfit. Even then it would appear that the local authority is under no obligation to find the house to be unfit following the inspection.

In deciding whether a home is UHH, the Environmental Health Officer will follow guidelines contained in DOE circulars, the Institute of Environmental Health Officer's circulars and case law.

---

*For basements special additional requirements apply; consult local Environmental Health Department for details).

What happens if the local authority decides that the home in question is UHH?

If a local authority receives a report from its officer that a home is UHH the local authority *must* take one of the following two courses of action:

- If it believes that the home *cannot* be rendered fit for human habitation at *reasonable expense*, it must make arrangements with all persons involved in the running of that property (owner, agent, mortgagee and so forth) to meet in order to discuss the future of the property with a view either to demolishing it, or to closing it down, or to buying it for short life use. For these purposes, *reasonable expense* is calculated by balancing the cost of the repairing work against the difference in value to the landlord of the premises as they are and the premises repaired (though still with the tenants in residence, which remains a contentious issue in law). An appeal against such a decision lies to the local county court.

If one of these courses of action is finally taken, the displaced occupiers will be entitled to be rehoused by the local authority and to receive certain financial compensation, depending on the length of time of their occupation (Home Loss Payments and Disturbance Payments: see pp. 398–99).

It should be noted that local authorities are loathe to undertake this course of action as it is open to abuse by bad landlords who simply allow their properties to deteriorate to such an extent that their tenants have to be rehoused by the council, with the council footing the bill.

- If it believes that the home *can* be rendered fit for human habitation at reasonable expense it must serve on the person 'having control of the house' (normally the person who receives the rent), a notice setting out the repair work to be done and the date by which it should be completed. Appeal against such a notice lies to the county court. Grants are payable to the person in control of the property by the local authority to assist in carrying out the repair work. Should the repair notice be ignored, or should the landlord be taking too long to do the work, the local authority has the power to carry out the works itself once the completion date has passed and furthermore to recover the cost of the work from the person having control of the property, either as a civil debt or by placing a charge on the property in the Local Land Charges Register. Intentional failure to carry out the work is a criminal offence.

Homes which are not UHH but are in a state of serious disrepair

There are two possible courses of action where homes in this category are concerned. (The contractual remedies between landlord and tenant outlined on pp. 373–77 are also available if the circumstances are appropriate. They can be used as an alternative remedy or in parallel.)

The local authority can serve a section 190/191 Notice (Housing Act 1985)

If local authority Environmental Health Officers, having carried out an inspection of a home in disrepair, do not consider it to be UHH (see p. 388), they can still serve a *repairs notice* on the person in control of the property, if they are satisfied that:

- the home is in disrepair having regard to its age, character and locality and substantial repairs are necessary to bring it up to a reasonable standard; *or*
- the disrepair of the property is such that the condition of the home interferes with the material comfort of the occupying tenant, *and* the tenant has complained about its condition to them.

All the conditions concerning repairs notices for properties that are UHH but repairable at reasonable expense apply to repairs notices under s. 190/191 (see p. 389).

Note also that improvement works and works to the common parts can be incorporated in this notice.

Repairs grants are available to landlords to carry out these repairs as for houses that are UHH.

It should not be forgotten that all the powers under this section are discretionary and will depend upon local authority initiative and co-operation.

The statutory nuisance procedure can be invoked

Any premises in such a state as to be prejudicial to the health of the occupants (i.e. injurious, or likely to cause injury to health) or a nuisance (i.e. the source of something unhealthy that is interfering with a neighbour's enjoyment of their land, for example by the escape of unsavoury smells from rotting wood or carpets) are described by law as a *statutory nuisance*.

This definition applies *whether the premises are in the private or the public sector*. Local authorities have a duty to inspect their areas for statutory nuisances. Where a statutory nuisance is found to exist there is a set procedure that the Chief Environmental Health Officer is supposed to follow. If the local authority does not follow this procedure, and the statutory nuisance continues to exist, any person suffering as a result of its existence can take the landlord to court.

It will be seen from the above definition that there are two distinct ways in which a statutory nuisance can arise. In practice it is the first type of statutory nuisance, where premises are prejudicial to the health of the occupants, that provides the most common course of action to a person who is living in premises that are in bad disrepair.

WHAT DOES *PREJUDICIAL TO HEALTH* MEAN?

There are few helpful guidelines on what the law means by the phrase *prejudicial to health*. It could be said that premises are 'prejudicial to the health of the occupants' so long as a qualified medical practitioner certifies this to be the case. Thus if an already ill person is made worse by enduring the consequences of disrepair, e.g. damp, draughts etc., those premises are 'prejudicial' to their health. Certainly, the evidence of a GP is of great importance in these circumstances. The word 'prejudicial' can incorporate not only actual, but also potential, damage to health and thus it has been decided in

391

one case that dangerous wiring can be 'prejudicial to the health' of the occupants. Similarly, if the occupant has a particular sensitivity, such as asthma, that is a relevant factor in determining whether the premises in which they live are 'prejudicial' to *their* health.

WHAT SHOULD THE OCCUPANT OF PREMISES THAT ARE A STATUTORY NUISANCE DO ABOUT IT?

Anybody who is suffering from the presence of a statutory nuisance (i.e. they are a 'person aggrieved by it', whatever their legal status in the property) should report the existence of the statutory nuisance to the local authority Environmental Health Department. The Environmental Health Department will come and inspect the premises. If they are satisfied that the statutory nuisance exists, they must serve a notice on the person responsible for it, telling that person to *abate* the statutory nuisance (i.e. to get rid of it). The only circumstances in which they are not obliged to serve such a notice are if they decide to use the Unfitness procedures described above (see pp. 387–90)

The 'person responsible' is the owner of the property if the statutory nuisance is caused by a structural defect (e.g. dampness caused by inadequate cavity wall insulation), otherwise it is the person who is responsible for causing the nuisance to exist or continue. This latter definition sometimes causes problems as it can be suggested that some statutory nuisances are caused by the occupants' own lifestyles, in which case the Environmental Health Officers will not agree to serve a notice on anybody else. It is up to the occupants in these circumstances, perhaps with the help of a law centre or an expert voluntary surveyor who may be supplied by a local CAB scheme, to argue that the statutory nuisance emanates not from their life style, but from the fact that they are alive!

CAN THE OWNER ABATE THE STATUTORY NUISANCE BY EVICTING THE OCCUPANTS?

At first sight this would appear to be a risk to the occupier. In practice however the landlord can only take this course of action if an *abatement notice* has not yet been served at the time of the eviction, and nobody is moved into the premises after the eviction has taken place (in order to show that there is no 'person aggrieved' living in the premises). And Chapter 10 has demonstrated that in general terms landlords have to follow fairly lengthy procedures before they can evict occupants, even licensees. Once an abatement notice has been served the landlord cannot seek to abate the nuisance by evicting the occupants, unless it can be shown beyond any doubt that the premises will not be relet, e.g. a *closing order* has been served on the premises. In these circumstances the occupants will in any event have a statutory right to be rehoused (see Chapter 10, p. 334) and also to receive compensation (see p. 398).

WHAT HAPPENS IF THE STATUTORY NUISANCE IS NOT ABATED?

If the statutory nuisance is not *abated* within a reasonable period it is the duty of the local authority to bring the matter before the local magistrate's court where a magistrate will issue a summons against the person responsible. A date will be set for the hearing. The local authority as complainant will take responsibility for proving the matter at the hearing, and the occupant need not be involved, except as a witness. As the proceedings are criminal proceedings there is a heavy burden of proof on the local authority to prove their case, and in particular to show that the statutory nuisance is still in existence *or likely to recur* at the date of the hearing, which may be some months after the date that the summons was issued. This is of particular importance when the alleged statutory nuisance is weather related, e.g. the disrepair causes rainwater to enter the premises, or there is seasonal damp. Advisers should be alert to the dangers of agreeing to hearing dates at which the statutory nuisance may well have temporarily disappeared and where likely recurrence will be hard to establish.

WHAT HAPPENS IF THE LOCAL AUTHORITY SATISFY THE MAGISTRATES THAT A STATUTORY NUISANCE EXISTS AT THE DATE OF THE HEARING?

If the case is proved, the magistrates will impose another abatement order on the person responsible for the statutory nuisance and may also impose a fine. They also have powers to instruct the local authority to carry out the necessary remedial works in default and to compensate the occupants of the premises for any damage they may have suffered either to their health or to their property. The willingness of magistrates to make such compensation orders varies considerably from court to court.

CAN THE OCCUPANT OF PREMISES SUFFERING FROM A STATUTORY NUISANCE
THEMSELVES APPLY TO THE COURT TO ISSUE A SUMMONS WITHOUT USING
THE LOCAL AUTHORITY?

The law does allow an individual to issue a summons against the
person responsible for a statutory nuisance if they are a 'person
aggrieved' by it. Legal aid is not, however, available to conduct such a
case (see Chapter 1) and unless they have the assistance of voluntary
organizations such as a law centre, the applicant should be advised to
leave the matter to the local authority to handle, however slow and
frustrating this may be. Better to put pressure on the local authority
to speed up the proceedings than bear the cost of conducting the
prosecution.

The one exception to the above advice is where it is the local
authority who is the 'person responsible' for the statutory nuisance
because, i.e. the local authority is the landlord. In these circumstances, because most local authorities refuse to serve abatement
notices on themselves, it will be necessary for the 'person aggrieved'
to issue the summons themselves. Practical advice on how to do so
can be obtained from the *Shelter Public Health Practice Notes:
Statutory Nuisance* and s. 99 Public Health Act 1936.

Homes which are not in disrepair but which are lacking in one or more *standard amenity*.

There are a number of complicated provisions contained in the 1985
Housing Act that deal with the rights of people whose homes are not
in disrepair but which lack *standard amenities* such as baths and hot
water, to receive assistance from the local authority towards the
installation of such amenities. The full list of standard amenities is set
out in Chapter 4, p. 100. The rights of individual tenants to have
standard amenities installed will depend on whether the area in which
their home is situated has been declared a Housing Action Area
(HAA), a General Improvement Area (GIA) or nothing. In any
event the relevant assistance will only be available if the property in
question was constructed before 3 October 1961. The first stage is
therefore to obtain this information from the Town Hall Information
Service or the Local Authority Planning or Environmental Department.

If the house is in a HAA or a GIA, local authorities have powers to serve notices* on the person in control of the house requiring them to install any standard amenities that are lacking, provided this can be done at reasonable expense. Grant aid is available to carry out this work. The procedures are, however, complex. Those who wish to acquire a detailed knowledge of the law on this subject should consult Wright, C. (1986) *Housing Improvement and Repair* (Sweet and Maxwell). But, as in any area of housing finance, the policy guidelines are constantly changing so any publication should always be checked to see if it is up to date. (see also the effects of the Local Government and Housing Act 1989.)

If the house is not in a HAA or a GIA, the powers of the local authority are less and depend very much upon the degree of initiative that the tenant is willing to exercise. If the tenant is prepared to make written representations to the local authority that their home is lacking one or more basic amenity, the local authority can serve notices on the person in control of the property in like manner as for houses in a HAA or a GIA.** The difference is simply that a local authority cannot do so on their own initiative; they must be requested to do so by a tenant.***

ATTITUDES AND POLICIES OF THE COUNCIL

It cannot be stressed strongly enough that the majority of the rights to achieve better housing conditions that have been detailed above are heavily dependent upon the willingness of a local authority to enforce these rights. A few of the enforcement procedures set out above have been described as legal duties which means that the local authority has no choice, they must take action. The majority of the enforcement procedures are not duties, they are merely powers, which means that the local authority will only use the procedure if it has both the political will and the finance to do so. Even where the enforcement procedure is a duty and not a power there will always

*Since the 1988 Housing Act EHO notices operate as local land charges.
**The council now also has power to appoint a receiver where there is an absentee landlord who is not doing repairs. (see Landlord and Tenant Act 1987).
***The Local Government and Housing Act 1989 is likely to make changes to some of the above.

remain the problem of what to do if the local authority does not carry out its duties. How can it be forced to do so? There are court procedures available in these circumstances (see Chapter 3, p. 81) but they are costly and time consuming. Advisers should therefore always be aware that persuasion based on knowledge of rights is their strongest weapon, and enforcement through legal process is an unlikely panacea for a large number of these rights.

OTHER SPECIAL POWERS OF LOCAL AUTHORITIES TO DEAL WITH SUB-STANDARD ACCOMMODATION.

There are a number of further miscellaneous powers vested in local authorities to enable them to deal with specific housing problems as follows.

Emergency orders where there is a serious risk to health

In cases where there are serious health risks, e.g. blocked drains or toilets, badly leaking rooves, or flooding, the Environmental Health Department do have emergency powers under the Building Act 1984 to serve a 9-day notice to abate the nuisance, which is a procedure it might use if sufficient pressure is placed upon it. For full details on this see Webster, C. (1981) *Environmental Health Law* (Sweet and Maxwell); Hughes, D. (1987) *Environmental Law* (Butterworths) and Luba, J. (1986) *Repairs: Tenants' Rights* (Legal Action Group).

Orders in respect of dangerous buildings

If a local authority believes a building, or part of a building, to be dangerous it has the power to apply to the local magistrate's court to request that an order be served on the person having 'control of the house' (see p. 383) requiring them to execute any works necessary to render the building safe. Any queries regarding this power should be addressed to the local Environmental Health Department.

Orders in respect of verminous or infested premises

Where premises are verminous, or in such filthy or unwholesome

396

condition as to be prejudicial to health, the local authority has a duty to serve a notice on either the owner or the occupier of the premises ordering them to take steps to remedy their condition. It is an offence to fail to comply with such a notice and the local authority may also do any necessary remedial work themselves and charge the defaulter, should the notice be ignored.

Where premises are infested with mice or rats the local authority must take steps to destroy them (if the land belongs to it) or to ensure that they are destroyed (if the land belongs to another).

Orders in respect of unsightly gardens, vacant sites or other open land

Where it appears to a local authority that the condition of any of the above three categories is so unsightly that it seriously offends the look of the immediate area, it has the power to serve a notice on the owner or occupier of the land ordering them to do something to improve the condition of the land. Enclosed sites e.g. a banker's yard, are not covered by this provision.

Further information

For further information on all the rights and powers set out in the above section advisers should consult any of the following:

Luba, J. (1986) *Repairs: Tenants' Rights* (Legal Action Group).
Baublys, K. (1986) *Your Rights to Repair* (SHAC).
Public Health Practice Notes obtainable from Shelter Publications, 88 Old St, London EC1V 9HU (Tel 01 253 0202).
Webster, C. (1981) *Environmental Health Law* (Sweet and Maxwell).
The Law of Statutory Nuisance and *The Law Relating to Houses in Multiple Occupation* both obtainable from the Institution of Environmental Health Officers, 48 Rushworth St, London SE1 (Tel: 01 928 6001).

For an excellent booklet setting out the basic structure of a house, and ways of dealing with common building defects see *The Bazaar Property Doctor* (BBC) which can be obtained from the Royal Institute of Chartered Surveyors, 12 Great George St, London SW1

(Tel: 01 222 7000), or local bookshops. See also *Which: Getting Work done on Your House* (Hodder and Stoughton)

A concise checklist of defects that can be found in houses and their effects is Ormandy, D. *Effects of Defects* (Shelter).

Finally, it should be noted that the following organization is willing, in cases of need, to provide free independent advice, house inspections, experts' reports and other environmental investigations from a team of independent and experienced advisers. It operates throughout the country: Health and Housing Group, 189 Old Brompton Road, London SW5 0AR (Tel: 01 373 8028).

HOME LOSS AND DISTURBANCE PAYMENTS

Any person who is displaced from their home in any of the following circumstances may (in addition to being rehoused: see Chapter 10, p. 334) be entitled to financial compensation in the form of a *home loss payment* and/or a *disturbance payment*. The circumstances are if displaced:

1. Following compulsory purchase.
2. By a local authority that has previously acquired the land and now wish to redevelop or improve it.
3. By a local authority or housing association following the issue of a *closing or demolition order* under the unfitness provisions (see p. 389)
4. By a local authority following the issue of an *improvement notice* under the Housing Act 1985.

All these circumstances will lead to compensation rights for private tenants and most housing association tenants, but only the first two will lead to compensation rights for local authority tenants.

Home loss payment

A home loss payment is paid by the local authority (or the Housing Association, if under the third head above) to any occupier of a home in the relevant premises who had a legal right to be there, and had lived there continuously as their main or only home for a period of at least 5 years at the date of the displacement. The claimant may

398

be the tenant, or a person living with the tenant. If the claim is by joint tenants the payment will be split equally between them. If the claimant has lived in a series of dwellings within the same building, for example in a succession of bedsits, during the 5-year period they will still be eligible. If the claim is under the first head the claimant does not have to remain in occupation until required by the local authority to leave, so long as they are in occupation on the date that the local authority are given permission to buy the property.

The amount of the home loss payment is 3 times the rateable value of the home from which the claimant has been displaced subject to a minimum of £150 and a maximum of £1500. The rateable value of the property can be obtained from the Rating Department of the local authority. If the home has not been separately rated, as will often be the case for example when it is a bedsitting room in a large HMO, an application will have to be made to the local valuation officer (different from the Rating Department) to work out a percentage figure on the rateable value of the whole property.

All claims must be made within 6 years of the displacement on a special form provided by a local authority. The form can also be obtained from a local Citizens' Advice Bureau, a Housing Aid or Action Centre or a local law centre.

Disturbance payment

A person who is entitled to claim a Home Loss Payment is also entitled to claim a Disturbance Payment. This is a sum of money to cover the reasonable expenses they have incurred as a result of their displacement and settlement in another home. It can thus cover not only removal expenses, but also the costs of setting up a new home, which may be substantial. Even if a person is not entitled to a Home Loss Payment, e.g. because they have not lived in the premises for at least 5 years, the local authority still has a discretion to make them a disturbance payment.

Is there an appeal against a refusal to make either of the above payments or the level of a disturbance payment?

Yes. An appeal lies to the Lands Tribunal, which is one of the few tribunals for which legal aid is available (see Chapter 1).

The address of the Lands Tribunal is: 48–9 Chancery Lane, London WC2 1JR.(Tel: 01 831 6611).

GETTING THE COUNCIL TO HELP: THE POSITION OF THE COUNCIL TENANT

The contractual obligations of a landlord to do repairs are the same in both the public and the private sector, and have been set out on p. 373. In addition, it has been stated there where disrepair gives rise to a *statutory nuisance* it is open to the *person aggrieved*, in this case the council tenant, licensee or any person living with them, to issue a summons in the local magistrate's court requesting that the landlord council be ordered to *abate* the nuisance, hopefully by carrying out any necessary repairs or improvements in the process. It should, however, be stressed that whilst this course of action provides a good way of taking direct action against the council landlord, the applicant cannot receive legal aid to help with their legal costs, and they should therefore be very careful to ensure that they make the best use of voluntary surveyor schemes at local CABs, or the special skills of law centres in this area.

Can a council tenant do their own repairs and send the bill to the council?

A council tenant (and any *secure tenant*: see Chapter 10, p. 337, 343) is in exactly the same position as a private tenant in this respect, i.e. they can do the repairs themselves and deduct the cost from future rent providing the repairs are the responsibility of the council and the council is given prior notice of this intention (see p. 375)

There is in addition a special scheme for secure tenants including council tenants, called the Right to Repair Scheme, which is a formal procedure allowing tenants to carry out certain repairs to their own homes and claim the cost back from the council. Although the scheme has been criticized because it simply formalizes existing rights of tenants and adds nothing new, it does nevertheless offer a proper claims procedure where previously nothing existed. The repair must be one for which the council is liable (see p. 373) and which would cost the council between £20 and £200 if they did it. It must not be a repair to the structure or exterior of a flat.

A claim under this scheme is made on a special form, the *Tenant's Repair Claim. Form 1* on which the tenant will explain:

- what they intend to repair;
- why the repair is needed;
- what works they intend to do;
- what materials they intend to use.

The council should reply within 21 days, either accepting the claim or refusing it, in which case reasons must be given.

A detailed leaflet explaining more about the scheme *Right to Repair: a Guide for Public Sector Tenants: Housing Booklet No. 2* can be obtained from the Department of the Environment.

REDUCING THE RENT

Position for tenants with Rent Act protected tenancies still in existence on 15 January 1989: the rent officer service

If a tenant in this category finds it difficult to pay the rent, they should consider whether they can use the rent officer service (also known as the fair rent system). This service enables rent officers, who are under the general supervision and control of the Department of the Environment and work from regional offices spread throughout the country, to register a fixed rent on certain privately rented premises, that will be the maximum sum that the landlord can charge for renting those premises for the next 2 years (see p. 404).

What premises does the rent officer service cover?

The service applies to any premises that are let to a tenant on a protected tenancy or statutory tenancy (see Chapter 10) where the tenancy was in existence prior to 15 January 1989 and still subsists. It does not therefore apply to public sector lettings, unprotected lettings, licenses or any lettings that commenced on or after that date.

Who can apply to register a fair rent?

Any tenant or landlord of premises in the above category may apply to register a fair rent. A local authority can also apply, even though they have no interest in the property. In practice, it is rare for a local authority to do so.

Are the means of the tenant or the landlord a relevant consideration?

No. The fair rent will be registered on the property not on the tenant and consequently the means of both the landlord and the tenant are irrelevant and are never taken into consideration. If the tenant's means are particularly low, they can always consider applying for housing benefit in addition to (or instead of) applying to register a fair rent, as housing benefit *is* means tested (see below p. 407)

How does a rent officer set about fixing a fair rent?

In fixing a fair rent, the rent officer follows a formula set out in the Rent Act 1977 supplemented by internal codes of guidance and case law. The formula takes into account a number of factors, in particular the age, character, locality, state of repair and quality of the furniture provided in the letting. The rent officer is supposed to discount any scarcity of similar accommodation in the locality, in other words to ignore the fact that in the open market scarcity of that particular type of accommodation might be forcing its rental value higher.

Anybody thinking of applying to register a fair rent should also be aware that rent officers are very influenced by *comparables* when fixing the rent on a particular property, i.e. the rents that have already been fixed on similar properties in the area. As all information on fair rents is public information, it is thus advisable for anybody considering an application first to inspect the register at their local rent office, to check the comparables currently operating in their area. Even this information should, however, be treated with caution because it may not include sufficient detail on such matters as the state of internal decoration and repair which could have influenced the decision. A figure for inflation should also be added if the registration date was some time in the past.

402

What is the procedure for applying to fix a fair rent?

The procedure is very straightforward. The applicant obtains a form from the local rent officer service (address in local telephone directory) and fills out a request for rent registration providing basic details about the property. The rent officer then informs the other party (whether landlord or tenant) of the application, and arranges a date to visit the property. Both landlord and tenant are invited to attend the inspection, should they so wish, and to make any representation they wish. In cases of complexity or controversy, a further meeting at the rent officer's office can sometimes be arranged. Once the rent officer has obtained all the necessary information, a fair rent is fixed on the premises (which will be exclusive of rates and other services) and this sum will be communicated to the parties as the maximum rent chargeable on the premises.

Is there an appeal against a rent officer's decision?

Yes. Either party may appeal against an unfavourable registration to the local Rent Assessment Committee (RAC) a specialist tribunal, normally with three members, set up to adjudicate on matters relating to housing cost. The RAC will consider the application afresh, will visit the premises and will make their own decision following a hearing which can be attended by all parties together with their representatives. As legal aid (see Chapter 1) is not available for RAC hearings, the cost of legal representation (at least for tenants) is normally prohibitive. There are, however, voluntary surveyor schemes operating in some parts of the country which can provide representation in such matters. For details consult a local CAB.

Tenants should be warned that RACs have a tendency to *increase* a rent officer's registration by an average of around 10 per cent and it is less common for a tenant to achieve a reduction in the rent officer's fair rent registration.

From what date will a fair rent be effective?

The answer to this question will depend on a number of factors and in any event is not simple. As landlords often make mistakes on this particular matter, tenants in any doubt should consult a law centre,

CAB or housing aid centre for advice. The answer in summary is as follows:

- In any event the earliest date from which the registered rent is payable will be the date of registration not the date that the application was filed (which may be several weeks earlier).
- During the *contractual period* of the tenancy, i.e. the period before either a fixed term tenancy or a Notice to Quit expires, the maximum rent chargeable is *either* the existing rent *or* the new registered rent, *whichever is the lower*. For further details on the contractual period see Chapter 10 p. 356.
- During the statutory period of the tenancy, i.e. the period after the contractual period has ended, but whilst the tenant remains in occupation under the protection of the Rent Act the registered rent will be the new rent payable. If this new rent amounts to a rent increase it will not become operative on the premises until a Notice of Increase (a special formal document) has been served on the tenant. If the rent is decreased by the rent officer, a Notice of Increase will obviously be unnecessary and the decreased rent will be the effective rent from the date of registration.
- If a Notice of Increase has to be served, the increase will be further subject to phasing. This means that the landlord will not be able to charge the *full* fair rent for a year. For the first year, the maximum amount chargeable will be one half the increase.

How long will a fair rent remain effective on a property once registered?

Once registered, a fair rent will normally remain effective on that property indefinitely, *or* until one of two things happens (there are other special circumstances which are too rare to warrant special mention here):

- The landlord has the registration removed from the register. This is however only permissible once 2 years have passed since the registration date and then *only* if there is no protected statutory tenant living on the premises at the time of the application to remove. If a new tenancy with a new tenant begins the relevant law will now be that contained in the Housing Act 1988 (see p. 406).

- Normally an application to register a new fair rent can only be made once 2 years have passed since the last application (although an application can be made by a landlord after 21 months to become effective as soon as the 2 years have expired). The exception to this rule is where there has been such a substantial change in the terms of the tenancy, e.g. as a result of improvements, refurnishing and so forth, that the existing fair rent is no longer 'fair'. Note, however, that whilst 'improvements' might allow the landlord to re-apply within the 2 year period, 'repairs' will not. (On the distinction between 'improvements' and 'repairs' see p. 374).

N.B. The rent is registered on the property not the tenant, and therefore the fair rent will continue to operate regardless of any change of tenant. This important rule only applies however if the letting is of the same property, i.e. if for example, the rent was registered on the premises as an unfurnished letting and the premises are now let furnished, the registered rent will not apply. Similarly, if the new letting is an assured on assured shorthold tenancy, the registered rent will no longer apply. (see p. 406).

What can a tenant do if they find out that the landlord has been charging them in excess of an existing registered rent?

If a tenant finds, by searching the rent register, that they are being charged more than the fair rent registered on the premises, they can claim back from the landlord the excess paid, up to a maximum of 2 years' overpayment. This can be done either by deducting the money from future rent, or by an action for debt in the local county court. The letting must however be for an identical letting as that which was subject to the fair rent registration.

Can a tenant register a fair rent and claim housing benefit?

Yes. Although the Government is theoretically committed to paying housing benefit on full market rents in all new types of tenancies under the Housing Act 1988, it could insist that it will only pay housing benefit up to the level of a fair rent for tenancies that *could* be registered under the fair rent scheme. It is therefore likely that for those of small means the dual approach will be quite common.

Rent control for assured tenants

There is no restriction on the rent which landlords can initially charge assured tenants. Rent officers have no jurisdiction over the rents of assured tenants. At the end of the contractual period of the tenancy the landlord can increase the rent so long as the correct notices are served (advice should always be sought on this matter by the tenant, to check the validity of notices). In some circumstances, if the tenant wishes to object to the new rent, they can apply to the local rent assessment committee, which will then fix the rent following a number of set procedures. This rent will not, however, be a 'fair rent' along the lines of rents fixed by rent officers on Rent Act protected tenancies. It will be the rent at which the tenancy 'might reasonably be expected to be let in the open market by a willing landlord under an assured tenancy'. The records of other rents fixed under this system are available for public inspection. If the tenant cannot afford the rent they can apply for housing benefit though this is subject to a means test (see p. 407). For more detail on these procedures see Arden and Hunter (p. 370)

Rent control for assured shorthold tenants

Tenants in this category can apply to the rent assessment committee to determine what rent they should pay if they are dissatisfied with the amount. The rent assessment committee will not alter the rent, however, unless it considers that the rent is significantly higher than the amount which a landlord might reasonably be expected to obtain for similar tenancies in the locality. The committee can only do this if there are sufficient numbers of similar properties in the area on which to make a comparison. It seems unlikely therefore that there will be many applications to rent assessment committees under this category.

HOUSING BENEFIT: FINANCIAL ASSISTANCE IN PAYING THE RENT AND RATES (COMMUNITY CHARGE)

For those who have difficulty meeting their housing costs, i.e. rates (community charge) and/or rent, it is always worth considering the possibility of applying for Housing Benefit (HB). The benefit is available both to *tenants*, to help with rates (community charge) and rent and to *owner occupiers*, to help with rates (community charge) though *not* mortgage repayments. The benefit is means tested.

What follows below is a summary of how to claim HB. For more detailed information consult one of a number of guides as follows: *The National Welfare Benefits Handbook* (CPAG); Ward, M. and Zebedee, J. *The Guide to Housing Benefit* (Institute of Housing and SHAC); *Benefits Guide for Single People* (CHAR); *How to Claim State Benefits; a Guide to Every Citizen's Rights* (Rathfelder/ Northcote House). For a detailed and more expensive annotated guide to all the relevant legislation see Findlay, L. (1988) *CPAG's Annotated Housing Benefit Legislation* (CPAG).

The DSS also produce a Fact Sheet on HB; DSS Leaflets RR2 *A Guide to Housing Benefit;* and DSS Leaflet RR1 *Help With Housing Costs*. Both leaflets are available from local councils and RR1 can also be obtained from post offices. The detailed manual that DSS officers themselves use when assessing HB is *The Housing Benefits Guidance Manual* (DSS).

How is HB claimed?

HB is a Government scheme that is administered by local councils. It is claimed by filling out a detailed form that is supplied by the local authority DSS (for all claimants in receipt of income support; see Chapter 8) or otherwise by the local authority HB section.

How is a claimant's entitlement to HB calculated?

Whatever a person's source of income, the same formula will be used for calculating whether or not they are entitled to receive any HB. The process appears complex, but if the stages set out below are followed, the claimant or their adviser can quickly gain a clear idea of their level of entitlement.

Stage One: is the claimant in receipt of income support (see chapter 8)?

If the claimant is in receipt of income support, they will be entitled to receive the maximum level of HB, which will be 100 per cent eligible rent and 80 per cent rates (community charge) (but see p. 409 on what exactly is meant by *eligible rent*). They must however claim their HB separately from the IS (i.e. there is no automatic payment to an income support claimant).

If the claimant is *not* in receipt of income support proceed to Stage Two.

Stage Two: calculate the claimant's capital

Any capital below £3000 will be disregarded. If the claimant has between £3000 and £8000, this capital will be deemed to generate £1 weekly income for every £250 (or part of £250) in excess of £3000. Thus a claimant with capital of £4400 will be deemed to generate income of £6 per week from their capital. (On the distinction between capital and income see the *National Welfare Benefits Handbook*.) Capital includes money in bank and building society deposits, premium bonds, unit trusts, stocks and shares, lump sum redundancy payments and cash savings. A child's capital is not treated as belonging to the claimant (but above a certain capital level the child cannot be included as a dependant). There are special rules on charitable payments (see *National Welfare Benefits Handbook*). Some items of capital are entirely disregarded. These are the same items that are disregarded for the purposes of a claim for income support (see Chapter 8 p. 263). Any claimant with capital in excess of £8000 will be ineligible for HB.

Stage Three: calculate the claimant's applicable amount

The formula for this calculation is exactly the same as for calculating eligibility for income support (see Chapter 8, p. 264) but for the purposes of HB it is of course being applied to those who (for whatever reason) are not in receipt of income support. The amount will vary considerably according to the age and level of disability (if any) of the claimant and any dependants.

Stage Four: calculate the claimant's income

The formula for this calculation is again the same as for calculating eligibility for income support (see Chapter 8, p. 268).

Stage Five: calculate the claimant's eligible rent and rates or community charge, i.e. amount against which they may claim benefit

RENT

Some parts of rent charges are not eligible for HB; i.e. they must be deducted by the claimant from their rent before filling out the form. The following charges are all ineligible: charges for meals, laundry, leisure facilities, cleaning (except for common areas), transport, medical and nursing care, and alarm systems (except on accommodation for sick and elderly or disabled people).

Service charges are eligible for HB, i.e. they can be included on the form, so long as they are reasonable and have to be paid as part of the tenancy. They would include such things as contributions towards the upkeep of lifts, common refuse chutes, and play areas. There are further complex rules regarding rent which includes fuel charges, some of which will not be included in the eligible rent according to a scale that can be found in any of the handbooks.

RATES (OR COMMUNITY CHARGE)

The eligible rates/community charge is 80 per cent of the amount actually paid by the claimant. Water rates are not eligible.

Stage Five: compare income with applicable amount

- If income is less than applicable amount, maximum HB is payable, i.e. 80 per cent rates (or community charge) and 100 per cent eligible rent).
- If income is higher than applicable amount the following formula is applied:
  1. Work out excess of income over applicable amount.

409

2. Apply following tapers to *excess*:
   65 per cent of excess for eligible rent;
   20% of excess for rates (or community charge).

Deduct the sums thereby arrived at from the maximum eligible rent and rates (or community charge) and the resulting figures will be the HB payable. (No HB will be paid if the figure is less than 50p per week.)

Example: Alan and Joan are both in their late 60s. Alan's retirement pension is £41.15, Joan's is £24.75. Alan also gets an occupational pension of £8.00 per week. They have savings of £4000. They live on their own. They are council tenants with an eligible rent of £15 per week and rates or community charge of £6.00 per week. Their HB will be calculated as follows:

A. Subtract Alan and Joan's applicable amount from their total income (£77.90, i.e. the three pensions plus a notional income of
   £4 per week from the £4000 capital (see p. 408).
B. Apply per cent tapers to the resultant figure (65 per cent for eligible rent £15 and 20 per cent for eligible rates or community charge).
C. Deduct the figures obtained at B from the maximum HB payable (80 per cent of rates, community charge, i.e. £4.80, and 100 per cent of eligible rent, i.e. £15.00).

Stage Six: deductions from HB where there is a *non-dependant* living in the claimant's home

A *non-dependant* is someone who lives in the claimant's home and is not dependent on them, e.g. an adult relative (unless they are dependent), a child for whom the claimant does not receive Child Benefit, a friend or a lodger. Where there is a non-dependant living in the claimant's home there will be an automatic deduction from the HB otherwise payable, according to a set scale: see Table 11.1. This deduction is intended to reflect the amount of contribution that the non-dependant make to the housing costs, *regardless of whether they do make any such payment.*

Table 11.1

Non-Dependant Deduction Chart

(1) Attendance Allowance   Constance Attendance Allowance
(2) Income Support

Reproduced with the permission of Benefits Research Unit (Service) Ltd, from *Guide to Housing Benefit* (Nottinghamshire Welfare Rights Service).

What happens if the local authority considers that the rent is too high?

If the local authority responsible for paying HB considers that the rent is too high or that the accommodation is too large or expensive, it can restrict the level of benefit accordingly. It cannot do this, however, if the household includes any of the following:

- someone aged 60 or over;
- a sick or disabled person;
- a child or young person.

Alternatively it could insist the tenant applies to the Rent Officer to register a fair rent or (post-15 January 1988) to the rent assessment committee (see p. 406)

Is anybody excluded from claiming HB?

A person cannot claim HB if they are in any of the following categories:

- a boarder* but see p. 269 on Board and Lodging Regulations and see also *Shelter Advice Notes on Board and Lodging Regulations and Their Implications*) (Shelter);
- in a residential home (but see Chapter 9, p. 295) regarding the elderly in residential accommodation;
- the tenancy is too informal, i.e. they are renting on a non-commercial basis from a friend, or from a close relative or partner.

Special rules for students

There are special rules relating to the rights of students to claim HB, which are dealt with in detail in the *National Welfare Benefits Handbook* (CPAG) and Ward, M. and Zebedee, S. *Guide to Housing Benefit* (SHAC and Institute of Housing). Students living in halls of

*Since October 1989 hostel residents can calim HB even if receiving board (see *Welfare Rights Bulletin* August 1989 3–4.

residence or similar college accommodation for which they pay rent to an educational establishment are not eligible at all for HB during the 'period of study' which amounts to both term time and Easter and Christmas vacations (but *not* the summer vacation). All other students are eligible to claim HB, subject to special rules and restrictions. For a useful article on students and HB see *Legal Action* (1988)

What is the maximum period for which HB can be paid?

The maximum benefit period is 60 weeks, though local authorities have a discretion to make the payments for a shorter period. Once the period has expired the claimant must resubmit their claim.

Can HB be backdated and claimants be forced to repay overpayments?

Local authorities have the power to backdate HB for up to 52 weeks. They can also recover overpayments in certain circumstances. It is likely that they will have some incentive to claw back overpayments (unless they were themselves grossly negligent in the initial payment) and also not to backdate unless absolutely necessary as they will get a lower subsidy on any such payments.

Can HB be paid direct to a landlord?

HB will normally be paid direct to the landlord in the following circumstances:

- where the claimant or their partner is receiving IS and the DSS decide to pay part of the benefit to the landlord to cover arrears;
- where the claimant has rent arrears of 8 weeks or more.

In addition, the local authority *may* agree to pay the HB direct to the landlord if the claimant has so requested or if the local authority decides it is in the best interests of the claimant's family. In all these circumstances both the landlord and the tenant must be notified of the decision. The claimant can request a review of an unfavourable decision.

413

Can a dissatisfied claimant appeal against an adverse HB decision?

A procedure exists enabling a claimant to appeal (known as a review) against any decision regarding their claim. There is no independent tribunal appeal system but there is a two-stage review procedure consisting of an internal review and an application to a review board. (The latter can only be requested after an internal review has been carried out.) The request for an internal review must be in writing – a letter will suffice – and it must arrive at the local authority no later than 6 weeks from the date that the letter of notification of the decision was posted. A request for a further hearing before a review board (which will consist of local councillors) must be made within 4 weeks of the posting of the notification of the decision of the internal review. For further details on the review procedure consult one of the detailed guides mentioned on p. 407.

Index